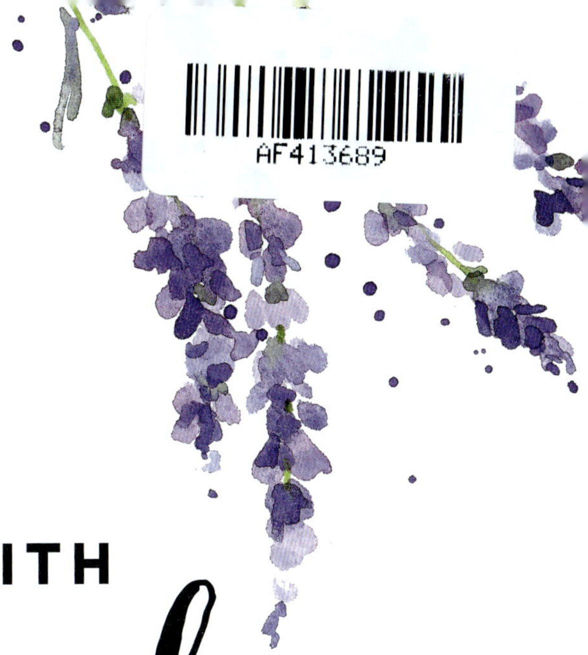

FUN WITH
Watercolor

45 Beginner-Friendly Projects to Create Frame-Worthy Art

ANNA KOLIADYCH

Author of *15-Minute Watercolor Masterpieces* and *Gouache in 4 Easy Steps*

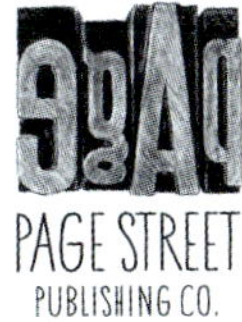

PAGE STREET
PUBLISHING CO.

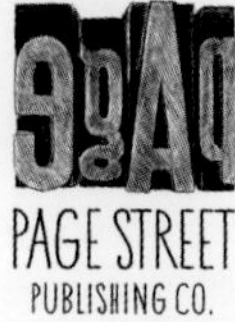

PAGE STREET
PUBLISHING CO.

TO MY FATHER, PAVEL, WHO GAVE ME THE
LIGHT INSIDE ME THAT I HAVE CARRIED
THROUGHOUT MY LIFE. AND TO MY
MOTHER, OLGA, WHO IS ALWAYS BY
MY SIDE, EVEN WHEN SHE DOESN'T
UNDERSTAND ME.

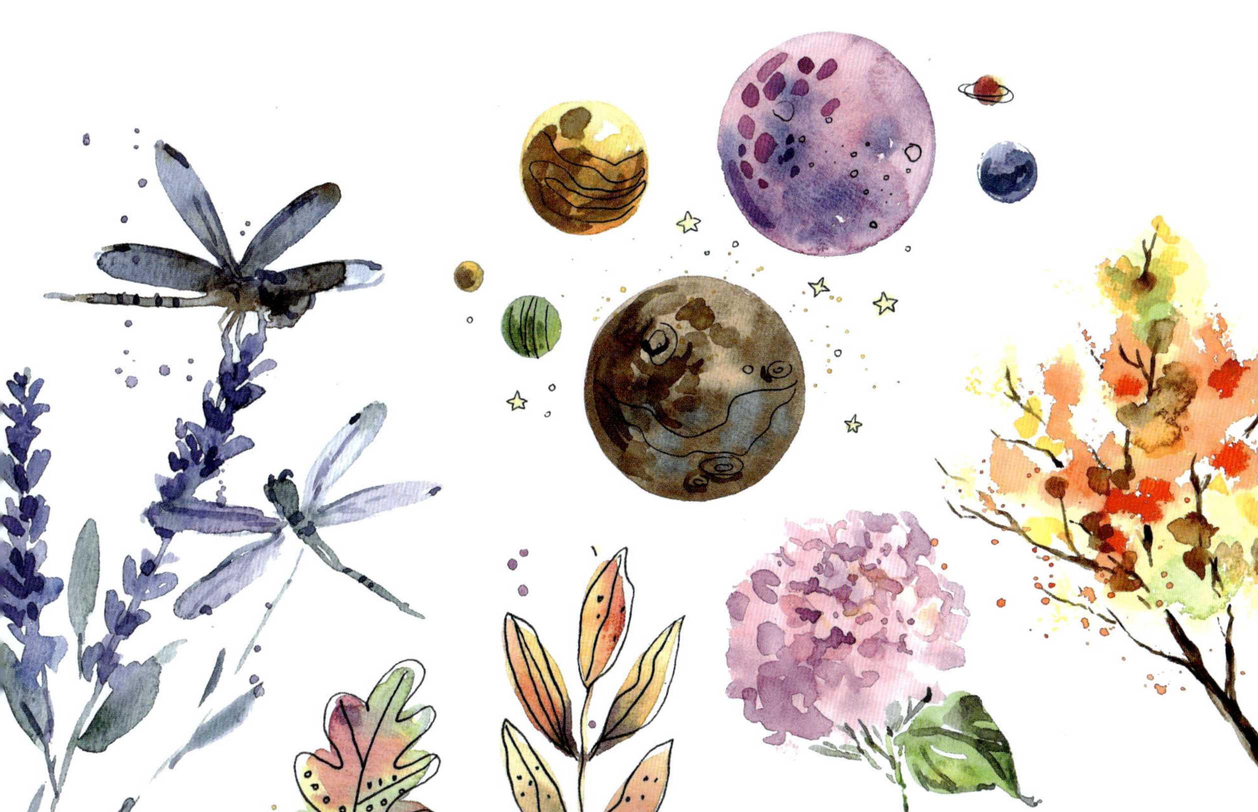

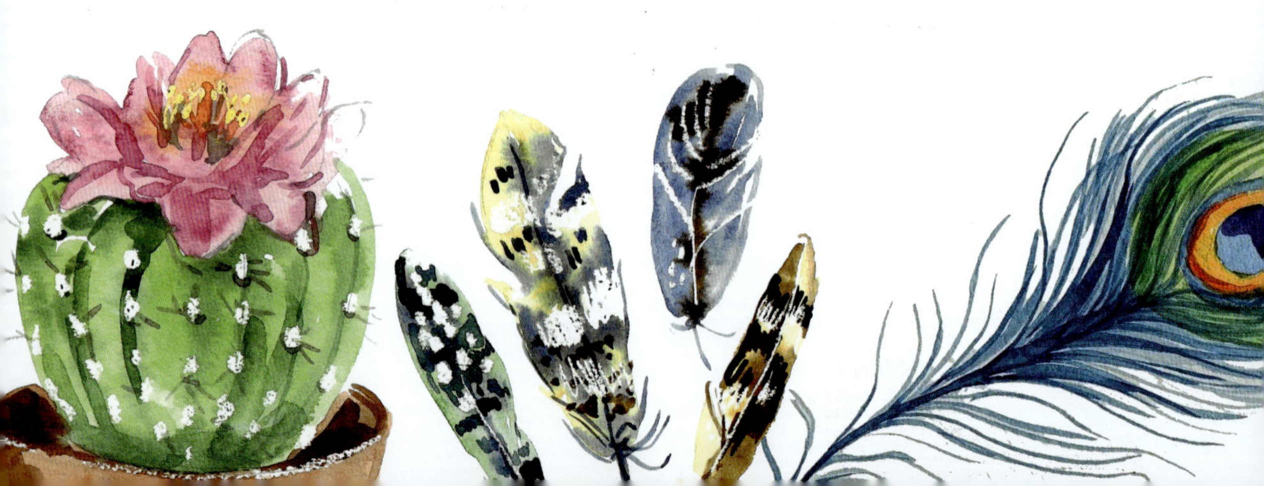

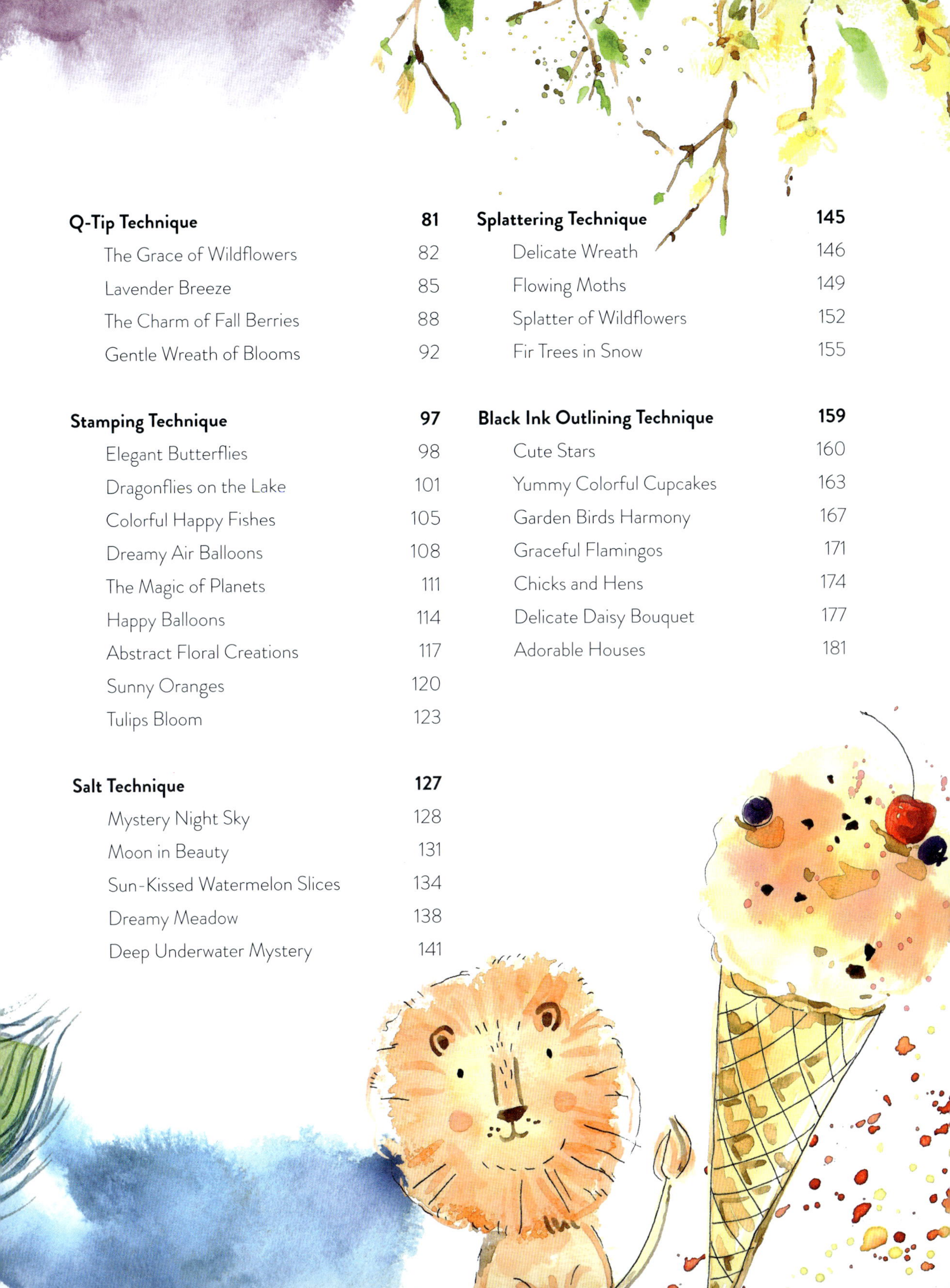

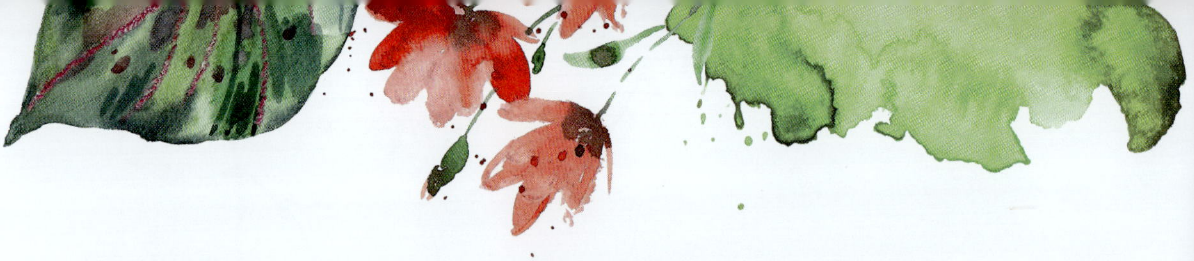

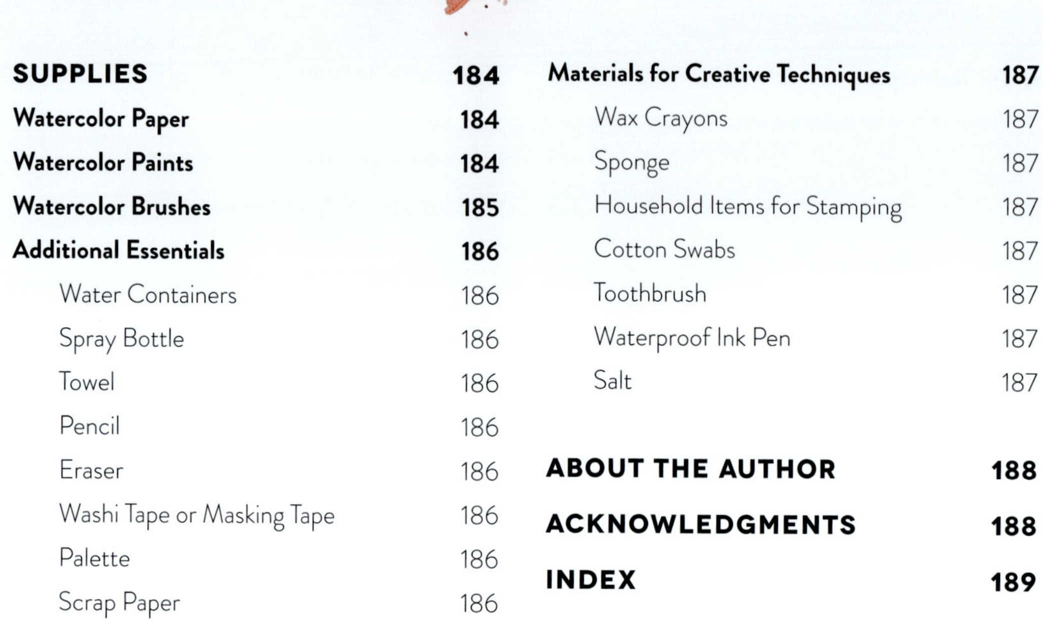

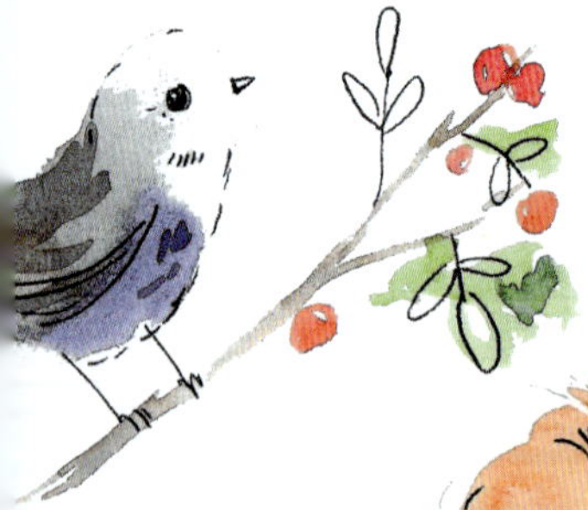

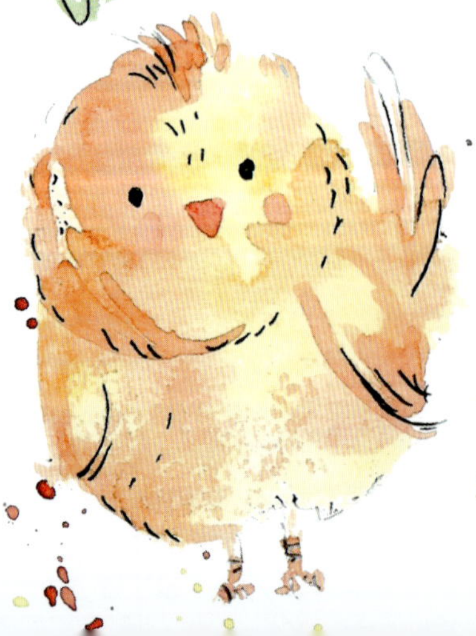

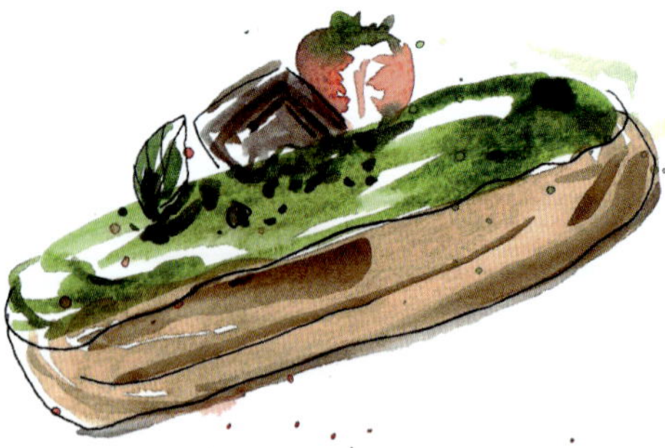

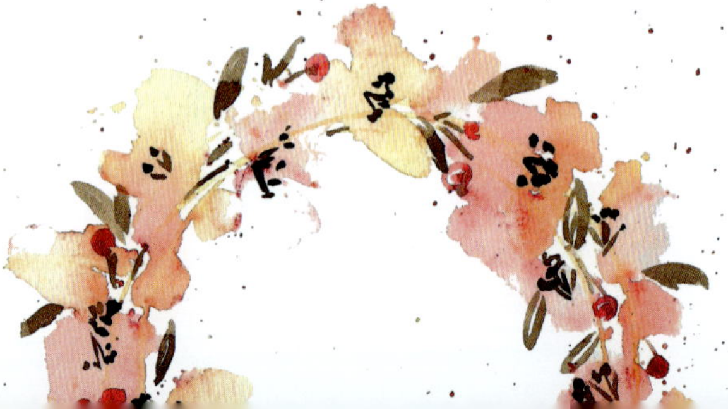

INTRODUCTION

Hey, I'm Anna, a watercolor artist and teacher, as well as a happy mom and wife.

My story and my watercolor journey started around eight years ago. When I was a kid, I loved to paint, especially with watercolor and gouache, but my parents didn't support me. They thought it wasn't good for me because, in real life, art wouldn't give me support or money. As I got older, I studied at a technical university and earned a master's in engineering. After that, I worked as a graphic designer for a long time. When I met my future husband, I told him that I wanted to paint and start everything over from the beginning. He gifted me my first watercolor paper, brushes, and watercolors, and I was so excited—it felt like a dream come true. I started teaching myself watercolor.

After some time, I became a freelance watercolor illustrator. I got a lot of jobs—different projects like creating food illustrations, watercolor logos, and illustrations for books. I've worked on hundreds of projects and gained a huge amount of experience. At some point, I started learning watercolor more seriously—through courses, classes, and workshops. One day, I began teaching watercolor to others because I felt I had something to share and wanted to help people start their own journeys. It's not just a faraway dream; it's a dream that can happen anytime, at any moment, when you say to yourself: "I want to start."

I've never regretted choosing this path. For the last five years, I've been teaching people all around the world. I truly believe everyone can paint and that painting and art are healing. I hope to open more hearts to watercolor by helping others to start, enjoy themselves, and find their own way.

If you're flipping through this book, chances are you're curious about watercolor, and I'm thrilled to be your guide on this fun journey.

In these pages, I've whipped up something special—a mix of projects that use traditional techniques and techniques that are easier and more fun. Forget about spending hours on end on one project— this book is all about quick and enjoyable painting.

You'll start with the basics, where you can find all the information about watercolor techniques, how to achieve the desired paint consistency, which colors to pick for your essential palette, and how to mix colors. It's everything you need to know to get started.

Then, you will dive into 50 fun watercolor projects. These projects each have a list of project colors and are broken down into steps. The steps will include images for you to reference as well as detailed instructions. At the end of each project, you'll find directions on how to use the knowledge you gained from that project to create your own project and continue practicing with watercolor.

The last chapter of the book is dedicated to tips and advice. You can use these as inspiration and motivation when you're having a bad day or feeling overwhelmed. All my suggestions from years of experience using watercolor are included here to make your watercolor journey easy and enjoyable.

You will also find a chapter on the supplies you will need for watercolor painting, from essentials to specific items you will need for creative and fun techniques.

This book isn't just about painting—it's about feeling the joy of creating, making mistakes, and finding your own style along the way. It's about having fun with watercolor, enjoying art, and relaxing throughout the process. Whether you're a newbie or already have some experience, there's something here for everyone.

I hope this book brings you joy. You will come to understand that art is not something we create; rather, art creates us. And I hope that you start to *feel* watercolor—that it becomes intuitive and natural. With some practice, if you follow the guidance in this book, you will have a great experience and become more advanced in your watercolor journey.

Believe in yourself. Even if you make mistakes, accept them. Even if you don't successfully execute the project on your first attempt, give yourself second, third, and fourth attempts. Explore watercolor, explore all the techniques, and try to find your favorite ones.

Grab your brushes and let's paint together. This book is your door to a world of watercolor fun!

With love,

Anna

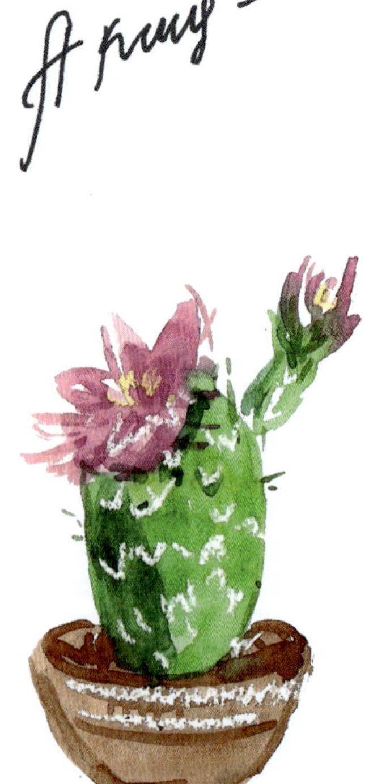

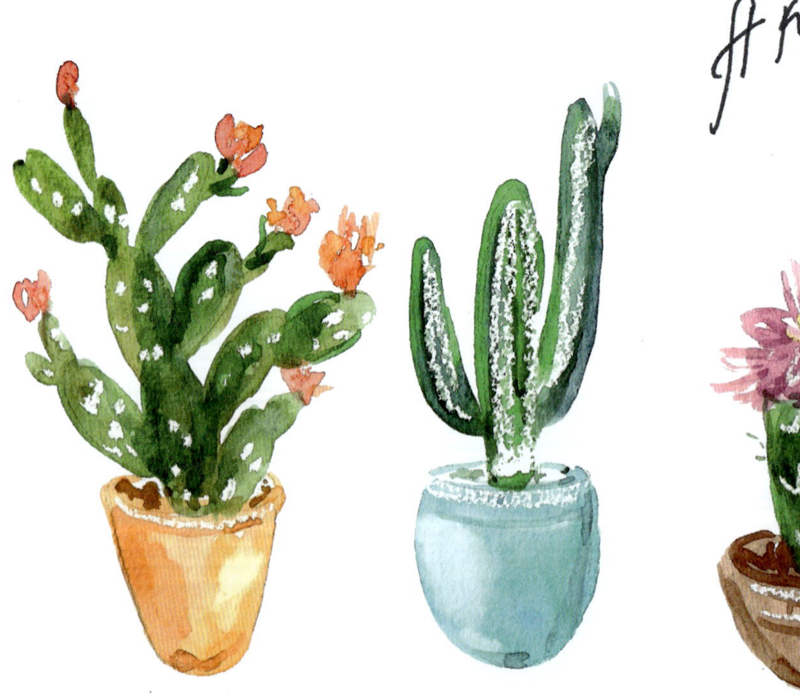

MASTERING WATERCOLOR: PRINCIPLES AND TECHNIQUES

WHAT WATERCOLOR IS, ITS FEATURES, AND SPECIFICS AS A MEDIUM

Before we dive into the fun and creative projects in this book, let me introduce watercolor paint. I'll explain what it is, how it works, and what makes it special.

Firstly, watercolor is a very popular and trendy medium that people love all around the world. Kids, adults, absolute beginners, and professionals all enjoy using it. I think its popularity comes from its versatility. With watercolor, you can create many different kinds of projects. They can be something simple, like a cute watercolor card, or something detailed and realistic, like a painting of a landscape or flowers. You can also make illustrations, portraits, or even mix watercolor with other mediums to create unique styles. There are no limits. You can paint in different styles, explore various themes, and enjoy endless possibilities.

Another great thing about watercolor is that it doesn't require many supplies to get started. All you need is a good-quality watercolor set, watercolor paper, and some brushes. That's it! Compared to other mediums, it's simple and affordable. Plus, it's incredibly flexible. You can paint outdoors, at home, in a studio, or wherever else you like.

Watercolor paint is unique because it's a water-soluble medium. This means it activates when you use water. By controlling the amount of water in the paint, you can create very transparent washes and layers or more opaque effects. On one hand, this gives you a lot of creative freedom. On the other hand, it can be tricky. You need to control the water carefully to get the right paint consistency for your project.

To sum it up, watercolor is a truly magical medium and so much fun to use. Through the projects I've prepared for you in this book, I hope to show you how enjoyable and magical watercolor can be. So, let's learn some basics and dive into the projects together!

TRANSPARENCY AND PAINT CONSISTENCY

As mentioned in the previous section, watercolor is a water-soluble medium, and it activates with water. You can control the consistency of your paint by adding water. With different consistencies, you can achieve different levels of transparency, from very transparent to opaque. Let's figure out how it works and how to achieve the desired level of transparency.

First, you need to activate your paint. If you are using watercolor pans, just spray a little water on them, and they will be ready to use. If you are using watercolor in tubes, squeeze some paint onto a palette or plate and add water.

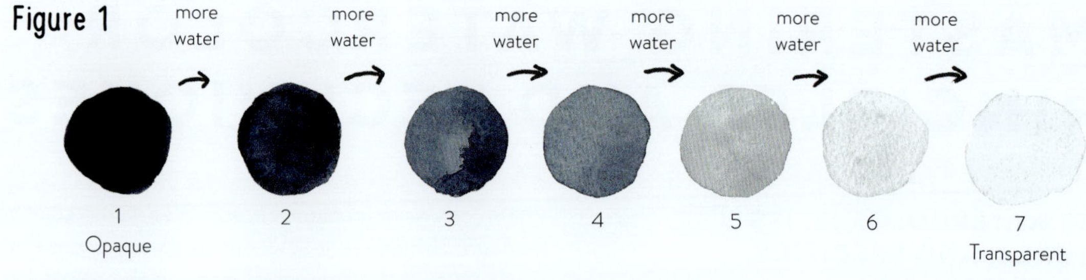

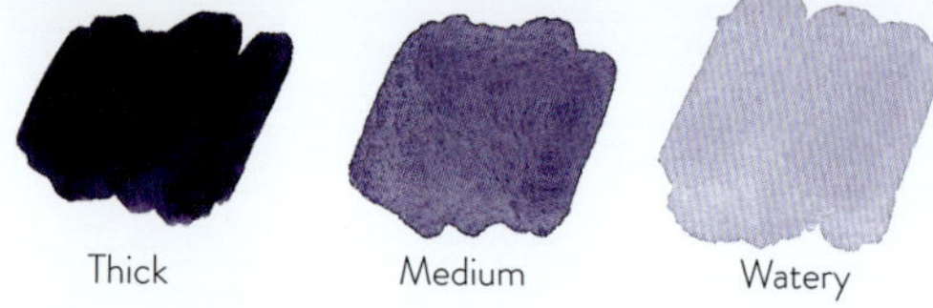

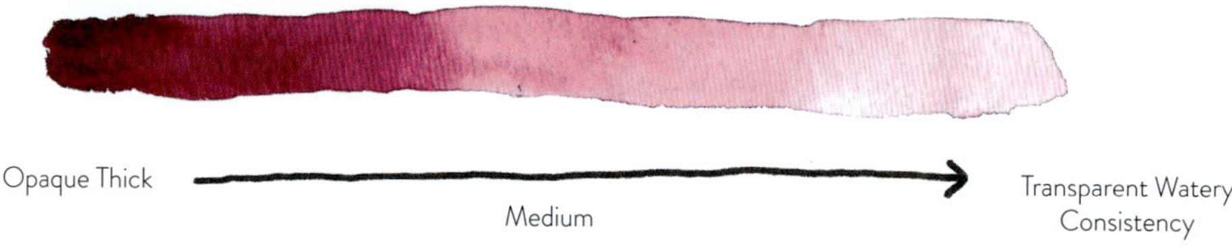

Once the paint is activated, you can start working with it. Mix your paint with a small amount of water creating a creamy, thick consistency. Paint a simple shape like a circle. With this consistency, you will get an opaque layer (see Figure 1-1).

Next, add a little more water to your paint and create another shape or wash (a circle in my case). You will achieve a less opaque, more transparent layer (see Figure 1-2).

Each time you add more water, the layer becomes more transparent. Keep adding water until you create a very transparent layer (see Figure 1-7).

We can divide transparency into three main levels: thick, medium, and watery (see Figure 2).

Thick consistency gives you an opaque layer.

Medium consistency creates a medium level of transparency.

Watery consistency gives you a very transparent layer.

In your projects, if I direct you to prepare paint in a watery consistency, you need to add a lot of water. For medium consistency, you add less water, just enough to achieve a "tea-like" consistency. Finally, if I ask you to make a thick consistency, you need to create creamy, thick paint to achieve an opaque layer or add details.

This means that the tonal value of a color depends on two things: how much water you add and the color itself. For example, a very watery consistency Permanent Red might still look darker than a thick layer of lemon yellow. So, when you plan your painting, remember that each color has its own natural tone, no matter what consistency of paint you use (see Figure 3).

BASIC COLOR PALETTE

Before we start mixing colors, it's important to figure out what colors you will need for practicing with this book. Let's start with the colors you already have. I recommend making a swatch card.

A swatch card is a piece of watercolor paper on which you paint a small sample of each color in your watercolor set. Prepare your paints by adding a little water to them. Then, paint each color one by one (in any order) on your swatch card. After you finish swatching all the colors, write the name of each color under it. This makes it easier to recognize your colors when you are painting (see example in Figure 4).

If you have more than one watercolor set, make a swatch card for each one and title them. Some watercolor brands already include blank swatch cards in their sets that you can fill. I recommend keeping your swatch cards nearby when you paint. This will help you see the colors clearly and choose the ones you need until you are more familiar with them.

To help you get started, I am sharing the exact colors I used in this book (see my essential color palette in Figure 5). I call this palette my essential color palette because, over many years, I have found it to be the most effective and useful for me.

1. Yellow Ochre
2. Cadmium Yellow
3. Lemon Yellow
4. Cadmium Red
5. Primary Red (or Permanent Red)
6. Opera (or Quinacridone Rose)
7. Alizarin Crimson (or Rose Madder)
8. Crimson (or Carmine)
9. Violet
10. Ultramarine Blue (Ultramarine for short)
11. Prussian Blue (or Cobalt Blue)
12. Indigo
13. Viridian
14. Hooker's Green

Figure 4

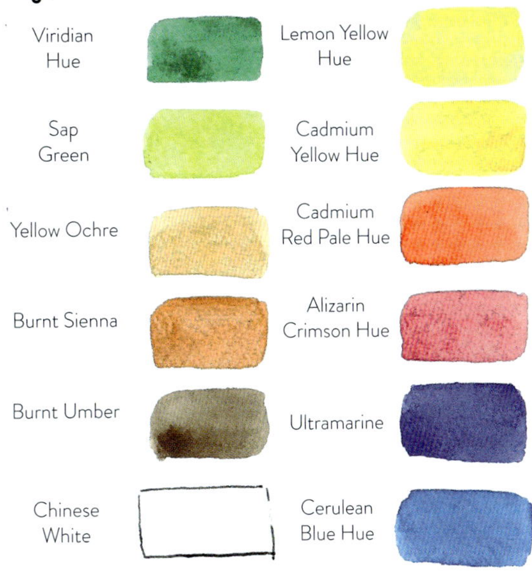

Figure 5

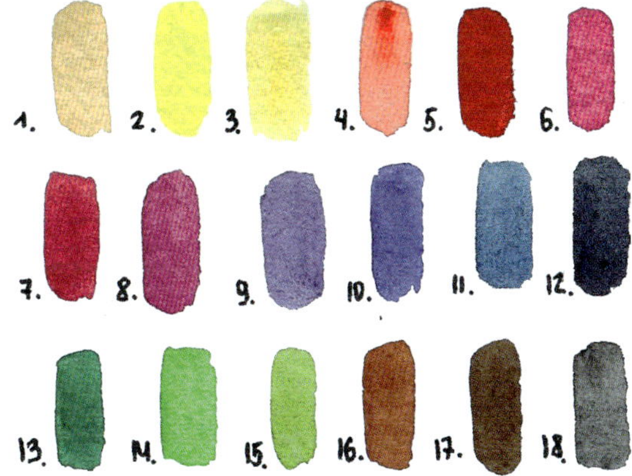

15. Sap Green
16. Burnt Sienna
17. Burnt Umber
18. Ivory Black

These colors are just my recommendations. If you have similar colors in your watercolor set, feel free to use those instead for the projects in this book.

Figure 6

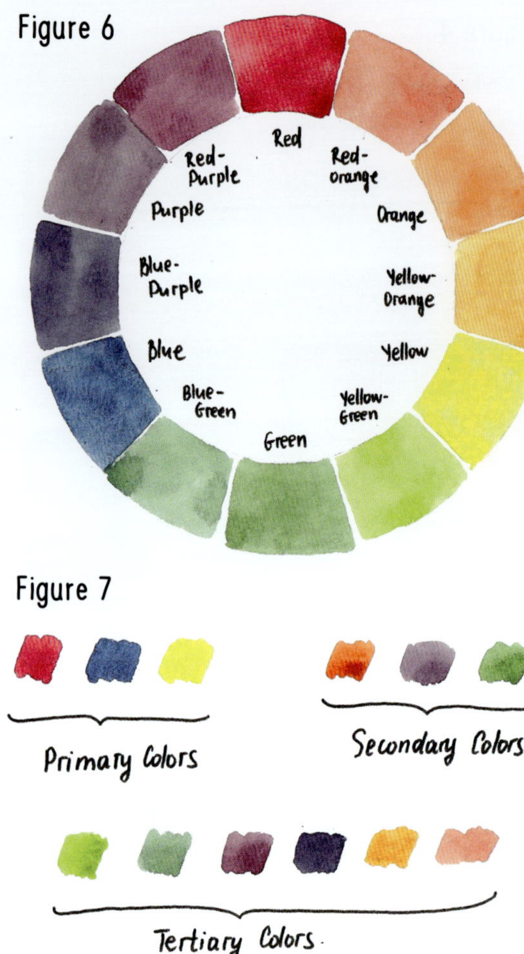

Figure 7

In the next section, I will share information on how to mix your own colors using the colors you already have. This will help you create many new shades on your own.

While mixing colors is fun, I believe some colors are essential to buy. For example, Yellow Ochre is one of the best yellow shades, in my opinion. I also think Opera, or a similar color, is very important. Other must-have colors (or similar shades) are Lemon Yellow, Ultramarine, Prussian Blue, Indigo, Burnt Sienna, and Burnt Umber.

These colors, or close ones, form a strong foundation for your palette. You can mix them to create many more colors to suit your needs.

Figure 8

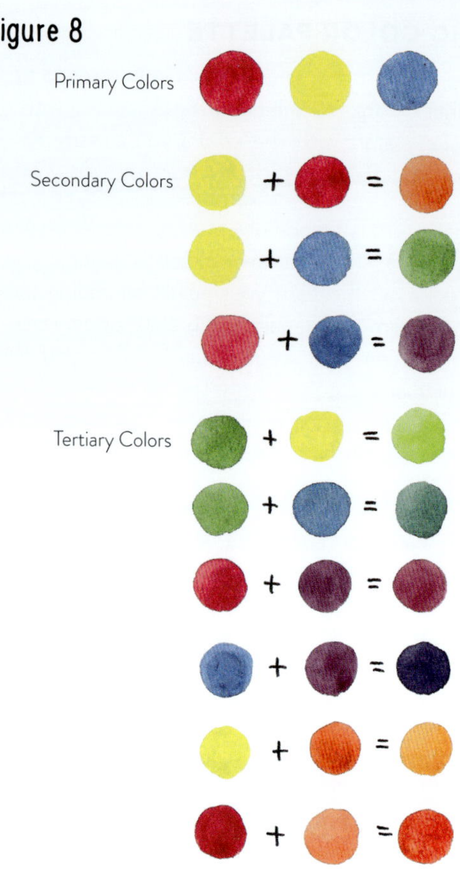

COLOR MIXING

Color mixing is based on color theory, which is essential knowledge for painting in any medium. So, let's dive into some basics and figure out how to mix colors, guided by the color wheel (see Figure 6).

The color wheel is a circle (though it can be shown in other forms) divided into twelve colors, arranged based on how they relate to one another. These colors are divided into three main groups (see Figure 7):

Primary colors: red, yellow, and blue. These are called "primary" because they cannot be created by mixing other colors (see Figure 8).

Secondary colors: orange, purple, and green. These are made by mixing two primary colors in equal amounts: Yellow and red make orange, yellow and blue make green, and red and blue make purple (see Figure 8).

Tertiary colors: These are six colors made by mixing a primary color with a secondary color. They are yellow green, blue green, red purple, blue purple, yellow orange, and red orange (see Figure 8).

Colors opposite each other on the color wheel are called complementary colors. When you mix complementary colors, they mute each other, creating a softer or more natural tone. For example, adding a little red to green will make the green less intense. If you add a little bit of orange to blue, you will mute it. The more orange you add, the closer it will get to gray. This is a useful approach for your painting process (see example in Figure 9).

Exercise: Creating a Color Wheel

Creating a color wheel is a simple and fun exercise that will help you understand how to mix colors and see their relationships. I recommend creating one on your own.

To start, draw a simple circle and divide it into twelve equal sections. Then, choose the colors you want to use as your primary colors.

For the most effective and bright primary colors, I recommend using Opera for red, Lemon Yellow for yellow, and Cobalt Blue for blue. You can also experiment with the red, yellow, and blue you already have in your palette.

Begin by filling in the sections of your color wheel with the primary colors in medium consistency (see Figure 10-1). Next, mix your primary colors to create the secondary colors and fill the sections between the primary colors (Figure 10-2). Finally, create the tertiary colors by mixing a primary color with a secondary color and add these to the remaining sections of the circle (see Figure 10-3).

Once your wheel is complete, you can use it as a guide for mixing colors in your paintings. The shape of your wheel doesn't need to be perfect; what matters is understanding the relationships between the colors. The more you practice with color mixing, the more confident you'll feel in choosing and mixing colors for your work.

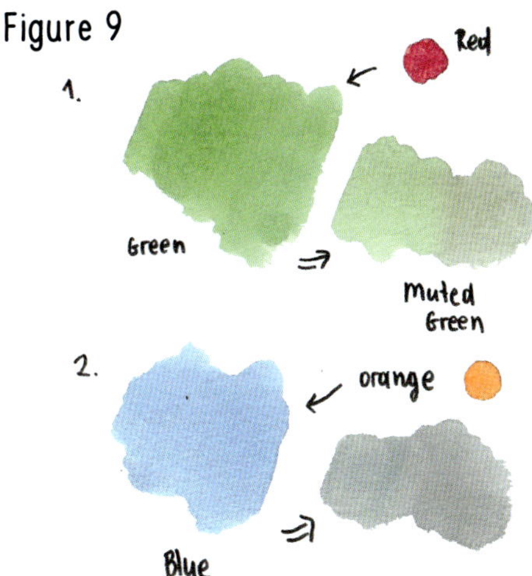

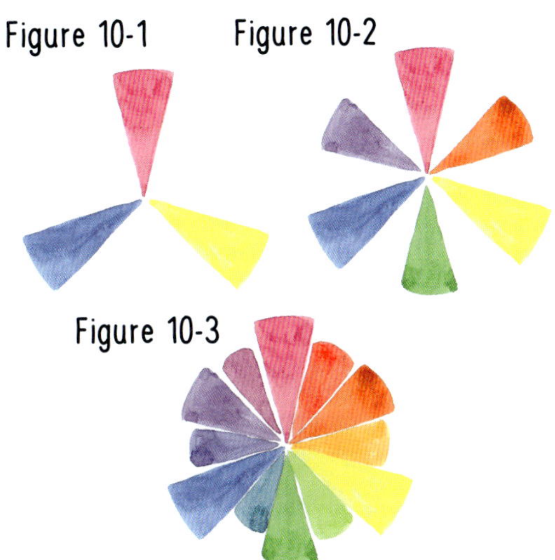

Mixing More Than Two Colors

You can mix more than two colors to create new ones, but I don't recommend mixing more than three colors. This often results in muddy tints. Watercolor is all about achieving clear and bright colors. Even when you want to mute a shade, you can do it without losing its clarity.

These are some of the basic principles of color mixing. This information will be enough to help you feel confident and have fun executing the projects in this book.

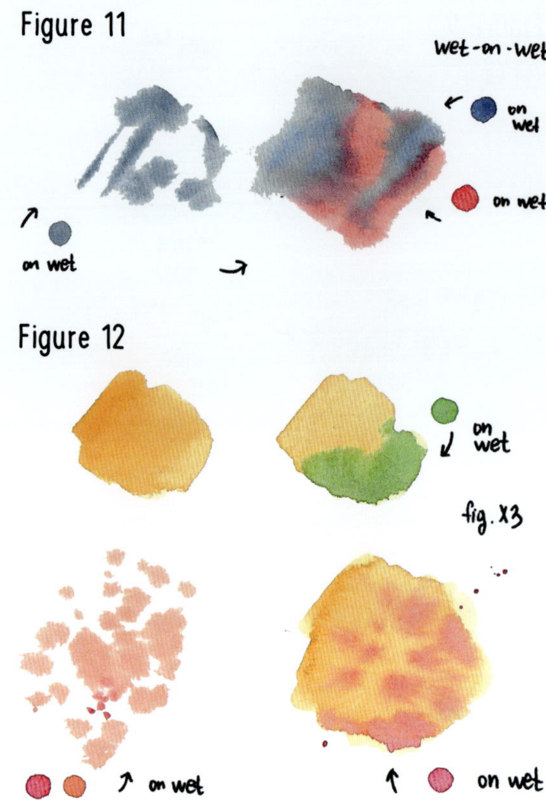

BASIC TECHNIQUES

In this chapter, I will explain the essential watercolor techniques. Practicing these techniques will help you feel comfortable with watercolor, make it easier to follow the projects in this book, and, most importantly, help you enjoy the process of painting. These techniques will also help you develop your own unique style.

Let's look at each technique in detail.

Wet-on-Wet

Wet-on-wet, also known as "painting on wet" or "blending," is a basic technique that showcases one of the unique features of watercolor: the ability to blend colors directly on paper. There are two ways to practice this technique.

For the first method, start by wetting the area of the paper where you plan to paint. While the paper is still wet, add your first brushstrokes or touches. The paint will spread across the wet surface. You can add more strokes, even with different colors, and the colors will blend directly on the wet paper (see Figure 11).

For the second method, paint a layer first, then add some details (brushstrokes) while the layer is still wet. The paint will blend naturally on the wet surface (see Figure 12).

Please note that the spreading and behavior of watercolor on a wet layer will vary depending on how much water you use, how wet the layer is, and how long the layer has been drying. Keep this nuance in mind.

The wet-on-wet technique is perfect for painting base layers, creating smooth transitions between colors, and achieving blending effects. Almost every project in this book uses this technique. You will see how effective it is for achieving amazing and varied results.

This technique can be combined with the splattering technique. First, wet the layer with water, then add some splatters on top. The splatters will spread across the wet layer. You can also add splatters to a still-wet paint layer; they will spread and blend with the base wet layer (see Figure 12).

Layering

Another essential and must-know technique is layering, also known as "glazing" or "painting on dry." This means painting on dry paper or over a dried layer.

To practice layering, first paint an abstract shape in a watery consistency with any color, aiming for a transparent wash. It should not be opaque. Once the layer is dry, you can paint another layer on top with the same or a different color, again in a watery consistency.

Repeat this process, allowing each layer to dry completely before adding the next. You can create as many layers as you like (see Figure 13).

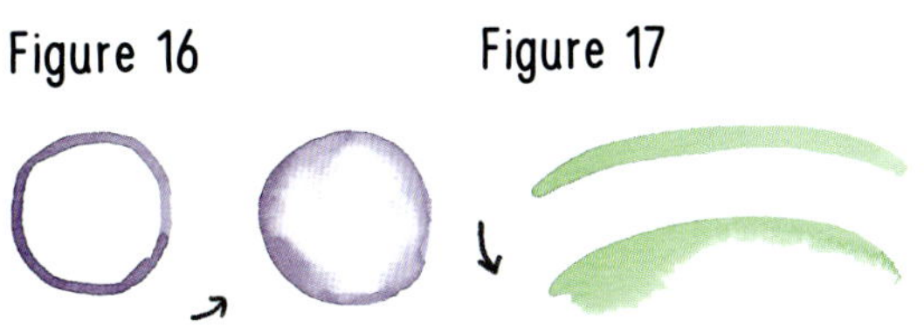

Figure 13

Figure 14

Figure 15
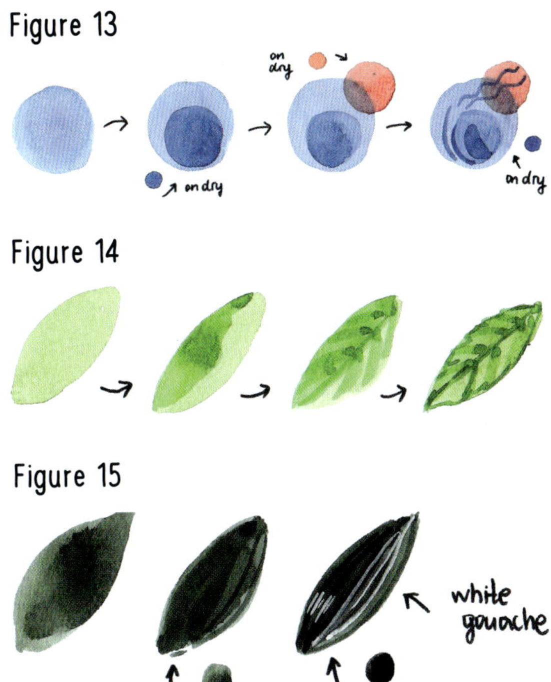

Figure 16

Figure 17

Painting a simple leaf provides a great example of layering (see Figure 14). Start with a transparent base, then add the details "on dry."

If you start with an opaque layer, the results will be different. Thick, opaque washes make it difficult to see the differences between the layers. On a thick, opaque layer, you can add some details with gouache, such as white or pastel colors. In this case, the layering technique is also applied (see Figure 15). This is why layering works best with light, transparent layers added gradually. This is also why, in watercolor, layers are usually planned and built from light to dark.

When using the layering technique, you usually need to allow the previous layer to dry completely. This can take some time, especially if you have applied a lot of water. However, you can use a hair dryer to speed up the drying process.

Layering is used as a fundamental principle of painting and is usually combined with different techniques. For example, you can use salt or splattering techniques on a still-wet layer, allowing each layer to dry before adding the next.

Softening

The next essential and must-know technique, in my opinion, is softening, also known as "blurring." Softening is not just a technique but a way of using watercolor to create blurred or soft edges for outlines, lines, or layer edges.

To practice, paint a circle (or any other shape) but do not fill it in. Then, clean your brush and use clean water to blur the edges inside the circle. This softens the shape and creates a delicate effect (see Figure 16).

You can also try this with a curved or wavy line. Paint the line first, then use a clean, wet brush to blur one side of it (see Figure 17).

Softening is helpful when you want to create smooth transitions or reduce the sharpness of edges. It can be especially useful in a realistic painting style. However, you don't need to use it all the time—only when you want to make edges, details, or layers smoother and more delicate.

Softening can also be used alongside other techniques—for example, the stamping technique. In this book, you will find a project based on the stamping technique, in which I use a paper roll to create stamps. To make the edges inside the stamped shapes smoother, I used the softening technique. This makes the stamping appear more delicate and the shapes softer and more refined.

Softening is also often used in projects based on the splattering technique. I often use it below the splatters to form particular shapes, and it works perfectly. Basically, all you need is a clean, wet brush to blur some splatters and shape them into recognizable forms.

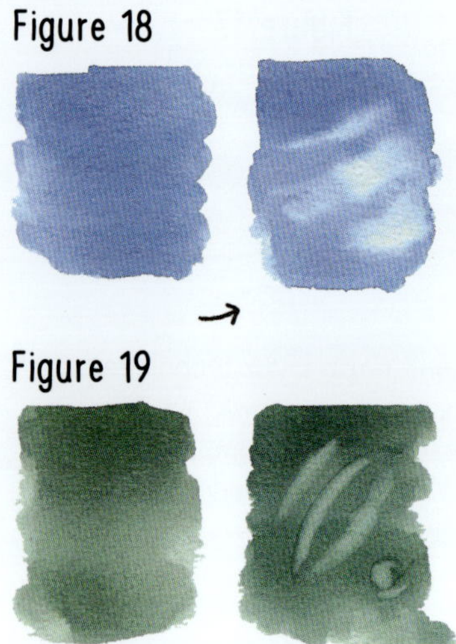

Figure 18

Figure 19

Figure 20

Figure 21

Figure 22

Figure 23

Lifting Paint

The last technique in this section is lifting paint. The name speaks for itself. You can use it to remove paint from the paper using a brush, sponge, or paper towel. This can be done on wet or dry layers.

To lift paint from a wet layer, paint a wash with one or more colors. Then, clean your brush, dampen it, and press it onto the wet layer to absorb the paint. Repeat this process to lift more paint (see Figure 18).

To lift paint from a dry layer, paint a shape and let it dry completely. Then, use a clean, wet brush to press and lift the paint. You can also use a paper towel or sponge to dab the wet layer and create highlights or textures (see Figure 19).

Lifting is great for adding highlights, fixing mistakes, or creating textures. I use it in some of the projects in this book. Keep in mind that this technique works best on thick, high-quality watercolor paper.

CREATIVE TECHNIQUES

In this section, I will provide detailed explanations of the creative techniques used in each of the projects in this book, including how these techniques work, how to use them effectively, and some variations, tricks, and advice. These techniques are not traditional, but I believe they bring joy and enhance the process of creating and enjoying watercolor.

Watercolor Resist Technique with Wax Crayons

The watercolor resist technique with wax crayons is used in the Watercolor Resist Technique chapter (page 23). Here, I will show you how to use wax crayons to create different effects and how to combine them with watercolor to achieve unique results.

What is this technique? It involves using wax crayons (or wax pencils, oil pastels, or even white candles) to resist watercolor.

First, draw with a wax crayon. Any color can be used, but I most often use a white crayon to create areas that will resist watercolor. For example, you can draw simple abstract lines. If you want to apply this technique to particular areas or inside a shape, you first need to sketch the shape with a pencil so you can see where you should draw with the crayon. Then, apply watercolor on top of the crayon—the crayon will resist the paint, creating an effect that will appear through the watercolor wash (see Figure 20).

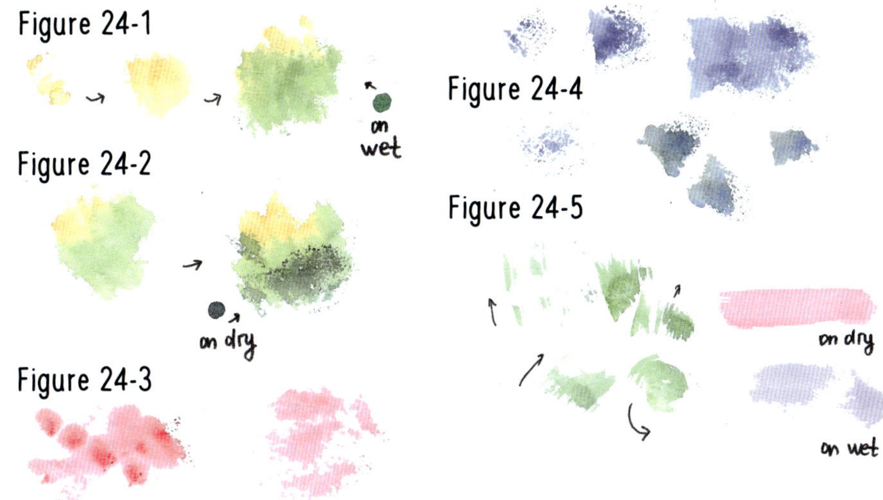

You can apply more layers on top of the wax crayon details, and each time, the crayon will resist the watercolor. Essentially, this combines the layering and resist techniques (see Figure 21).

This technique is a simple alternative to using masking fluid. However, unlike masking fluid, which can be removed after painting, wax crayon marks cannot be removed. Instead, the wax stays on the paper, which can be useful for different projects.

As mentioned earlier, you are not limited to using white wax crayons. You can also use colored crayons (see Figure 22) or experiment with colored oil pastels (see Figure 23).

TIP: Make sure your crayons are sharp enough to draw small details. If not, you can use a knife or office knife to sharpen the crayons.

Adding specific details with a white wax crayon can be challenging since the crayon is not visible on white paper. In this case, begin by creating a black outline of what you would like to draw with the white wax crayon. Then, place your watercolor paper on top of the outline and trace the drawing using a lightbox or a window. This allows you to see where you're applying the wax crayon. After tracing, you can apply watercolor over the wax crayon marks to reveal the design. We will use this method in some of the projects in the Watercolor Resist Technique section (page 23).

Sponge Painting

The next technique is sponge painting. This technique is great for creating fluffy shapes, forming specific shapes, making prints, adding texture, and even building layers. Through the sponge painting projects in this book, you'll see how fun and effective it can be.

To get started, you'll need a simple sponge (a cheap kitchen sponge works well) or, even better, a sponge cut into two or four small pieces. Then prepare watercolor in a medium consistency in any color. Always make sure you have a generous amount of paint ready. Ensure your sponge is clean, wet it with clean water, and squeeze out the excess water. Load it with watercolor and then dab it onto the paper. Keep pressing the sponge onto the paper to form the shapes or texture you need. You can change colors and start adding more sponge prints on top either before the first layer dries (see Figure 24-1) or after (see Figure 24-2).

You can also use this technique on a wet surface. First, wet the area where you want to apply paint. Then, using the sponge with paint on it, press and lift it up repeatedly (see Figure 24-3). You can experiment with the level of wetness on the paper when applying the sponge technique.

In Figure 24-3, you can see two examples of the sponge technique applied on wet layers. In the first, I applied the sponge immediately on a super wet layer, while in the second, on the right side, I waited a little. The sponge texture in the second example appears more defined and doesn't spread as much on the wet paper.

The types of prints you create using the sponge technique depend on how much pressure you apply, how you hold the sponge, how you make the prints, and, of course, whether you're working on a wet or dry surface (see Figure 24-4). You can also not only press and lift the sponge but press and move it slightly on the paper before lifting it up (see Figure 24-5). Another option is to use the sponge to fill areas with paint, which I've found especially effective on wet layers (see Figure 24-3).

This technique may seem simple, but I always recommend practicing creating prints on scratch paper to get a feel for the technique and refine your process before using it on a real project.

Using a sponge is not only fun but can also save you time, especially for large projects that involve painting trees or landscapes. It's much faster than using just a brush. I also encourage you to experiment with different types of prints using this technique. Personally, I love sponge painting, especially for creating landscapes, flowers, and fluffy shapes when painting animals.

Stamp Technique

The next technique is called the stamp technique, or simply stamping. This method is not very traditional for watercolor painting, but it adds a lot of fun to the process. I personally love and use this technique a lot.

The idea is to use an object with a specific shape, like a circle, heart, oval, or drop, load it with watercolor paint, and press it onto watercolor paper to make a stamp. The result is usually an outline in watercolor (see Figure 25). You can then continue working with this shape by blurring the inside or filling it with one or more colors (see Figure 25). This technique works with almost any shape, and in this book, I share some project ideas you can try.

Figure 25

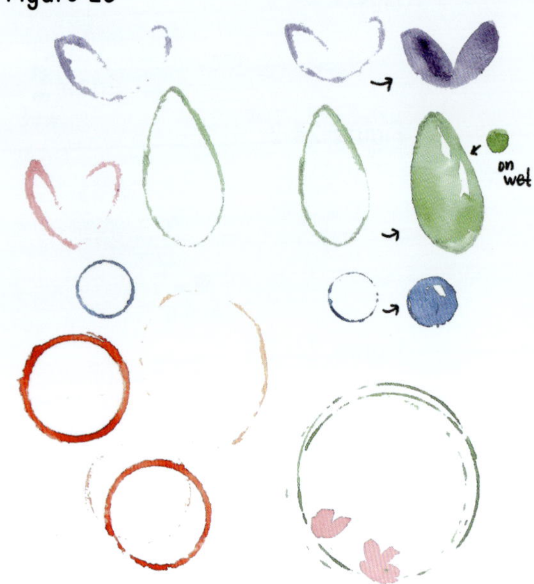

I especially enjoy using recycled materials for stamping, like paper rolls, and shaping them into different forms (see examples in Figure 25). When using a paper roll, if you need to change colors, you can cut off the used part and load it with a new color. I also recommend keeping a piece of scrap paper nearby to test your stamps before using them in your project.

You can also use household objects, like jars, cups, or bowls, to make circular stamps. One of my favorite ideas is to press the object down and then move it slightly in circles, creating overlapping or shifted shapes for a wreath base (see Figure 25).

For smaller objects, like bottle caps, you can create fun shapes like planets or Christmas ornaments. There's no limit to the shapes and designs you can try, and you can experiment with different objects to make unique stamps. The only rule is to load watercolor paint onto the edge of the object, press it onto the paper, and lift it up. That's it!

Enjoy the process of stamping with watercolor and have fun! This technique is great for kids, as there's something magical about pressing an object, lifting it up, and seeing a shape appear. Stamping is also quick and easy, especially if you need to create many similar shapes. It can save a lot of time and effort.

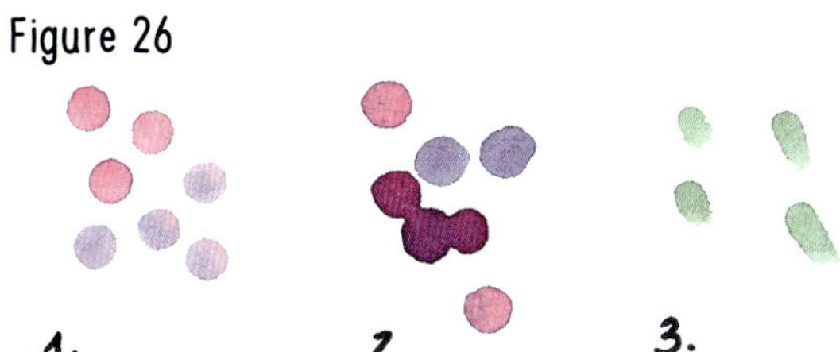

Figure 26

Q-Tip Technique

The next fun technique is the Q-tip technique. It involves making small prints with cotton swabs. This works well with watercolor, but you can also use it with other paints.

To use this technique, wet your cotton swab with clean water, then load it with the desired color at the consistency you want. Usually, a medium paint consistency works best. Press the swab onto watercolor paper, lift it up, and repeat. This will create round prints on the paper (see Figure 26-1). If you press a little harder, you will get a larger print (see Figure 26-2), as the swab spreads the water and paint more. If you tilt the swab slightly while pressing, you can create a drop-shaped figure, like the ones shown in Figure 26-3.

If you want to change the color, simply use a new cotton swab or flip the one you're using to the other side. I usually clean and dry my cotton swabs so I can reuse them later.

This technique is perfect for making quick and fun prints, such as blossoms, flowers, small leaves, berries, or branches. You can use it for any creative project you like. Making blossoms or wreaths with this technique is especially fun and quick.

In the Q-Tip Technique chapter (page 81), you will find some projects in which you can apply this method to create beautiful and impressive artwork.

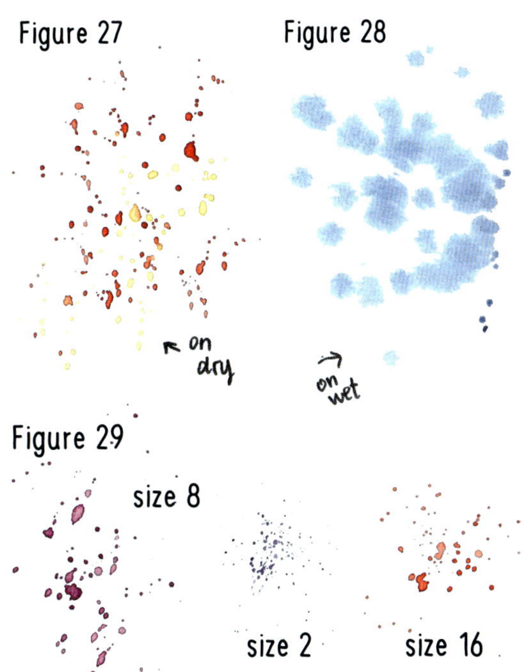

Figure 27 **Figure 28**

Figure 29

Splattering

The next technique I want to introduce is the splattering technique. This is one of the more common creative techniques in watercolor painting, but it's not for everyone. Splattering is usually combined with other techniques—either to complete the project or to start with, in order to build creative flow and direction. Personally, I find it super fun and use it all the time, especially for sketchbook painting. Sometimes, splattering is the perfect final touch in my works. In this book, this technique is featured in the Splattering Technique chapter (page 145) as a base. Splattering is also used in many other projects in this book as an additional technique. So, let's learn how it works.

You can use any round brush for this technique and experiment with different consistencies of paint. To create splatters, load your brush with paint and then flick it onto the watercolor paper one or two times. You can, of course, use multiple colors if you like (see Figure 27). Additionally, you can add splattering to a wet layer (see Figure 28). The size of the brush also affects the appearance of the splatters, so try using brushes of various sizes and see which ones are most effective for you (see Figure 29).

Figure 30

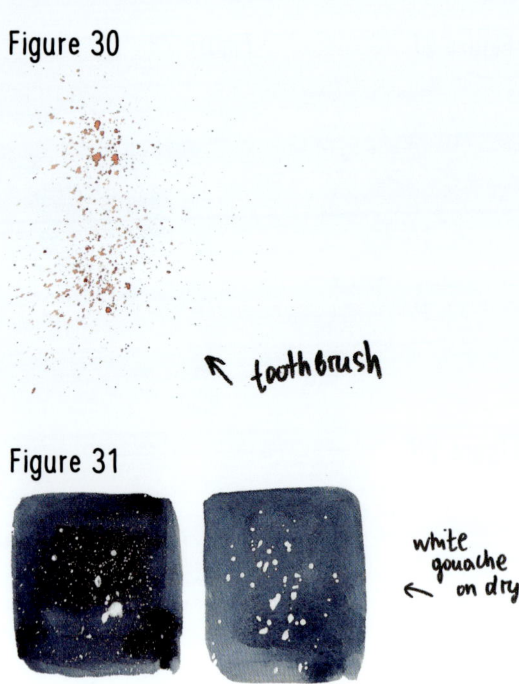

Figure 31

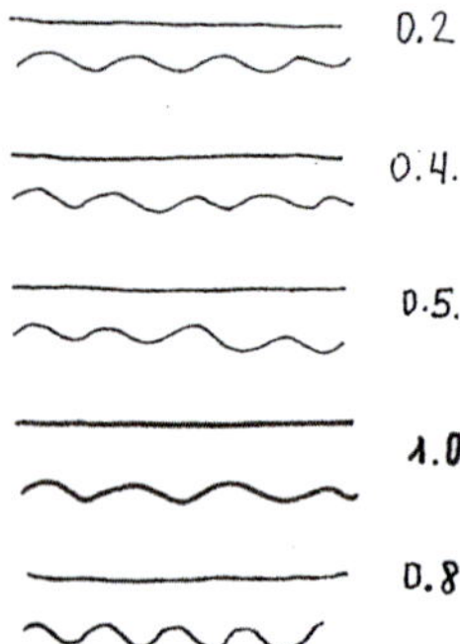

Figure 32

Figure 33

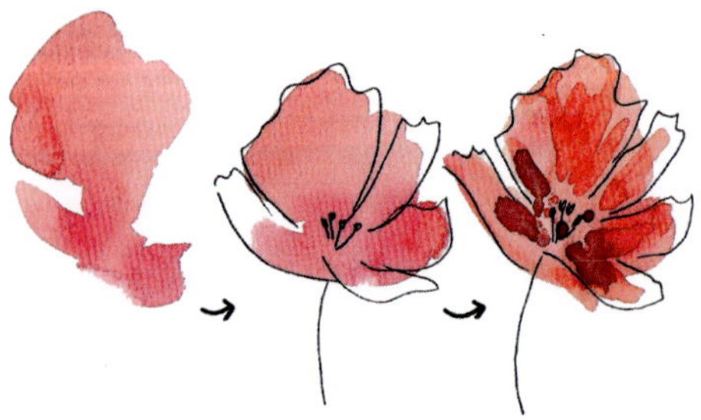

I also recommend trying a toothbrush for splattering—it's so much fun! Simply load the toothbrush with watercolor paint and spray the paint by pressing and flicking it with your fingers. This technique creates a beautiful, fine mist of splatters (see Figure 30).

I especially love using splattering to add accents with white gouache (see Figure 31). It's magical and especially effective for starry sky effects or snow.

When using splattering, just make sure to cover your table with something to protect it, as this technique can get quite messy. But if you're brave enough to embrace the mess, you'll find splattering to be both fun and highly effective.

TIP: Before adding splattering to your artwork, I recommend testing it on a scrap piece of paper, especially if you're new to the technique.

Enjoy this technique and don't be afraid to experiment with it. It will give you so much freedom and creativity!

Outlining with Ink Pens

Sometimes, I call this technique black ink outlining. It's a variation of the layering technique, but with the addition of outlines and details using a black ink pen. You can use any pen, but I usually recommend a waterproof ink pen because it allows you to add more details with watercolor if needed. In some projects from the Black Ink Outlining Technique chapter (page 159), I specifically recommend using a waterproof pen.

Waterproof ink pens come in different sizes, ranging from very thin (like 0.1 mm or less) to thicker ones (like 1.2 or 1.5 mm). Personally, I prefer using 0.5- and 0.8-mm pens—they're my favorites (see Figure 32).

Let's learn how this technique works. First, paint a layer with watercolor and let it dry completely. Then, take your black ink pen and start adding details. These details can include defining shapes or adding dots, spots, or specific features like eyes. After adding the ink lines, I always recommend waiting one or two minutes to let the ink dry completely. Once it's dry, you can paint over it again with watercolor if needed (see Figure 33).

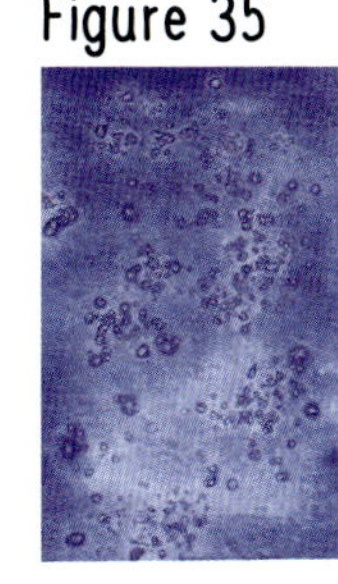

Figure 34

Figure 35

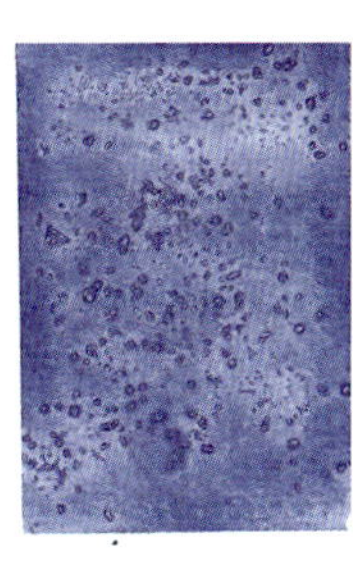

Figure 36

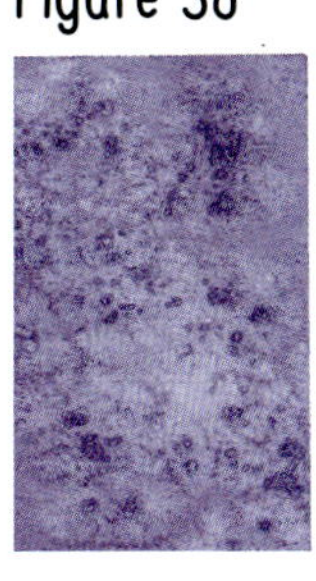

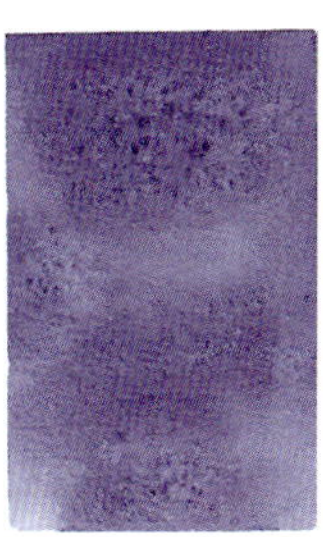

Using this technique is so simple, and I especially love it for creating cute watercolor illustrations. It gives you so much freedom—you can define or correct shapes with the pen and add intricate details. The paint serves as a base color, while the black ink adds contrast and completes the project.

In this book, I've created some super fun and cute projects for you to practice outlining with the black ink technique, and I hope you'll enjoy them. Maybe the ink pen will even become a part of your personal style. It's a highly effective technique and a lovely addition to watercolor projects, especially for children's book illustrations, whimsical watercolors, landscapes, or urban travel watercolors.

So, experiment with this technique and enjoy adding black ink outline details to your projects.

Adding Salt

The next technique is, let's say, a creative one, but it's more traditional for watercolor painting and is widely used to make special textures. The idea is to sprinkle salt onto a wet watercolor layer, where the salt reacts with the watercolor paint to create a unique texture.

Let's try it. First, paint a wash with watercolor. While the layer is still wet, sprinkle a pinch of salt onto it. Be careful not to add too much salt. Let the layer dry completely, and once it's dry, gently brush off the salt to reveal a unique and beautiful effect (see Figure 34).

You can try using different types of salt to get different results, such as fine salt or crystal salt (see Figure 34). The level of wetness in the watercolor layer also affects the results. Try adding salt to a very wet layer and then to an almost dry layer to see the difference (see Figure 36). It's also important to note that the result can vary depending on how the salt dries. If you let it dry naturally, it will look different than if you use a hairdryer.

NOTE: When working with salt, especially when removing it from the watercolor paper after it has dried, make sure you don't smudge the darker colors onto the lighter areas, as this can damage your painting. I've experienced this many times when I thought the watercolor and salt were completely dry, but there was still some wetness. When I started removing the salt, the dark paint stained the lighter areas.

I've included some fun projects using this technique. The results can vary greatly, and I especially love how the salt effect works in watercolor landscapes and abstract art. But there are no strict rules. Feel free to experiment with salt in different projects. You might even enjoy it so much that it becomes part of your style!

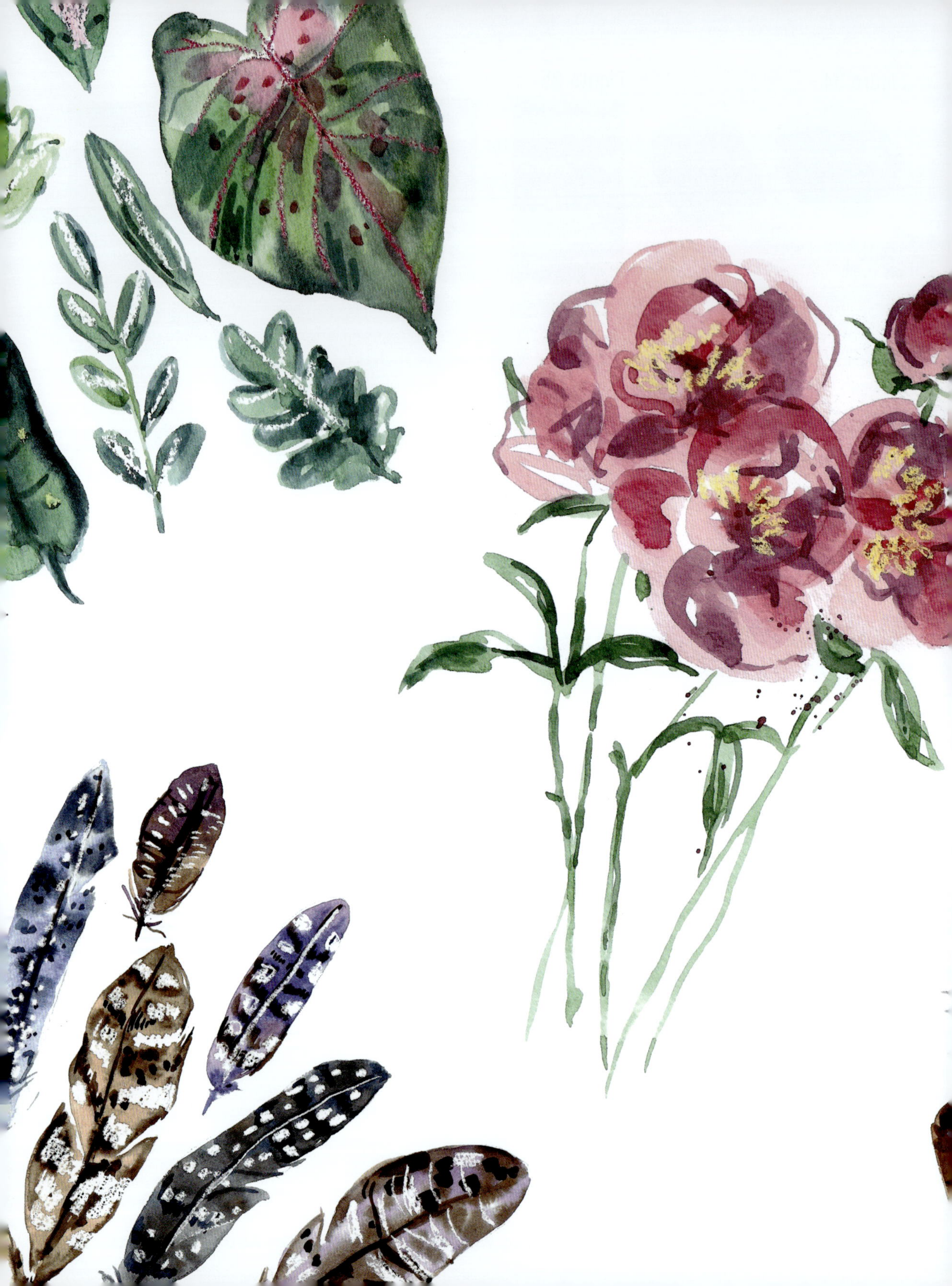

45 WATERCOLOR PROJECTS

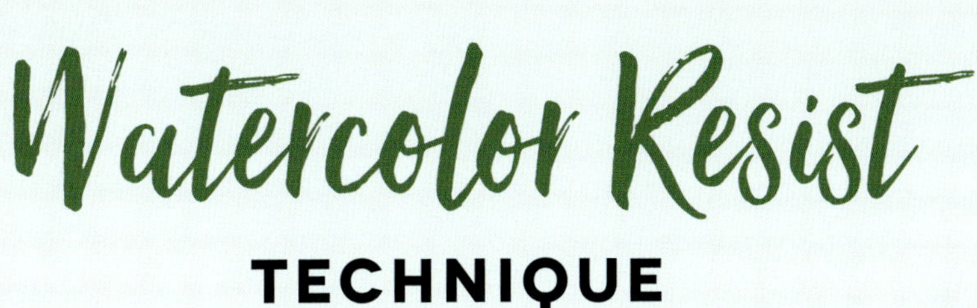

Watercolor Resist
TECHNIQUE

TECHNIQUES USED IN THIS CHAPTER

Wet-on-Wet Technique (page 14)

Layering (page 14)

Lifting (page 16)

Watercolor Resist Technique (page 16)

Sponge Technique (page 17)

Splattering (page 19)

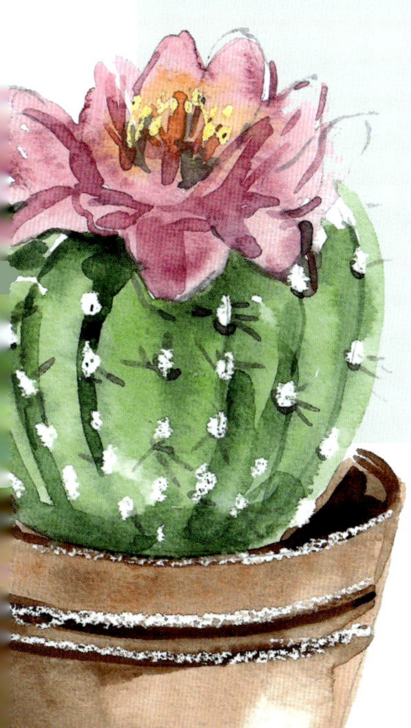

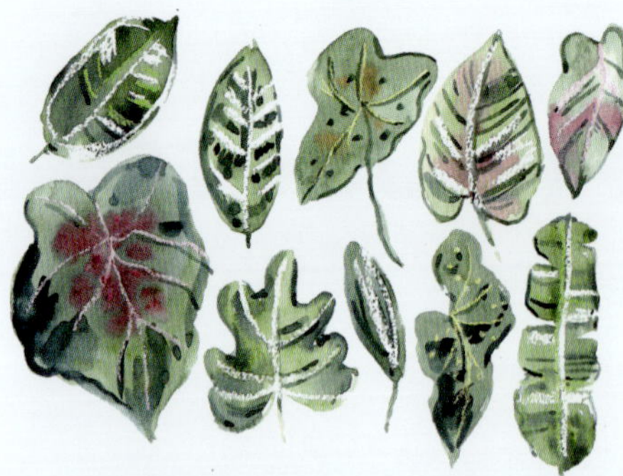

Vibrant Leaf Collection

Let's paint beautiful and vibrant leaves. We'll create a leaf set using a magical trick and, of course, watercolor. We will use wax crayons to make the leaves simple yet colorful and contrasting, catching anyone's eye. This project would look really pretty framed and hung on the wall, and it's so easy to do if you know the method. So, let's enjoy this lesson together.

SUPPLIES

- Watercolor paper
- Washi tape or masking tape (optional)
- Pencil and eraser
- Wax crayons (white, yellow, light green, pink, Alizarin, or Crimson)
- Round brushes: small (sizes 1–4) and large (sizes 10–12)

TIP: Make sure your crayons are sharp enough to draw small details. If not, you can use a knife or office knife to sharpen the crayons.

TIP: If you don't have Indigo in your watercolor set, you can use any blue. If you want to make it deeper and more saturated, you can add a little bit of Burnt Umber to your blue. This will make it darker and perfect for adding details.

PROJECT COLORS

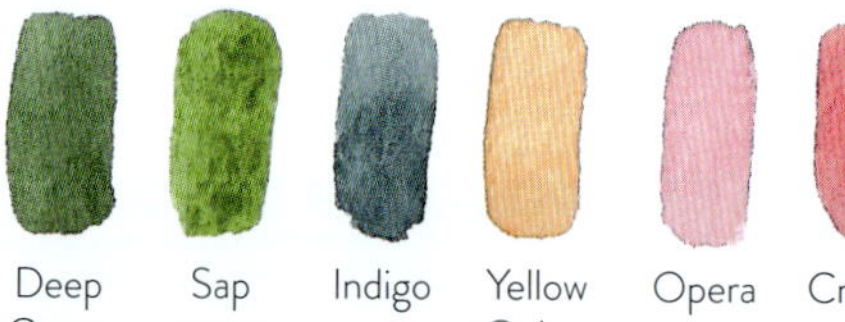

| Deep Green | Sap green | Indigo | Yellow Ochre | Opera | Crimson |

COLOR MIXING

- Deep green: Mix Sap Green with a little bit of blue. I use Indigo. If you don't have Indigo, you can use Prussian Blue or any other cool shade of blue you have.

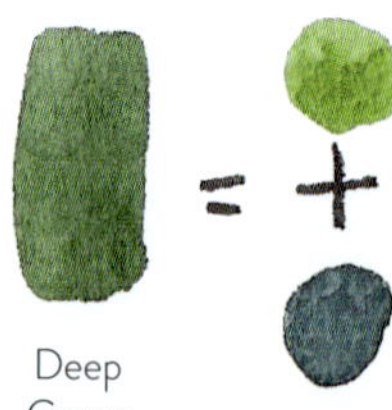

Deep Green

NOTE: If you use wax crayons, such as those from a kids' set, just find colors that are as close as possible to the required colors. For example, if the list of required colors includes Crimson or Alizarin, you need a dark pink tint. If you don't have it, that's okay; you can use a pink one or try using red, for example.

PREPARATION WORK

First, if you would like, you can secure your paper with washi tape to prevent any wrinkling when we add watercolor to it. Second, make a preliminary sketch. In my sketch to the right, you can find the outline of the composition I created. You can copy the same composition or create your own based on the set. You can use just the shapes of the leaves to create your own composition.

The Sketch

When you do the sketch, you don't need to add all the details inside the leaves. We will add these details with crayons in the first step. So, once you have secured your paper and made a preliminary sketch, proceed to the first step.

STEP 1

Let's start our painting by exploring how the project will be done. In Figure 1, you can find the four steps to create one leaf. We need to understand how to make one leaf, and then we can repeat it for the set. As you can see, we will start by creating details inside the shape of the leaf with a wax crayon. In the second image, you can see the applied watercolor. You can apply it on wet or dry paper—it's up to you—but I prefer to do this on wet paper, which looks softer. While it's still wet, you can add some details using the wet-on-wet technique. Finally, on dry paper, I recommend adding extra details to bring more contrast to your painting and give the leaf its final look.

For all of the leaves, we will use this method. In this step, we already have a sketch: an outline of all the leaves. Now, take your wax crayons and start adding the details with all the colors, including white crayons. Be careful and don't rush; take your time to add the details, especially the veins of the leaves. When working with white crayons, you need to look at the paper from an angle to see where you're adding lines. It's much easier to add wax crayons in other colors because you can see them. Once you're happy, you can follow the same details as in my example, or create your own unique details. Once you are satisfied with the result, you can proceed to the next step.

Sketch

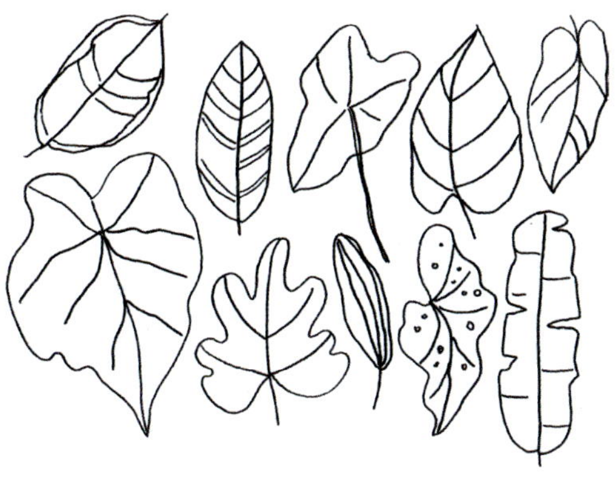

Figure 1

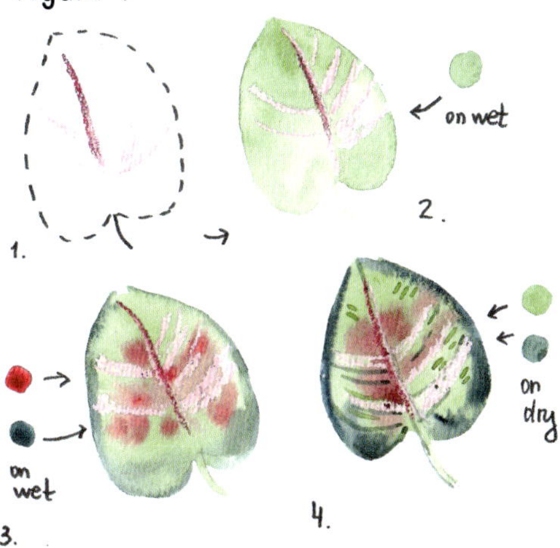

Step 1

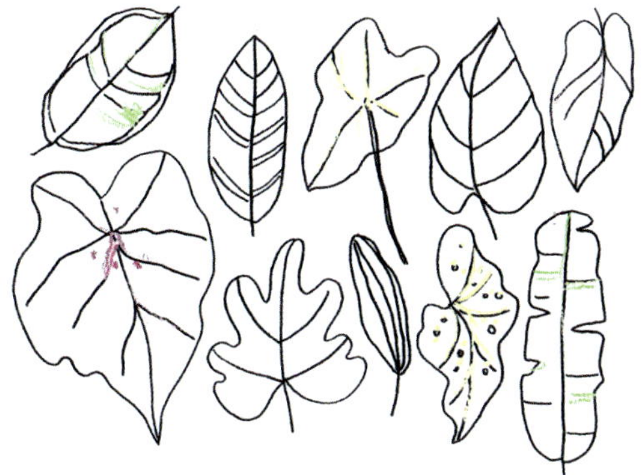

Step 2

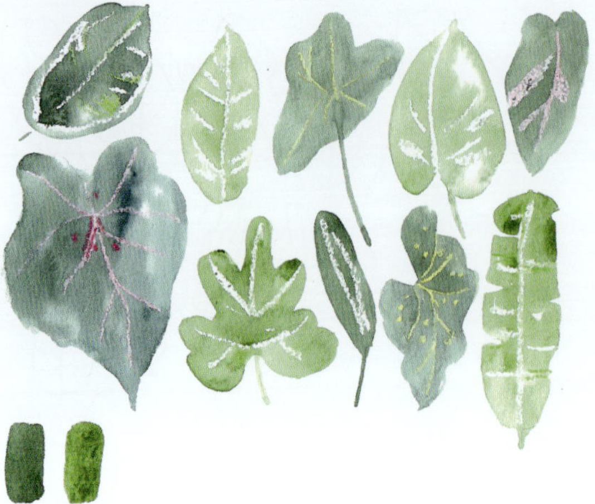

Step 3

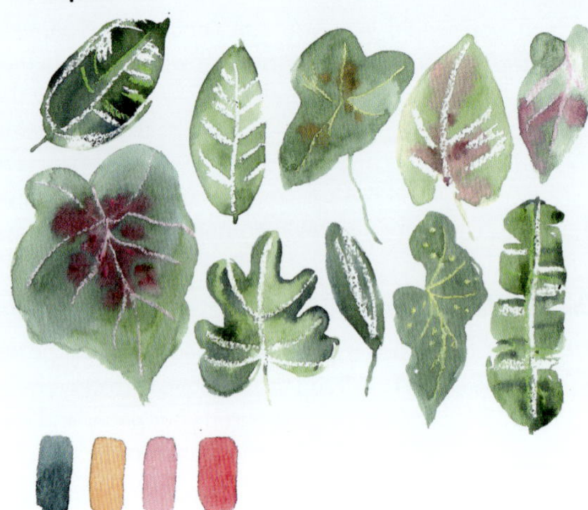

STEP 2

For this step, prepare medium consistency deep green and Sap Green. You will need to move quickly between steps two and three, so in addition, prepare medium consistency Indigo, Yellow Ochre, Opera, and Crimson.

We will fill all the shapes of the leaves with watercolor. I advise you to use a large round brush. Remember, work quickly because we will add some extra details while the paint is still wet in the next step.

First, fill the inside of each leaf shape with one of the green colors. Carefully touch the brush to fill inside the shape. You will already see how the wax crayon details appear through the watercolor washes. It's such a magical technique, and I think it's really fun to see how the wax resists these details.

Repeat this for all the leaves in the set. You can choose either color for each leaf, or you can follow my color choices for the leaves. Once you have completed the first layer, immediately proceed to the next step.

STEP 3

While the first layer of the leaves is still wet, we need to quickly add details. Keep working with the same large brush or switch to a small round brush. Use the following colors in medium consistency: Indigo, Yellow Ochre, Opera, and Crimson. Add extra details to the wet layer with these colors, as shown in the example, or create your own design by adding details as you think will look best. The colors will blend within the shapes of the leaves, creating a beautiful effect. I especially like to add dark colors like Indigo to the edges inside the shapes of the leaves, as it creates a 3D effect and makes the leaves look alive.

Once you are done adding these details, allow everything to dry completely before proceeding to the next step.

TIP: If you want to avoid the risk of the first layer drying before you add details to the wet layer, you can complete steps two and three for each leaf, one at a time.

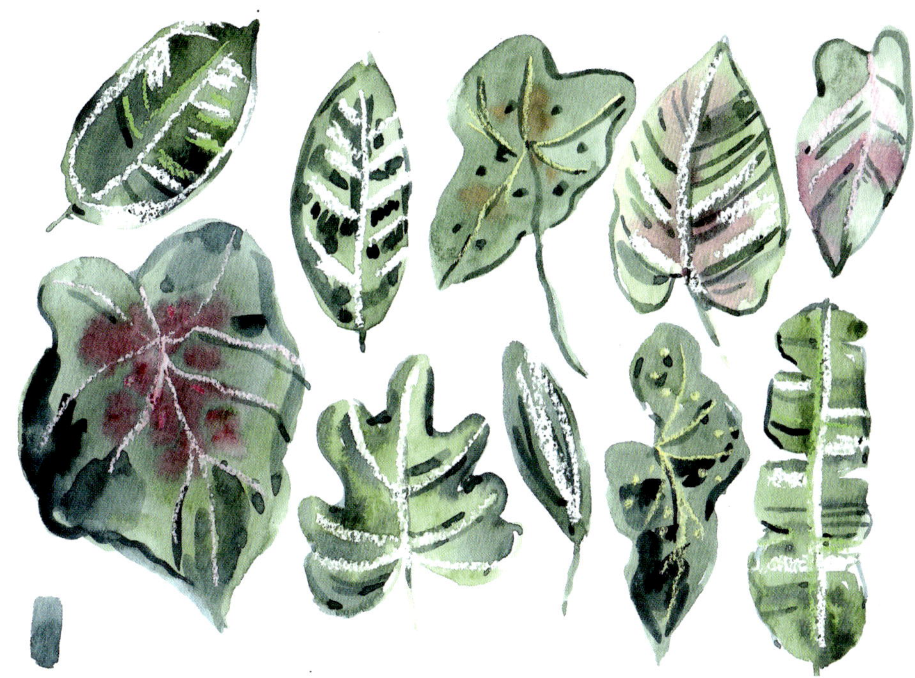

STEP 4

We are at the final step, and we just need to add the final details to complete our beautiful and vibrant set of leaves. Prepare Indigo in a thick consistency. You can, of course, use some additional colors from our project, but I advise using just one color to make the composition look cohesive and unified. One color will unite all the objects in our composition.

Use a small round brush, or you can use a large round brush if you prefer to add broader brushstrokes. Start adding details and some extra brushstrokes. I especially advise you to add details to the edges of the leaves and brushstrokes to emphasize the veins. These brush-strokes, combined with the wax resist details, will create a lovely contrast and a complete look.

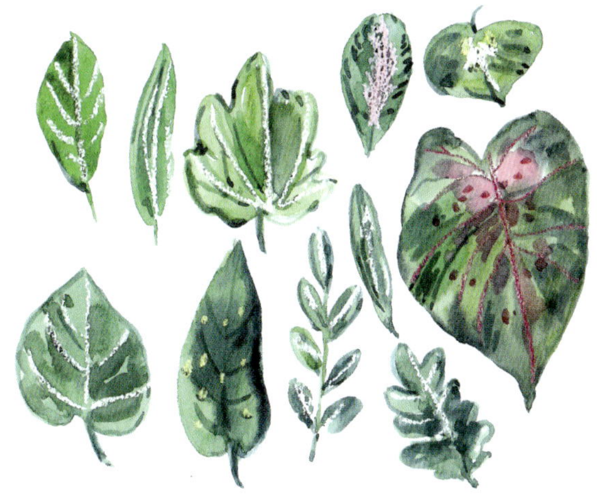

You can follow the details as shown in the example or give yourself the freedom to add your own. Once you're happy with the result, avoid adding too many more details. And that's it—your painting is done!

Try experimenting with different details, colors, and compositions!

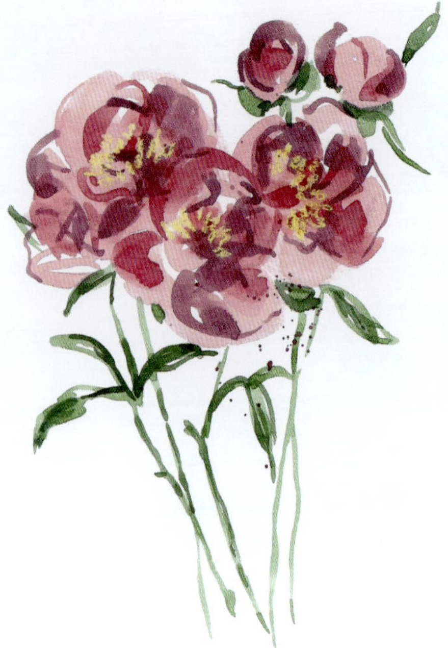

Elegant Peonies in Bloom

In this project, I will show you how to paint peonies, one of my favorite flowers, in a very easy way. I have always been captivated by the beauty of peonies, their variety, and the way their colors change as they bloom. If you are still struggling to paint watercolor peonies and capture their specific characteristics simply, you will definitely enjoy this lesson. After much experimentation, I believe I have found a method that simplifies the process, yet effectively captures the flowers' essence. I hope you enjoy this project as much as I do.

SUPPLIES

- Watercolor paper
- Masking tape (optional)
- Pencil and eraser (optional)
- Wax crayons (Yellow or Yellow Ochre)
- Quill brush (size 4, optional)
- Round brushes: small (sizes 1–4) and large (sizes 10–12)

NOTE: For this project, you can use round brushes, both small and large, or you can use a quill brush, which is perfect for creating loose brushstrokes. This is ideal for painting peonies in the loose style we use in this project.

PROJECT COLORS

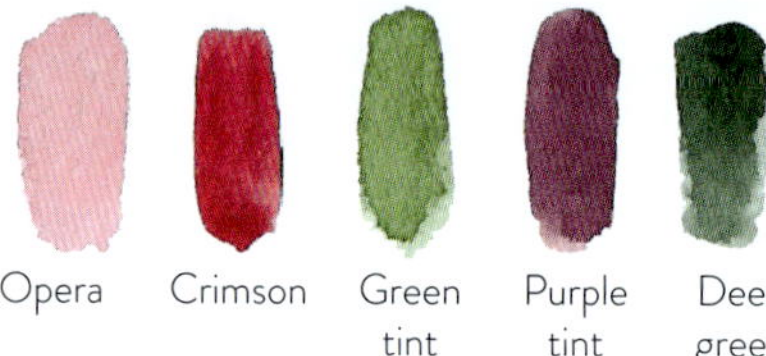

Opera   Crimson   Green tint   Purple tint   Deep green

COLOR MIXING

- Green tint: Add a bit of blue to Sap Green (I use Indigo).
- Purple tint: Mix Opera with Crimson and a little blue.
- Deep green: Mix Sap Green with a little Indigo.

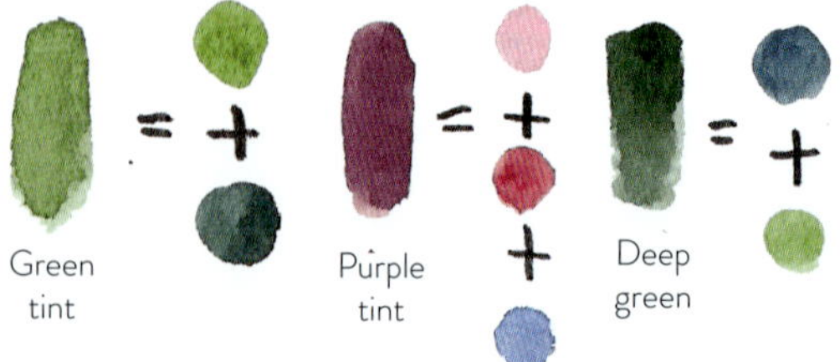

Green tint   Purple tint   Deep green

PREPARATION WORK

Let's prepare everything so that we can start painting confidently and enjoy the process. First, secure the paper to the table with washi tape, if using. Then, decide what you are going to paint by creating a composition. You can follow my composition or create your own. This project should be done in a loose style, which means it doesn't require any detailed preliminary sketching. However, you can make a very basic sketch to help you feel more confident. If you look at Sketch, you will see that I demonstrate the bud of the peony, an almost open peony flower, and a fully opened peony flower. You will notice that each of these types has a circular shape. For a preliminary sketch, you can draw very light circles or ovals in different sizes to create a composition with very light pencil lines. This may help you when you start working with watercolor. If you're comfortable with loose painting, you can move directly to the painting process.

STEP 1

In this project, we will use the watercolor resist technique to create beautiful peonies easily. I suggest taking a Yellow or Yellow Ochre wax crayon and starting to draw the stamens, the central yellow details of the opened or almost opened flowers.

If you have a basic sketch, it will be easier for you. If you don't have a sketch, just take a look at my example. Once you are ready, you can start painting with watercolor.

STEP 2

For this step, you will need Opera and Crimson paints in a watery consistency. Also, prepare to use a large round brush or, even better, a quill brush, if using. Prepare a substantial amount of the Opera color and begin painting the peony with loose brushstrokes. You need to shape the petals of the peonies, ensuring they fit within a circle. The flowers should not be perfect or identical. You can either follow my image to try to copy the shape or create your own. Also, ensure there is some space between your brushstrokes to add airiness to your painting.

When you apply Opera over the top, you'll notice that the paint does not cover the details drawn with the wax crayon. The wax prevents the watercolor from spreading to these areas.

Sketch

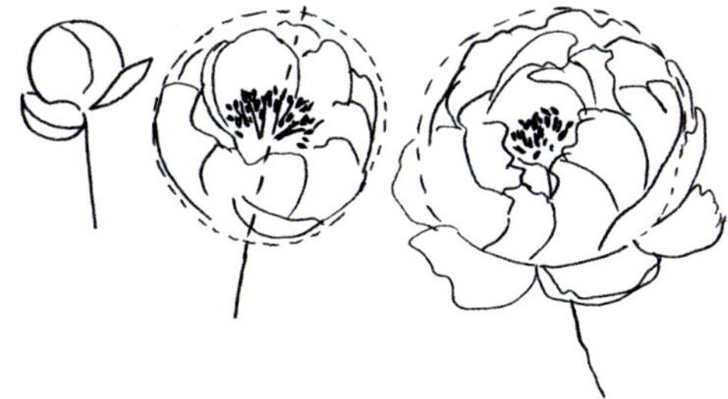

Step 1

Step 2

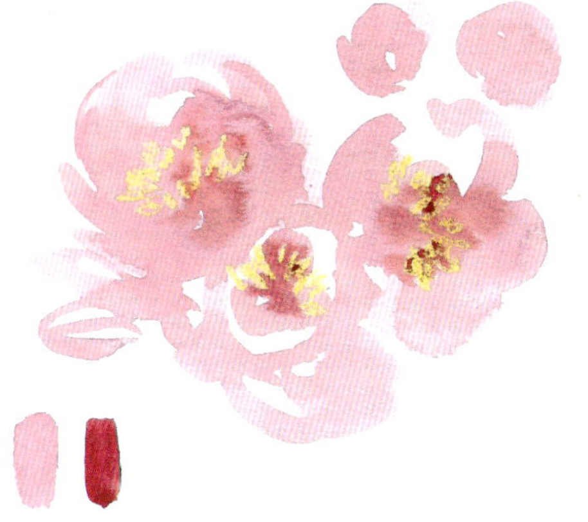

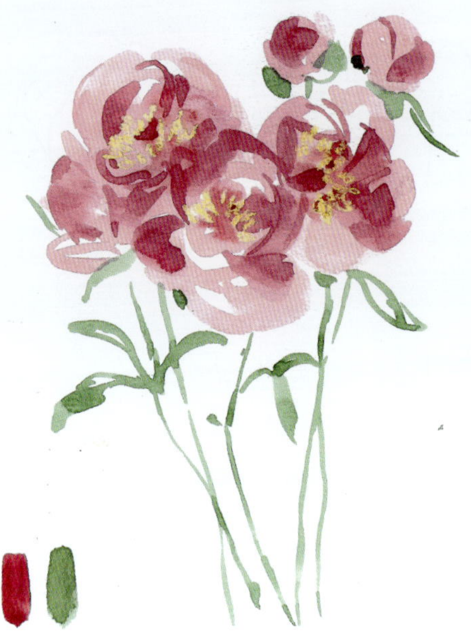

Figure 2

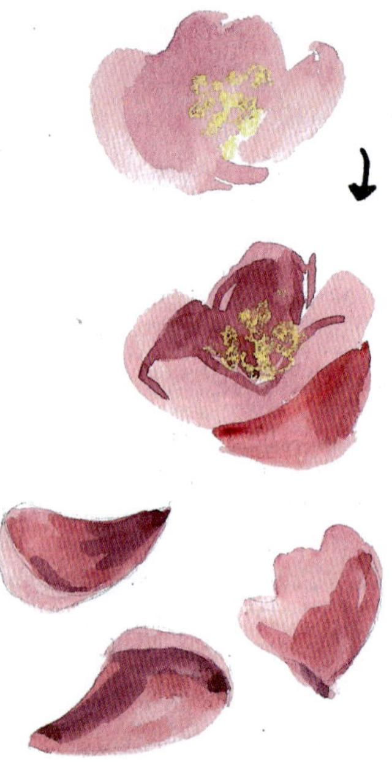

Once you are happy with the first layer and the shape of your flowers, take a little Crimson on your brush and add a few strokes to the center of each flower on a still-wet layer, including the buds of the peonies.

Once you are satisfied, allow everything to dry before moving on to the next step.

STEP 3

Take a look at Figure 2, where you can see how we are going to build depth in our peony. This will help us depict a specific peony flower while maintaining a very loose style. I start with a flat layer and then create the impression of a more voluminous flower by adding just one darker layer on top. I mostly add these accents towards the center of the flower because the petals surrounding the center are lighter due to the light they receive, and the petals inside are much darker. The darker areas give the illusion of depth inside the flower. Adding extra brushstrokes can also enhance the volume. In this figure, you can see how adding dark brushstrokes on petals serves to create shadows and mid-tones. I advise first adding mid-tones on the initial layer and then the darkest accents to achieve this volume and depth in your peony. It's important to maintain balance and not add too many details while still ensuring the petals distinctly resemble those of a peony and maintaining the overall spherical shape of the flower.

Let's begin by adding mid-tones to the peony using Crimson. Prepare the color in medium consistency, then take a large round brush or a quill brush, if using, and start adding brushstrokes that bring depth to our peonies. You can follow my example or try your own approach, but remember not to overdo it. Once you are satisfied, you can start adding the green parts of the flowers: first the stems, then some leaves, and finally the details on the buds. You can follow my design or paint your own. Remember, you can always make the stems thicker, so start with thinner lines and then thicken them as needed.

Once everything is done, let it all dry completely before moving on to the final step.

STEP 4

And now we are ready to add the final details. We already have a beautiful composition in a loose style done with watercolor, but the final, darkest accents on the flowers and the green parts complete the painting, bringing it into harmony. The first thing I advise you to do is to prepare some tints of purple and deep green in medium consistency. Then you can take your small brush if you feel more comfortable. You might prefer to use a quill brush, if using, or the tip of a big round brush.

I start by adding the accents and shadows and the darkest parts of the flowers and buds using the tint of purple. Mostly, I'm adding these details to the center of each flower. I also add a few extra brushstrokes to emphasize the shadows from each petal. I work with the buds and add a few touches with a tint of purple.

Once I feel it's enough, I change the color on my brush to deep green and start adding some accents with it. You can add these details from one side to emphasize the darker side on the leaves, stems, and details, or you can opt for a freestyle approach and randomly add these accents—it's up to you. When you feel it's enough, you can just take a little bit of Crimson or also a tint of purple and make a splattering, which will be a great final touch to your painting.

Try experimenting with different details, colors, and compositions!

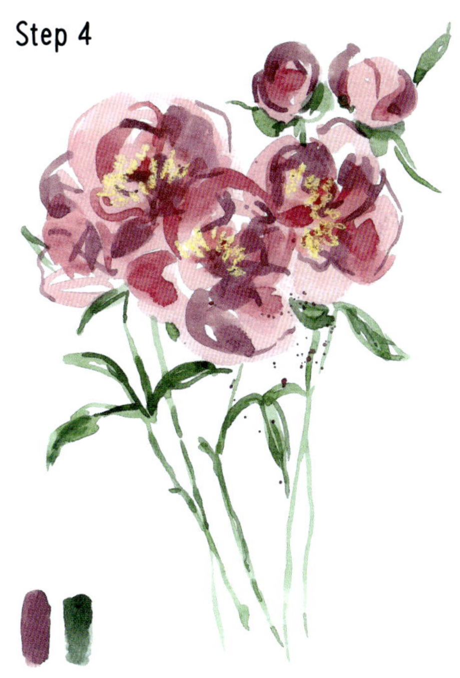

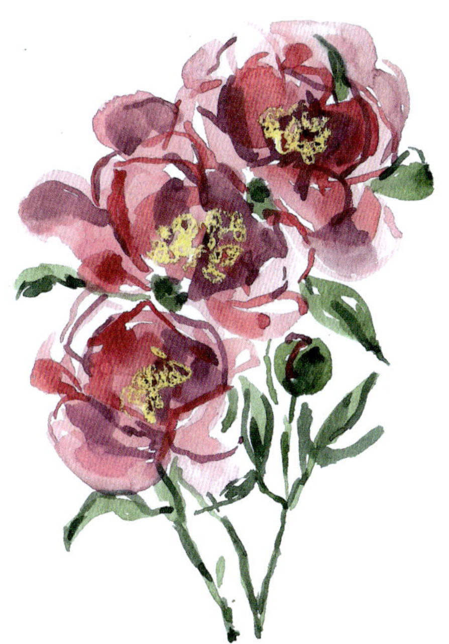

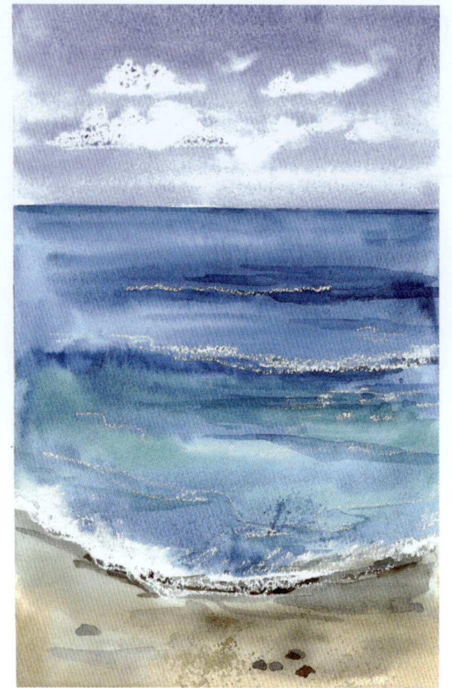

Calm Seascape

Let's dive into this beautiful seascape painting using the watercolor resist technique. On one hand, this project is done in an abstract, loose, and expressive style, while on the other, it incorporates a variety of techniques, both creative and traditional. Together, we'll create a stunning seascape painting, and you'll discover how many possibilities and variations of seascapes you can later create using this method.

PROJECT COLORS

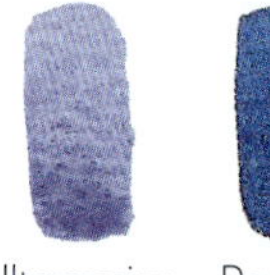 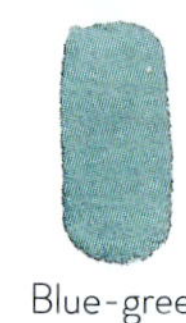 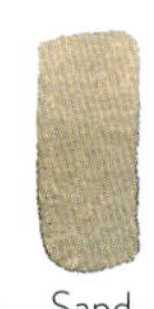 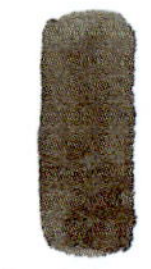 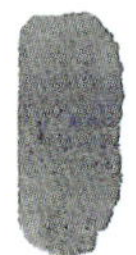

| Ultramarine | Prussian Blue | Blue-green tint | Sand tint | Dark brown tint | Cool gray tint |

SUPPLIES

- Watercolor paper
- Washi tape or masking tape
- White wax crayon or thin white candle
- Round brushes: small (sizes 1–4, optional) and medium (size 8)
- Quill brush (size 4, optional)
- Sponge

COLOR MIXING

- Blue-green tint: Add a little Viridian to Prussian blue.
- Sand tint: Mix Yellow Ochre with some Burnt Umber and a little Ultramarine.
- Dark brown tint: Add a little Ultramarine to Burnt Umber.
- Cool gray tint: Add some Burnt Umber to Ultramarine.

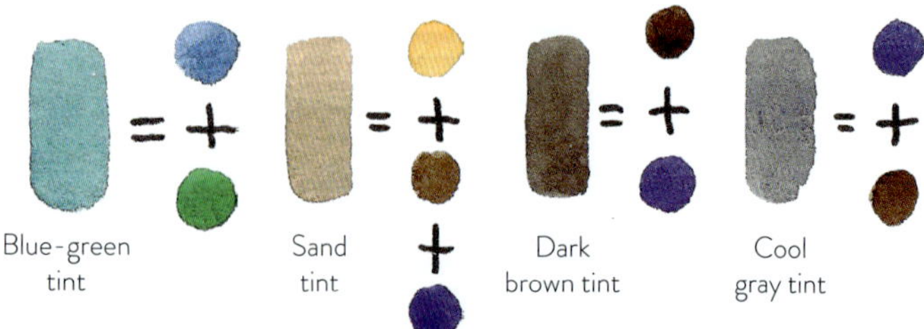

| Blue-green tint | Sand tint | Dark brown tint | Cool gray tint |

NOTE: To complete this project, you'll only need one medium round brush, as long as it is soft and of good quality. You can also use a small brush for adding details if that works best for you. If you have a quill brush for wetting the paper, you can use that as well.

PREPARATION WORK

For this project, we will not do any preliminary sketching. However, we will create a watercolor resist drawing with wax crayon before starting to paint.

First, secure the paper with washi tape. Then, using the tape, divide your vertically positioned paper into two sections in a 1:2 proportion—one part for the sky and two parts for the sea, with a small portion for the sand area. Use the washi tape to further divide the paper below the horizontal line.

Once your workspace is prepared, take a white crayon and, following the outline sketch in Sketch, begin drawing. Start by drawing the clouds and the white areas on the water. Draw small dashes and lines to represent the foam of the waves, and include smaller waves closer to the beach.

Also, draw a wide foam line with some texture close to the area where the water ends. Be sure to mark the line where the water ends and where the foam from the waves gathers. You can refer to the outline in the sketch to the right for guidance.

TIP: Since the white crayon won't be easily visible on the paper, you'll need to draw carefully. If you'd like more control, try viewing the paper from different angles to better see the wax marks. Once you're finished with this, you can proceed to the first step.

STEP 1

Now we will apply the wet-on-wet technique to paint the sky area. Since we have already drawn the clouds with wax crayon, we will also be using the watercolor resist technique.

Prepare Ultramarine in a medium, watery consistency. Then take your medium brush and start wetting the sky area. Don't wet it too much, just a little. I usually add a small amount of water and spread it over the area I need. Next, start adding the Ultramarine. To achieve an even effect, spread the watercolor consistently from the top to the horizontal line where the washi tape divides the sections. If you want more intensity, you can add a thicker consistency of Ultramarine to the top part to make it look deeper. Once you're happy with the result, you can either leave it to dry completely or use the lifting technique. By using an almost-dry brush, you can absorb some areas around the clouds to make them softer. I like this effect, and you can try it as well. If you use the lifting technique, allow the sky area to dry completely afterward.

Sketch

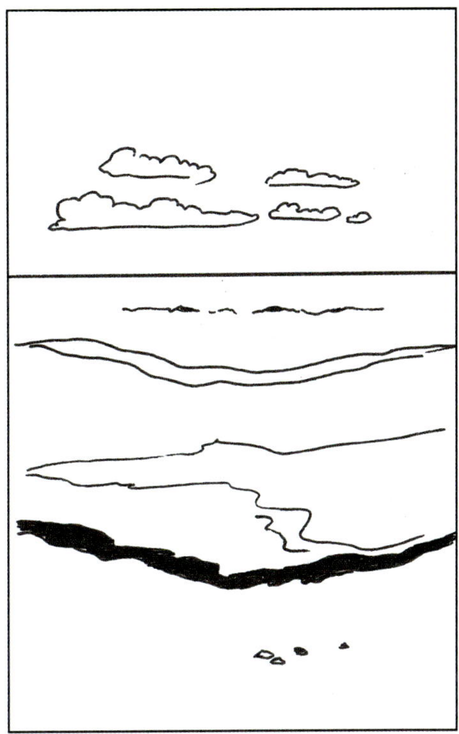

Step 1

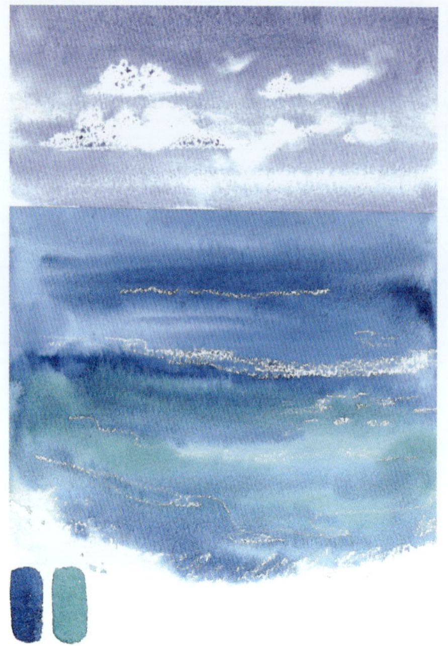

Step 2

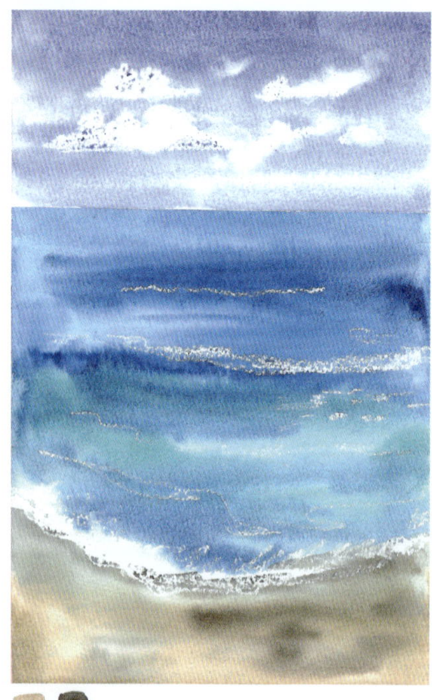

Step 3

STEP 2

First, prepare Prussian Blue and blue-green tint in a medium consistency. Keep working with a medium round brush, or use a quill brush if you prefer.

Now that the sky area is dry, you can remove the washi tape that was placed below the horizontal line. Next, apply washi tape above the horizontal line, over the sky area.

Let's paint the sea area with Prussian Blue and blue-green tint using the wet-on-wet technique.

Wash the sea area with clean water, covering almost the rest of the page, even going slightly into the sand area. To achieve an even result, start with Prussian Blue, applying brushstrokes from top to bottom. Then, add the blue-green tint while the layer is still wet. Continue adding the blue-green tint until you reach the white crayon line. Blur the blue-green with water to achieve a transparent effect.

In this step, aim for a gradient from Prussian Blue to blue-green, transitioning into transparency, and finishing with transparency in the sand area.

Once you're done, you can either leave it to dry completely or add some additional wet-on-wet brushstrokes with Ultramarine to make the sea area more interesting.

Once everything is done, allow the painting to dry completely.

STEP 3

Now, you can remove the tape that divided the sky and sea areas. Let's continue painting our first layer by adding the sand area. Prepare the sand tint and dark brown tint in medium consistency and keep working with a medium round brush. Wash the paper from the bottom, going slightly above the white crayon line. You can even gently wash a bit of the sea area. While the area is still wet, start adding the sand tint from the bottom, moving up to the white crayon line. You can also apply very transparent washes of this color on the water area.

On the still-wet layer of sand, add a few brushstrokes or spots of dark brown tint to create the effect of watercolor blending on the paper. Once you're finished, allow everything to dry completely before proceeding to the final step.

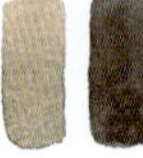

STEP 4

Our seascape already looks beautiful with some accents and blended colors, but the final details will bring more contrast and give it a more complete look. First, prepare your medium and small round brushes, if using. Also, prepare Prussian Blue, blue-green tint, dark brown tint, and cool gray tint in medium to thick consistency.

Start by using the medium round brush to add shadows on the sand with the cool gray tint. Apply the shadows randomly and emphasize the foam line where the water ends with this color. Then, using the layering technique, use dark brown tint to paint small stones and further emphasize the line where the water ends.

Next, with Prussian Blue, gently emphasize the horizontal line. If you're unsure, you can place washi tape directly onto the horizon just above the water so you can add the accent line without worrying about painting into the sky area. With this color, you can also make the white details more visible by adding some accents beneath them. Additionally, you can use blue-green tint to add a few more details to the water, but don't overdo it, as too many details might overwhelm the painting.

The final touch for this project is adding texture using the sponge technique. Apply dark brown tint on a damp sponge and gently add texture to the sand in medium consistency. Use Prussian Blue with the sponge technique to create a splatter effect, mimicking sea spray.

Once you're happy with the details, let everything dry completely, and then remove the tape.

Try experimenting with different details, colors, and compositions!

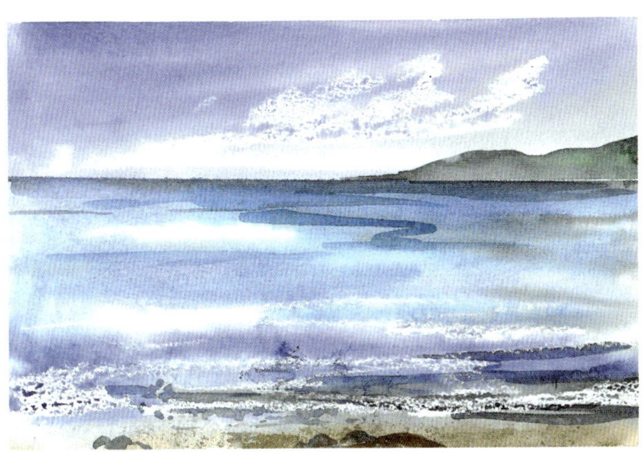

Step 4

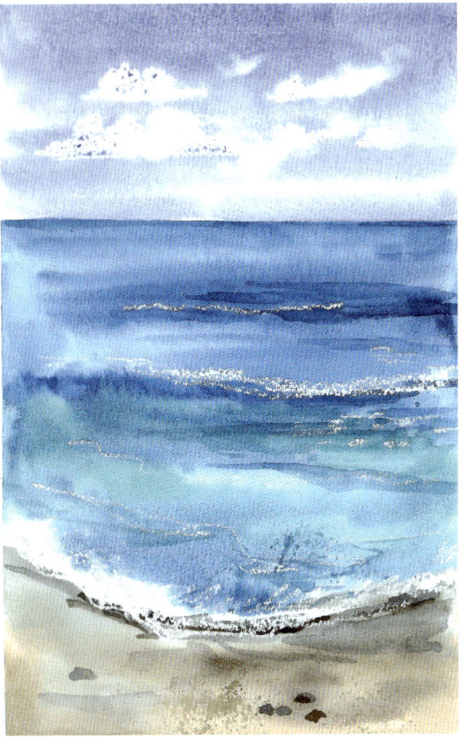

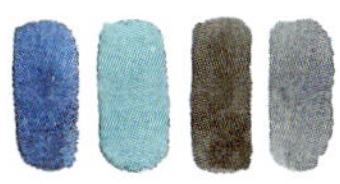

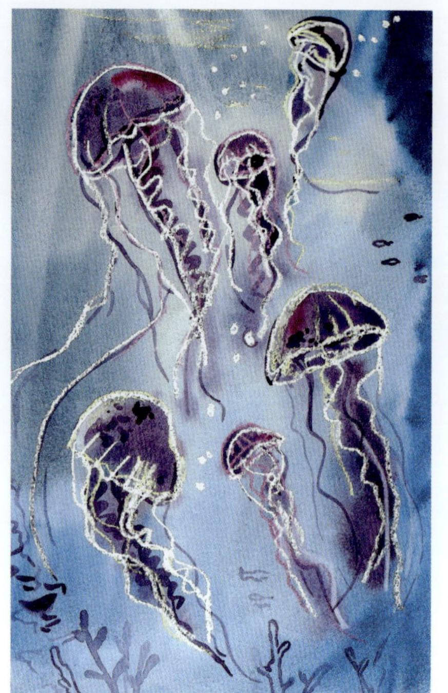

Dancing Jellyfish

This project beautifully highlights the charm of water-color combined with wax crayons, resulting in a piece that features deep colors and bold contrast. If you've seen jellyfish in real life, you know how meditative and impressive they are. With watercolor and crayon, we can easily capture that beauty on paper. Although this project is simple, it offers a wide range of creative possibilities.

PROJECT COLORS

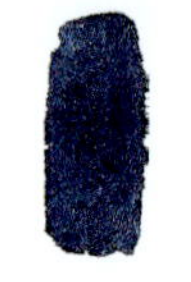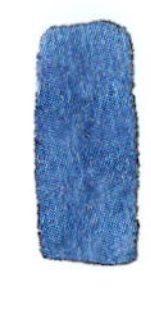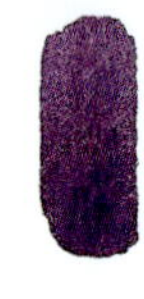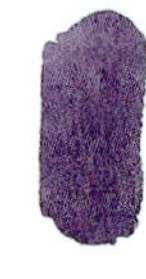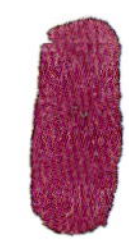

Dark blue (I use Indigo)   Prussian Blue   Purple tint   Violet tint   Cool rose tint

COLOR MIXING

- Purple tint: Mix Ultramarine with a bit of Alizarin.

- Violet tint: Add just a little Alizarin to Ultramarine.

- Cool rose tint: Mute Alizarin with a touch of Ultramarine.

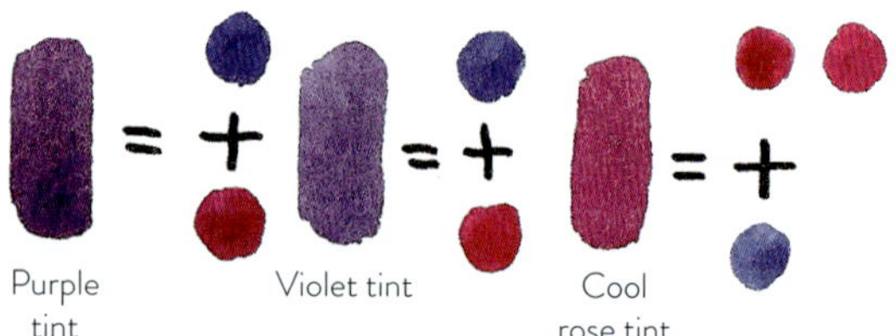

Purple tint   Violet tint   Cool rose tint

NOTE: You can use any color similar to Alizarin, like Rose or Madder Rose, for mixing the required colors.

NOTE: Please note that the purple tint, violet tint, and cool rose tint are all mixed from the same two colors—Ultramarine and Alizarin—in different proportions. This allows you to create various shades and tints by adjusting the ratios of these two colors for use in step 2. Don't worry about matching my exact colors.

SUPPLIES

- Watercolor paper

- Washi tape or masking tape

- Pencil and eraser

- Black marker or pen

- Colored wax crayons (white, purple, pale yellow)

- Round brushes: small (sizes 1–4), medium (size 8), and large (sizes 10–12)

- Quill brush (size 4)

- Flat brush

- Light box (optional)

NOTE: If you don't have a quill brush, you can use any large round brush, like a size 10, for example. The most important thing is that it has natural hair or an imitation of natural hair, which will give you the ability to work on a large background. Also, if you don't have a flat brush, you can use your large round brush instead.

Sketch   Step 1   Step 2

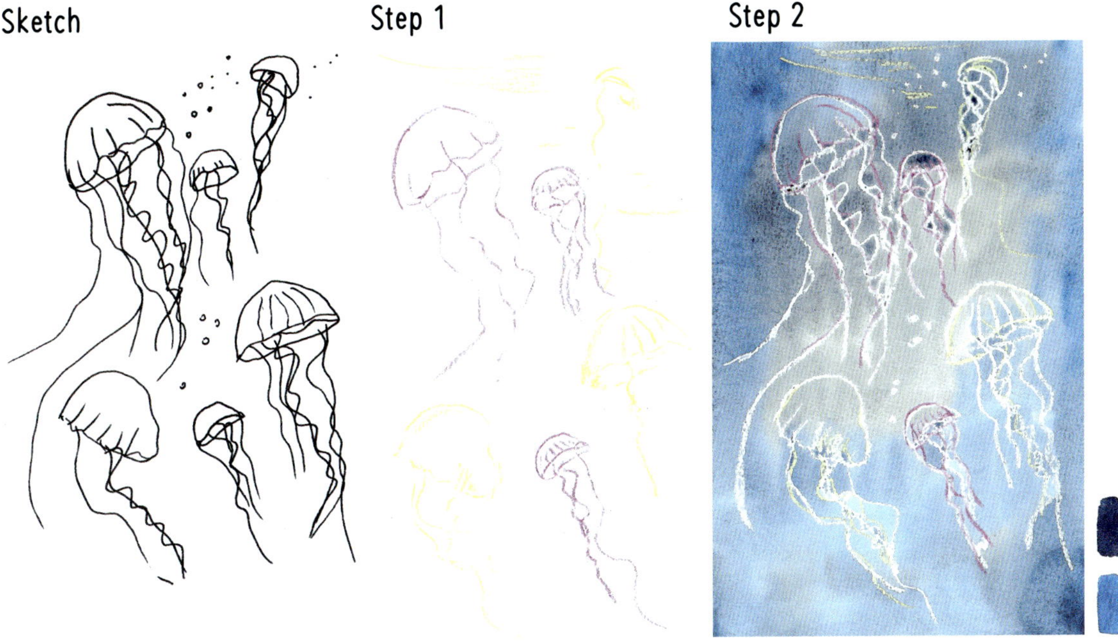

PREPARATION WORK

Let's start our project by securing the paper with washi tape. This will prevent the paper from wrinkling and create neat, beautiful edges, like a white frame around your piece.

Once this is done, we need to prepare the template that we'll use for tracing the outlines onto the watercolor paper with wax crayons. In Sketch, you can see the sketch of our project. Once you've drawn it with a pencil, I recommend going over it with a black marker or pen. We'll use these outlines of the jellyfish for tracing with wax crayons in step 1.

STEP 1

In this project, we will use the watercolor resist technique with wax crayons. I use white, pale yellow, and purple for this.

Start by tracing the outlines of the jellyfish using a window or a light box, if using. You can follow along with me—I trace each jellyfish with white first, then add details to some of them with pale yellow and purple. I also add spots with white to create a shine on the water and horizontal dashes to emphasize the water. Feel free to be creative, but I particularly recommend making the jellyfish tentacles with white,

as it gives them a delicate, lively appearance. Once you've finished drawing all the outlines with wax crayons, you can move on to the next step and start painting with watercolor.

STEP 2

This is where the magic happens. Since we've already traced the drawing with wax crayon, when you apply the watercolor, you'll see the drawing appear through the paint. The thicker and more saturated the watercolor, the more clearly the drawing will show.

For this step, prepare blue colors with a medium to thick consistency. I used Indigo and Prussian Blue, but if you don't have these, feel free to use any blue shades you have. First, using a size 10 round brush or a quill brush if using, dampen the watercolor paper just enough to spread the water from the initial brush stroke. Then, on the wet layer, start adding the blues. I begin in the center with Indigo and gradually spread it toward the edges, adding Prussian Blue along the edges. This creates the illusion of light coming from the sides. Once you're done with this, immediately move on to the next step to add details while the surface is still wet.

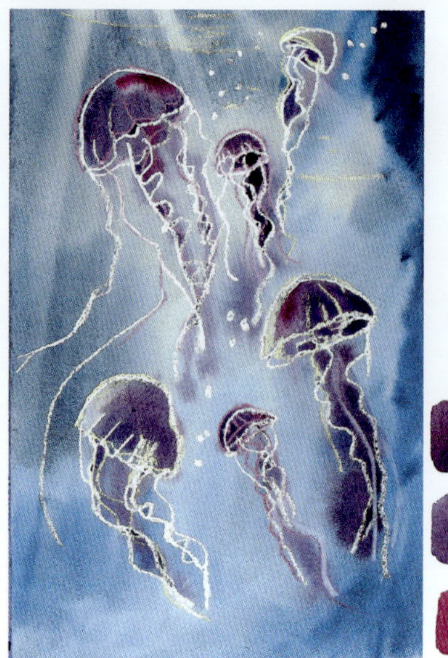

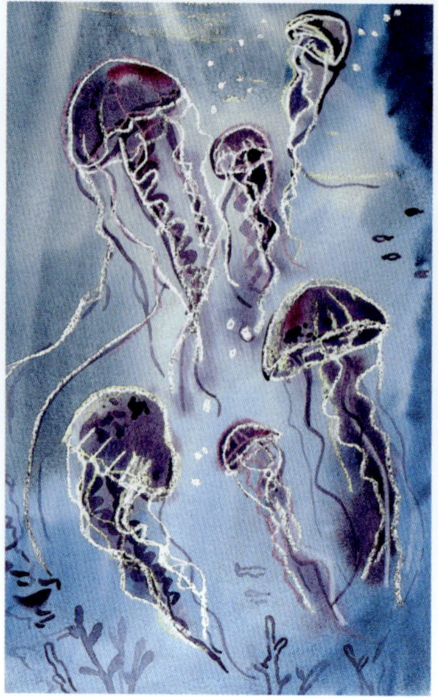

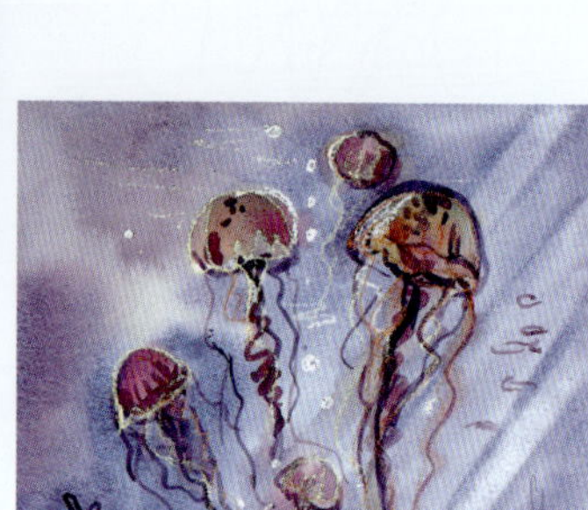

STEP 3

While the layer is still wet, you can add additional colors to blend directly on the paper. Prepare the following colors in medium consistency: purple tint, violet tint, and cool rose tint. Now, pick your round brushes—both a large one and a medium one will work depending on the size of the jellyfish. Start randomly adding these colors to the areas where the jellyfish are. You can also use purple tint to emphasize the larger tentacles of the jellyfish. You can follow my instructions or go your own way, but be careful not to add too many colors or details while the paper is still wet, as it can make things look messy. I recommend simply coloring inside the jellyfish with these tints, and that's it.

While the layer is still wet, you can also use a size 10 round brush or a flat brush, if using, for lifting paint. With a clean, damp brush, start lifting color from the surface to create rays going through the water. I recommend using the lifting technique on the top part of the scene, just above the jellyfish. Start at the top and move downward just a little bit. Don't go all the way to the bottom of the page. Then, clean your brush and repeat in another area. Once you're happy with the result, let everything dry before proceeding to the final step.

STEP 4

We've created a beautiful painting with bold contrast from the crayon details and a deep watercolor background. It's time to add the final details.

Prepare purple and violet tints in a thick consistency and begin adding details with your small round brush. First, paint the tentacles of the jellyfish and emphasize their shapes using purple.

When painting the jellyfish tentacles, it's important to keep them thin. Even if the lines are a bit broken or interrupted, that's much better than making them too bold.

Additionally, you can add more details to the jellyfish body using violet and purple tints.

I also recommend adding some background elements—use medium consistency purple and violet tints to paint silhouettes of fish, seaweed, or stones, but be careful not to overdo it.

Once you're satisfied with the result, let it dry completely, then carefully remove the washi tape. And there you have it—your Dancing Jellyfish painting!

Try experimenting with different details, colors, and compositions!

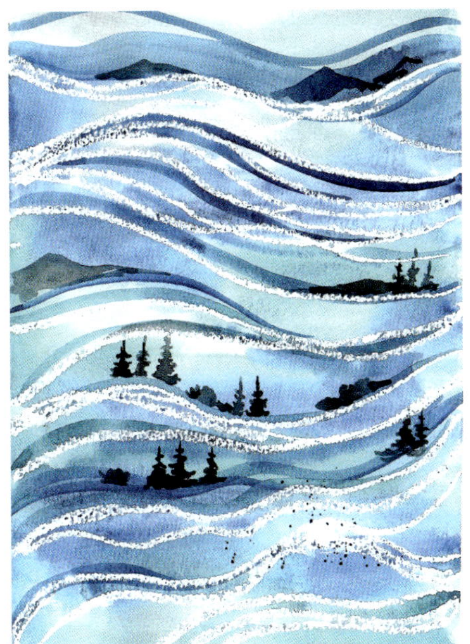

SUPPLIES

- Watercolor paper
- Washi tape or masking tape
- White wax crayon or thin white candle
- Black marker or pen
- Light box (optional)
- Round brushes: small (sizes 1–4), medium (size 8), and large (sizes 10–12)
- Quill brush (size 4, optional)

NOTE: Instead of using a quill brush, you can use a large round brush with natural or imitation natural hair.

PROJECT COLORS

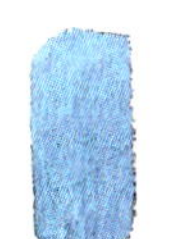
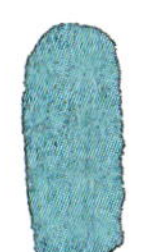
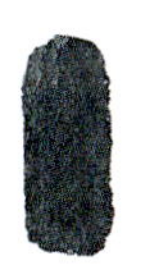

Prussian Blue   Blue-green tint   Deep green tint

Delightful Abstract Waves

Abstract projects always look beautiful and captivating in interior design, but with watercolor, creating an eye-catching painting can be challenging. In this project, I will share a simple and lovely technique to create abstract waves. This project is not only enjoyable and relaxing but also gives you the chance to practice mixing colors, creating contrast, and adjusting the paint's consistency to achieve the desired level of transparency. All of this comes together in one easy and fun project. It's a perfect warm-up exercise. If you're unsure of what to paint, just grab a wax crayon and watercolor and enjoy the creative process.

COLOR MIXING

- Blue-green tint: Mix Prussian Blue with a little Viridian.
- Deep green tint: Add a little Burnt Umber to Prussian Blue.

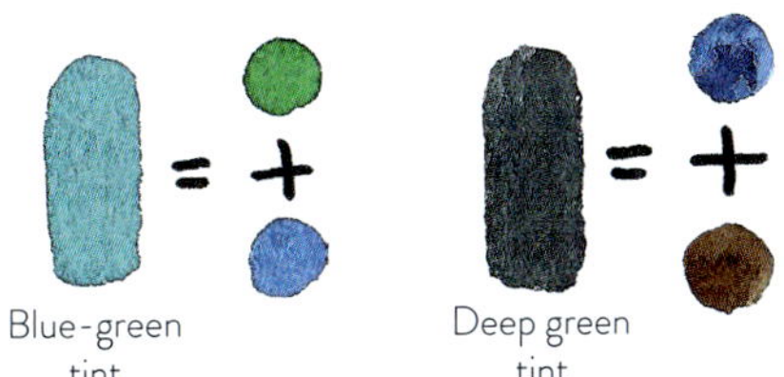

PREPARATION WORK

Start the project with some basic preparations. First, frame your watercolor paper with washi tape. This will create neat and beautiful borders for the painting, making it look more delicate. The abstract style of painting requires a clean frame to maintain accuracy and avoid a loose look. Once you've framed the paper, we'll draw the lines—essentially waves—using a wax crayon. The thinner the lines, the neater your final abstract painting will look.

(Continued)

Step 1

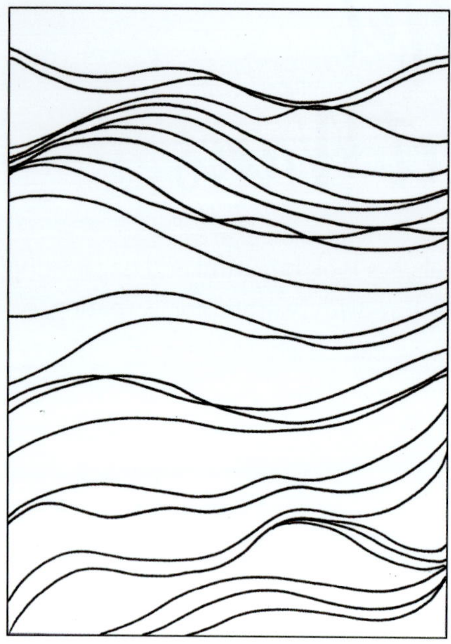

Step 2

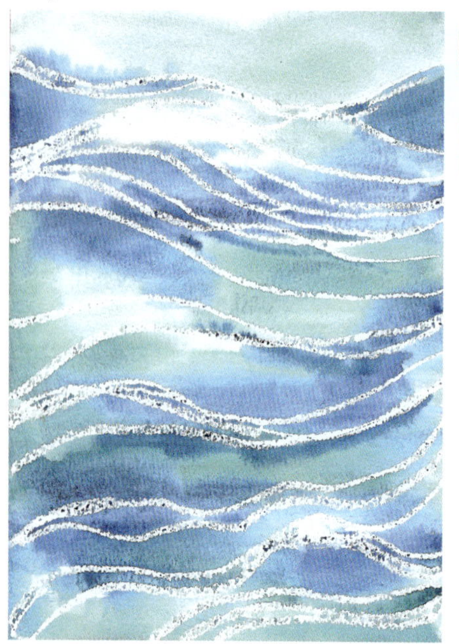

TIP: Make sure your crayons are sharp enough to draw small details. If not, you can use a knife or office knife to sharpen the crayons. I also suggest preparing a large amount of the project's colors with medium consistency in advance. This project doesn't require a preliminary sketch before painting with watercolor. However, you do need to draw the pattern of waves with the crayon in the first step.

STEP 1

Let's create our beautiful painting! Since white crayon on white paper is almost invisible, I suggest the following: First, sketch your pattern with a black liner, pencil, ink pen, or black pen. You can follow my image or create your own wave design (see the image to the left). Then, using a window or light box, if using, trace your sketch with the white wax crayon onto the watercolor paper.

Once that's done, you're ready for the next step.

STEP 2

Since we already have the design drawn with white wax crayon, we can now apply watercolor. You can use any technique at this point, but we will focus on the wet-on-wet technique for creating the background.

First, pick up your quill brush and start wetting the paper. Make it damp, but not too wet, and work quickly because we need to apply the colors while the paper is still wet. For this background, we will use Prussian Blue and blue-green tint. The consistency of both paints should be medium— closer to water, but thick enough for the white pattern to resist the paint and create a contrast effect.

While the paper is still wet, randomly add both colors, filling the entire piece with these shades. If you feel that certain areas need an extra wash of Prussian Blue or blue-green tint, feel free to add a few more brushstrokes. Once you're satisfied with the background, allow everything to dry completely.

STEP 3

Now we have a beautiful design, but let's add more contrast. This time, prepare medium and small round brushes. Use the same colors as in the previous step (Prussian Blue and blue-green tint), but this time in a medium to thick consistency. Using the medium and small round brushes, start adding extra waves on top of the dried layer.

Step 3

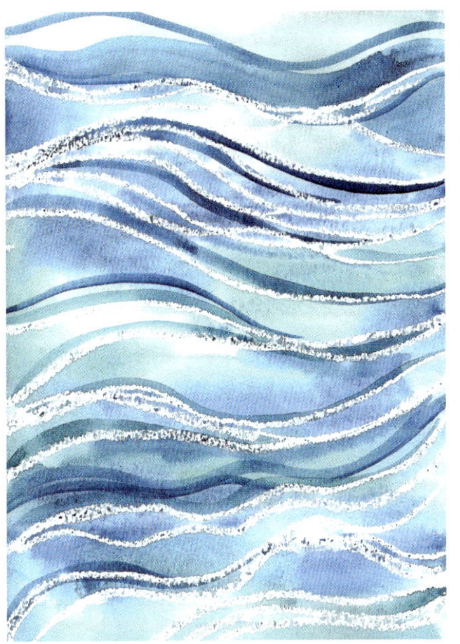

Add the waves randomly. I suggest focusing on areas close to the white crayon lines, as this will emphasize the contrast effect. The key is to avoid making them symmetrical or identical—keep them varied to make the design more interesting and natural. Remember, perfection doesn't exist in nature, so embrace the irregularity. At the same time, you can use repetition in certain areas to create a rhythmic effect in your composition.

Don't add too many lines, just a few to enhance the overall design. You can follow my pattern or create your own if you'd like. Once you're done, let everything dry completely.

STEP 4

Let's finish our painting. You can stop at step 3, and it will be a complete abstract watercolor piece. However, I encourage you to keep going and add some extra details. This time, let's focus on more specific elements like small trees, bushes, or even the silhouette of mountains. For this, I recommend using blue-green and deep green tints in a thick consistency. A small round brush works best for this step.

You can add your own designs, ideas, and silhouettes, or follow mine. I suggest placing them randomly to create something like a scene within your abstract piece, as this will add more interest and focus to your painting. Small details will naturally draw the viewer's eye. You can use the waves as abstract hills or landscapes in your painting.

As a final touch, which I always appreciate, you can add some splattering using a medium round brush with the same colors for a beautiful finishing effect, though this step is optional. Once you're happy with the result, allow everything to dry completely and remove the washi tape.

Try experimenting with different details, colors, and compositions!

Step 4

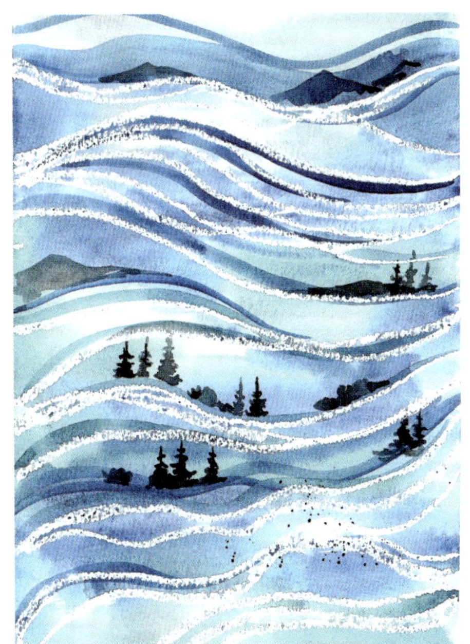

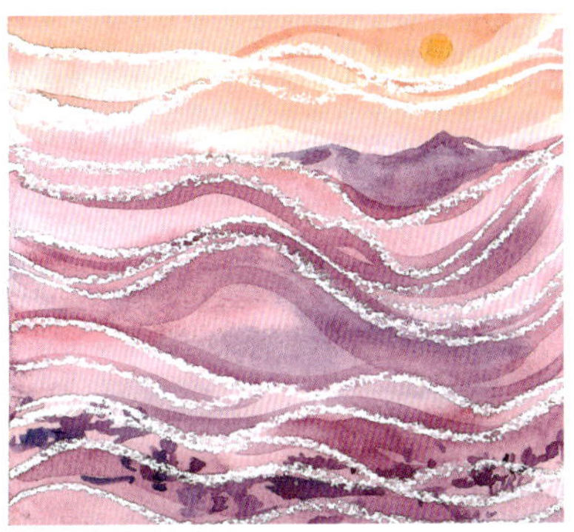

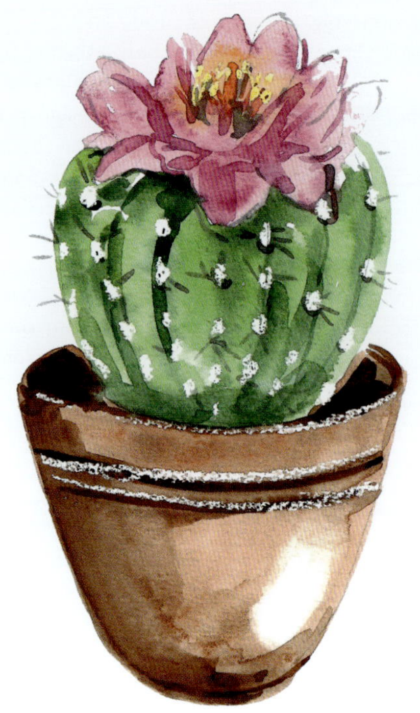

Blooming Cactus in a Pot

Let's paint a colorful blooming cactus in a pot with a beautiful, detailed, and slightly loose watercolor style. I've broken down the process of creating this watercolor illustration into steps, so it will be easy for you to recreate. Additionally, based on this lesson, you can create more colorful illustrations. We'll do everything using wax crayons and the watercolor resist technique. So it will definitely be fun, easy, and enjoyable. Let's create a colorful splash of summer on watercolor paper!

SUPPLIES

- Watercolor paper
- Masking tape (optional)
- Pencil and eraser
- Wax crayons (white and yellow)
- Round brushes: small (sizes 1–4) and large (sizes 10–12)

PROJECT COLORS

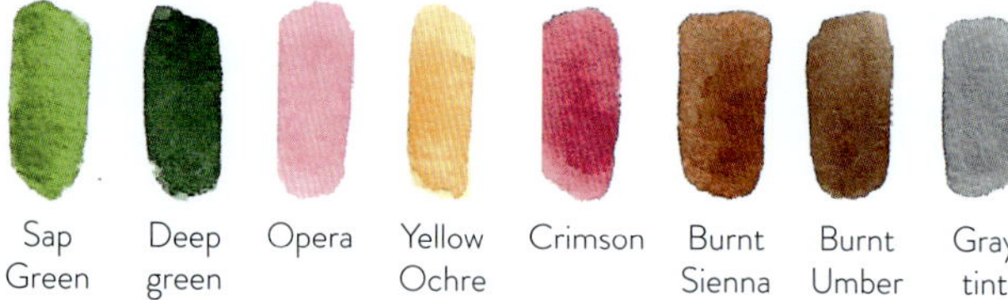

| Sap Green | Deep green | Opera | Yellow Ochre | Crimson | Burnt Sienna | Burnt Umber | Gray tint |

COLOR MIXING

- Deep green: Mix Sap Green with a little Indigo.
- Gray tint: Mix Opera with Sap Green and a little Yellow Ochre.

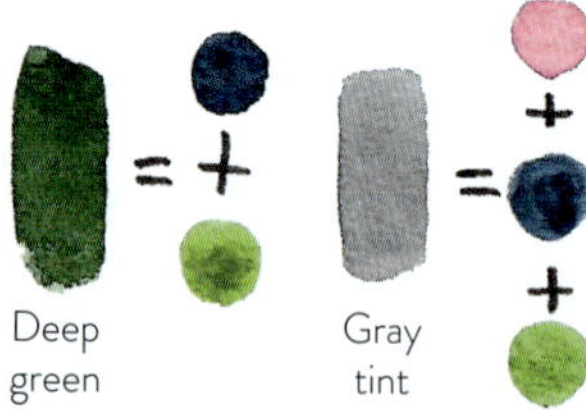

NOTE: If you are using a small watercolor paper, you can use a medium round brush in sizes 6 to 8 instead of a large round brush.

PREPARATION WORK

In this project, we will not paint a background, so it's not necessary to secure the paper along all the edges. However, you can do so if you feel more comfortable. Alternatively, you can fix the corners of the paper onto a table using washi tape.

Next, we need to do a preliminary sketch. You can repeat or follow my sketch or create your own. Try not to make the sketch very detailed; just outline some basic elements. The most important part is to define the areas of the cactus, the flower, and the pot.

TIP: Make sure your crayons are sharp enough to draw small details. If not, you can use a knife or office knife to sharpen the crayons.

Once you are done with the sketch, use an eraser to make the pencil lines less visible. Then, with a white crayon, draw the spines of the cactus in an orderly manner. Create a pattern or some details on the pot. You can experiment here or follow my example.

NOTE: The spines can be drawn in different shapes, like dots, spots, ticks, lines, dashes—anything you would like. In this project, the spines are drawn as spots.

Once you are done, take a yellow crayon and add some details to the center of the cactus flower. After that, we can start painting with watercolor.

STEP 1

Take a large round brush. I use size 10, and my brush has a thin tip, which is very important. Then, prepare two colors: Sap Green and deep green. I recommend using both colors in medium consistency. This provides color intensity, contrast, and transparency.

Next, pick up Sap Green on your large brush and start filling the shape of the cactus. On the still-wet layer add some details with deep green. Since we have details drawn with wax crayon, the Sap Green and deep green paints will spread around and resist those details. We already have the shape of the cactus visually because we can see the spines, which are spots in our case, and by painting with Sap Green on wet paper, we have created the base for our cactus.

Once it's done, allow the painting to dry completely, then move on to the next step.

Sketch

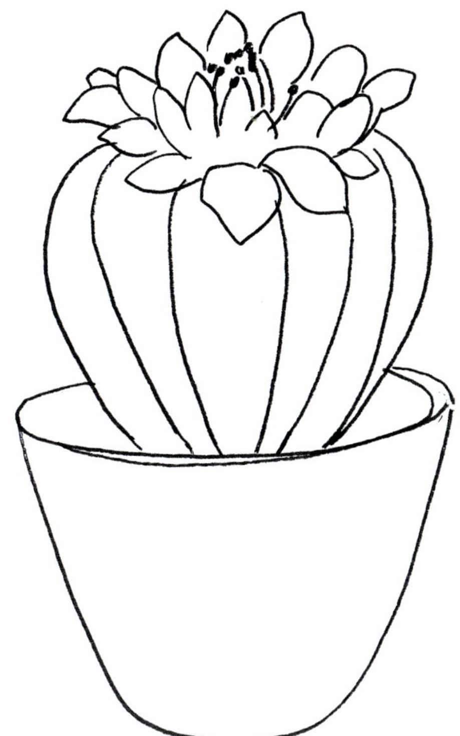

Step 1

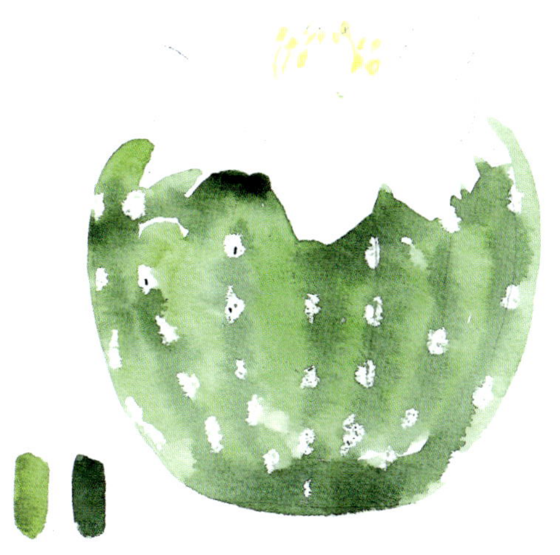

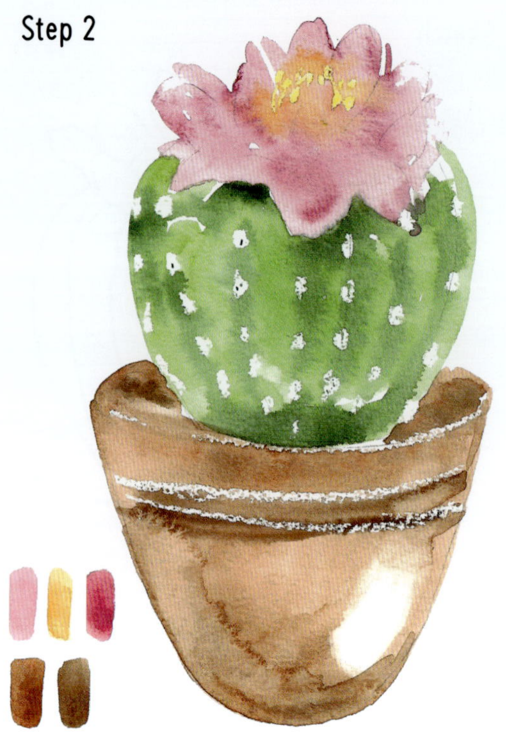

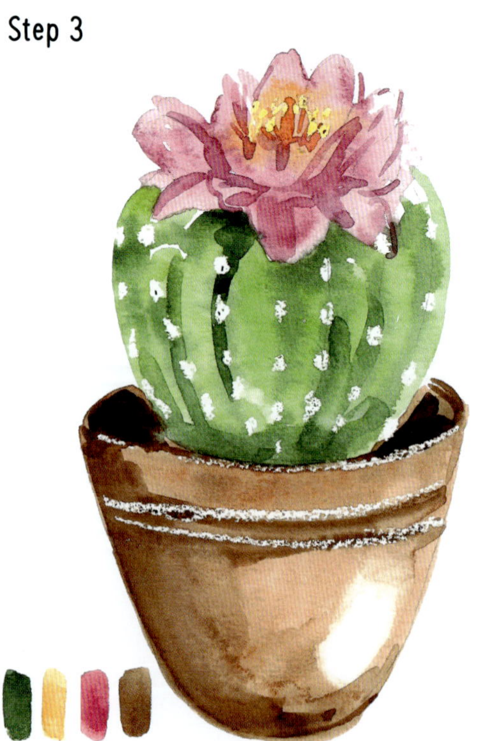

STEP 2

Let's continue painting with watercolor for the rest of our project. The first thing you need to do is prepare the following colors in medium consistency: Opera, Yellow Ochre, and Crimson for the flower, and Burnt Sienna and Burnt Umber for the pot.

Take your large round brush and start by filling in the flower with Opera. Then, on the still-wet layer, add Yellow Ochre to the center of the flowers. Next, take some Crimson and add just a few brushstrokes to the flower to emphasize the petals, specifically making the lower petals darker.

Once that's done, you can move on to the pot. First, use Burnt Sienna to fill the pot and the visible inside of the pot. Then, on the still-wet layer, add a little bit of Burnt Umber. You can also emphasize the lines on the edges of the pot with Burnt Umber and add some details to the soil in the pot.

Additionally, you can add some Burnt Umber to one side to emphasize the darker part of the pot. While it's still wet, clean your large round brush with water and remove excess water with a fabric towel. Then, with this dampened brush, lift some paint on the side of the pot opposite the shadow. This creates highlights on one side and shadows on the other, giving the pot dimension.

Allow everything to dry completely before moving on to step 3.

STEP 3

In this step, we will add the second layer to the flower, the cactus, and the pot using the layering technique.

First, prepare the following colors in medium consistency: Crimson, Yellow Ochre, deep green, and Burnt Umber. I also suggest switching to a small round brush and using it throughout this step.

The first thing we need to do is define the flower more. Let's maintain its transparency but bring more contrast. I suggest adding just a few brushstrokes of Yellow Ochre to the center of the flower, then using Crimson to add extra details and define the petals, especially at the bottom. Make sure not to add too many details—less is more.

Once you're done with the flower, use deep green to define some shadows and vertical lines on the cactus. They don't need to be perfect; in some places, make them curve. Also, add a shadow to the bottom of the cactus using the same color.

Next, use Burnt Umber to add a second layer to the pot. Define the area inside the pot to make it darker and bring more depth to the shadow opposite the highlight area. Add depth to the bottom of the pot with a few brushstrokes.

If you want to soften these brushstrokes, use a dampened brush to blur them into the paper with clean water.

By adding a second layer to each element of our project, we aim to bring more depth while keeping a loose style, airiness, and contrast.

Allow the painting to dry completely before adding the final details.

STEP 4

We already have a beautiful and colorful watercolor illustration, but some extra details bring more interest and always make the painting look more complete. For this, I used the same brush, a medium size 4, with a thin tip, and I prepared medium consistency paint in gray tint and Burnt Umber.

With Burnt Umber, you can add some extra detail to the pot. Just make sure your pot is symmetrical. You can also add some extra detail to the bottom of the pot to bring balance to your project.

With the gray tint, I suggest adding some sharp spines, and you can also add shadows under the white spots you created with the white crayon. Additionally, you can use the same color to add details to the flower, perhaps to the center, or to outline some petals. This will further emphasize the flower and make it look more complete.

Keep the painting balanced; don't add too many details. Just ensure your painting looks complete and that you are happy with it.

Try experimenting with different details, colors, and compositions!

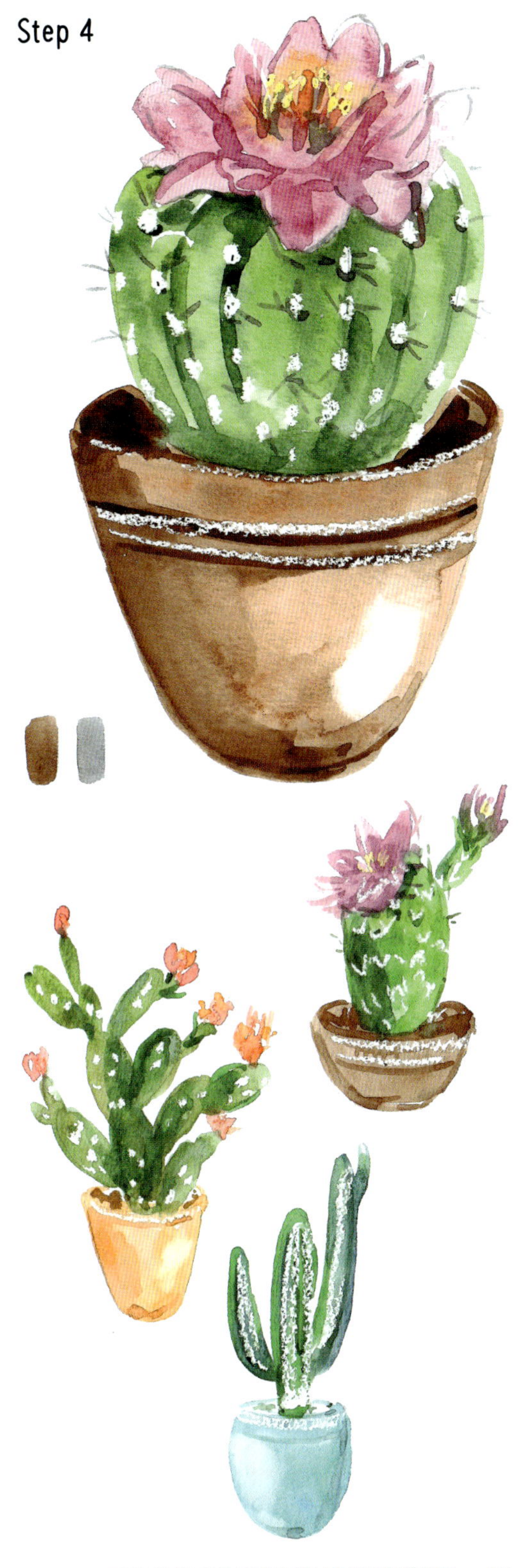

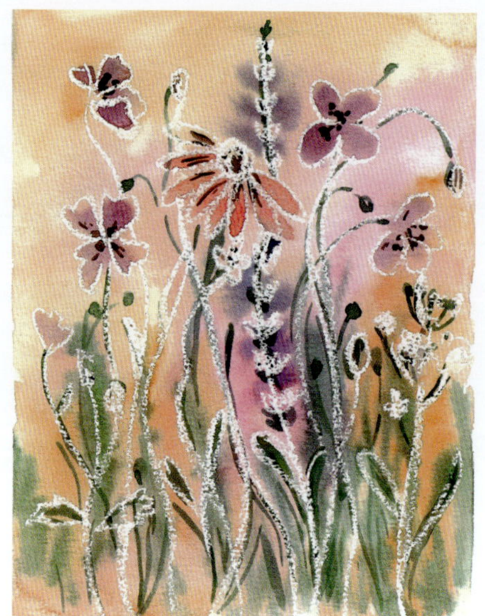

Elegant Wildflowers

Let's paint elegant wildflowers with watercolor, using a white wax crayon for gradients. It's a magical joy when the delicate outlines of wildflowers and herbs appear through watercolor blends and colors, resulting in a beautiful piece. This lesson is simple yet enjoyable and teaches you about composition, colors, and contrasts.

COLOR MIXING

- Green tint: Mix a little blue with Sap Green. I use Indigo as the blue in this mixture.

- Violet tint: Mix Crimson with Ultramarine.

- Warm rose tint: Mix Opera with a little Yellow Ochre.

- Purple tint: Mix Opera with a little Ultramarine.

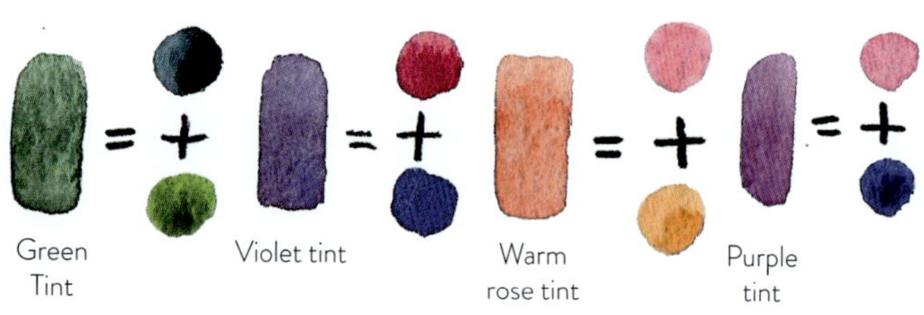

NOTE: If you don't have a quill brush, which is perfect for painting projects that use a lot of water and the wet-on-wet technique, you can instead use a large round brush with soft bristles.

SUPPLIES

- Watercolor paper
- Washi tape or masking tape
- White wax crayon or thin white candle
- Pencil and eraser (optional)
- Black marker or pen
- Light box (optional)
- Round brushes: small (sizes 1–4) and large (sizes 10–12)
- Quill brush (size 4, optional) or a large round brush

PREPARATION WORK

In this project, we need to do some preliminary preparation work. We will start with a special sketch in the first step. Before we begin, make sure to secure your watercolor paper with washi tape to prevent any warping and wrinkling, as we will use a lot of water and the wet-on-wet technique. Also, prepare a white wax crayon and make sure it is sharp. If you don't have a wax crayon, you can use a white candle, like those for birthday cakes, but ensure it is made of wax and is white in color. Using white will create the perfect contrast for this project.

TIP: Make sure your crayons are sharp enough to draw small details. If not, you can use a knife or office knife to sharpen the crayons.

PROJECT COLORS

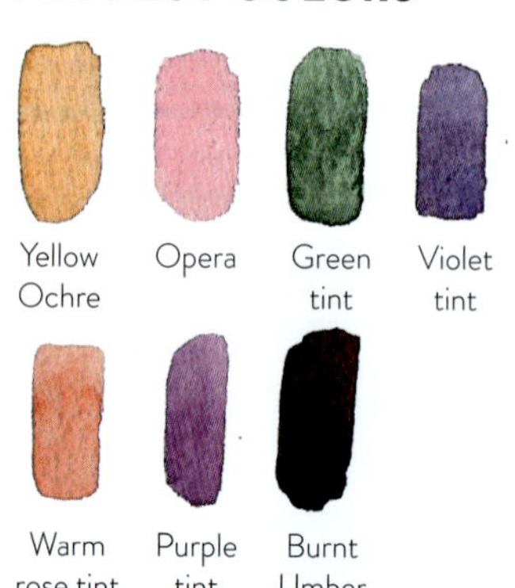

TIP: I advise you to prepare all the colors for the project in advance because we will be using the wet-on-wet technique. Especially between steps 2 and 3, you will not have time to prepare the required colors: green tint, violet tint, purple tint, and warm rose tint. Each of these colors should be prepared to a medium consistency.

STEP 1

Let's start our project by drawing outlines with a wax crayon. Drawing with white on white paper is not easy, so I recommend first sketching with a pencil or creating a black outline. If you start with a pencil, you can later cover it with a black marker, or you can start with a black marker. In Step 1, you will find the composition for this project.

Once you have outlined this composition, I recommend tracing it using a window or a light box, if using, onto another piece of watercolor paper with a wax crayon. This way, you will know where to draw the lines. Once you have completed this, you can proceed to the next step.

STEP 2

Now, let's use watercolor. In the first step, we prepared everything for the watercolor resist technique. We will now apply watercolor on wet paper using the wet-on-wet technique.

For this step, we will need two colors: Yellow Ochre and Opera. Prepare these colors to a medium consistency. It's best to use a quill brush for this step, but if you don't have one, a large round brush will work as well.

First, moisten the entire paper. Make sure it is wet enough to apply watercolor. Once the paper is moistened, start adding Yellow Ochre from the top, working your way down. Leave a few areas free of paint and then add a few spots of Opera in those areas. The colors will blend directly on the paper, creating a beautiful effect and a lovely first layer. You will already see how the white outlines appear through the watercolor washes, making a beautiful contrast.

Once the first wash is done, immediately proceed to the next step.

Step 1

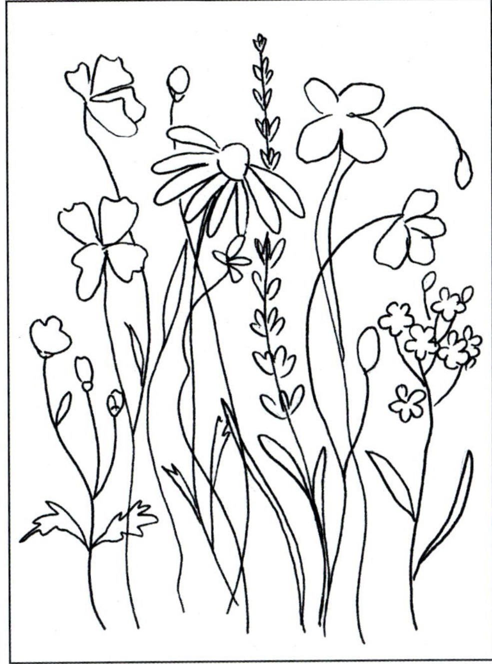

Step 2

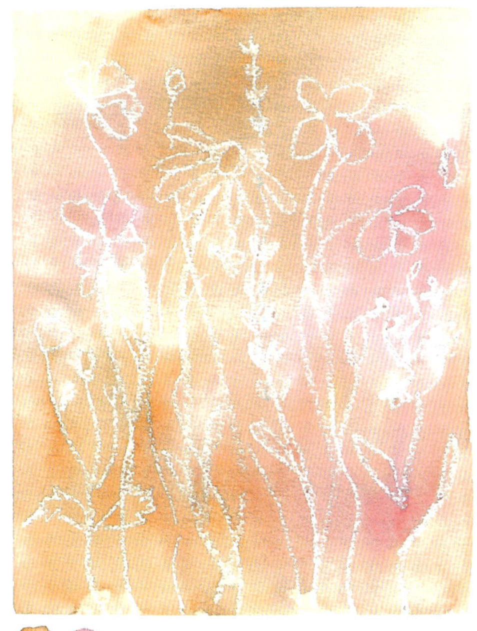

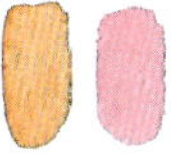

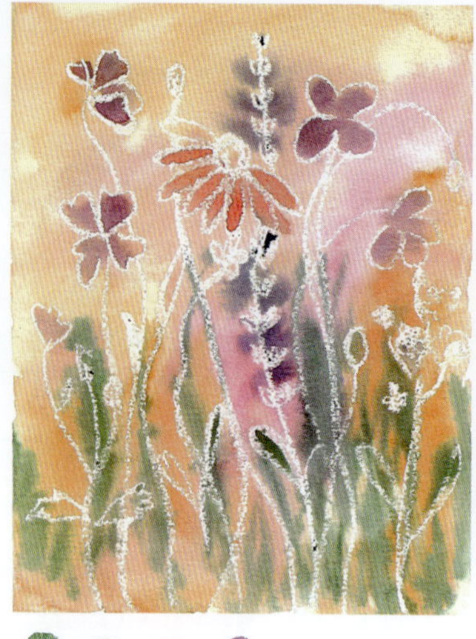

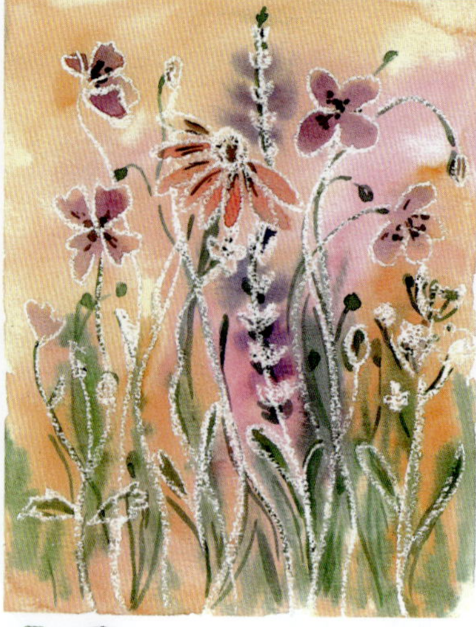

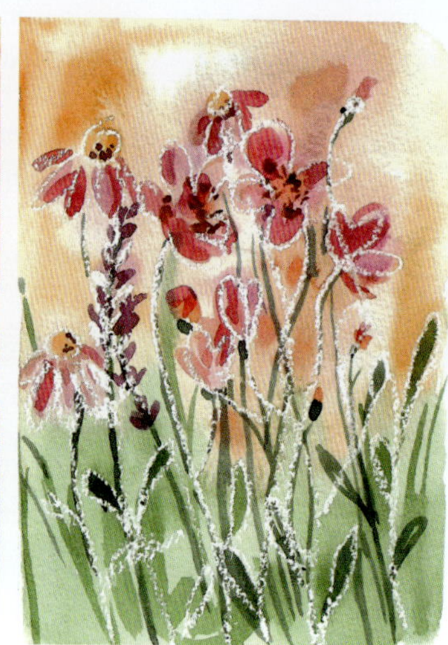

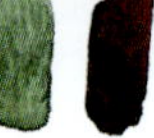

STEP 3

While the layer is still wet, you can add some brush-strokes and extra colors to make your background more interesting and richer. You will use the colors you prepared in advance: green tint, violet tint, warm rose tint, and purple tint. Each of these colors should be prepared to a medium consistency.

You can continue with the same quill brush, if using, or switch to a large round brush and start adding colors on the wet paper. Start with the green tint, making brushstrokes at the bottom to imitate stems and grass in the scenery. Then, color the outlines of the wild-flowers with the purple tint, violet tint, and warm rose tint. You can follow my example for coloring the petals and blossoms of the wildflowers, or you can choose your own approach.

Once you are happy with your work, allow everything to dry completely before proceeding to the final step.

STEP 4

We are at the final stage, and it already looks so pretty and elegant. We have contrast, beautiful watercolor blends, and lovely colors, but these final touches and details will make the painting complete.

Arm yourself with a small round brush and prepare the next two colors in medium consistency: Burnt Umber and green tint. If you prefer even better contrast, you can use a thicker consistency. I especially recommend adding details with Burnt Umber to the centers of the flowers to emphasize their colors. Use green tint to add extra stems, leaves, and green details. Feel free to be creative and make some unique additions, or you can follow my composition. It's important not to overdo the painting; when you feel it's enough, just stop. Once you feel everything is done, remove the washi tape, and your painting is complete.

Try experimenting with different details, colors, and compositions!

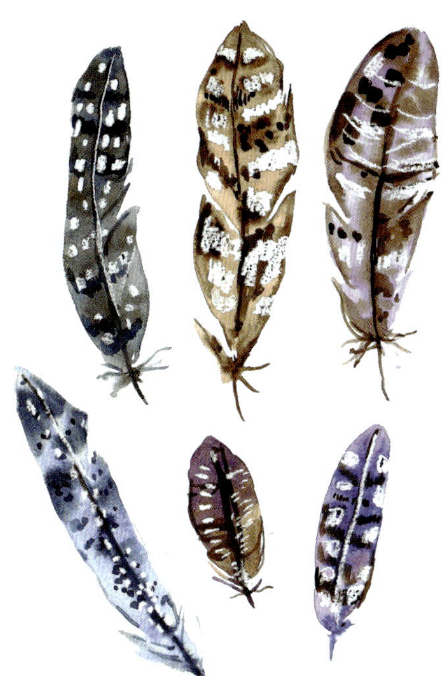

Airy Feathers

Let's paint beautiful, airy feathers using the watercolor resist technique. This method is very easy and allows you to create stunning textures and patterns on the feathers. Watercolor adds a sense of airiness and transparency, while extra details bring the feathers to life, making them absolutely stunning. I love this project because it's not only fun and relaxing, but also can be used as a beautiful decoration for your home.

PROJECT COLORS

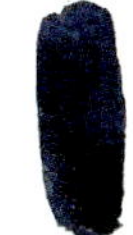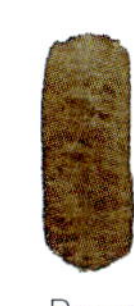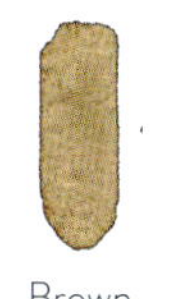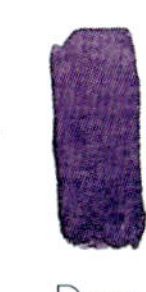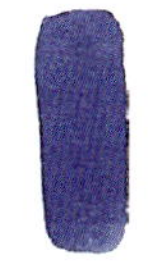

Indigo   Burnt Umber   Brown tint   Deep purple   Ultramarine

COLOR MIXING

- Brown tint: Add a little Burnt Sienna to Burnt Umber.
- Deep purple: Mix Ultramarine with Alizarin or Crimson.

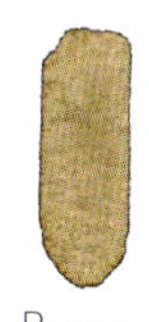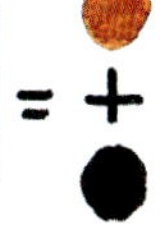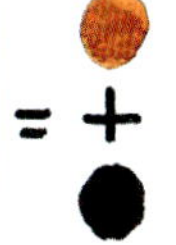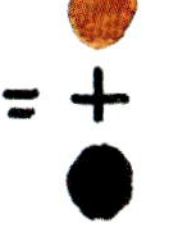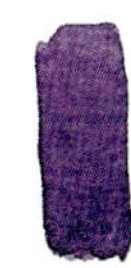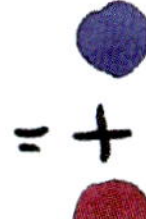

Brown tint   Deep purple

NOTE: The colors for this project are not strict, so you can choose them on your own. However, I advise you to limit the color palette and especially recommend using deep colors like Indigo or, for example, brown tones such as Burnt Umber. For other colors, feel free to experiment and make your own choices.

SUPPLIES

- Watercolor paper
- Washi tape or masking tape (optional)
- Pencil and eraser
- White wax crayon or thin white candle
- Round brushes: small (sizes 1–4) and medium (sizes 6–8)

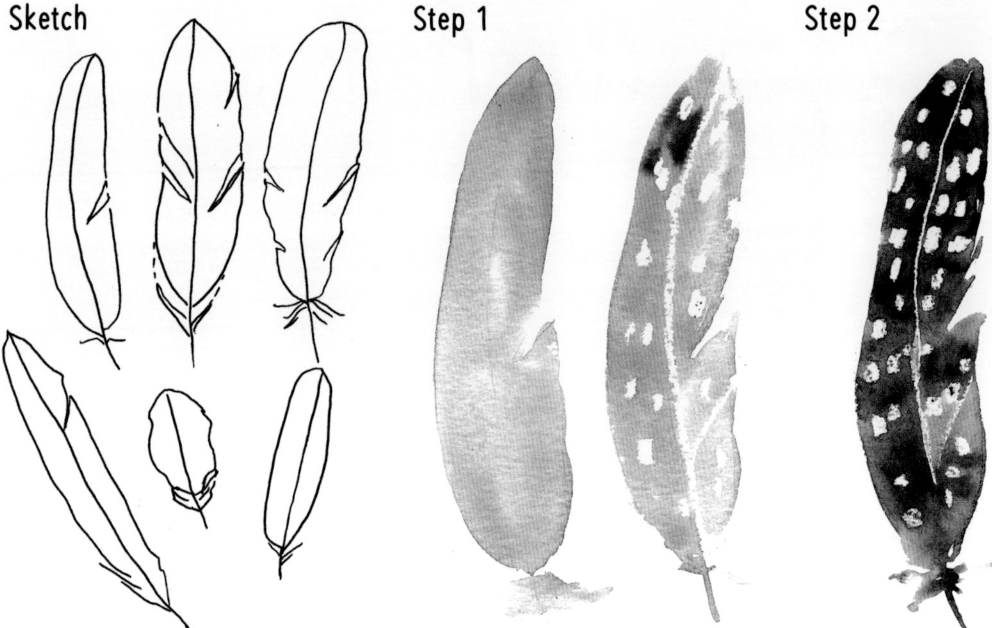

PREPARATION WORK

If you'd like, you can secure the paper to the table or a board using washi tape, but this step is not mandatory for this project.

Next, you'll need to create a sketch or preliminary drawing of your feathers with a pencil. You can refer to Sketch as an example of my feathers, but the most important thing is to keep it very simple: just basic lines without any details. Focus primarily on the shapes of the feathers. Then, using an eraser, lighten the pencil lines so they are barely visible.

STEP 1

Let's now create some magic using a white wax crayon and the watercolor resist technique.

Use a white wax crayon to draw details within the shapes of the feathers. I recommend experimenting here. Try adding different types of spots, dots, lines, and dashes. For one feather, you can even combine various types of details. You might also add a central line, like a vein, to emphasize the feather's symmetry.

Once you've added all the details inside the feather shapes with the white wax crayon, move on to the next step.

TIP: If you want your crayon to create neater details or thinner lines, you can use a knife or a utility knife to sharpen your crayons. Also, instead of using a wax crayon, you can use a candle if it has a thin tip.

STEP 2

Let's color our feathers. First, pick your medium round brush, wet it, and use clean water to wet the first feather inside its shape. At the bottom, wet it a little more because we'll add some fluffy barbs while it's still wet.

On the wetted feather shape, use the same brush to pick up Indigo paint in medium consistency and fill the inside of the feather. While the layer is still wet, you can add more details. I used medium consistency Burnt Umber. The watercolor will naturally spread on the wet layer but won't cover the areas where we used the wax crayon to create patterns. You'll notice how the white details appear through the watercolor.

Once you're finished, use the tip of your brush to add some extra small fluffy barbs at the bottom of the feather. For this, paint a few short brushstrokes on both sides of the bottom of the feather. They shouldn't be perfect, straight, or too similar. Simply add a few on one side and a few on the other, making sure they aren't symmetrical. Now, let everything dry completely.

Step 3   Step 4

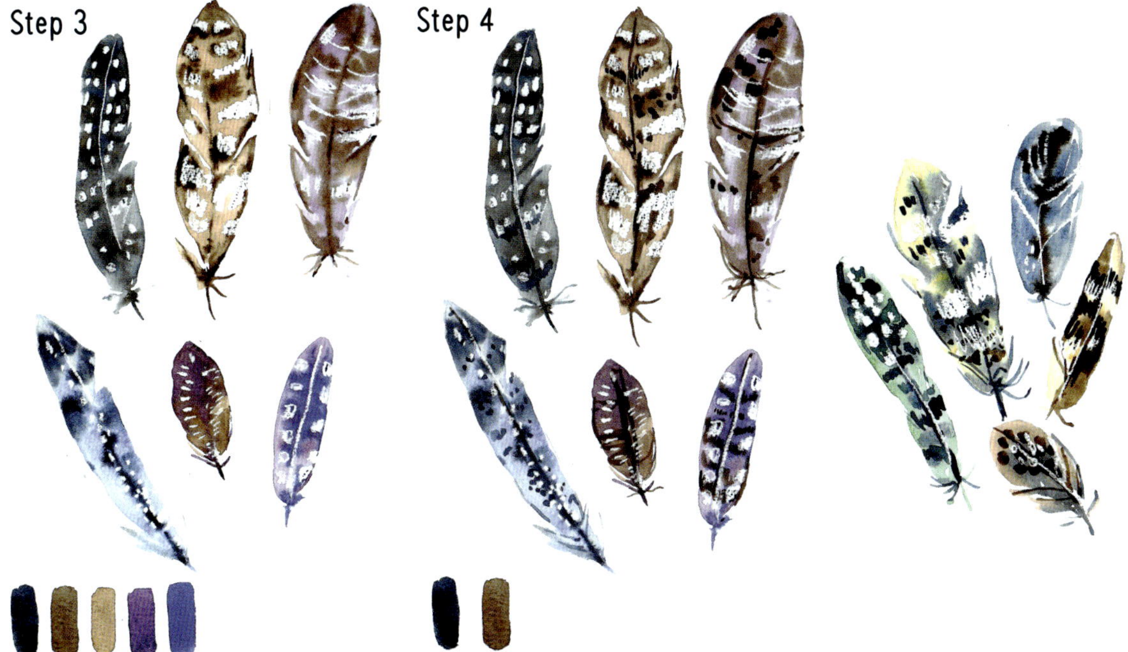

STEP 3

Let's keep working with the same medium round brush. Prepare the following colors in medium consistency: Indigo, Burnt Umber, brown tint, deep purple, and Ultramarine. You can experiment with the consistency by using more water for the first layer if you want a more transparent and airy effect.

Now, let's color the rest of the feathers using the same principles we followed for the first feather in the previous step.

For the second feather, wet the feather shape, start with a brown tint base, and add Burnt Umber on the wet layer. For the third, use deep purple as the base and add brown tint. For the next feather, use Ultramarine with Indigo, then deep purple with Ultramarine for the smaller feather. Finally, use brown tint with deep purple for the smallest feather.

Remember, for each feather, first wet the entire shape, then add the base color while it's wet, and finally add extra details on the wet layer. Don't forget to include the small fluffy barbs at the ends of each feather, as they add a more natural look.

Once you've colored all the feathers, let them dry completely before moving on to the next step.

STEP 4

Our feather details base layer is complete and dry, so now we can add the final details to make the feathers more complete and natural-looking. For this step, switch to a small round brush or use both small and medium round brushes. Prepare Indigo and Burnt Umber colors in medium to thick consistency.

Add different types of details to the feathers, such as spots, dots, dashes, or lines of various sizes. Try to vary the details and emphasize the white spots created with the white crayon. You can also highlight the feather's ridges for added texture. The most important thing is not to aim for perfection—experiment with different details and let the feathers look natural.

Don't forget to emphasize the fluffy barbs and add some extra details there. Once you're happy with the result, avoid overloading the painting with too many details, and let it dry completely.

Try experimenting with different details, colors, and compositions!

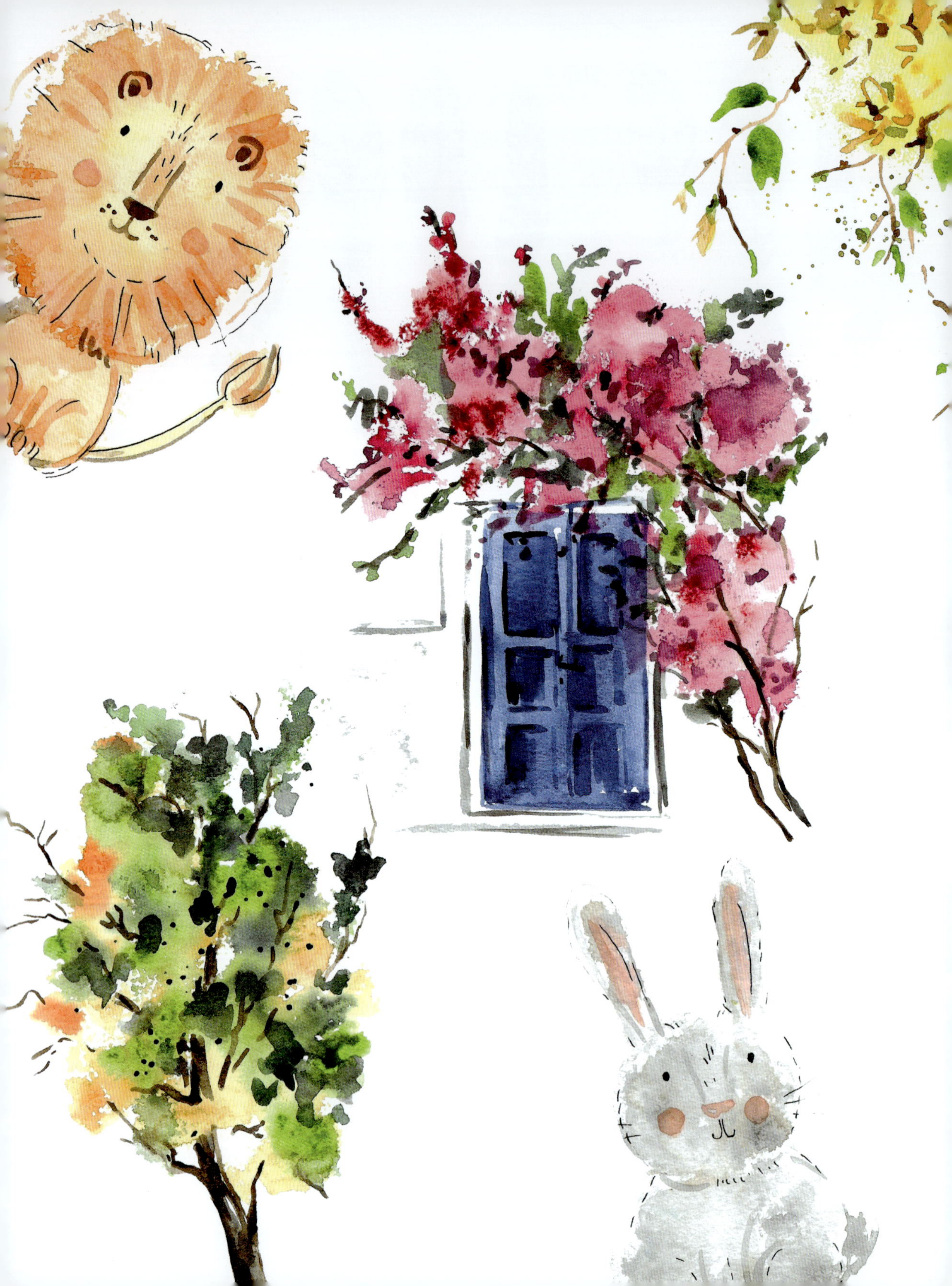

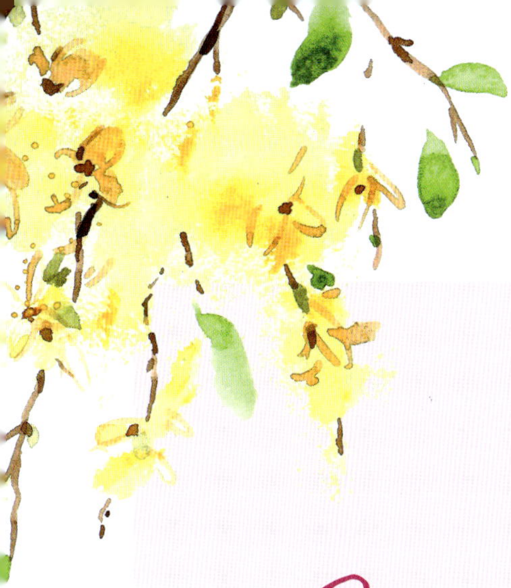

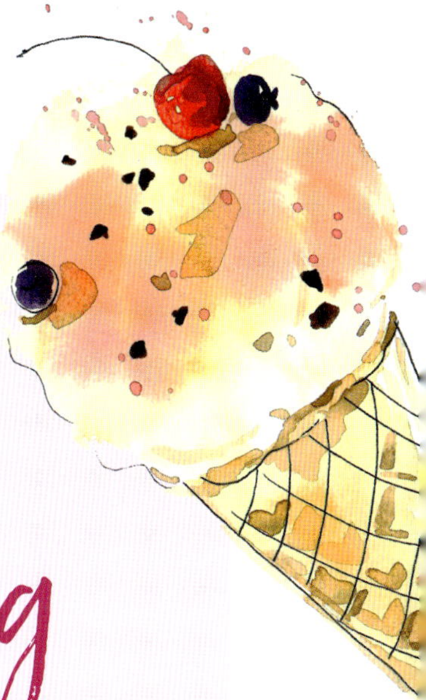

Sponge Painting
TECHNIQUE

TECHNIQUES USED IN THIS CHAPTER

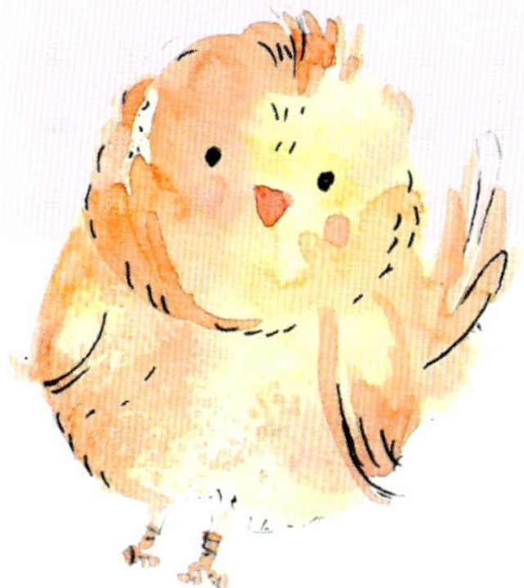

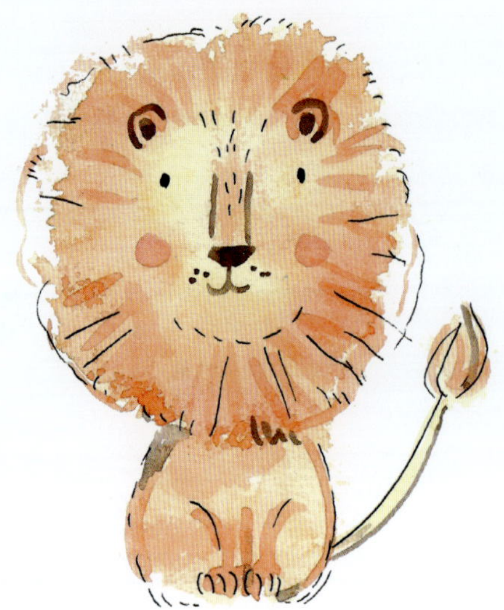

Whimsical Lion

In this project, we will create a very cute whimsical lion illustration with kitchen sponges. It's a very fun yet quite effective project. Through this, you can learn to create illustrations in children's book style. You will learn how to apply a base layer and shape it using a sponge and watercolor. I will show you how to create beautiful texture. Let's explore all these techniques and methods together.

SUPPLIES

- Watercolor paper
- Washi tape or masking tape (optional)
- Pencil and eraser (optional)
- Kitchen sponge
- Round brushes: small (sizes 1–4) and medium (sizes 6–8)
- Pointed black ink pen (size 0.8 mm), or any ink pen

NOTE: I recommend using a simple kitchen sponge, which you can buy at any store that sells household items. Cut it into different-sized pieces. I also suggest practicing the sponge technique.

PROJECT COLORS

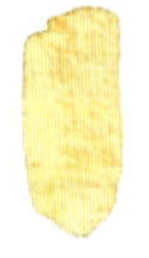 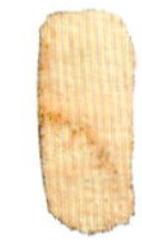 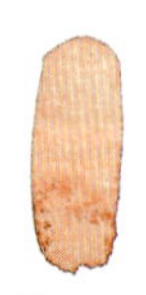 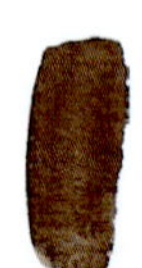 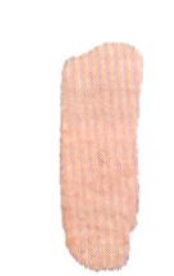

Cadmium Yellow	Yellow Ochre	Orange yellow	Burnt Umber	Pastel warm pink

COLOR MIXING

- Orange yellow: Mix Cadmium Yellow with Cadmium Red.
- Pastel warm pink: Mix Opera with a little Yellow Ochre.

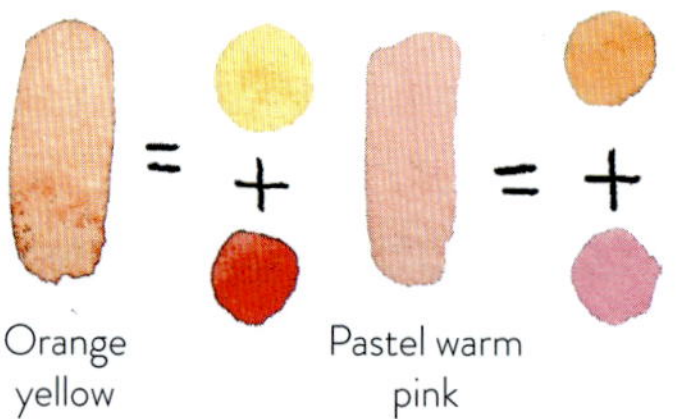

Orange yellow

Pastel warm pink

PREPARATION WORK

This project doesn't require any preliminary sketching, and neither do we use techniques that require a lot of water, so it's not necessary to secure the paper on the table with washi tape. However, if you feel more comfortable doing so, you can. You can also choose to use a pencil to make a very basic preliminary sketch to mark the base shapes.

STEP 1

We'll begin by painting the base layer using the sponge technique. What do you need? First, prepare three colors. We'll use Cadmium Yellow and Yellow Ochre in watery consistency and orange yellow in medium consistency.

Once you've prepared your colors, take a sponge piece, moisten it in clean water, and squeeze out excess water. Once the sponge is damp but not too wet, start shaping your lion. Pick up Cadmium Yellow with the sponge and form the shapes of the lion by making prints with water. Begin with the head. While the layer is still wet, incorporate Yellow Ochre using the same sponge technique.

Once the head is done, create the body of the lion and its fluffy tail using the sponge. Use Cadmium Yellow as a base and then add Yellow Ochre while the layer is still wet.

We've created a very fluffy base layer. While it's still wet, use a small round brush (size 3 or 4) to add extra color to the head with orange yellow, like rays coming out, as shown in the example (but leave the center of the head unchanged.) This adds volume to our illustration.

Once done, allow the painting to dry or use a hairdryer to speed up the drying process.

NOTE: The first layer shouldn't be very thick; it's better to achieve a transparent layer because we will need to add details later, and an opaque layer won't allow us to do this.

STEP 2

In this step, we'll paint the second layer on dry.

We'll use orange yellow in medium consistency and Cadmium Yellow in watery consistency. Take your medium size round brush (size 6 to 8). I use size 8 with a thin tip. Begin by making some corrections to the base layer using the brush. Try to make the shape of the head rounder by adding some brushstrokes to balance it out. Also, emphasize the lines and details of the body.

Start adding some details. Emphasize the ears and add some details to the hair and the rays. Also, add some details to the end of the tail. With the medium consistency orange yellow, pick a clean, dampened sponge squeezed of excess water and use the sponge technique to add some extra texture to the first orange yellow layer. Randomly add some prints to the head, especially emphasizing the nose of the lion.

Pick up a small round brush (size 1 to 4) and, with watery consistency Cadmium Yellow, paint a line to connect the body and the fluffy end of the tail. Try to make a thin line. Once everything is done, allow everything to dry or use a hairdryer again.

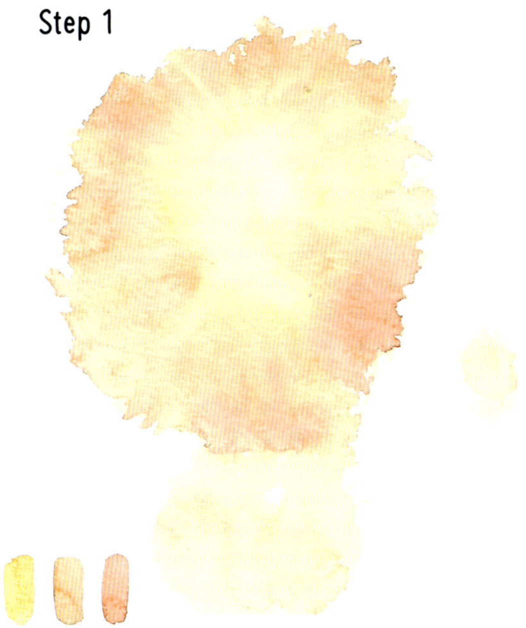

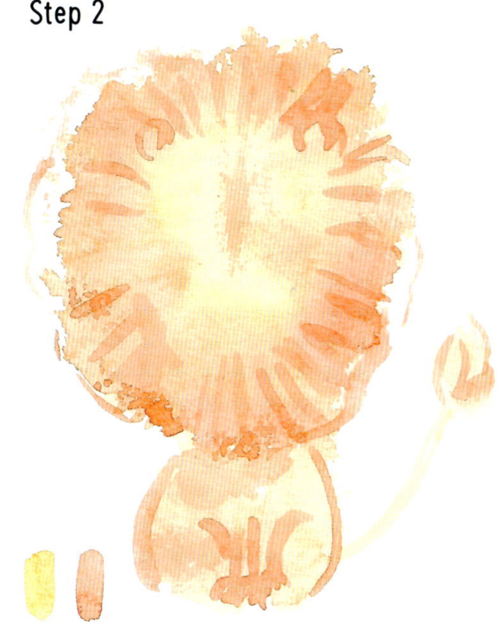

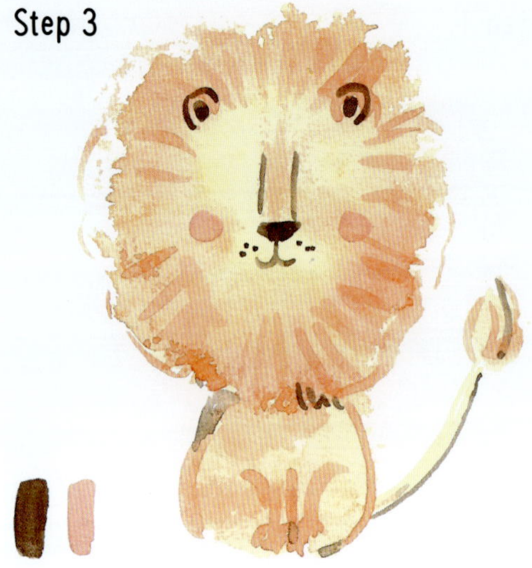

Step 3

STEP 3

It's time to bring more details to our cute illustration. Prepare Burnt Umber in medium consistency, closer to thick paint, and watery to medium consistency pastel warm pink.

Pick a small round brush. Just make sure the tip of the brush is pretty thin. We will add all the details on dry. Paint the ears, nose, and mouth. Also, randomly add a few details such as a shadow under the head. Use my image as a reference, or you can decide what details to add on your own. Always add some random asymmetrical details.

Now, with watery to medium consistency pastel warm pink, add a light blush to the painting. If you don't want to add blush, you can leave it like this. Again, allow the painting to dry completely or use a hairdryer.

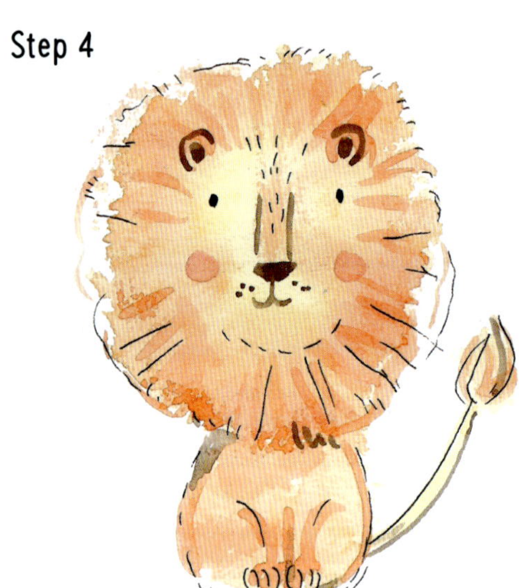

Step 4

STEP 4

So, we are at the final stage, and our illustration is almost recognizable as a lion! But we need to add the final details. I used a black ink pen (size 0.8 mm), but you can use any ink pen.

On a dry layer, let's add some details. First, draw the eyes of our character, then emphasize the lines of his head, body, and tail. Also add texture, such as little strokes around his hair to imitate fluffiness.

These lines and strokes, along with some white areas of paper, will create an illusion of a fluffy head and complete the illustration. You can use the same approach for the body. Also, with some strokes of the pen, add texture like dashes to the nose. I advise you to emphasize the lion's chin as well. And that's it—our cute illustration is done.

You learned how to create cute illustrations and fluffy animals with the sponge technique! You also learned how to combine different techniques in this project.

Try experimenting with different details, colors, and compositions!

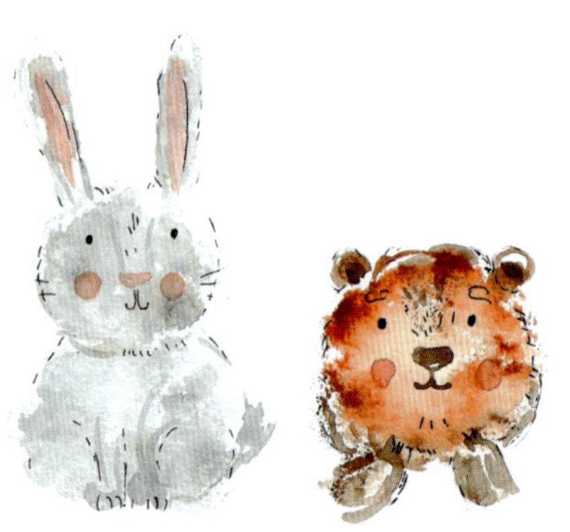

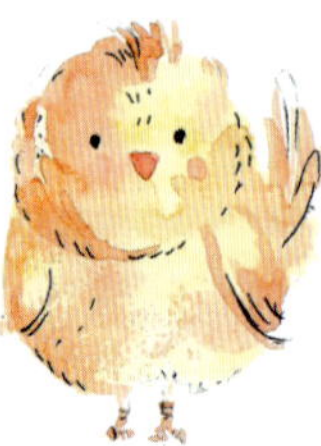

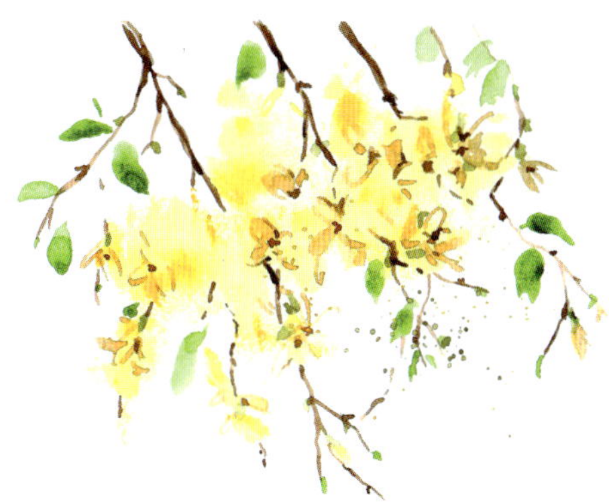

Sunny Spring Blossom

This Sunny Spring Blossom project invites you to dive into inspiration by creating a dimensional painting using a sponge. Every spring, I am always amazed and deeply inspired by the sight of blossoms—from the tender pinks and whites to the beautiful purples, yellows, and violets. These colors fill me with such inspiration that I can't resist depicting them on paper. The key here is capturing this beauty without overworking the painting, and I believe I've found the perfect method. You'll discover how easily a sponge can bring transparency and airiness to your work, while combining it with traditional watercolor techniques to build a complete and beautiful piece. I hope you also find it helpful in strengthening your watercolor skills. Enjoy the process, and don't forget to experiment and try again with other blossoms.

SUPPLIES

- Watercolor paper
- Washi tape or masking tape
- Pencil and eraser (optional)
- Kitchen sponge
- Round brushes: small (sizes 1–4) and medium (sizes 6–8)

NOTE: I recommend using a simple kitchen sponge, which you can buy at any store that sells household items. Cut it into different-sized pieces. I also suggest practicing the sponge technique.

PROJECT COLORS

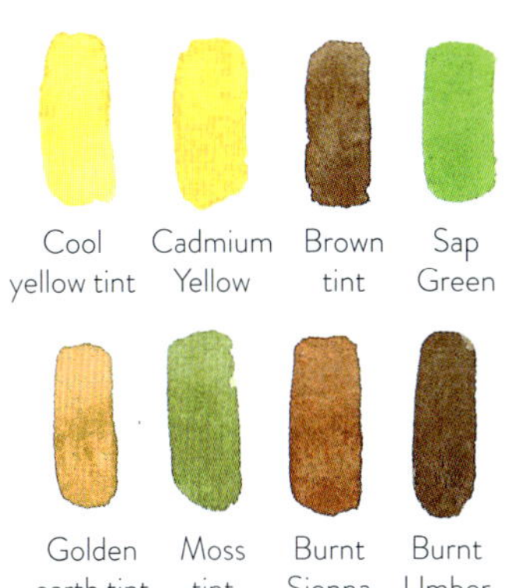

Cool yellow tint · Cadmium Yellow · Brown tint · Sap Green

Golden earth tint · Moss tint · Burnt Sienna · Burnt Umber

COLOR MIXING

- Cool yellow tint: Add a little Yellow Ochre to Lemon Yellow.
- Brown tint: Add a hint of Burnt Umber to Burnt Sienna.
- Golden earth tint: Mix Yellow Ochre with a little Burnt Sienna and just a bit of Sap Green.
- Moss tint: Add a little Burnt Sienna to Sap Green.

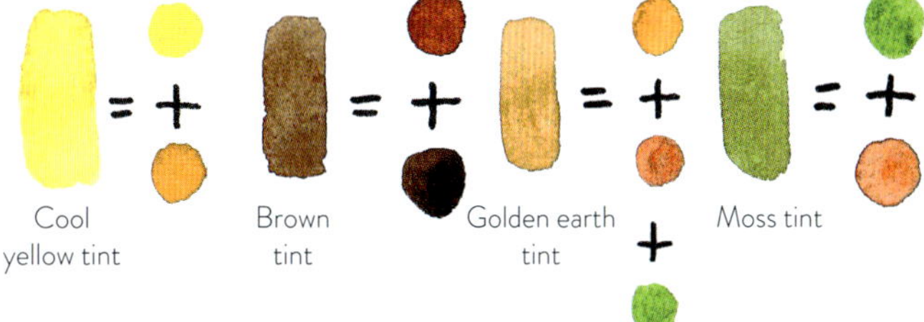

Cool yellow tint · Brown tint · Golden earth tint · Moss tint

Sketch

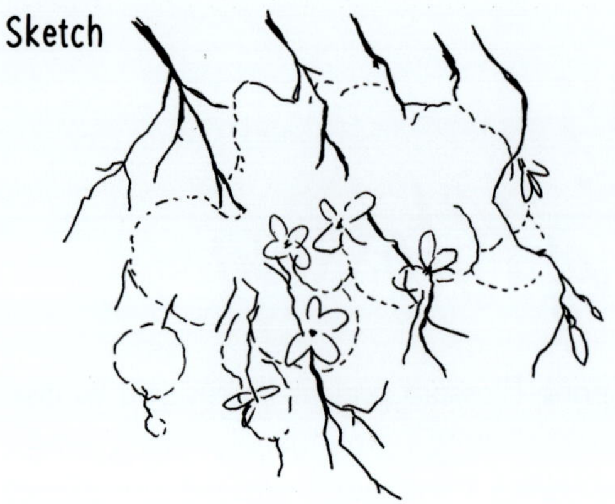

Step 1

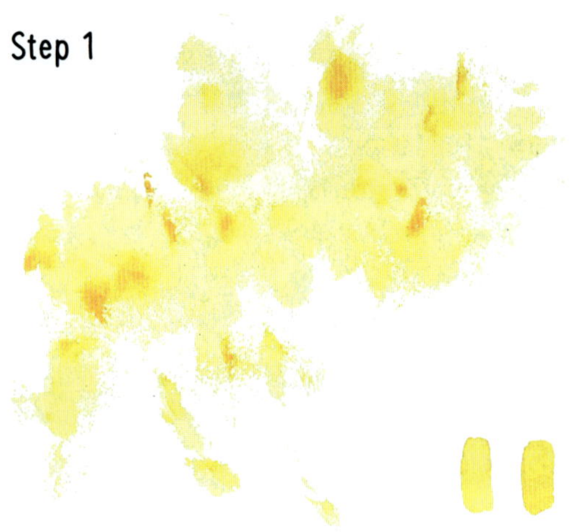

Step 2

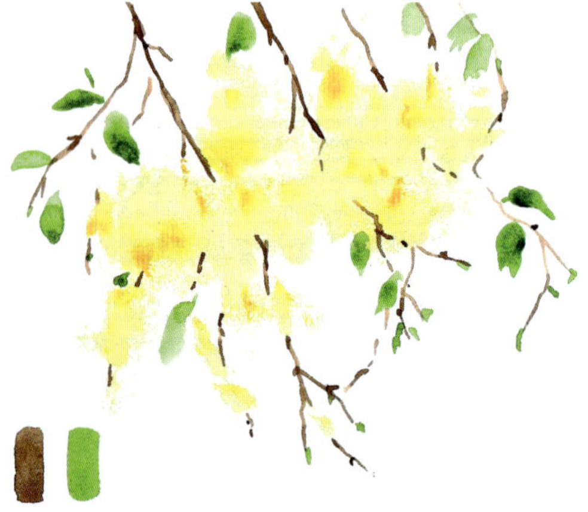

PREPARATION WORK

Secure the paper to the table with washi tape. This step is important to prevent wrinkling and create a border, giving the final piece a delicate, airy look.

Once that's done, you can make a light sketch, marking the main branches of the blossom as shown in Sketch. Avoid sketching the blossoms or flowers—we'll define those later with watercolor. This simple sketch will give you confidence as you proceed.

Also, prepare a generous amount of cool yellow tint and Cadmium Yellow, both in medium consistency, in advance.

STEP 1

To create a beautiful layer of blossoms, we will use the sponge technique. First, pick a small sponge (I recommend cutting it down to size so you can pinch it between your fingers), then wet it and squeeze out the excess water. Load it with the cool yellow tint, making sure to absorb enough paint. If needed, you can always reload the sponge to absorb more paint during the process.

Start forming the blossoms with the cool yellow tint by pressing it onto the paper and creating textured prints. You want to achieve a fairly transparent layer, but not too transparent. Once you're done, load the sponge with Cadmium Yellow and add accents to the still-wet layer. This way, you're combining both the sponge technique and the wet-on-wet technique.

NOTE: It's important to consider the direction in which the branches grow. Toward the ends of the branches, the blossoms become fewer, with more buds and neighboring blooms. Compositionally, the blossoms should be concentrated in a specific area, while at the tips of the branches, there should only be a few small clusters of blossoms. These can also be adjusted using various techniques.

STEP 2

Let's keep adding details to our blossoms, this time focusing on branches and leaves. You'll need both a small and medium round brush, as well as brown tint and Sap Green in medium consistency.

Start by adding the branches. If you did a sketch, simply color them in with the small brush and brown tint, making sure the tips of the branches are thin. Then, with the medium brush, add some leaves using Sap Green. Vary the shape and size of the leaves for a natural look.

Once done, let everything dry before moving to the next step.

STEP 3

Now, let's add the second layer to our painting using the layering technique. For this step, you will need a medium round brush and golden earth and moss tints in medium consistency.

First, decide which flowers or blossoms you want to depict. Start by adding flowers with the golden earth tint, emphasizing and defining their shapes; paint some and outline others. You can also use this color to paint single petals over the base layer and some buds.

Once you're happy with the result, pick up some moss tint and add green details in certain areas: extra leaves, inflorescence bases, and unopened leaves or leaf buds. This will bring more detail to the painting. Allow everything to dry.

STEP 4

Now we need to add the final details. I suggest using the medium brush, focusing on the tip for looser details.

Prepare the following colors in medium consistency: Burnt Sienna, Burnt Umber, Cadmium Yellow, and moss tint. You can also use any other project colors. It's time to add the final details with the layering technique. First, use Burnt Sienna to add the centers of the flowers and emphasize certain blossoms.

Next, use Burnt Umber to thicken some branches and add accents. This will increase contrast, so don't hesitate to apply it.

Once satisfied, you can add a few more details. I recommend splattering with Cadmium Yellow by flicking your brush once or twice, and you can also use moss tint. And with that, our sunny spring painting is done!

Try experimenting with different details, colors, and compositions!

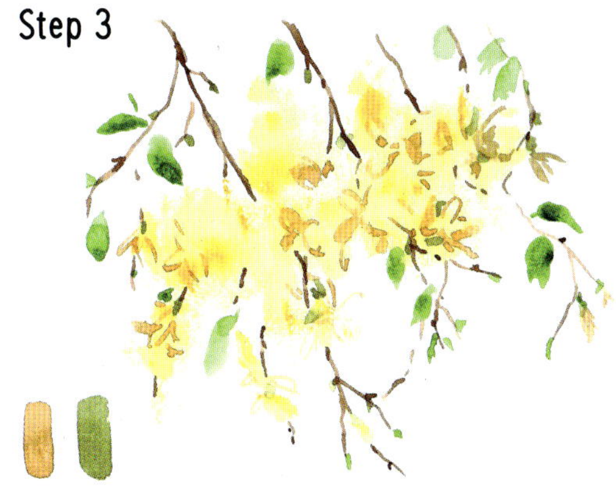

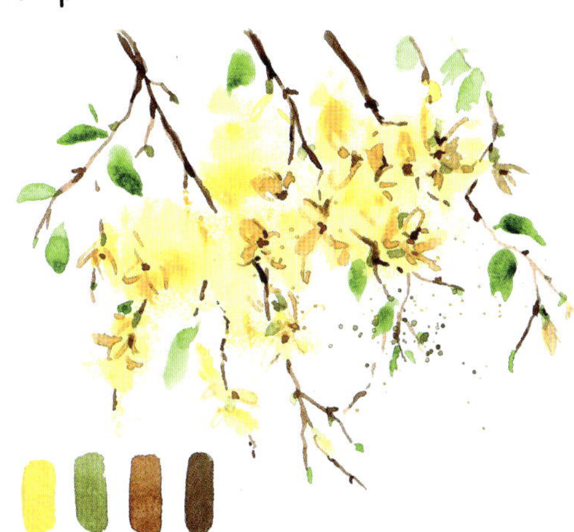

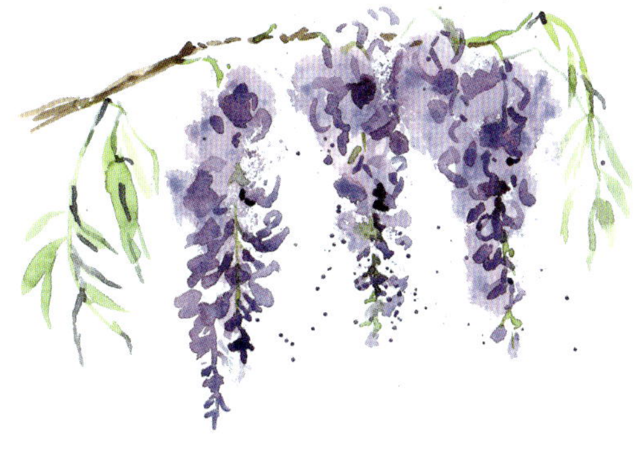

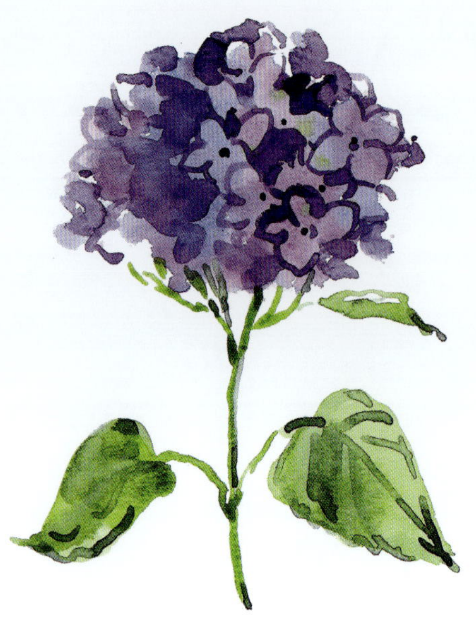

Hydrangea Elegance

Let's paint a beautiful hydrangea together. We'll form the entire shape of the blossom with a sponge, making this project super fun and enjoyable. I'm always amazed by how beautiful hydrangeas are, especially their colors, which are so unique. You can really play and experiment. Let's discover this project together!

PROJECT COLORS

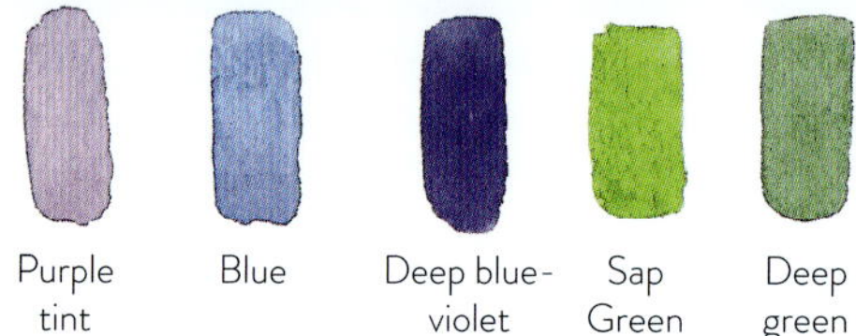

SUPPLIES

- Watercolor paper
- Washi tape or masking tape
- Pencil and eraser (optional)
- Kitchen sponge
- Round brushes: small (sizes 1–4) and medium (sizes 6–8)

NOTE: I recommend using a simple kitchen sponge, which you can buy at any store that sells household items. Cut it into different-sized pieces. I also suggest practicing the sponge technique.

COLOR MIXING

- Purple tint: Mix Opera with a little blue.
- Deep blue-violet: Add a little Opera to blue.
- Deep green: Mix Sap Green with a little blue.

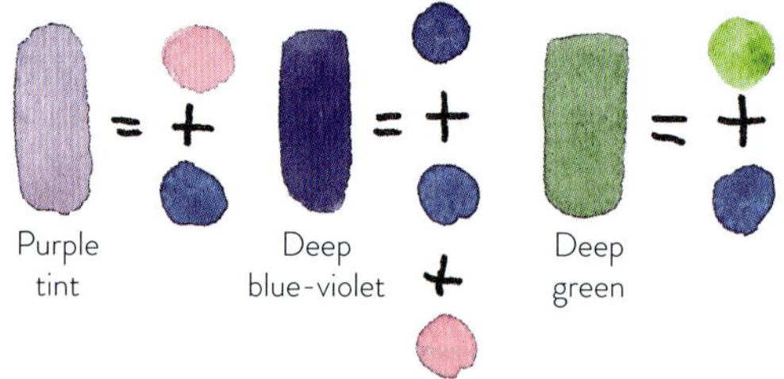

TIP: Please note that for this project, I use Cobalt Blue, but you can experiment with different blues you have, such as Ultramarine, Prussian Blue, or any other blue, to achieve beautiful purple and blue-purple tints, as well as deep green. Just make sure you choose one blue and use it for mixing all the colors we use in this project.

TIP: For this project, I especially recommend preparing all the colors in advance, and for the purple tint, make sure you have plenty of paint. This will help you work comfortably stress-free.

PREPARATION WORK

Before we start painting our hydrangea, we need to cover a few points. First of all, for this project, I recommend securing the watercolor paper to the table with washi tape. This prevents the paper from wrinkling or warping when using the wet-on-wet technique. Secondly, we need to plan the shape of our blossom and the overall composition. You can use a pencil to make a basic sketch to mark the stem of the blossom, where you'll place the leaves, and the shape of the hydrangea. However, for this project, I don't recommend drawing the shapes of the blossoms, as we will be using a sponge technique to create a loose, spontaneous style, adding an element of unpredictability to the project.

In Sketch, you'll find a sketch that helps you understand what the final project will look like, but it's just for reference.

Also, we need to prepare the sponge in advance. I recommend using a simple, thin sponge—not too thick. Cut it into halves or thirds so you can easily hold it with your fingers in one hand and control how it folds. This will give you better control and feel. I also recommend wetting the sponge with clean water before filling it with watercolor. Prepare another glass of clean water to rinse your sponge as needed.

STEP 1

Let's begin by forming the first layer of the hydrangea blossom. We'll be using the sponge technique, and for this step, we will work with a purple tint. Generously wet your sponge, then squeeze out the excess water so it's damp but not too wet. Next, prepare a large amount of paint in a medium consistency. Make sure you have plenty of paint ready, as the sponge will absorb quite a bit.

When you're ready to paint the hydrangea, load your damp sponge with the watercolor and start forming the blossom by pressing the sponge onto the paper. You can adjust the shape, creating an oval or round form, but it doesn't need to be perfect. The beauty of this technique lies in its ability to create airiness and transparency, while also adding texture and shape.

Once this is done, move immediately to the next step, as we'll need to add extra colors while the surface is still wet.

Sketch

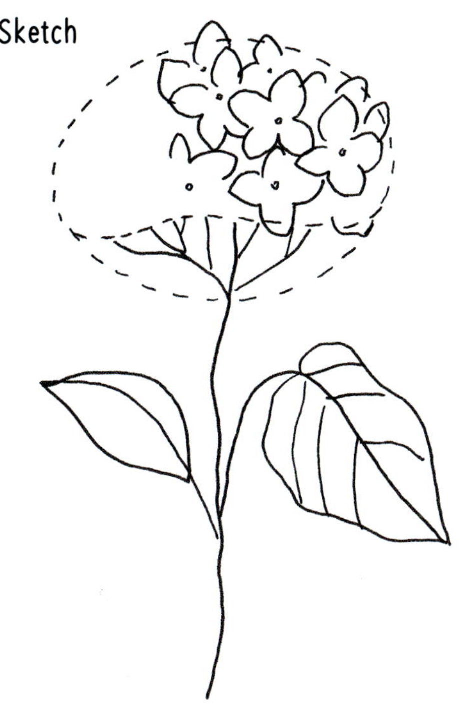

Step 1

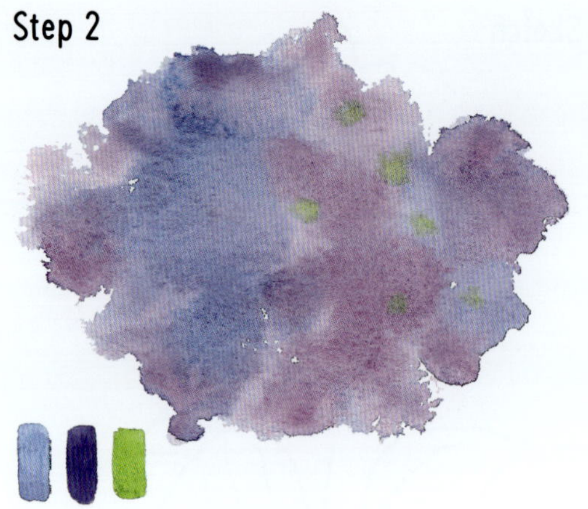

Step 2

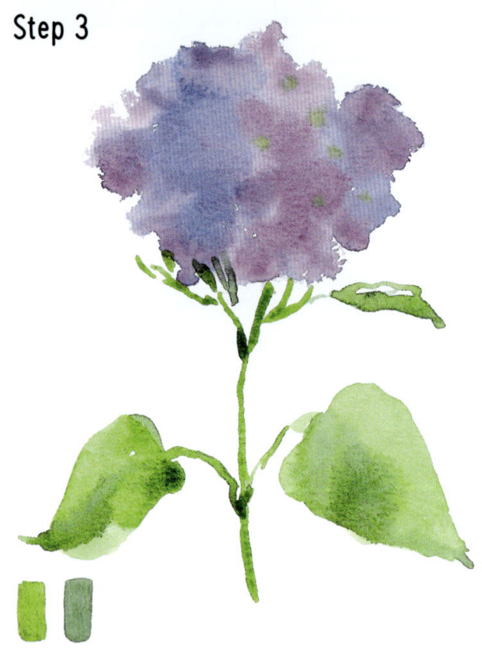

Step 3

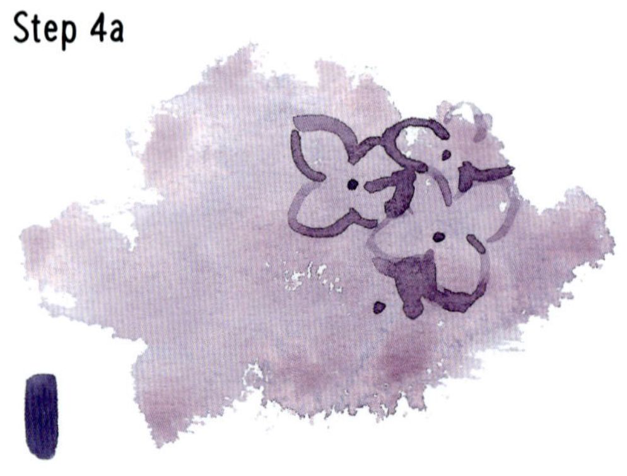

Step 4a

STEP 2

For this project, you'll need three colors in a medium consistency, which you should have prepared in advance: blue, deep blue violet, and Sap Green. Take your medium round brush and start adding color to the still-wet layer. First, I suggest adding blue and deep blue-violet tints, focusing mostly on one side to create a 3D effect. To achieve this, decide where the light is coming from. If the light is coming from the top right, the shadows will be on the left side and at the bottom of the blossom, as in my case.

You can also add a thicker consistency of purple tint if the first layer is too transparent. Finally, arm yourself with a small round brush and add a few spots of Sap Green. This will create an interesting color-mixing effect. Hydrangea petals naturally have some variation, so feel free to experiment, but don't add too much Sap Green—just a little, as shown in the example.

STEP 3

While the hydrangea blossom is drying, we can move to the bottom part of the flower to paint the stem, green details, and leaves. Prepare a medium consistency of Sap Green and deep green, and arm yourself with a medium round brush. Start by painting the stem, then add the leaves and other details using Sap Green. While it's still wet, add some touches of deep green to give the layer a natural look and avoid flatness. Let the colors blend on the paper to create a beautiful effect.

Allow all the painted layers and details to dry completely before proceeding to the next step.

STEP 4

In this step, we will use the layering technique. First, prepare a medium to thick consistency of deep blue-violet tint. Use a medium round brush; for small details, you can also use a small round brush. Now, we need to add the second layer. I recommend starting by painting random spots on the upper right side of the blossom. We are painting the centers of the flowers (see 4a). Outline some of the flowers within the blossom, then fill the space between them with color, making sure to paint outside the flowers, not inside them.

Next, move to the lower left corner of the blossom to fill in the shadows opposite the flowers you've just painted. Make wide brushstrokes one by one to imitate petals in shadow.

STEP 5

Our hydrangea already looks pretty and elegant, with some airiness and volume. Let's now add the final details. I recommend adding details to the greens—the leaves and stems. Using a deep green tint, apply extra details with the layering technique. You can add accents, veins, or shadows, keeping it random and organic—it doesn't need to be symmetrical or perfect. Just a few brushstrokes, and you can follow my example if you'd like.

Next, using a deep blue-purple color in medium consistency, add some extra petals, shadows, and details. Here, you can use your imagination or use a reference photo to finalize your painting.

Try experimenting with different details, colors, and compositions!

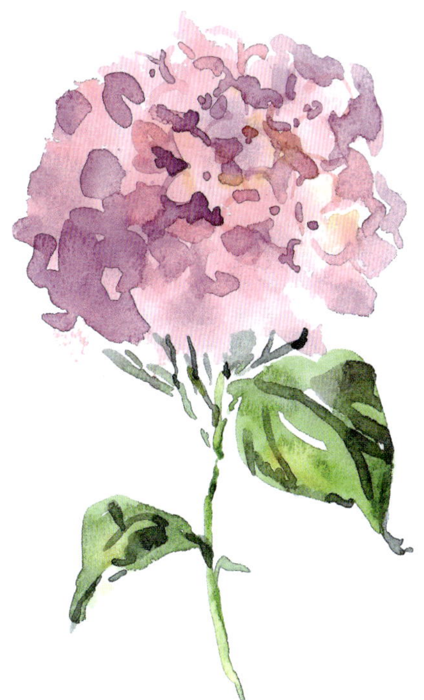

Step 4b

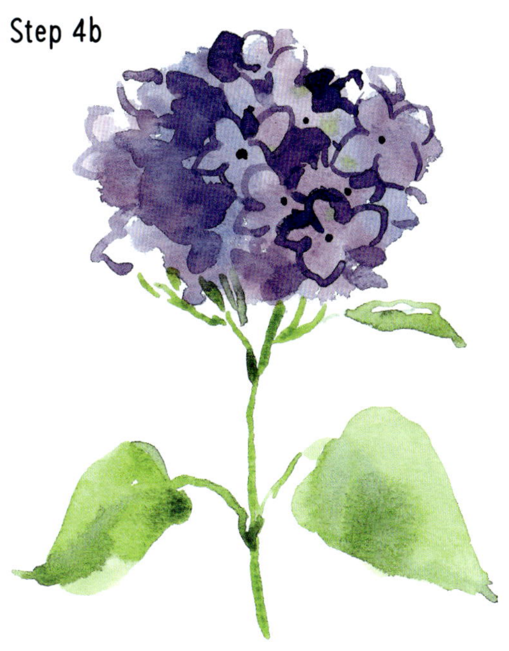

Step 5

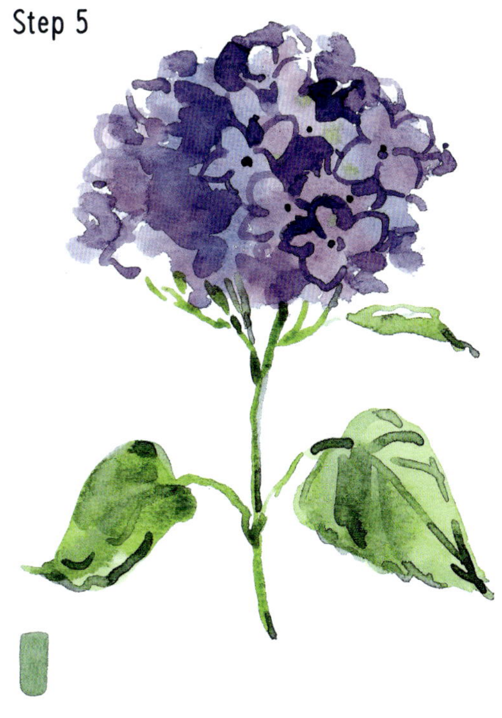

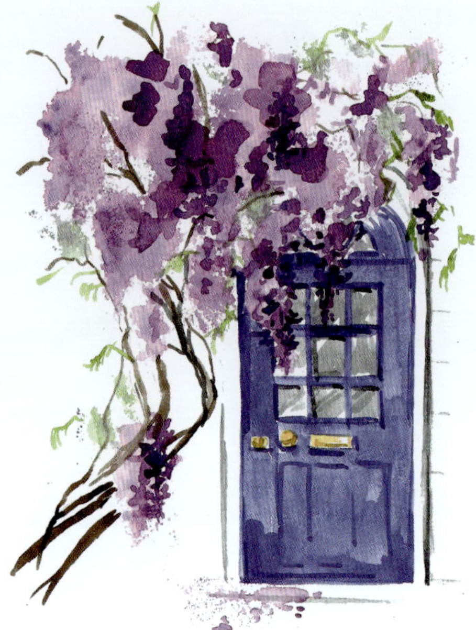

Blossoming Doorway

Let's paint a beautiful wisteria blossom around a door. This project may not be the easiest in this book, but using the sponge technique makes it much simpler and a lot more fun. I'll guide you through building the first layer of wisteria, creating volume, and achieving deep, vibrant colors. Then, we'll finalize the painting with detailed touches to achieve a truly delightful result.

On one side, the painting feels loose and free flowing, while the other side features a more structured and balanced composition. By applying the principles from this lesson, you can create a variety of scenes with doors and windows adorned with blossoms and flowers. Wisteria blooms are especially charming because of their beautiful purple and blue tints.

SUPPLIES

- Watercolor paper
- Washi tape or masking tape
- Pencil and eraser
- Kitchen sponge
- Round brushes: small (sizes 1–4) and medium (sizes 6–8)

NOTE: I recommend using a simple kitchen sponge, which you can buy at any store that sells household items. Cut it into different-sized pieces. I also suggest practicing the sponge technique.

PROJECT COLORS

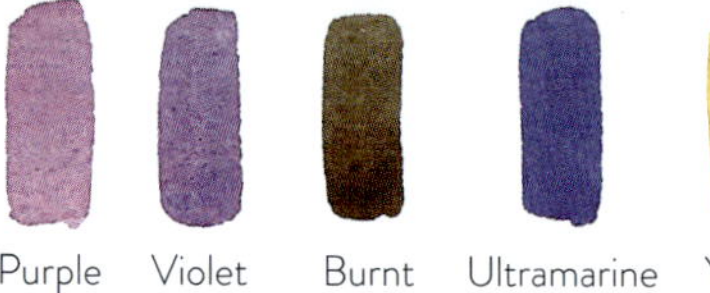

| Purple tint | Violet tint | Burnt Umber | Ultramarine | Yellow Ochre | Gray tint | Green tint | Sap Green |

COLOR MIXING

- Purple tint: Mix Opera with some Ultramarine.
- Violet tint: Mix Opera with Ultramarine, aiming for a slightly bluer tint compared to the purple tint.
- Gray tint: Mix Burnt Umber with Ultramarine.
- Green tint: Add a small amount of Ultramarine to Sap Green.

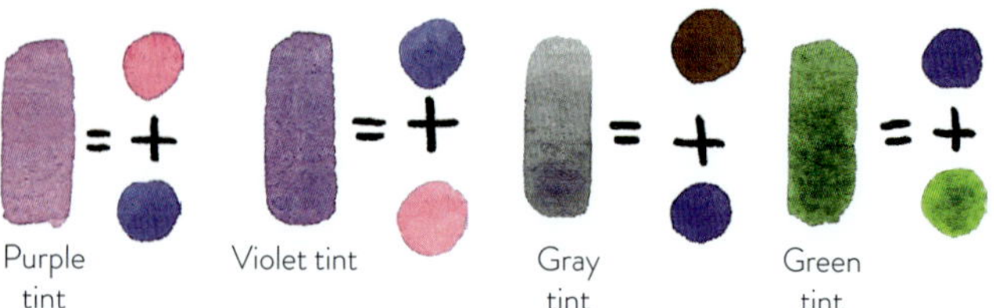

PREPARATION WORK

Let's start the project with some preparation. First, secure your paper to the table or board using washi tape.

Then, create a preliminary sketch based on the reference shown in Sketch. The main goal is to outline the door and include some details, especially the glass section. The more precise your sketch of the door, the more beautiful the final result will be.

For the wisteria, lightly mark the branches and faintly indicate where you plan to place the blossoms. Once you've finished the sketch, use an eraser to gently soften the pencil lines, making them less visible.

Prepare a large amount of medium consistency purple tint and violet tint in advance.

STEP 1

Let's start by building our wisteria blossom base layer using the sponge technique. Take a small piece of sponge, wet it with clean water, then squeeze out the excess water. Next, pick up the purple tint with the sponge and start adding the blossom by pressing the sponge on the paper and making textured prints. Make sure you have enough paint on the sponge, and continue adding until you feel that you've built the first layer.

On the still-wet layer, you can add the violet tint and spread it with the sponge to create texture. Here, two techniques are used: the sponge technique and the wet-on-wet technique. Once you're happy with the result, let everything dry completely.

Take a small round brush and, using medium consistency Burnt Umber, add the branches of the wisteria blossom. Don't add too many branches, just the main ones and some additional thinner branches. Make sure the main branches, which grow from the ground, are thicker; as you move upward make the branches thinner.

Once again, let everything dry completely, and then move on to the next step.

Sketch

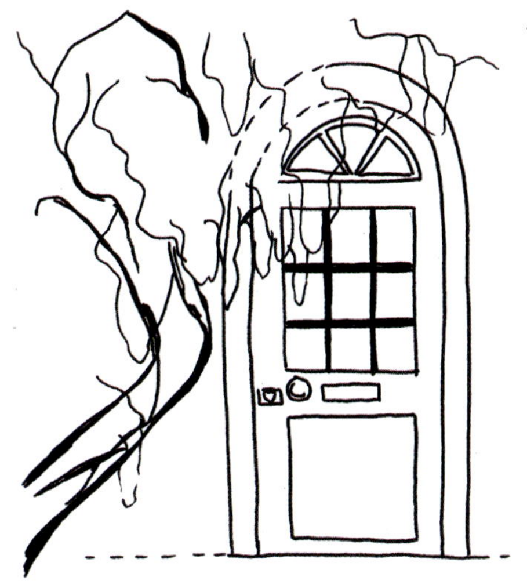

Step 1

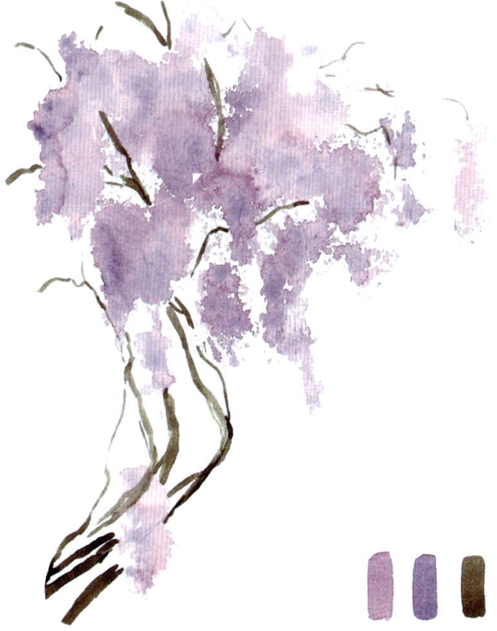

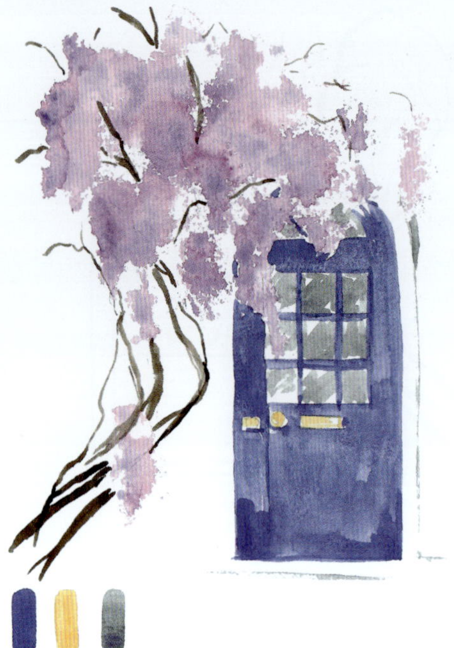

Step 2

We have the first layer of wisteria. Next, let's color the door. Prepare medium consistency Ultramarine and Yellow Ochre, as well as watery consistency gray tint. Prepare two brushes: a medium round brush and a small round brush.

With the medium round brush, fill the door with Ultramarine, leaving the glass and small details unpainted. Paint in one direction, such as from top to bottom, to make the door layer look even. Let it dry completely.

Switch to the small round brush and add details with Yellow Ochre. To make it look like gold, leave small white spots inside the details for a shimmering effect. Next, fill the glass sections with gray tint using the small brush. Don't color them completely; instead, leave some areas unpainted for reflections.

With the same gray tint, add small details around the door, such as the wall or parts of a house.

Once done, let everything dry completely, and move on to the next step.

STEP 3

Let's keep adding more layers to make our painting deeper, with richer colors and more details in the composition.

First, take a sponge, wet it, and prepare a green tint with medium consistency. Squeeze the sponge to remove excess water, dip it into the green tint, and start adding prints. Aim to create green leaves for the wisteria blossom, but don't add too many details.

Next, let's add a second medium layer to our wisteria blossom. For this, take a medium round brush and pick up some medium consistency purple tint. Start adding details randomly to create mid-tones of wisteria blossom. You don't need to depict the exact shape of the wisteria. Instead, add these details between shadows, around the branches, or to emphasize the structure of the wisteria blossoms and create depth. You can also use my example as a reference.

Once you're happy with the result, let everything dry completely, and move on to the final step.

Step 3

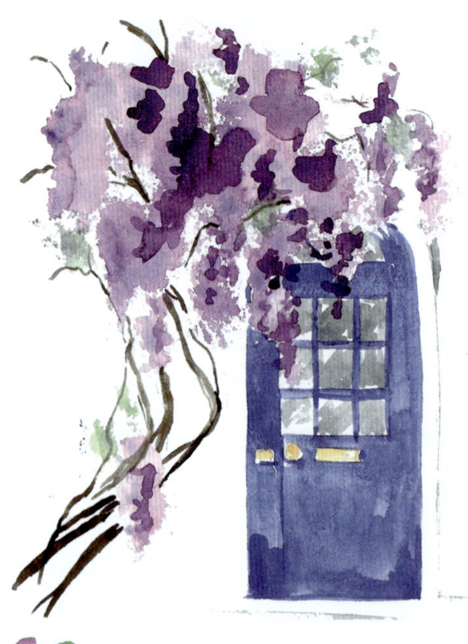

STEP 4

Let's add the final details to make our painting delightful. Prepare thick consistency purple and violet tints, along with medium consistency Sap Green, gray tint, Yellow Ochre, and Burnt Umber. Use medium and small round brushes, depending on the size of the details.

Start by refining the wisteria blossoms. Use violet and purple tints to define the shapes of blossoms closest to the viewer, especially under the door and on the bottom left side. Focus on small details and emphasize the stems.

Next, use Sap Green to define the leaves. Switch to Yellow Ochre to enhance the golden accents on the door's details. Then, use gray tint to emphasize the glass contours and add small details to the wall around the door. Finally, use Burnt Umber to refine or add branches as needed.

And voilà, your painting is ready! Remember, less is more. Add just enough final touches to enhance the composition.

TIP: For a finishing touch, use the sponge technique with purple tint to mimic fallen blossoms below the door.

Try experimenting with different details, colors, and compositions!

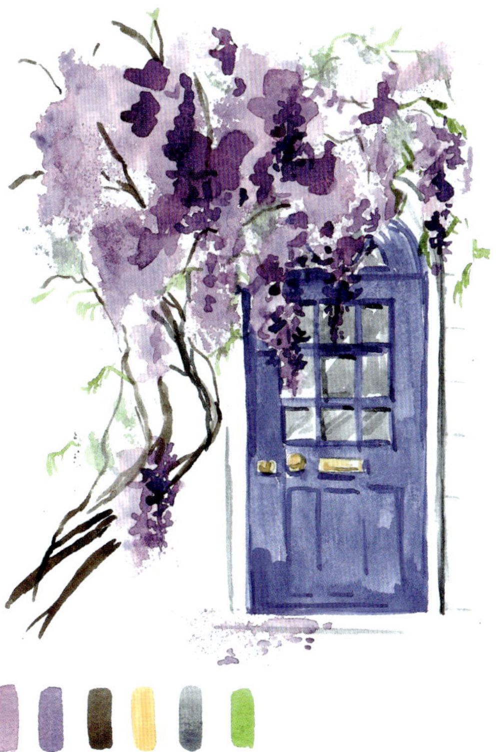

Step 4

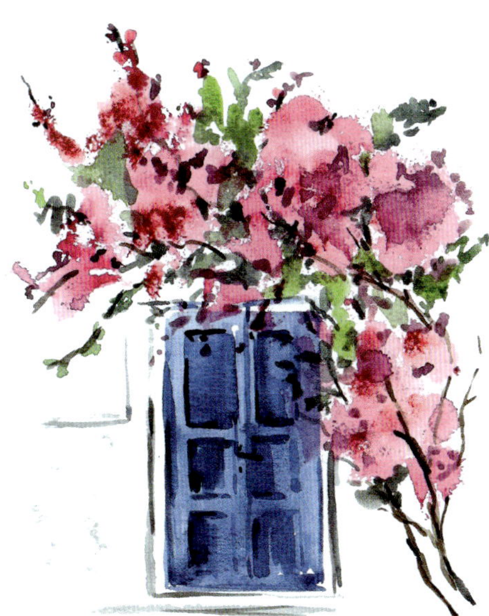

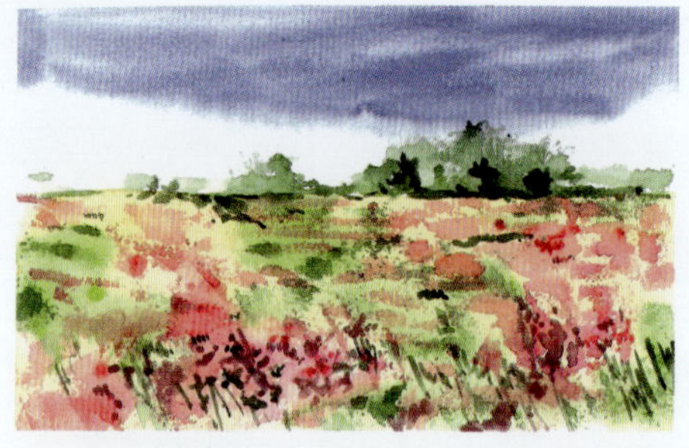

Summer Bloomscape

In this project, I invite you to try using the sponge technique to create a summer meadow landscape, which, at first glance, may look simple. We'll focus on textures and details, and you'll see how easy and enjoyable it is to create the flowering areas of the meadow, add grass details, bushes, trees, and everything else—all using the sponge technique. With the right guidance, you'll master it in no time. So, let's paint a meadow landscape!

SUPPLIES

- Watercolor paper
- Washi tape or masking tape
- Quill brush (sizes 1–4) or large round brush (size 8)
- Kitchen sponge
- Round brushes: small (sizes 1–4) and medium (sizes 6–8)

NOTE: I recommend using a simple kitchen sponge, which you can buy at any store that sells household items. Cut it into different-sized pieces. I also suggest practicing the sponge technique.

PROJECT COLORS

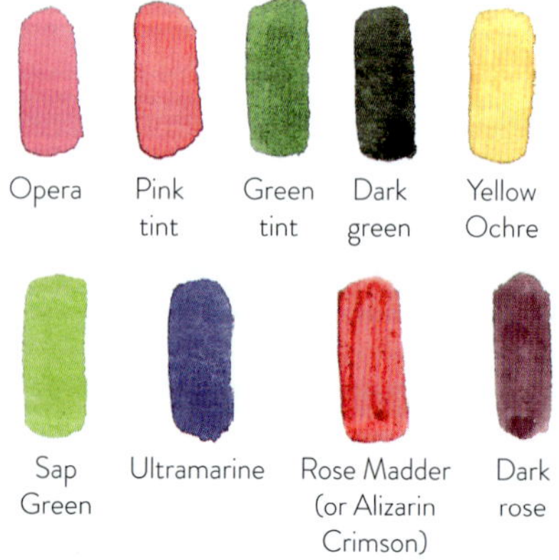

Opera | Pink tint | Green tint | Dark green | Yellow Ochre

Sap Green | Ultramarine | Rose Madder (or Alizarin Crimson) | Dark rose

COLOR MIXING

- Pink tint: Add a little Yellow Ochre to Opera.
- Green tint: Mix blue (I used Prussian Blue) with some Sap Green.
- Dark green: Mix blue (I used Prussian Blue) with Sap Green, and a little Burnt Umber.
- Dark rose: Add a bit of Viridian to Rose Madder.

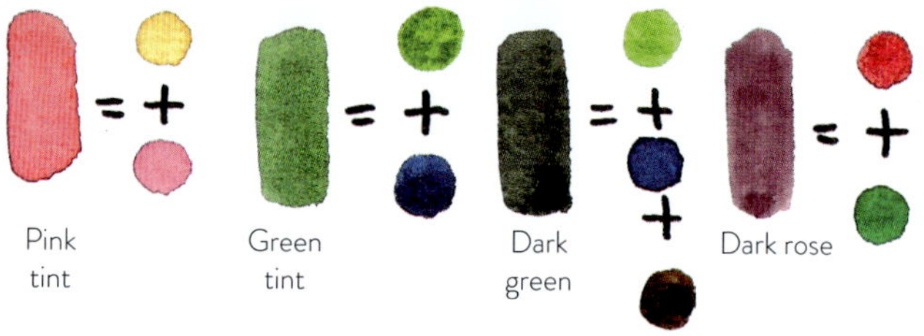

PREPARATION WORK

The first thing we need to do in this project is secure the paper to our table with washi tape to prevent any wrinkling or curving. In this project, the washi tape will also serve as a border, defining the edges of our landscape.

For this landscape, we don't need to do any detailed preliminary sketching. However, you can use washi tape to divide your landscape into the sky and meadow sections, securing it along the horizontal line, just above the horizon. I recommend creating this horizontal line in a loose style directly on the paper using a brush.

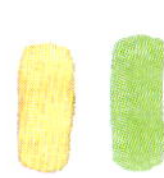

Step 1

TIP: I also advise you to prepare your colors in advance. You'll need a large amount of the following colors, in a medium consistency: Opera, pink tint, green tint, and dark green. For the remaining colors, prepare a moderate amount in a watery-to-medium consistency: Yellow Ochre, Sap Green, and Ultramarine. Use medium consistency for Rose Madder and dark rose. This preparation will save you time, especially since the sponge technique requires a generous amount of color.

Once all the preparations are done, move on to the first step.

STEP 1

Let's paint the base of the meadow area. Arm yourself with a quill brush or a large round brush.

First, wet the meadow area very slightly. Then, on the wet surface, start adding Yellow Ochre to cover the entire area. You can keep it very smooth, or in some areas, make it more saturated by adding more Yellow Ochre in a medium consistency, while other areas remain waterier. Or you can keep it even throughout.

While the layer is still wet, add some horizontal brush-strokes with Sap Green at random. Be careful not to add too much, as we'll be adding blossoming flowers to the Yellow Ochre base layer, so we don't want to cover everything with green. Once this is done, let it dry and move on to Step 2.

STEP 2

Now, let's paint the sky. If you used washi tape to create a strong horizontal line, you can remove it now. Continue working with the same brush and wet the sky area slightly. Then, start filling the sky with Ultramarine in a watery to medium consistency. You can make the sky even, or create a gradient from medium at the top to more transparent at the bottom. Also, you can add some extra brushstrokes of Ultramarine in medium consistency to add interest to the sky.

Step 2

Step 3

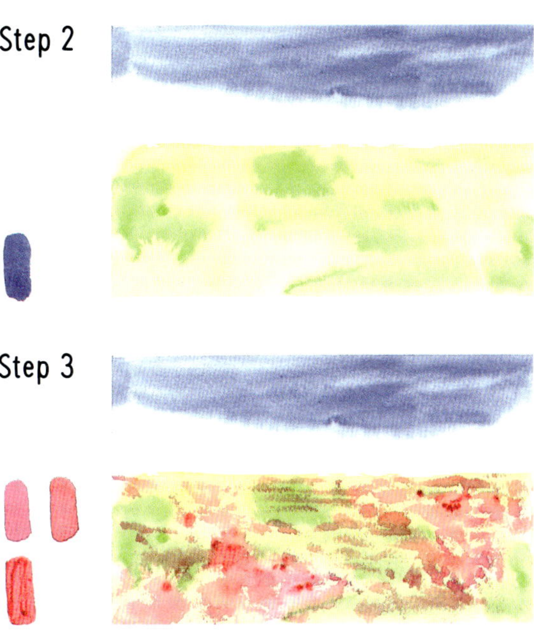

Once you're happy with the result, let everything dry completely before moving on to the next step.

STEP 3

Now that we have the base, the next step is to use the sponge technique to add blossoms to our meadow area.

To do this, pick up a sponge, wet it, squeeze out the excess water, then load it with Opera and start adding blossoms to the yellow area in the middle. Press the sponge to this area, varying your pressure and moving the sponge slightly to create different effects.

You can experiment here. The most important thing is to make these prints loose, random, and varied in size and shape. Be sure to add them mostly over the yellow base; although you can add some over the green, they may look slightly muted there, whereas on the yellow, the flowers will appear bright and colorful.

Then, you can add some extra sponge touches with pink tint on the still-wet area. Once you're happy with the result, take a medium round brush, load it with Rose Madder, and add a few random touches to the wet layer of blossoms for added contrast and interest, mimicking the natural accents in a flowering meadow.

Once you're satisfied with the result, let everything dry completely.

STEP 4

Let's continue working with the sponge technique. First, clean your sponge, then load it with green tint. Press the sponge onto the paper, lift it up, and move it in different directions over the green base in the meadow area. As with the flowers, make sure you create these prints in a variety of sizes and shapes.

Then, move to the horizon line. Just above the line, carefully start adding prints with the sponge technique in the same green tint to imitate bushes and trees on the horizon. While the area is still wet, you can add extra touches with a small or medium round brush, using the same color in a thicker consistency. This will enhance the effect, adding depth to the bushes and trees.

Once you're satisfied with the results, let everything dry completely before moving to the final step.

TIP: If you want to make your horizon line more defined and precise, allow everything to dry before adding the bushes and trees along the line. Then, carefully place washi tape just below the horizontal line to secure it and begin adding the bushes and trees using the sponge technique on the horizon.

STEP 5

It's time to add the final details. This step is important, but remember: less is more. Prepare dark green and dark rose in a medium consistency. Using a medium or small round brush, start adding details.

With dark green, first emphasize the horizontal line by adding shadow accents to the green horizon, as well as to the line of trees and bushes. Also, add some grass strokes to the foreground. Keep these details random, especially the grass, with variations in size. You can add small details to the middle area with green, but not too many.

Then, use dark rose to add accents to the flowering areas in the foreground. Remember to keep the flowers loose and not overly precise. With the same colors, add a few small touches to the background flowers to bring subtle emphasis and depth to certain areas.

Try experimenting with different details, colors, and compositions!

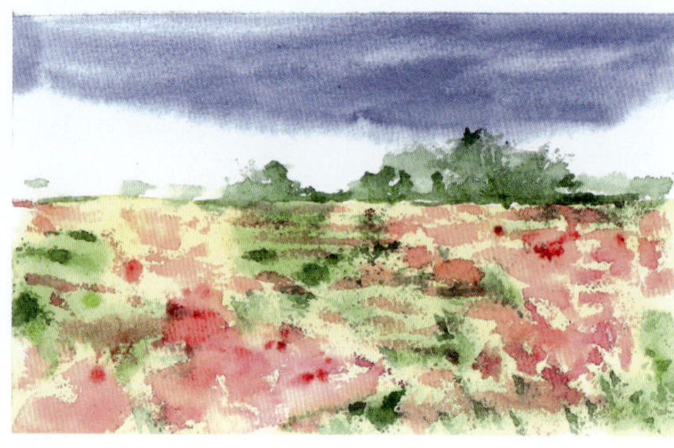

Step 4

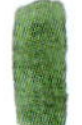

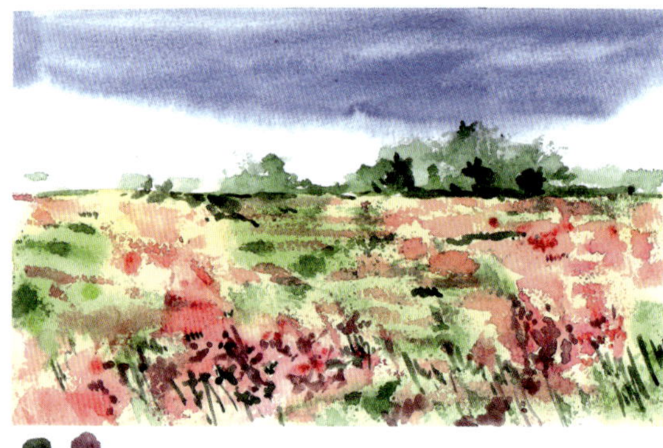

Step 5

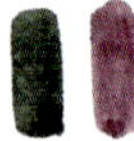

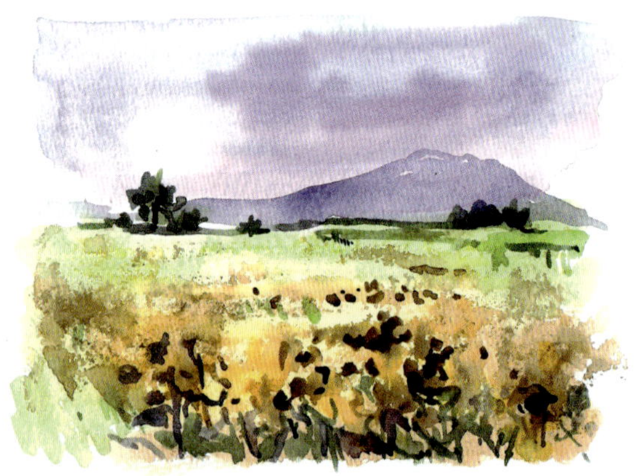

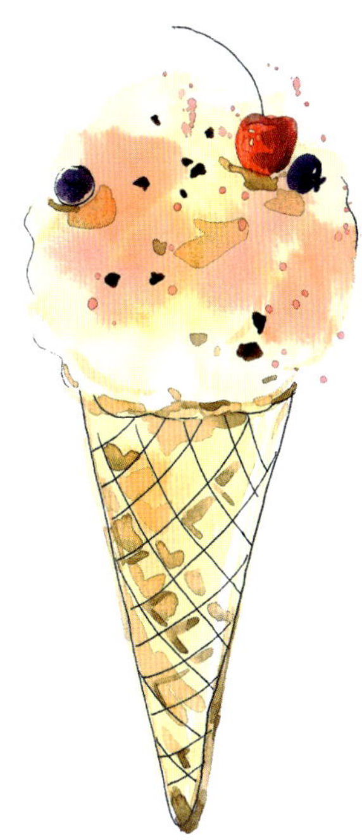

Fluffy Ice Cream

Let's paint a transparent and fluffy ice cream! You can experiment with different flavors, and each time you'll enjoy it because it's super easy, fun, and quick! This project is a great exercise for your imagination. So, let's enjoy it together.

PROJECT COLORS

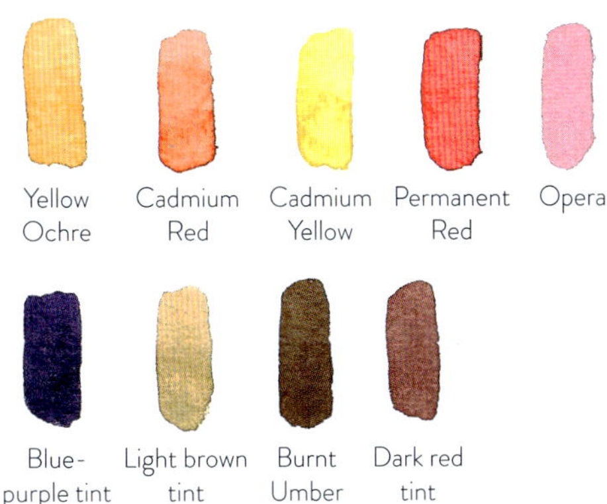

COLOR MIXING

- Blue-purple tint: Add a little Crimson or Alizarin to Ultramarine.

- Light brown tint: Mix Burnt Umber with Yellow Ochre.

- Dark red tint: Add a little Sap Green or any green to Permanent Red.

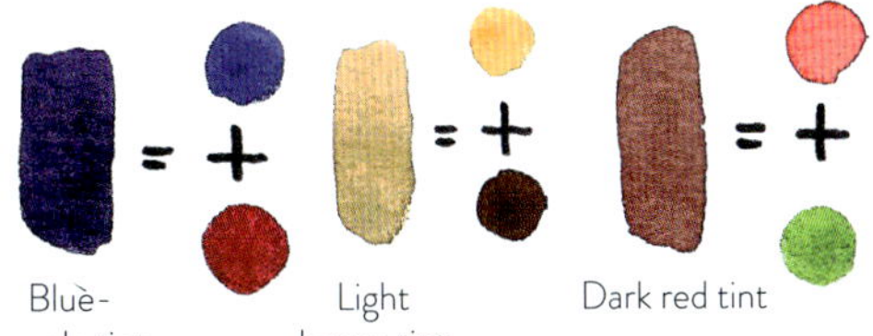

SUPPLIES

- Watercolor paper

- Washi tape or masking tape

- Pencil and eraser (optional)

- Kitchen sponge

- Quill brush (sizes 1–4) or soft round brush (size 8)

- Round brushes: small (sizes 1–4) and medium (sizes 6–8)

- Waterproof black ink pen

NOTE: I recommend using a simple kitchen sponge, which you can buy at any store that sells household items. Cut it into different-sized pieces. I also suggest practicing the sponge technique.

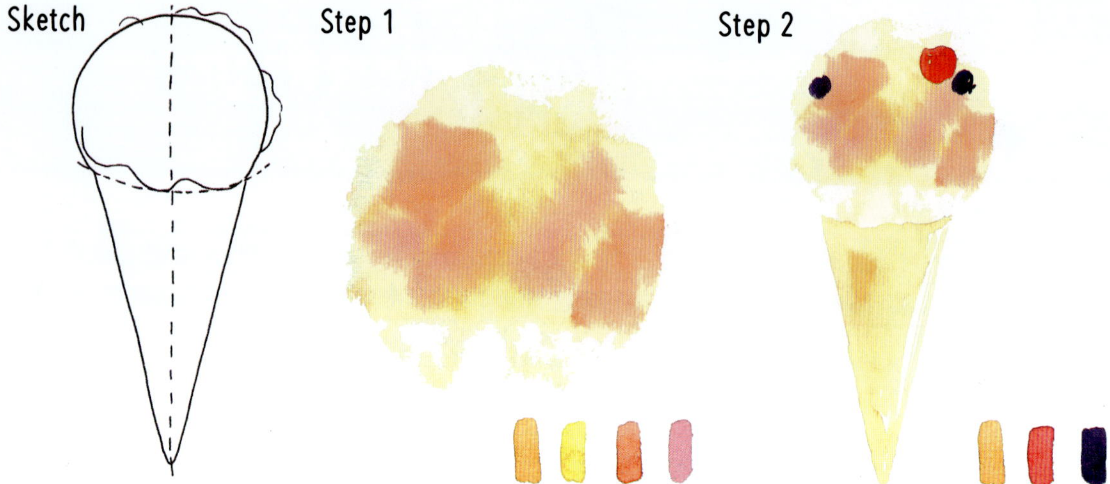

PREPARATION WORK

First, secure your watercolor paper with washi tape to prevent wrinkling.

Next, you can make a preliminary sketch, which is optional. If you decide to, lightly sketch the basic lines on your paper with a pencil, making them almost invisible. I recommend sketching only the cone with a pencil and leaving the ice cream to be created with watercolor, without any sketching.

Once that's done, prepare your sponge. I recommend using a small piece of sponge, so you can pinch it between your fingers easily. Prepare a generous amount of Yellow Ochre in a medium to watery consistency, as this will serve as the base for our ice cream. Also, prepare Permanent Red, Yellow Ochre, Cadmium Yellow, Cadmium Red, and Opera in medium consistency.

Once you're ready, proceed to the first step.

STEP 1

Let's start by making this fluffy ice cream using the sponge technique on a wet surface.

Wet the area where you plan to paint the fluffy ice cream using a quill brush. It should be wet but not too wet, slightly larger than the ice cream. Take your sponge, load it with water, squeeze out the excess, and then load it with Yellow Ochre. Press the sponge to form the ice cream shape. The watercolor will spread

and create a fluffy texture. Repeat to intensify the color if needed.

While it's still wet, pick up your medium round brush and start adding Cadmium Red, Opera, and Cadmium Yellow randomly to the wet layer. Be careful not to add too much of these colors—just a little bit to prevent the ice cream base layer from looking flat and to give it a colorful touch. Adding too many colors could create a messy result.

NOTE: The ice cream doesn't need to be a perfect circle. Some texture and imperfection will make it better.

Once you've finished, let the layer dry completely.

STEP 2

Now it's time to add more details to our artwork. First, prepare your medium round brush and Yellow Ochre in medium consistency, and start painting the waffle cone as shown in the example. It doesn't need to be perfect, but make the end of the cone especially thin to give your work a neat finish.

Next, if you'd like, you can add berries and toppings to the already dried ice cream layer. Using a small round brush, add a cherry with Permanent Red in medium consistency, and paint a few blueberries with blue-purple tint in thick or medium consistency. Once you're happy with these details, let the painting dry and move on to the next step.

STEP 3

It's time to add some more details, and this time we'll use a black pen. Draw details on the waffle cone, especially by outlining the inner shape of the cone and adding some extra patterns inside. You can also use the pen to emphasize details on the berries or toppings you've added—in my case, I'm adding details to the cherry and blueberries.

Additionally, you can add a few details to the fluffy top part of the ice cream, but not too many so as not to ruin the beautiful fluffy texture we created earlier. Just a few lines will be enough.

Let the black ink lines dry a little, then move on to the final step.

STEP 4

Let's finalize our illustration. You can use a small round brush and a medium round brush for this step. Prepare light brown tint, Burnt Umber, dark red tint, and Opera in medium to thick consistency.

First, pick a medium round brush and start adding shadows in light brown tint randomly to the fluffy top part of the ice cream, especially at the bottom of the berries or fruits if you've added them. Use the same color to emphasize and define some texture in the waffle cone.

Next, use Burnt Umber to add extra details to the waffle cone, particularly at the end of the cone. I also recommend adding some extra details with Burnt Umber, like chocolate pieces, and you can emphasize shadows as well. We're using the layering technique here. Then, with dark red tint, add shadows to the cherry. If you've included other fruits and berries, add shadow details to give them dimension and make them look more complete.

As a final touch, I suggest splattering a bit of color. I used Opera—one or two splashes will be enough—but you can use any color from your project. And that's it! Our fluffy, summery ice cream is complete.

Try experimenting with different details, colors, and compositions!

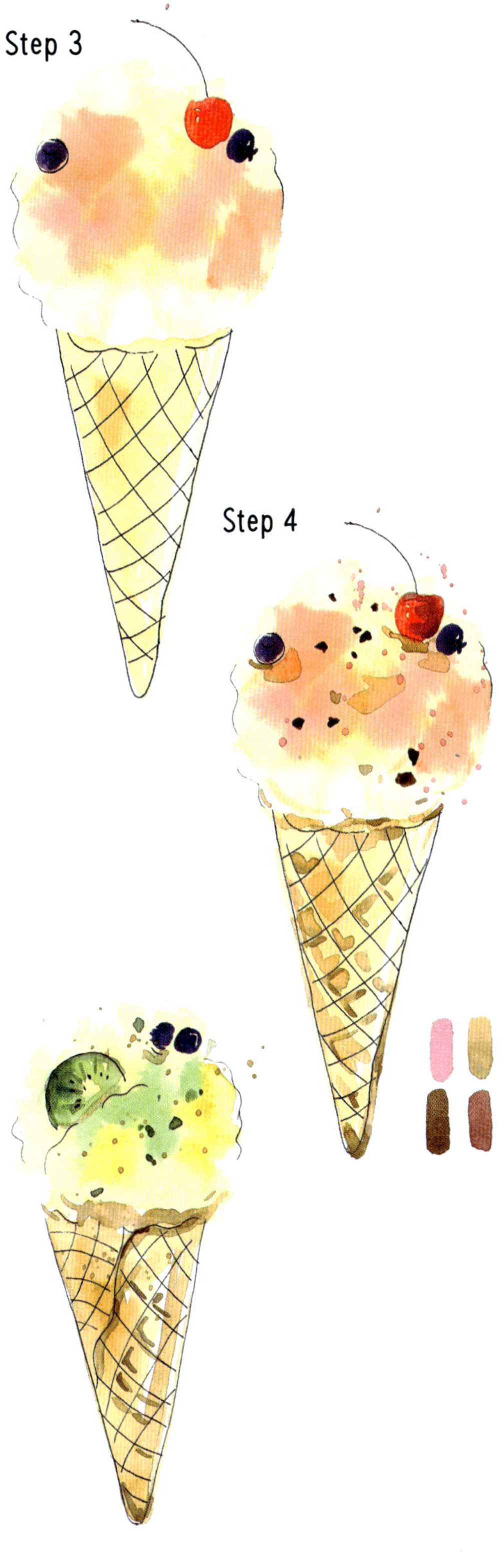

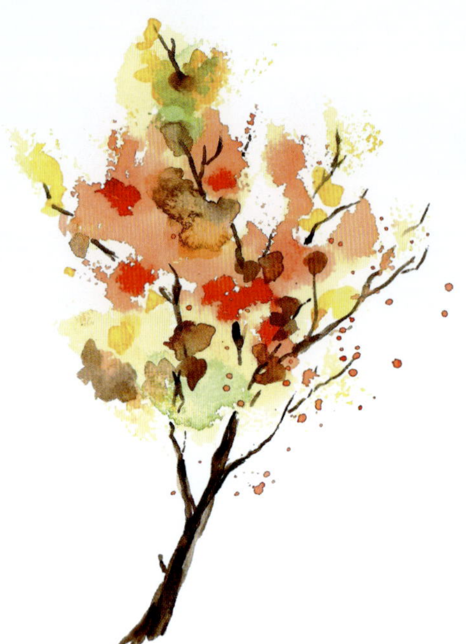

Bright Fall Tree

Let's paint an abstract tree in beautiful, vibrant fall colors. You'll see how easy it is to create a tree silhouette using the sponge technique and how interesting it is to add colors on a wet layer and let them blend. Let's have fun together!

PROJECT COLORS

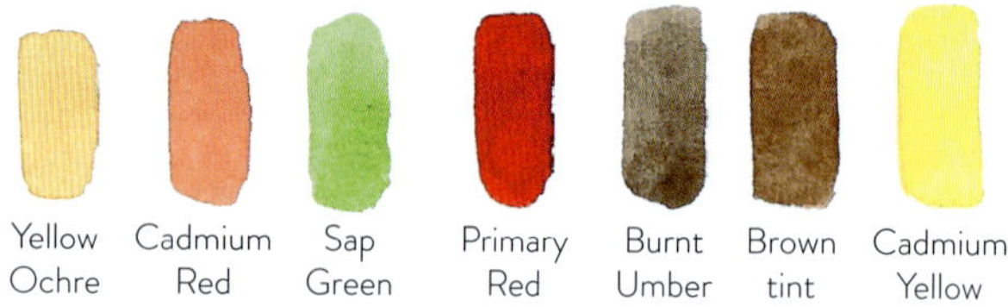

SUPPLIES

- Watercolor paper
- Washi tape or masking tape
- Pencil and eraser (optional)
- Kitchen sponge
- Round brushes: small (sizes 1–4) and medium (sizes 6–8)

NOTE: I recommend using a simple kitchen sponge, which you can buy at any store that sells household items. Cut it into different-sized pieces. I also suggest practicing the sponge technique.

COLOR MIXING

- Brown tint: Add a bit of Burnt Umber to Burnt Sienna.

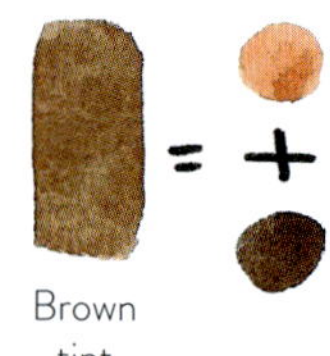

NOTE: The colors for this project are flexible. You can use Yellow Ochre as a base for the tree's crown and add different colors to experiment. Also, I recommend using brown, such as Burnt Umber, for the tree trunk, as this color is essential for the project.

PREPARATION WORK

Let's begin this project by preparing the paper for painting. While not mandatory, you can secure your paper to the table with washi tape to prevent any wrinkling or curling while using the wet-on-wet technique.

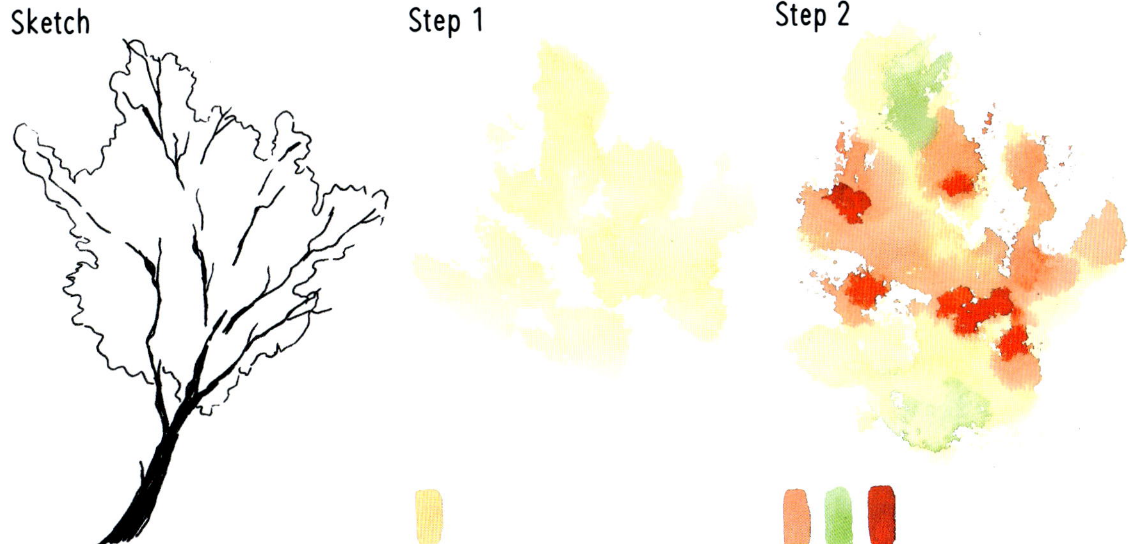

Next, decide where you'll place the tree on your paper. Planning in advance helps ensure you have enough space, especially at the top of the paper for the tree's crown. You can lightly mark the general edges of the tree crown or trunk with a pencil, keeping these marks very faint. Or, simply visualize where you'll place the tree, making sure to leave space for branches at the top of the paper. In Sketch, you'll find a sketch you can use as a reference for your preliminary outline.

Also, prepare the following colors in advance, mixed to a medium consistency: Yellow Ochre, Cadmium Red, Sap Green, and Primary Red. You'll need a larger amount of the Yellow Ochre mixture, as it will be applied with a sponge to form the tree's crown.

STEP 1

Let's start painting our abstract tree. Take a small piece of sponge, wet it with clean water, squeeze out the excess, and hold it pinched between your fingers.

Dip the sponge into the Yellow Ochre paint and begin forming the tree's crown by pressing the sponge onto the paper.

You only need to create a base for the crown with the sponge, not fill it in completely; we'll add more colors in the next step. Work quickly, as we'll be adding those colors on a still-wet layer. Once the crown base is ready, immediately proceed to the next step.

STEP 2

Now, pick up your medium round brush and start adding Cadmium Red, Sap Green, and Primary Red in a medium consistency to the crown of your tree.

Be careful not to place red and green too close to each other to avoid creating muddy colors on the crown layer. You also don't need to add too many touches with these colors, as the yellow base should remain visible.

NOTE: While the colors are still wet, you can use the sponge technique with medium consistency Yellow Ochre to add extra touches to the crown, especially around the edges.

Once you're satisfied with the result, let everything dry completely before moving to the next step.

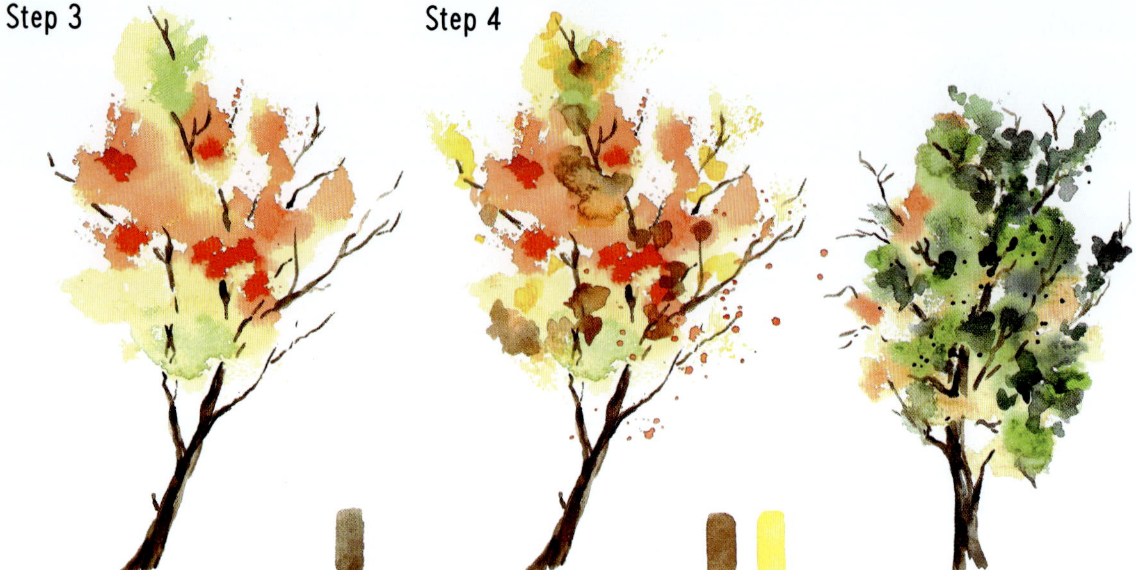

STEP 3

Switch to your small round brush, or keep the medium round brush if it's comfortable for you, and start painting the trunk with medium-consistency Burnt Umber. Then add the main branches, followed by the smaller ones, until you achieve the desired result. You can follow my example if you'd like. Make sure your branches look natural; you may want to refer to a real tree for inspiration on how the branches typically appear.

I also recommend using a very dry brush, especially for the small, thin branches that extend far from the trunk. To do this, dampen the brush slightly, remove excess water with a towel, then load it with paint. Use this almost-dry brush to add these branches, keeping them loose and avoiding perfect or symmetrical shapes. Once you're satisfied with the result, move on to the final step.

STEP 4

We've created a beautiful abstract fall tree, but in watercolor, it's always fun to add extra details and a layer on top.

Prepare a medium-consistency brown tint and Cadmium Yellow. Using a medium round brush, start adding details. With the brown tint, focus on creating subtle shadows. If the light is coming from above, the shadows will appear at the bottom of the tree clusters. Since we're working in an abstract, loose style, the shadows don't need to be perfect—just try to place them on one side and near the bottom.

Also, add a few touches of Cadmium Yellow, and if desired, add a hint of any other project color as detail. I don't recommend adding too many colors, as this might overwhelm the painting.

For the final touch, I suggest adding some splatters to the top of your painting with Cadmium Red, focusing on areas where you want to draw attention.

TIP: You can also use the sponge technique to finish the painting. Wet the sponge, squeeze out excess water, and use Cadmium Red to add a few extra prints, creating an interesting texture on the tree.

Try experimenting with different details, colors, and compositions!

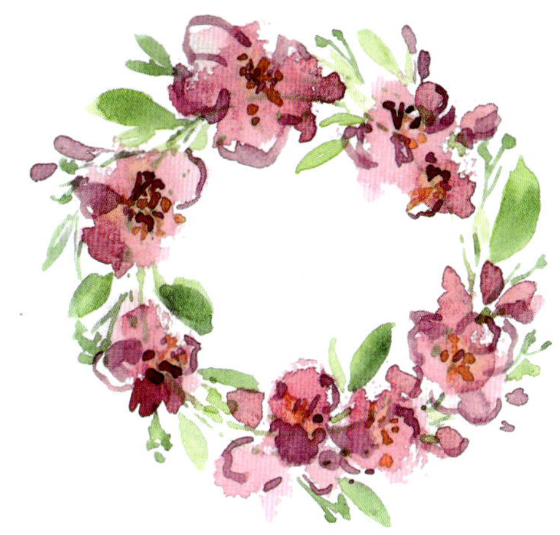

Tender Wreath

Let's paint an elegant, flowering watercolor wreath using the sponge technique. This project lets your creativity flow, as the sponge allows for unpredictable results, forming unique blossoms and flowers. At the same time, you can practice traditional watercolor techniques to refine the piece and turn it into a lovely wreath, making it perfect for a greeting card or framing as wall art. It's also ideal for recreation and exploring watercolor techniques, so let's have fun together!

SUPPLIES

- Watercolor paper
- Washi tape or masking tape
- Medium-sized rounded object (such as a cup, jar, or bowl)
- Kitchen sponge
- Round brushes: small (sizes 1–4) and medium (sizes 6–8)

PROJECT COLORS

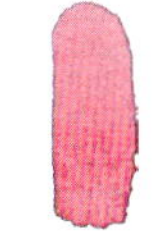 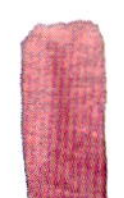  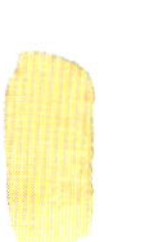 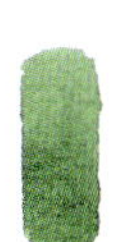

Opera (or any other pink or rose color)   Crimson   Yellow Ochre   Green tint

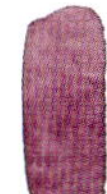 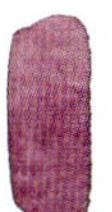 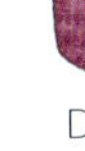 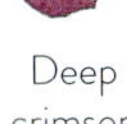

Burnt Sienna   Deep crimson   Sap Green

COLOR MIXING

- Green tint: Mix Sap Green with a bit of blue (I used Prussian Blue).
- Deep crimson: Add a little blue to Crimson.

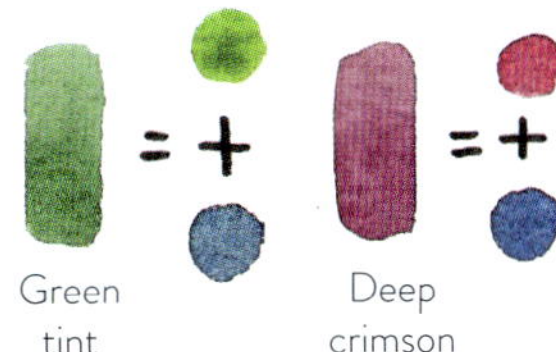

Green tint   Deep crimson

NOTE: I recommend using a simple kitchen sponge, which you can buy at any store that sells household items. Cut out a small piece. I also suggest practicing the sponge technique.

PREPARATION WORK

Let's begin the project by securing the paper to the table with washi tape. This project does not require any preliminary sketching. However, you'll want to find the center of your page, which will help you decide where to place the wreath. If you plan to add text, you may want to position the wreath slightly higher on the page.

On the next page, you'll find a basic sketch for the wreath we're going to create. This outline gives a general idea of where to place blossoms and flowers, but keep in mind that it doesn't need to be perfectly symmetrical. The flowers should have a natural, slightly random placement for an organic feel.

(Continued)

Sketch

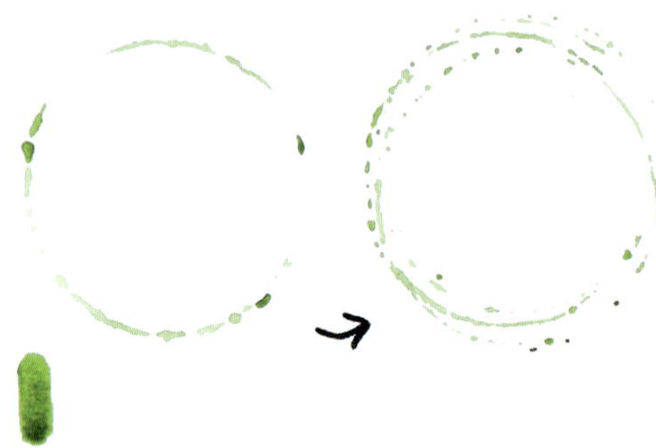

Step 1

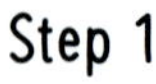

Step 2

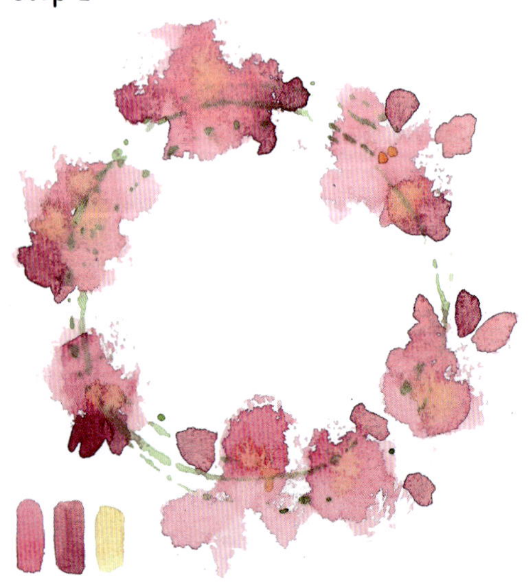

In Sketch, you'll see guidance on the direction of flowers and leaves. This will help you create a balanced composition.

Prepare the following colors in medium consistency: Opera, Crimson, Yellow Ochre, green tint, Burnt Sienna, and deep crimson. Also, prepare Sap Green in a watery consistency. Make sure to mix a generous amount of Opera, as we'll use it for the sponge technique.

STEP 1

Let's create the base of our wreath using the stamp technique. Pick a medium-sized rounded object; I'm using a medium-sized jar. With a medium round brush, paint the edges of the jar with watery consistency Sap Green. Then, at the spot where you're going to create the wreath, press the jar onto the paper, lift it up, slightly change the position, and press again. Repeat a few times until you have several overlapping circles that form a base, with each one slightly offset from the others. This will create a beautiful, natural base for our wreath.

Your circles don't need to be perfect; it's actually better if they are a bit interrupted. This makes it easy to add flowers on top. Once everything is done, let it dry completely, and move on to the second step.

STEP 2

Let's continue painting by adding flowers and blossoms to the wreath. Take a small piece of sponge, wet it, and squeeze out all the excess water. Generously load the sponge with the Opera paint mixture, press it onto the paper, then lift it up and repeat to create bold, textured prints with the sponge. Add flowers in different shapes and directions until you've filled most of the wreath with blossoms.

NOTE: To ensure you achieve a beautiful arrangement of flowers and blossoms with the sponge technique, you may want to practice on a separate sheet before working on your main piece.

While the flowers are still wet, use a medium round brush to add small flowers and buds with Crimson. These details can blend naturally with the flower shapes. Also, add one or two touches of Yellow Ochre to the center of each flower, allowing it to blend on the paper as well.

Once you're happy with the result, let everything dry completely before proceeding to the next step.

STEP 3

Now it's time to add green details to our wreath. Let's work with Sap Green and green tint, using a medium round brush. You can also use a small round brush for finer details.

Start by adding leaves and details with Sap Green. Begin with a few larger leaves, followed by smaller leaves, then add extra branches and small details as you go.

While the details are still wet, add some green tint to blend with the Sap Green areas, creating depth.

Be careful not to overdo the green details; the flowers should remain the focal point of your wreath. Keep a sense of direction for the leaves, with some leaves flowing in the same direction, or adjust slightly to add natural variation. If it helps, refer to my example image as a guide.

Once everything is complete, let it dry completely before moving on to the final step.

STEP 4

It's time to add the final details to our painting. You can continue working with the medium round brush or switch to a small round brush. Start by adding details to the centers of your blossoms using Burnt Sienna. Make them varied and natural-looking; don't aim for perfection. Let this layer dry a little.

Next, switch to deep crimson to add extra definition to the centers of the flowers, creating a lovely contrast. Using the same color, add additional details to the flowers, such as shadows, defined petals, and a few touches on the buds. You can also enhance the depth with some subtle accents.

Be careful not to add too many details. Once you feel that your painting has achieved a balanced and elegant look, it's time to stop. Your painting is now complete!

Try experimenting with different details, colors, and compositions!

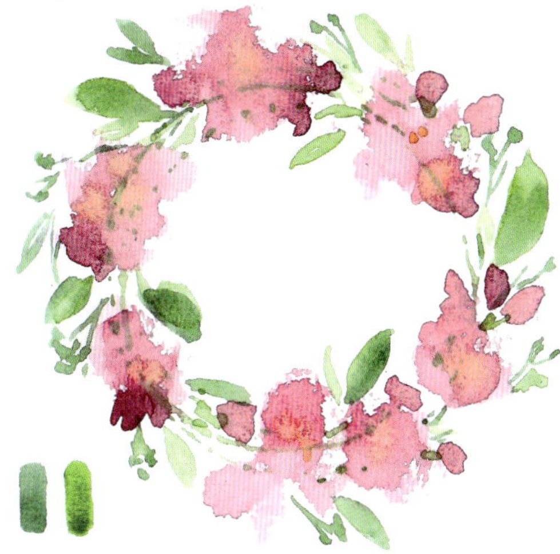

Step 3

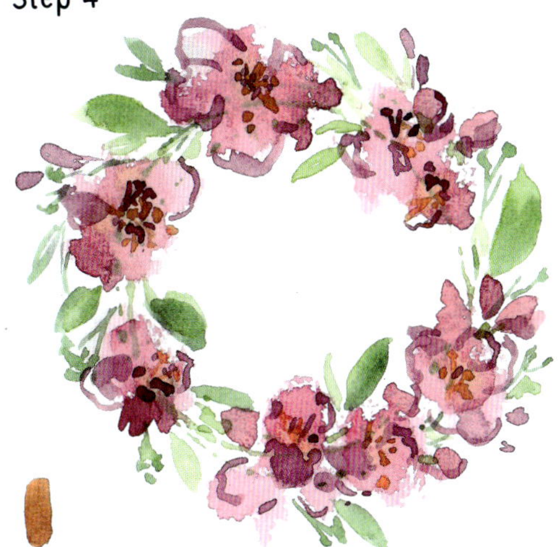

Step 4

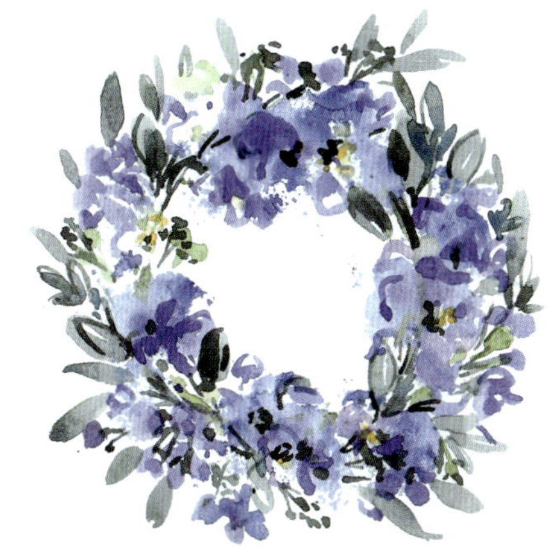

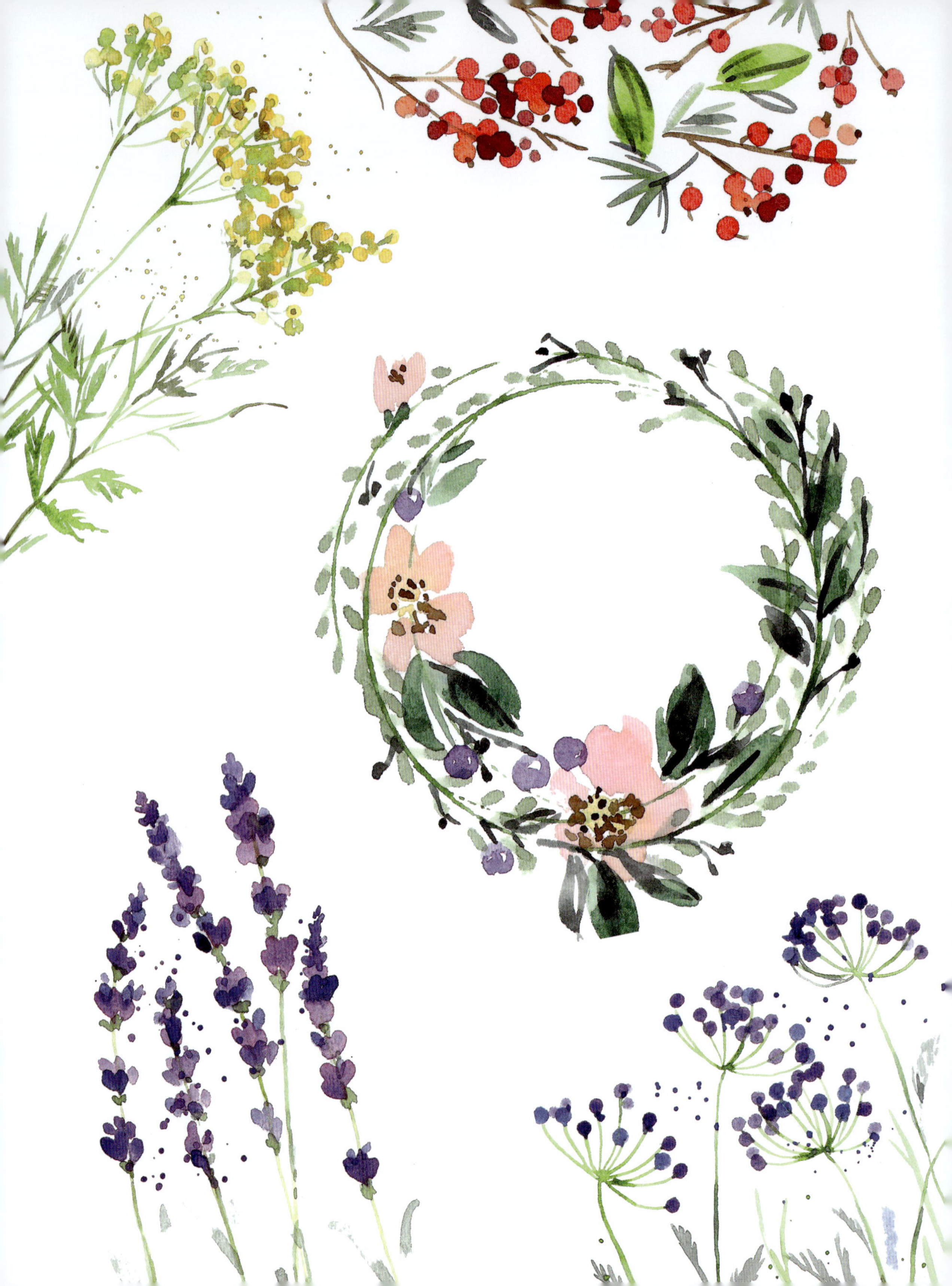

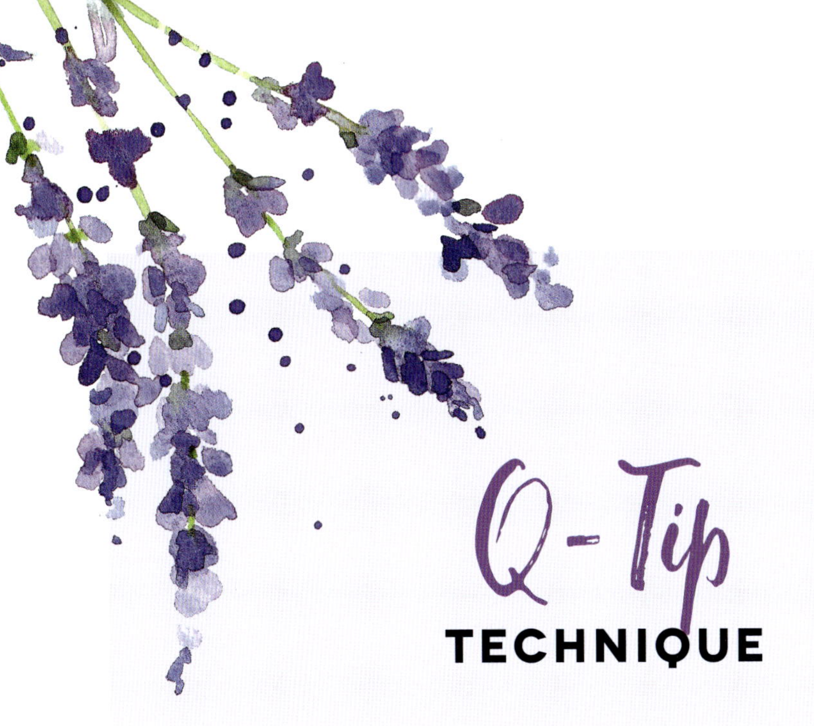

Q-Tip
TECHNIQUE

TECHNIQUES USED IN THIS CHAPTER

Wet-on-Wet Technique (page 14)

Layering (page 14)

Softening (page 15)

Lifting (page 16)

Stamp Technique (page 18)

Q-Tip Technique (page 19)

Splattering (page 19)

Outlining (page 20)

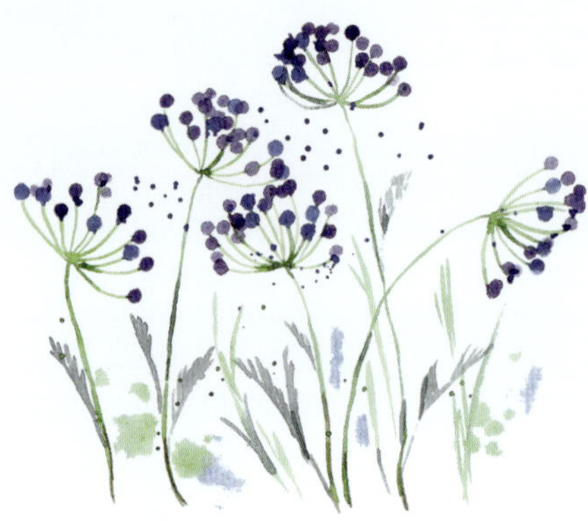

The Grace of Wildflowers

Let's create wildflowers full of grace, inspiration, and creative flow. You'll enjoy both the project and the process.

SUPPLIES

- Watercolor paper
- Round brushes: small (sizes 1–4) and medium (size 6)
- Cotton swabs
- Washi tape or masking tape (optional)
- Pencil and eraser (optional)

PROJECT COLORS

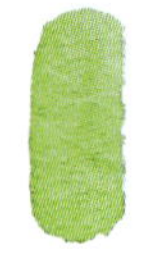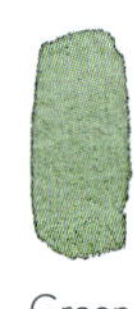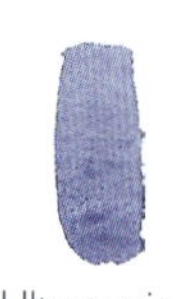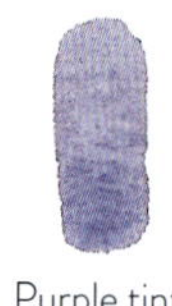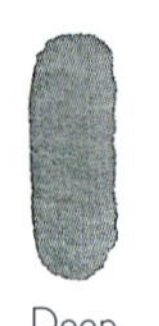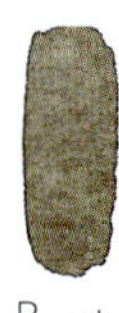

| Sap Green | Green tint | Ultramarine | Purple tint | Deep green tint | Burnt Umber |

COLOR MIXING

- Green tint: Add a little blue (I use Indigo) to Sap Green.
- Purple tint: Mix Ultramarine with Crimson.
- Deep green tint: Add a little Sap Green to blue (Indigo).

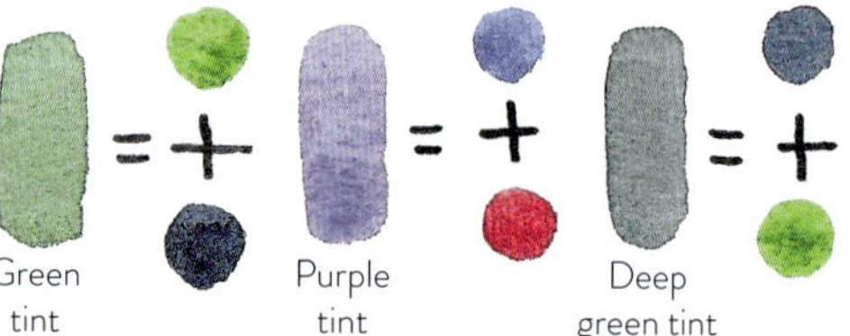

NOTE: Instead of Burnt Umber, you can use any other brown.

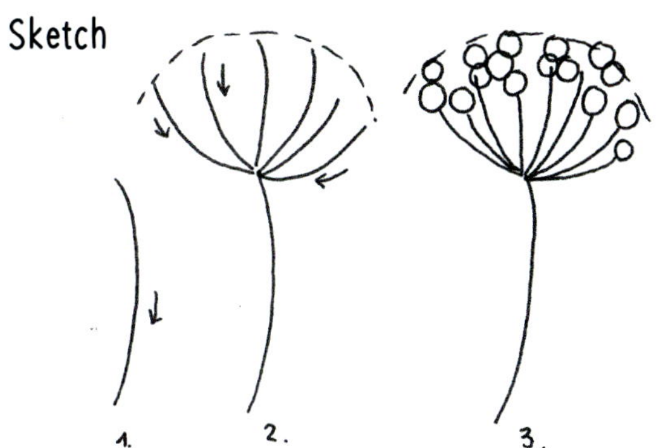

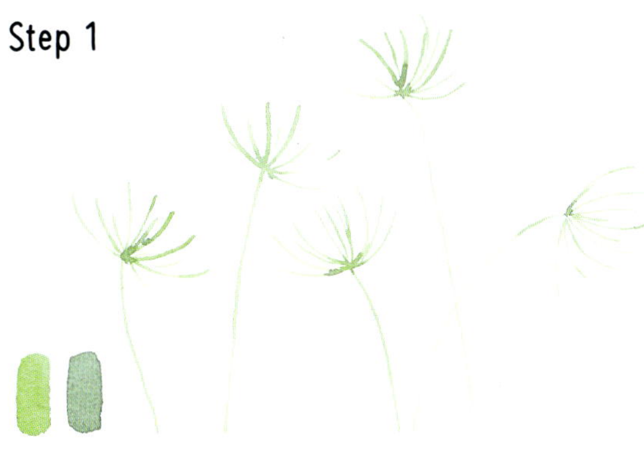

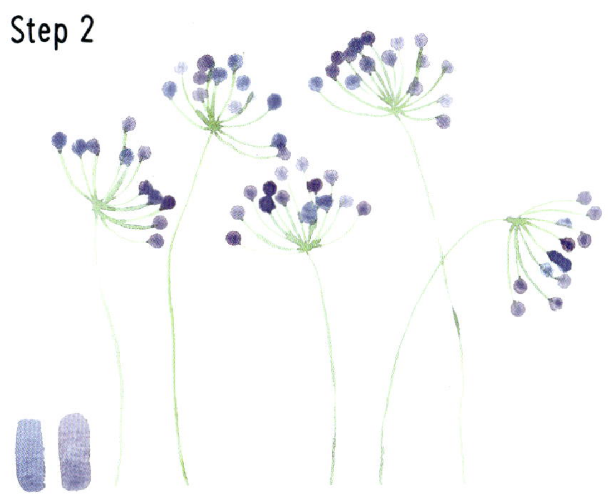

PREPARATION WORK

Begin this project by preparing the paper. I advise you to secure the paper to the table using washi tape. If you'd like, you can make a very light preliminary sketch and mark the stems of the wildflowers. However, I recommend letting go and painting the stems and other details with watercolor.

I also suggest preparing a large amount of paint in advance, especially Ultramarine and a purple tint in medium consistency. Next, I advise you to pick two or three cotton swabs and soak them in clean water to soften them slightly. After soaking, lightly blot them on a paper towel so they are wet but not dripping and ready for use in the Q-tip technique in steps 2 and 3.

Once you've completed these steps, move on to the first step of the project.

STEP 1

Begin the project by painting the stems and green parts of the inflorescence. To do this, prepare Sap Green and green tint in medium consistency. Take a small round brush with a thin tip, and use Sap Green to start painting the stems. I recommend painting from the center of the inflorescence down to the base of the stem (see the image to the right). Then, add the green parts (little stems) of the inflorescence by painting toward the center. Make sure that the small stems of the inflorescence have different lengths for a natural look.

While the Sap Green details are still wet, you can add a small touch of green tint in some areas. Repeat this process for the rest of the wildflowers. Once everything is done, let it dry completely before proceeding to the next step.

STEP 2

Now let's add inflorescence flowers using the Q-tip technique. The flowers may look abstract, but they still effectively represent this type of wildflower.

Prepare Ultramarine and purple tint in medium consistency, along with wetted cotton swabs. First, load a cotton swab with Ultramarine and add small, random spots to form the flowers. Then switch to another cotton swab, load it with purple tint, and add the remaining spots.

Vary the spot sizes by pressing the Q-tip harder or more lightly onto the paper. Some blending of purple and Ultramarine is fine and creates a nice wet-on-wet effect. Add spots to form both the arc and the center of the inflorescence. Let everything dry before moving on.

STEP 3

In this step, we'll add more details to the wildflowers to make the painting look even more refined and complete. Using a deep green tint in medium consistency and a medium round brush, paint some leaves. You can follow my example or create your own.

Next, use Burnt Umber to add accents at the base of the stems, near the roots. This adds contrast and mimics how wildflowers naturally appear thicker and earth-toned at the base.

Lastly, use the Q-tip technique to add more inflorescence flowers with a purple tint. You can layer them on top of the existing flowers or add more to complete the look.

Once you're satisfied, let everything dry before moving to the final step.

STEP 4

I recommend just a few extra details. First, wash some areas at the bottom of the piece with clean water. Then, using Ultramarine in medium consistency, make loose vertical brushstrokes in a chaotic, wet-on-wet technique. The paint will spread beautifully, creating a lovely transparent effect.

Next, using the same color in a thicker consistency, try splattering. Load a medium brush with Ultramarine and flick it two or three times onto the top part of the painting.

Then, with Sap Green in medium consistency, splatter on the wet bottom part, where the Ultramarine background has already been created.

You can also use purple to add small touches to the flowers, emphasizing certain areas to make them more interesting. Lastly, if you want, make a few adjustments to the leaves, but be sure to stop when you feel it's enough.

Try experimenting with different details, colors, and compositions!

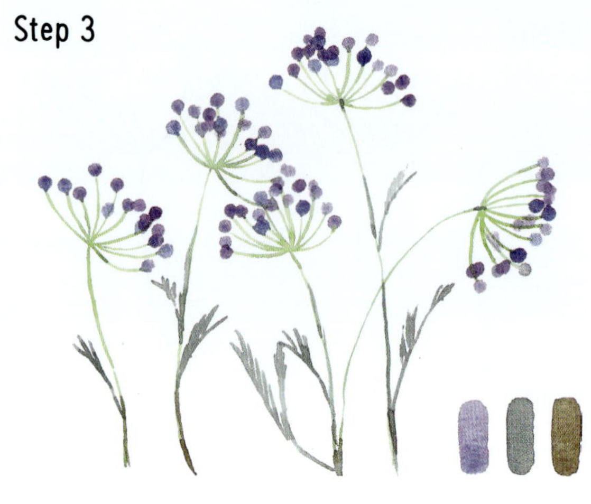

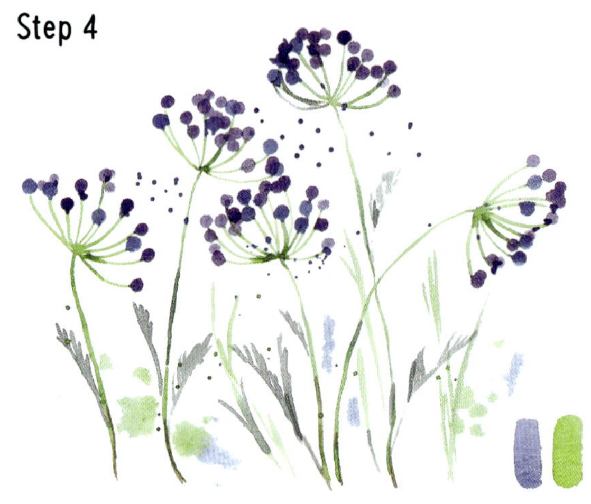

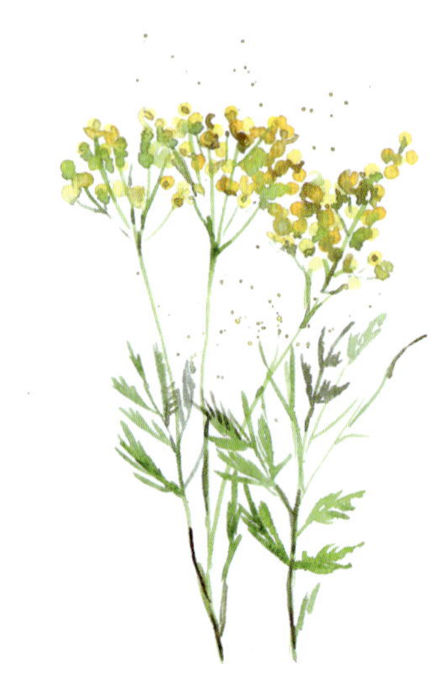

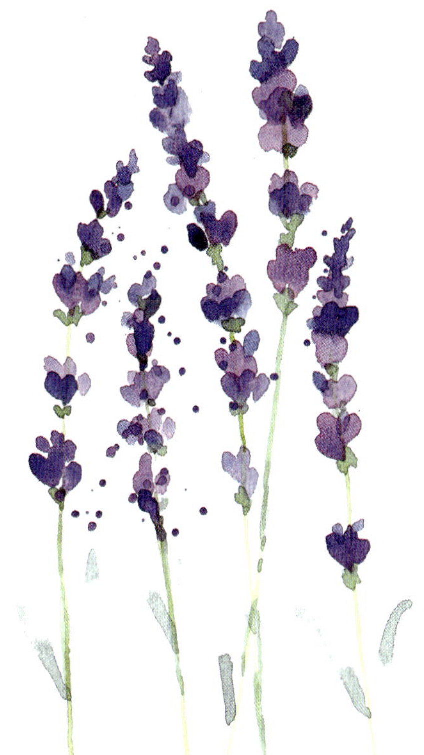

Lavender Breeze

Painting lavender with watercolor is such a pleasure because it's simple and you can always achieve beautiful results. But I encourage you to try a different way of creating a lavender painting. This project is done in a loose style, while still staying detailed with beautiful shades of purple and violet. The final result I call Lavender Breeze, because it not only depicts lavender but also gives that special feeling of a lavender field, with its smell and atmosphere.

I hope you fall in love with this project and learn from it to recreate in different variations.

COLOR MIXING

- Sap Green tint: Add a little Burnt Sienna to Sap Green.

- Purple tint: Mix Ultramarine with some Opera.

- Violet tint: Mix Ultramarine with a little Opera.

- Warm blue tint: Add a little Opera to Ultramarine.

- Earth green: Add a little Indigo (or another blue) and a bit of Burnt Sienna to Sap Green.

- Deep green: Mix Sap Green with some Indigo.

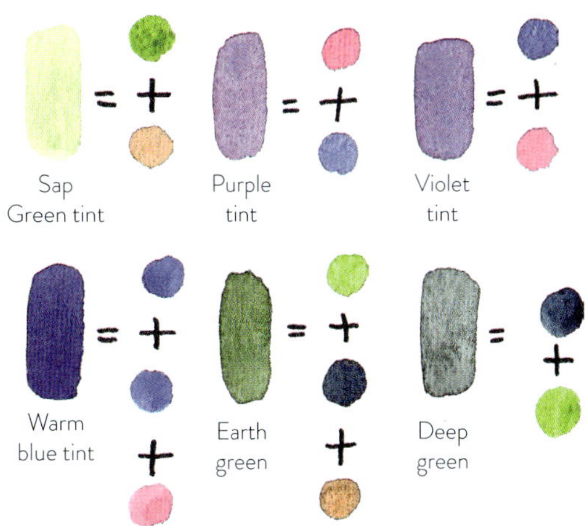

SUPPLIES

- Watercolor paper

- Washi tape or masking tape (optional)

- Pencil and eraser (optional)

- Round brushes: small (sizes 1–4) and medium (sizes 6–8)

- Cotton swabs

PROJECT COLORS

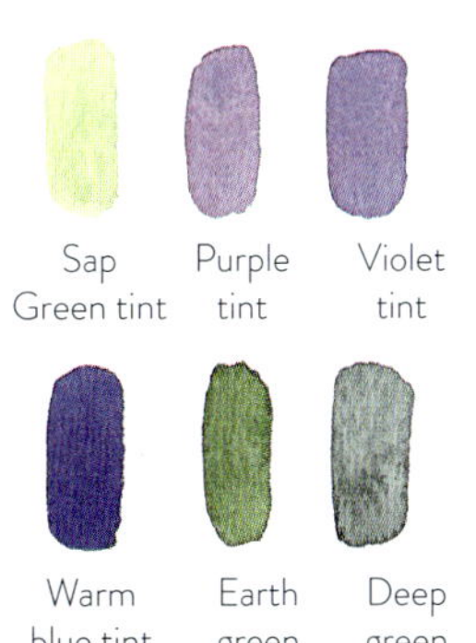

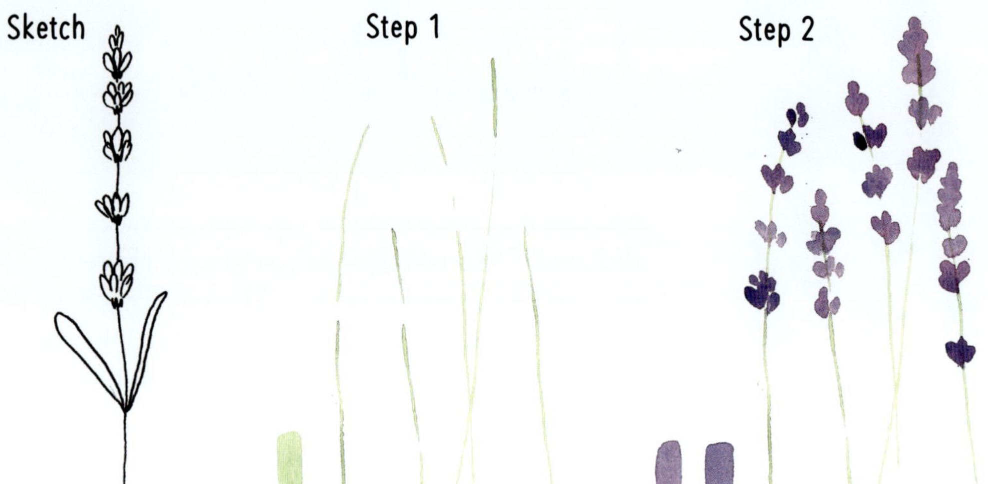

NOTE: For violet tint, purple tint, and warm blue tint, you mix very similar colors, but the key is in the proportions. For the purple tint, you need to add a little more pink—Opera in this case—while for violet, you add less pink to achieve a bluish tint. For the warm blue, we add even less pink to balance and set the rest of the colors for this project.

PREPARATION WORK

Let's begin our project by setting everything up. First, if you prefer, you can secure the paper with washi tape. Then we need to figure out the composition. I recommend following my composition and skipping any preliminary sketching. You just need to understand how each lavender branch grows. For this, you can refer to Sketch. However, if you feel you need help, feel free to make a preliminary sketch. You can take your pencil and make a few very light lines to mark where the lavender branches will be located.

STEP 1

Pick a small round brush, and using a fairly watery to medium consistency Sap Green tint, draw the branches—the stems of our lavender. I suggest making them as thin as possible, even leaving gaps in the stems, because you can always make them thicker later. I start from the bottom. You can add as many lavender stems as you'd like, but for the first time, I suggest limiting yourself to five to seven branches. Once that's done, let it dry completely before moving to the next step.

Figure 1

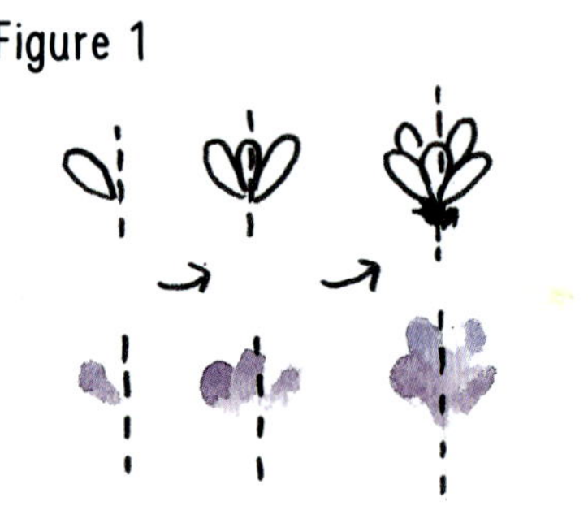

STEP 2

Now let's make all the magic happen using the Q-tip technique. Pick two cotton swabs and dip them in clean water, making them wet but not too wet. Prepare a generous amount of purple tint and violet tint in medium consistency. You'll start by dipping one cotton swab in the purple tint. You need to press the cotton swab with pigment onto the paper, holding it parallel to the surface. This way, you're not making a round print but creating a shape similar to a small lavender flower. You can even use your finger to control the pressure while pressing. Press and lift, press and lift, to make clusters of three flowers. You can see the progress of building a lavender flower cluster in the image above. After you've finished the first layer of purple flower prints, begin using the violet tint. In some areas, the purple and violet tints will blend, creating a beautiful, natural effect. Once all the flower prints are done, let everything dry completely.

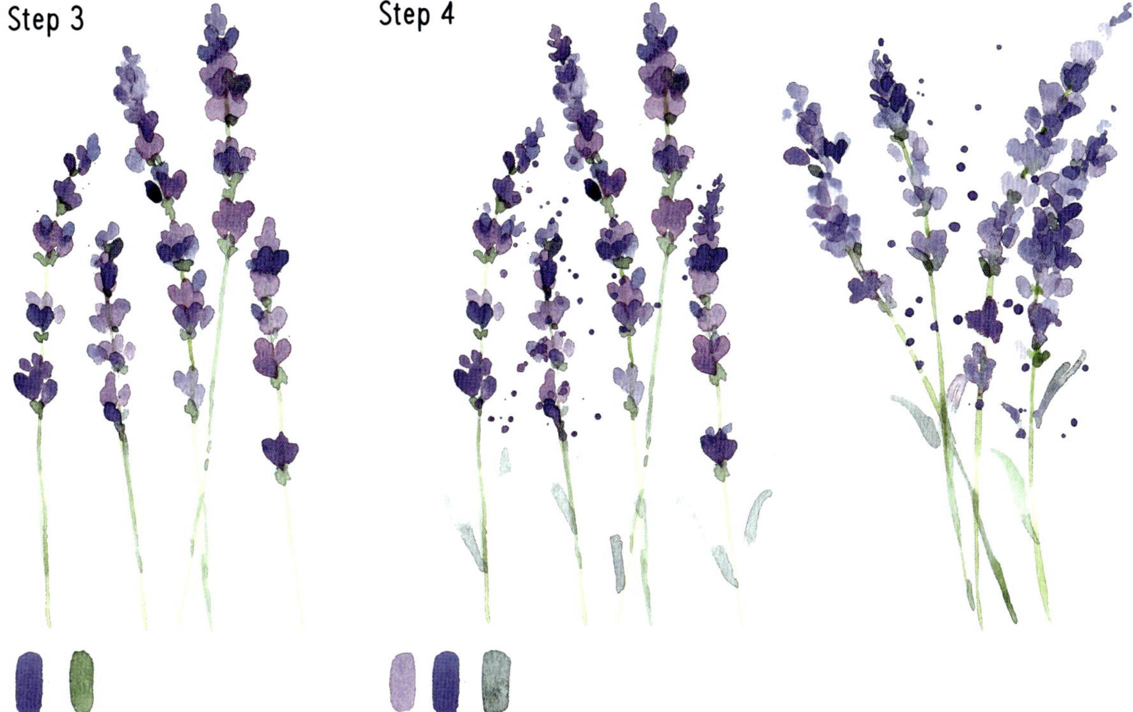

STEP 3

Prepare a medium consistency warm blue tint and earth green. Wet a cotton swab, then load it with a generous amount of warm blue tint, and start adding lavender prints on top of the previously added ones. You can add them randomly or add three extra flower prints per cluster, creating a 3D effect in some areas.

Once you're done with the lavender clusters and flowers, pick a small round brush and, using a medium consistency of earth green, start adding the green parts at the bases of the clusters, where the flowers are attached. Also, with the same color, make the stems more visible in certain places by adding extra brushstrokes. Once everything is done, let it dry completely before moving on to the final step.

STEP 4

We've already created a beautiful lavender composition, but let's add some finer details to give it a "Lavender Breeze."

First, using warm blue and purple tints, add accents to some of the lavender branches, making them thinner at the beginning of the branch. This is because the blossoms naturally taper off and become smaller, giving a delicate effect typical of lavender. These accents shouldn't look exactly like the flowers, but rather hint at them. Keep it random, and if you need help, you can refer to an image of real lavender for guidance.

Once you're satisfied with the result, prepare a watery consistency of deep green and, using a medium brush, start adding leaves. Again, if you look at a photo of real lavender, you'll notice the shape of the leaves. We'll simplify them here, keeping them as basic as possible to represent the overall shape.

Next, use a tint of purple, violet, or even warm blue tint to add some splatters by flicking the brush—just one or two flicks on the paper will be enough. That's it! Our beautiful Lavender Breeze artwork, created with the fun Q-tip method, is complete.

Try experimenting with different details, colors, and compositions!

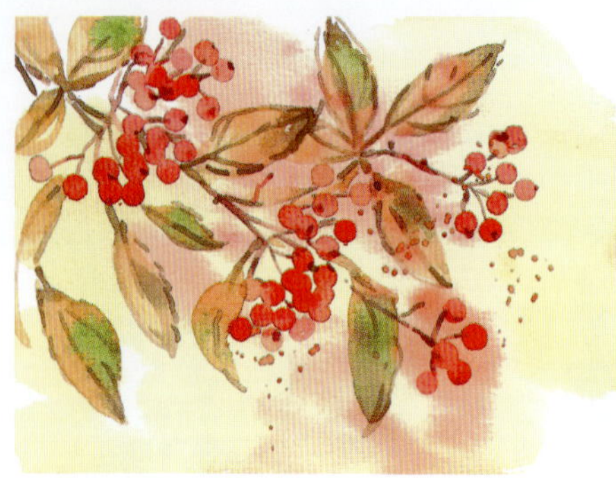

SUPPLIES

- Watercolor paper
- Washi tape or masking tape
- Pencil and eraser (optional)
- Quill brush (size 4) or soft round brush (size 8)
- Round brushes: small (sizes 1–4) and medium (size 6)
- Cotton swabs

The Charm of Fall Berries

In this lesson, you will learn how to paint a fall watercolor piece in just a few easy steps, using a magical technique and some helpful tricks. I'm always inspired by the colors, shapes, and contrast of autumn, and I love capturing this beauty on paper.

This artwork features lovely autumn colors and splashes, with a loose background and carefully placed accents added in the final stage. It's a celebration of fall's vibrant colors, and I'm sure you'll love this method. You can use it to paint a variety of scenes, especially if you want to capture the essence of nature with berries.

The result of this project is always so beautiful that you can frame it and hang it on your wall. So, gather your supplies, and let's create!

PROJECT COLORS

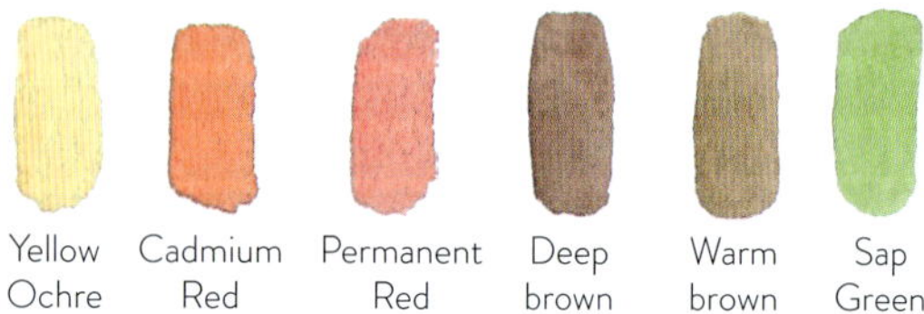

COLOR MIXING

- Deep brown: Mix Burnt Umber with Permanent Red.
- Warm brown: Add a little Burnt Umber to Burnt Sienna.

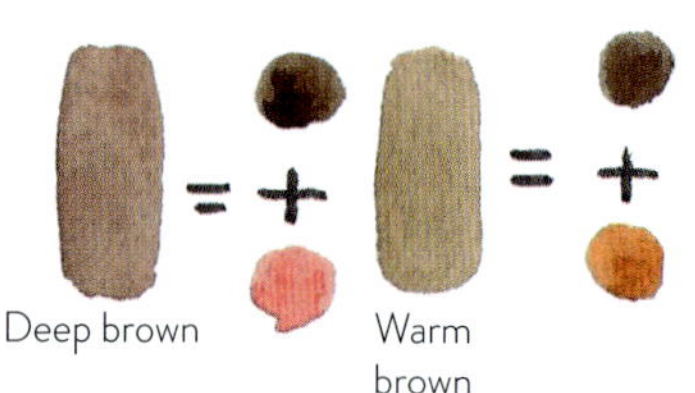

Sketch

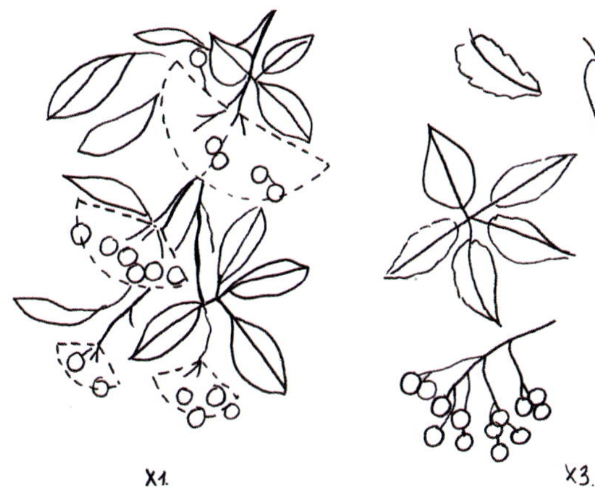

Step 1

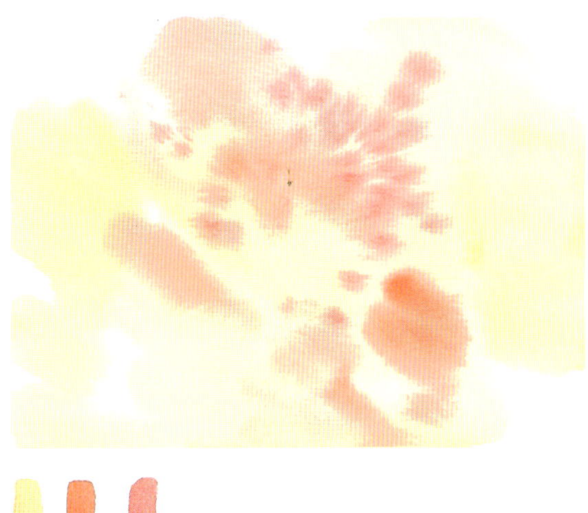

PREPARATION WORK

Before starting this beautiful project, you need to prepare your paper. I recommend using a smaller format because we will be creating berries with cotton swabs. The berries will be small, so the scale of the scene should be balanced to match their size. However, if you'd prefer a larger composition, it's fine to use a bigger paper format. Secure the paper to your table using washi tape along the edges.

You can make a very basic sketch at this point, following the example in Sketch. It shows a simple layout where you can sketch the branches and mark where the berry clusters and leaves will be. I don't recommend making a detailed sketch—keep it simple.

STEP 1

Let's start our project by painting the background using the wet-on-wet technique. Prepare your colors first: Yellow Ochre in a watery to medium consistency, and Cadmium Red and Permanent Red in a medium consistency. You'll need a quill brush and a small round brush for this step.

First, take your quill brush, moisten it with water, and lightly wet the paper. You don't need to wet the entire working area, but be sure to cover the central part of the paper. It's not necessary to wet all the borders of the work. Then, using the same brush, pick up some Yellow Ochre and apply it to the wetted area. The paint will spread on the wet paper by itself, and it's truly magical to see what watercolor can do!

Yellow Ochre will be the main background color, but let's bring more colors into our project. Switch to the small round brush and add a few random touches of Cadmium Red to the wet Yellow Ochre. Then, flick Permanent Red using the splattering technique— one or two times will be enough. The paint will spread beautifully, creating a stunning background. Don't overdo the splattering. Once all this is done, let the background dry completely before moving to the next step.

Step 2

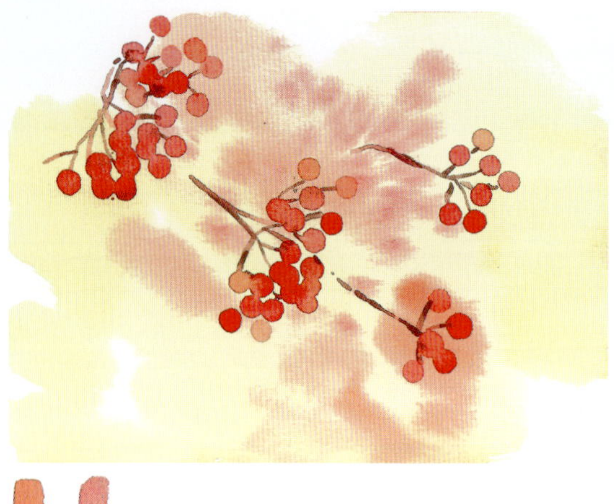

Step 3

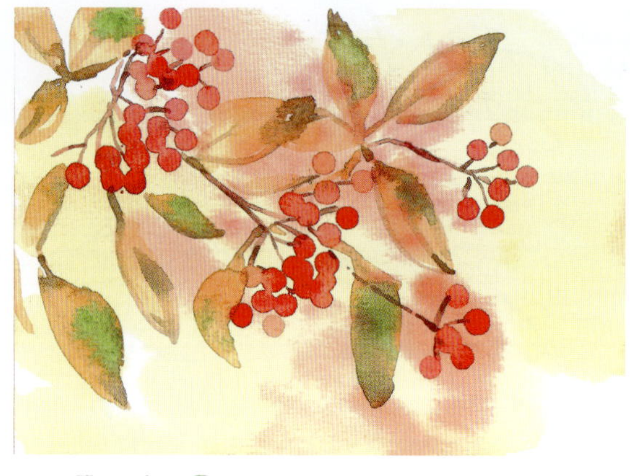

STEP 2

Let's add the berries using the Q-tip technique. Refer to Figure 1 for my sketch or follow your own.

Prepare Cadmium Red and Permanent Red in medium consistency. Moisten two cotton swabs by letting them sit in water for a minute or two. Dip one swab into each color. In one color first, press a swab onto the paper to create round spots. Repeat with the other color.

NOTE: In the images above, you can see how the berries should look and how they are connected. This is just for your understanding, and you don't need to copy it exactly.

Some clusters of berries can be bigger, and some smaller, which adds contrast to the composition and makes it more interesting for the viewer.

Once you're happy with the berries (you can add more later), use a small round brush and deep brown tint to paint the branches connecting the berries, as shown in the example. Let everything dry completely before moving on to the next step.

STEP 3

Now let's add the leaves. Once again, you can follow my composition, or you can create your own. In Figure 2, you'll see how the leaves typically look for this type of berry, but there's no strict rule here. You can change the appearance of the leaves. Prepare Yellow Ochre in a medium consistency, along with a warm brown tint and Sap Green.

In this step, I recommend using a medium round brush, preferably a soft one. If you feel comfortable, you can also use a quill brush to form the shapes of the leaves. Start by creating the shapes of the leaves with Yellow Ochre in medium consistency, painting them in different sizes and perspectives. While the leaves are still wet, randomly add warm brown and Sap Green to the wet layer. You can even experiment by adding a little deep brown to make the leaves look more realistic. Don't overdo it or add too many leaves. When everything is dry, move on to the final step.

Step 4

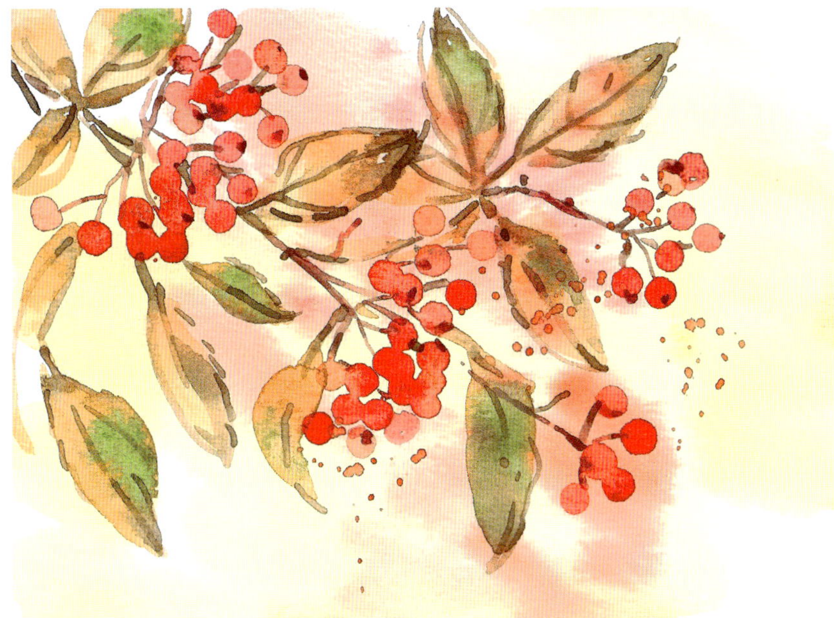

STEP 4

You can already see how beautiful the painting looks, but the final details and accents will make it look complete. First, prepare deep brown and warm brown in a medium to thick consistency. You will also need Cadmium Red in a medium consistency. Arm yourself with a small round brush with a fine tip.

Begin by adding details to the leaves using warm brown and deep brown. I recommend adding veins and outlines to some of the leaves. Vary the lines and brushstrokes for the leaf details. Use your creativity in this stage to make each leaf unique, as it's important to reflect how no two leaves in nature are exactly the same. You can also add wide brushstrokes to create shadows on some leaves, making them more visible and contrasted.

Once you are satisfied with the leaves, move on to the berries. Add small spots to some of the berries and extra branches to connect the berry clusters using deep brown. You can also use deep brown to make the main branches more visible and thicker.

For the final touch, pick up some Cadmium Red on your brush and flick it once or twice—your painting is ready!

Try experimenting with different details, colors, and compositions!

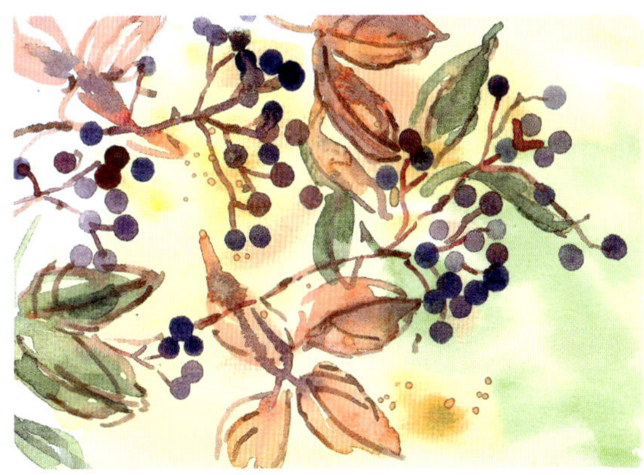

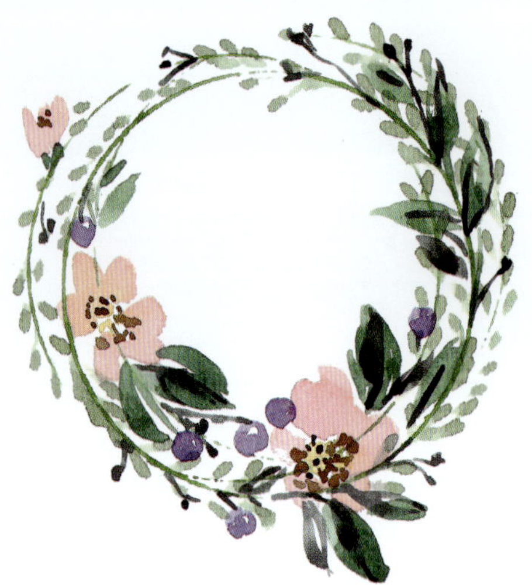

Gentle Wreath of Blooms

I love painting wreaths, especially those featuring florals, berries, and Christmas themes. I think wreaths are especially beautiful when created using the transparency of watercolor.

This project highlights the Q-tip technique, which I'll use to show you how to create a very delicate and neat leaf effect. After that, we'll use additional techniques to bring the entire wreath together into a stunning piece.

I'll also share tips and advice so you can use this project to create other wreath designs or apply the techniques to different projects. Let's take it step by step.

SUPPLIES

- Watercolor paper
- Washi tape or masking tape (optional)
- Pencil and eraser (optional)
- Round object (like a big cup or bowl) the desired size of your wreath
- Round brushes: small (sizes 1–4) and medium (size 6)
- Cotton swabs

NOTE: Instead of Burnt Umber, you can use any other brown.

PROJECT COLORS

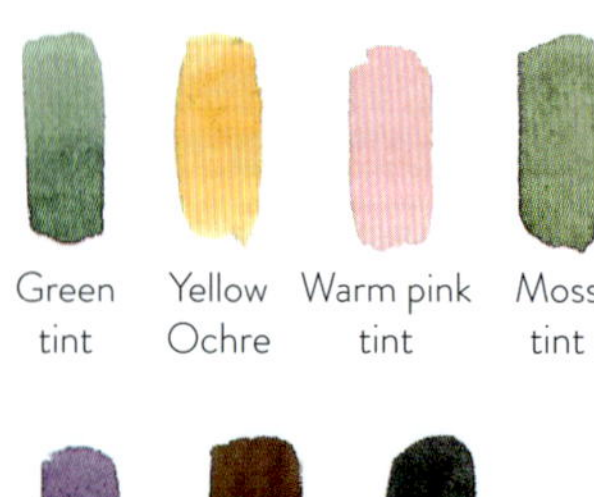

| Green tint | Yellow Ochre | Warm pink tint | Moss tint |

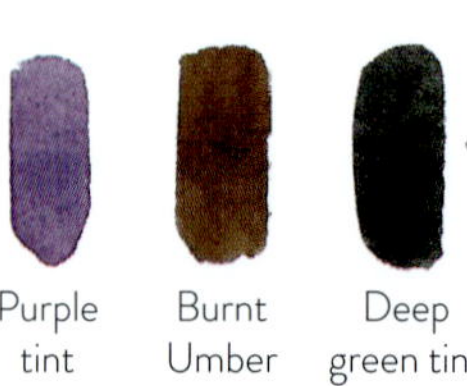

| Purple tint | Burnt Umber | Deep green tint |

COLOR MIXING

- Warm pink tint: Add a little Yellow Ochre to Opera.
- Moss tint: Mix Yellow Ochre with some Prussian Blue.
- Purple tint: Mix Opera with some Ultramarine.
- Deep green tint: Add some Sap Green to Indigo (or Prussian Blue).

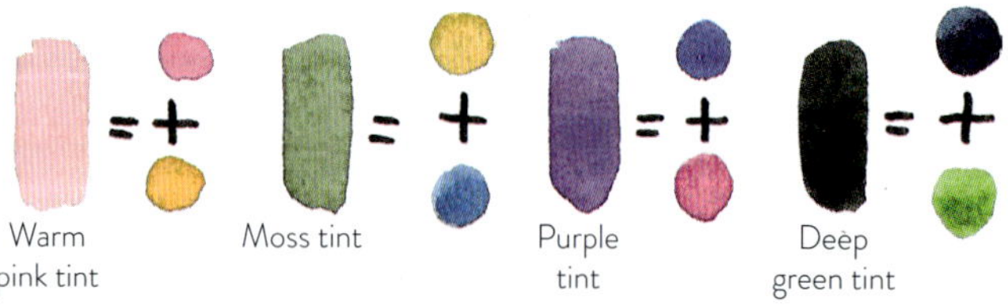

Warm pink tint   Moss tint   Purple tint   Deep green tint

PREPARATION WORK

If you prefer, secure the paper to the table with washi tape.

We will not do any preliminary sketching. However, you can lightly mark the center of your wreath with a pencil if you prefer.

I recommend preparing your colors in advance. This will make the project quicker and more enjoyable. Prepare the following colors in medium consistency: green tint, Yellow Ochre, moss tint, purple tint, Burnt Umber, and deep green tint. Prepare warm pink tint in a watery consistency. Make sure you have a generous amount of moss tint ready.

STEP 1

Let's start by making the base of our wreath. For this, pick your round object and apply green tint to its edges using a medium brush. Make sure the edges are fully covered.

Next, we will use the stamping technique. Take your round object and press it onto the paper, then lift it up. Slightly move it and press again, then lift it up. Repeat this a third and final time, again slightly moving it before pressing. This will create three overlapping circles with some gaps.

The circles should be slightly offset and not perfect. It's even better if there are some interruptions, as we will add elements of our wreath to these areas later.

Once you're happy with how it looks, let it dry completely before moving on to the next step.

STEP 2

It's time to add some elements to our wreath. Take your medium round brush and add the largest objects. These can be anything: flowers, birds, butterflies, big leaves, or anything else you like. The most important thing is that these two or three objects should be the largest ones.

For my design, I decided to add flowers. Start by painting the centers of the flowers using Yellow Ochre, and then add the petals with warm pink tint. Don't worry about making them perfect—just make sure the shapes are recognizable. I also added two buds.

Step 1

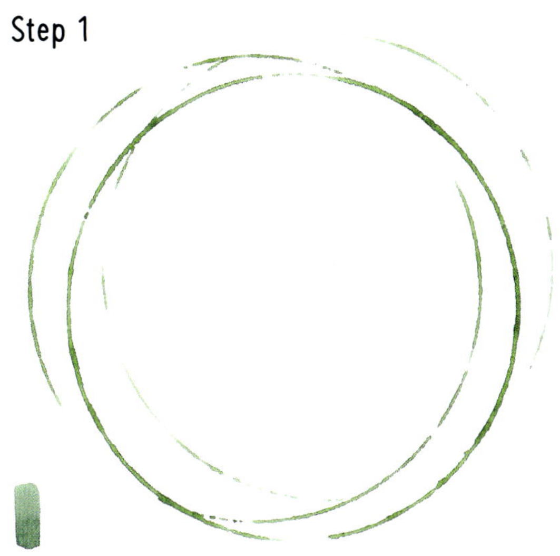

Step 2

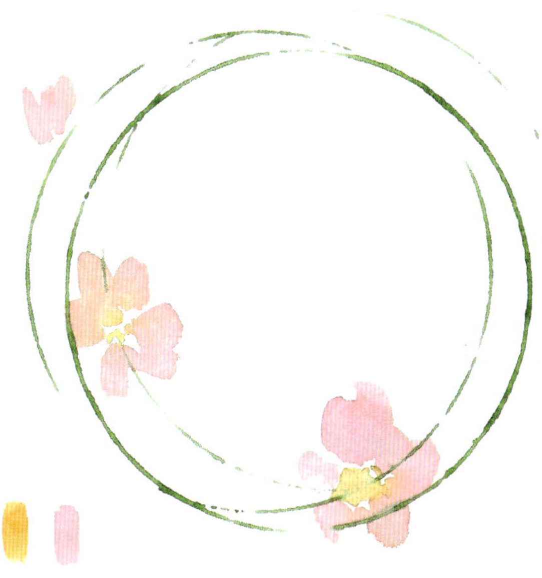

It's best to position these elements at the interruptions in your circles. However, if you don't have interruptions, it's fine to add them on top of the circles.

Now, let everything dry completely before moving on to the next step.

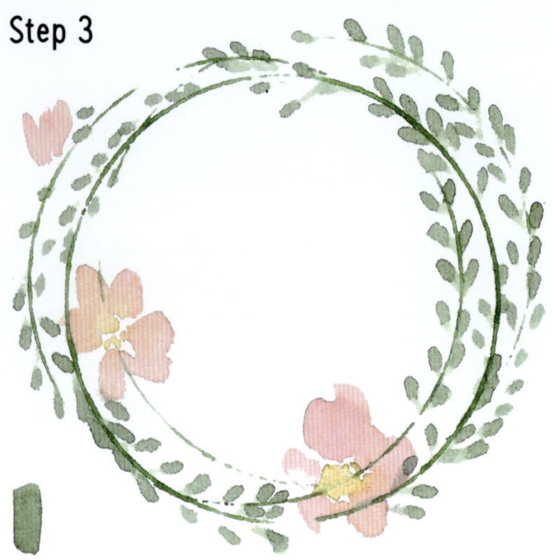

Step 3

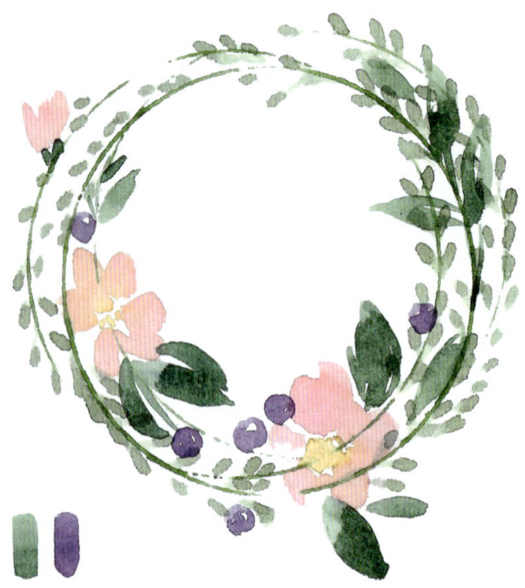

Step 4

STEP 3

Let's add small leaves to our wreath using the Q-tip technique.

First, take a cotton swab—you can use one or two if you prefer. Wet the swab generously, then remove the excess water so it's damp but not dripping. Next, load the swab with moss tint, and start adding small leaves one by one onto the branches of the wreath.

The key is to press the swab onto the paper and then lift it up. Repeat this process—press and lift. You can experiment with different patterns, such as symmetrical arrangements or more chaotic placements. The most important thing is that the branches of the wreath should follow one consistent direction.

Once you've filled almost the entire circle of the wreath using this technique, let everything dry completely.

STEP 4

Let's add more details. First, I suggest adding large leaves, which should be smaller than the flowers. Using green tint and a medium brush, add a few leaves around the flowers in different styles and sizes. You can also add small green parts to the buds of the flowers.

The leaves can overlap some of the smaller leaves we created in the previous step.

Another element to include in the wreath is berries. Switch to a small round brush and add some berries using purple tint. Add a few berries along the wreath, leaving some unpainted areas inside the berries for a highlight effect. Play around with these details to create a natural look.

Once you're happy with the result, let everything dry completely before moving on.

Step 5

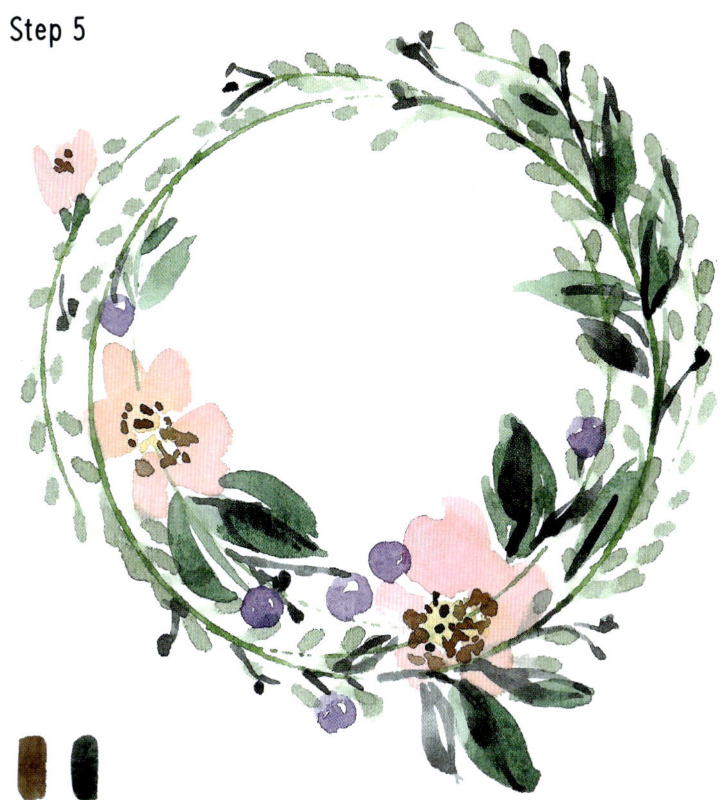

STEP 5

Our wreath is almost ready, but we need to bring more contrast and complete the overall look. You can use either a medium or small round brush.

Let's start by adding details to the centers of the flowers using Burnt Umber. Add small details such as dots, spots, and tiny dashes. Make sure these details are varied, not identical for each flower.

Next, for the final elements, I suggest using deep green to add details to the leaves, emphasize some branches, and add other small elements. You can experiment here, but the most important thing is to make the details noticeable to bring contrast to your work.

Avoid overdoing it. Make sure not to cover all the leaves created with the Q-tip technique.

Admire your delicate wreath.

Try experimenting with different details, colors, and compositions!

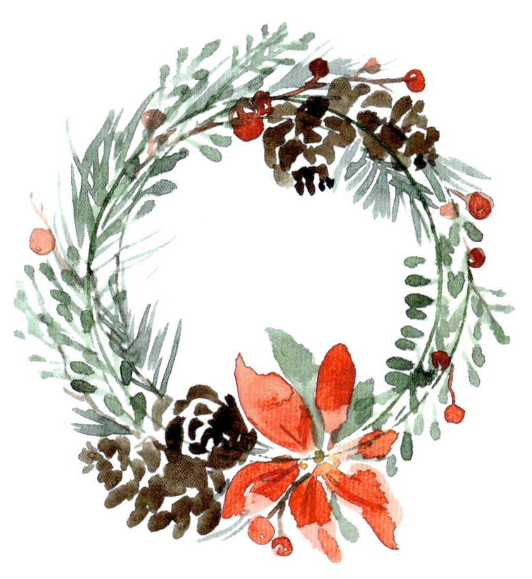

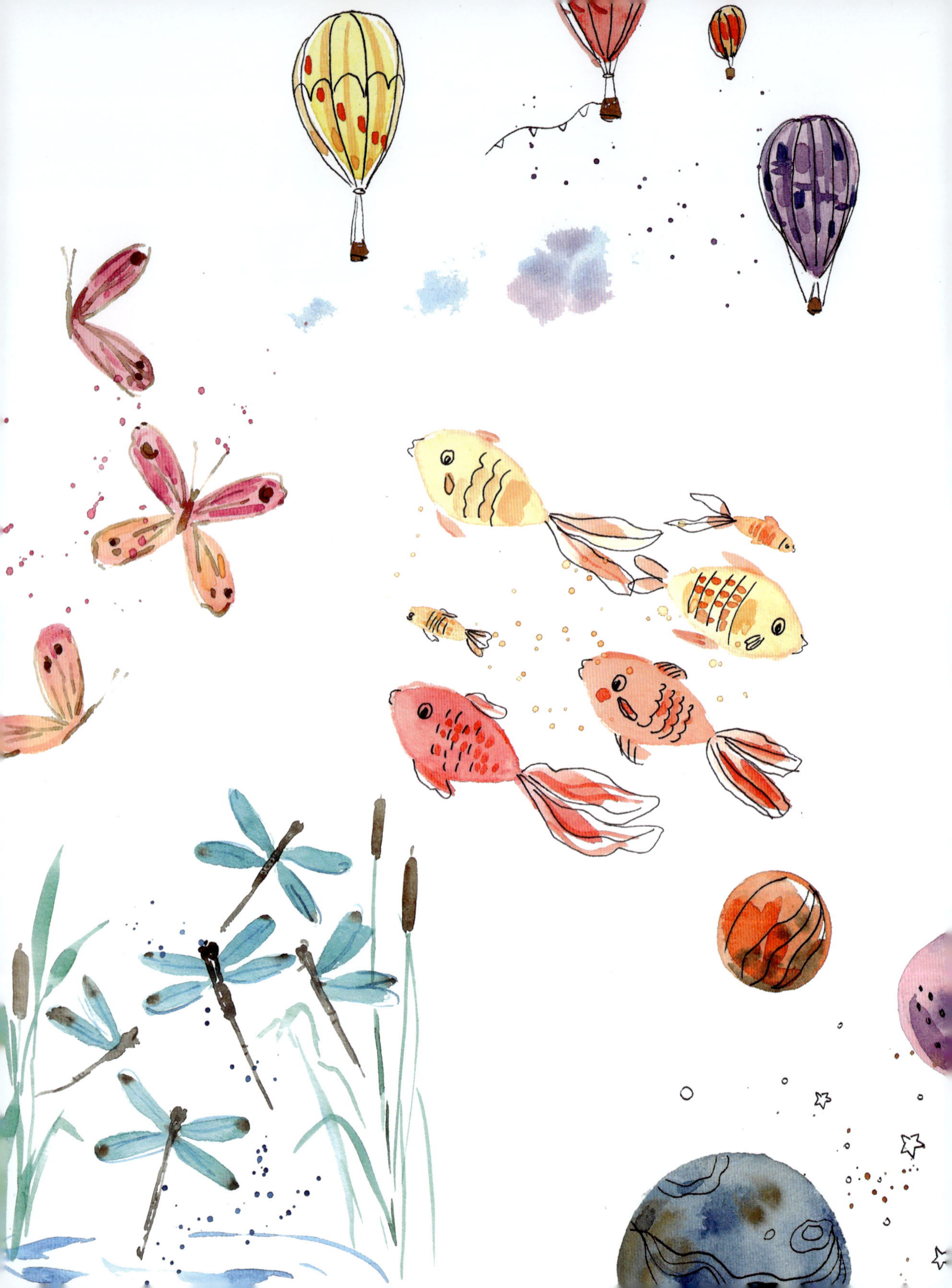

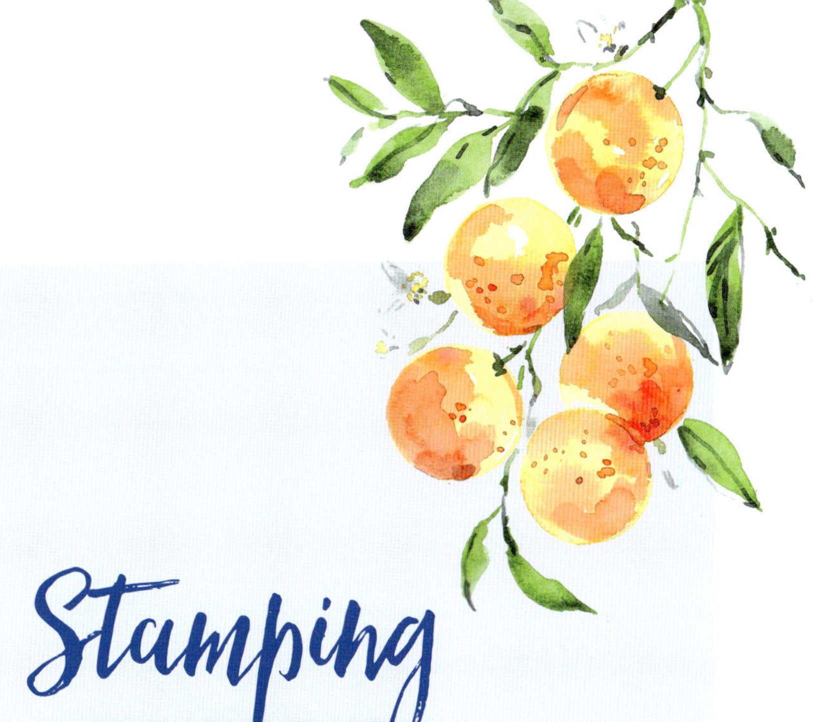

Stamping
TECHNIQUE

TECHNIQUES USED IN THIS CHAPTER

Wet-on-Wet Technique (page 14)

Layering (page 14)

Stamp Technique (page 18)

Splattering (page 19)

Outlining (page 20)

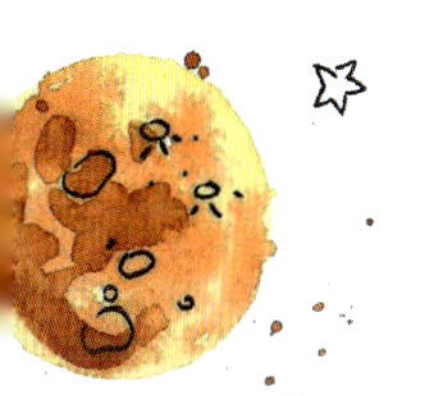

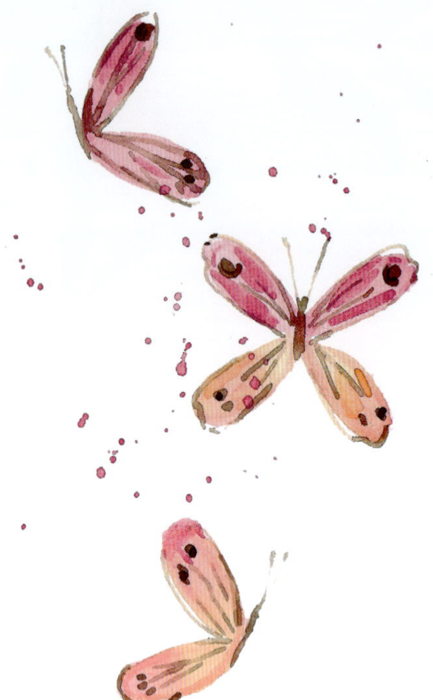

Elegant Butterflies

If you are looking for a quick project to use as a warm-up before starting a big project, this is perfect for you. You can achieve a very quick and impressive result by painting butterflies using watercolor and the stamping technique. The beauty of this project is not just that it is straightforward, quick, and enjoyable, but also that you can create an open, symmetrical butterfly. You will see how easy and fun it can be.

I also encourage you to share this project with your loved ones and kids. It always brings fun and creativity. Additionally, you can strengthen your watercolor skills by practicing and using all the techniques we'll cover.

SUPPLIES

- Watercolor paper
- Pencil and eraser (optional)
- Masking tape (optional)
- Toilet paper roll
- Round brushes: small (sizes 1–4) and medium (sizes 6–8)

NOTE: You can use any pink color, like Crimson or Alizarin, if you don't have Opera.

PROJECT COLORS

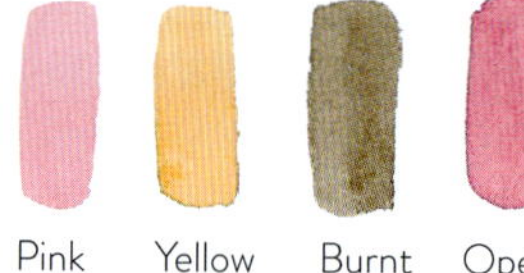

Pink tint   Yellow Ochre   Burnt Sienna   Opera

COLOR MIXING

- Pink tint: Add a little bit of Yellow Ochre to Opera.

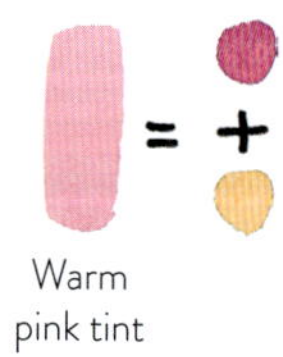

Warm pink tint

Figure 1

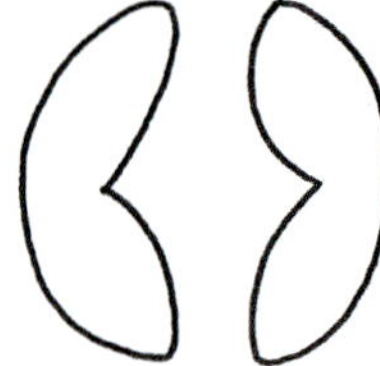
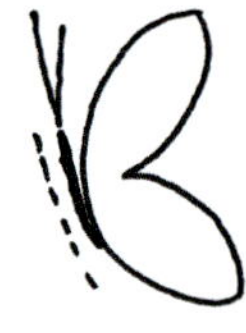

PREPARATION WORK

We will not use a preliminary sketch, but if you feel the need to mark at least the butterflies, you can use a pencil to draw them, mark their centers, or outline them. For the composition, you can either create your own or follow mine.

If you'd like, you can secure your paper with washi tape to prevent any wrinkling and to keep the paper in place, but this is optional.

Next, we need to prepare the paper roll so that it forms the outline shown in Figure 1. Squeeze the roll in the center to make it look like two closed butterfly wings, as shown in Figure 1.

To create the other part of the butterfly wings, simply turn the shaped roll 180 degrees, and you will have it. Depending on how you shape the paper roll, you can get different shapes for the butterfly wings; the key is to make both wings look similar (see Figure 2). If you're creating a butterfly with open wings using the stamping technique, you can make it symmetrical, which is very fun, quick, and easy.

Once your paper roll is ready, you can move on to the first step and start creating.

STEP 1

Look at Figure 3. You can see that we will start by creating the outline, then fill it in with one color or a few colors. You will be able to add details later if you'd like. In this step, we will only create the outlines.

Prepare a medium consistency pink tint. Load your shaped paper roll with paint, making sure the edges are evenly covered. I suggest you first make test stamps by pressing the paper roll onto scrap paper and lifting it up. Do this a few times to practice. Once you're satisfied with the results, you can use this method to create the outlines of your butterflies. You can follow my example or create your own composition.

In my composition, I have two closed-wing butterflies and one open-wing butterfly. To make the open-wing butterfly, stamp the first pair of wings with the stamping technique. Then, turn your paper roll 180 degrees and press it close to the previously stamped wing. This way, we create a symmetrical open-wing butterfly. Once you're done with this, proceed to the next step.

STEP 2

We've already created the outlines of our butterflies, and now we will fill them with color. Prepare the pink tint and Yellow Ochre in a medium, close-to-watery consistency.

(Continued)

Figure 2

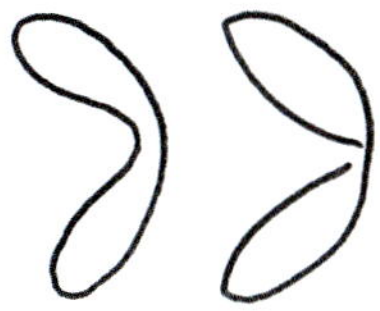

Step 1

Figure 3

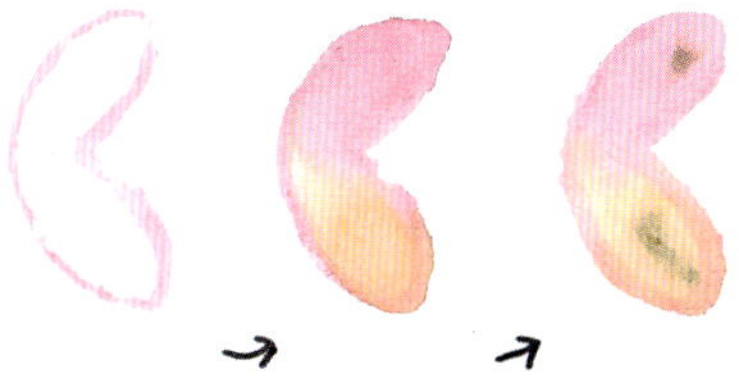

Step 2

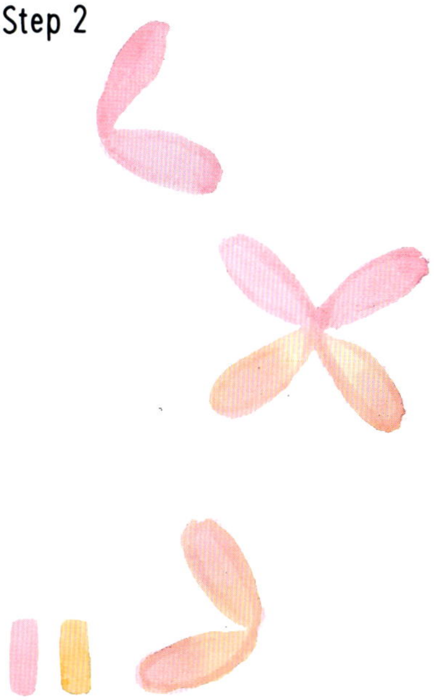

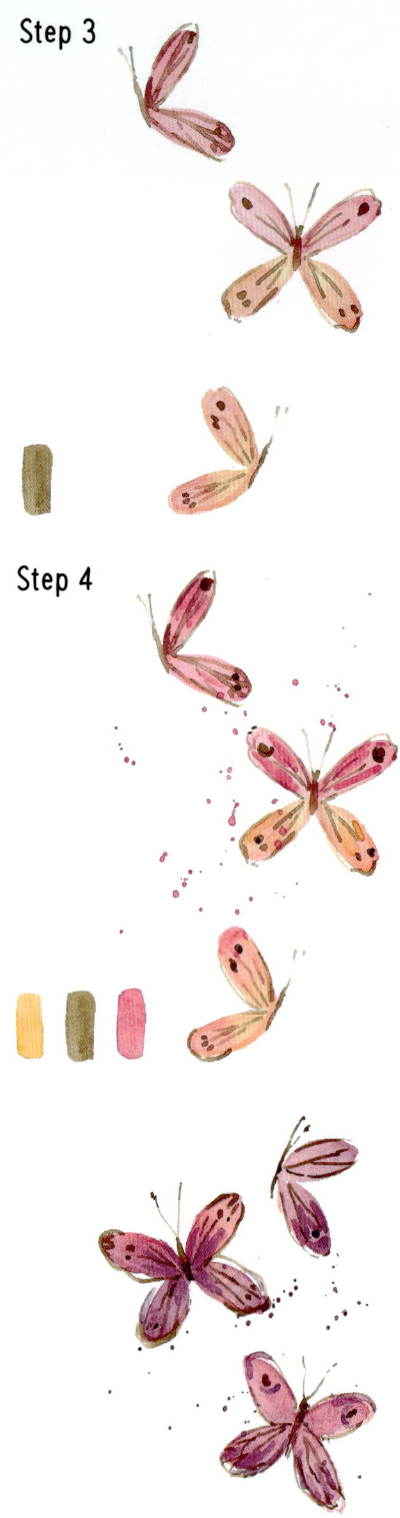

Using a medium round brush, start filling in the butterflies with these colors. You can decide how you would like to fill them or follow my method. I filled the top closed-wing butterfly with pink tint. Then, for the open-wing butterfly, I used pink tint for the top wings, added a little pink to the bottom wings, and added Yellow Ochre. For the bottom butterfly, I used both colors—pink tint and Yellow Ochre—again applying the wet-on-wet technique.

Now allow everything to dry completely before moving on to the next step.

NOTE: If you would like to add more butterflies, you can do so at this point—either open-wing or closed-wing butter-flies—and repeat steps 1 and 2. Just make sure that when you add the butterflies, your composition remains balanced.

STEP 3

It's time to add details and make our butterflies look more defined. Prepare a medium consistency Burnt Umber and take a small round brush. I suggest starting with the centers of the bodies and the antennas. Make the antennas thin to give your butterflies a sense of elegance and grace. You can add extra details like dots, spots, or lines inside the butterfly wings, creating your own design or following mine. In this step, by outlining, you can also adjust the wings and make them slightly different using brown outlines with your brush. Once you're happy with the result (be careful not to overdo the details), let everything dry completely before moving on to the final step.

STEP 4

Keep working with the small round brush and prepare medium consistency Yellow Ochre, Burnt Umber, and Opera. With these colors, you can add shading or extra details to the butterflies. I suggest using brown to add dots and clearer details, like spots on the butterfly wings. Be careful not to overdo it—just aim to make the butterflies look more saturated while keeping them transparent and airy.

Once you're happy with the result, I also recommend adding a splattering effect. I did the splattering with Opera, and I think it adds a great, beautiful final touch. And that's it—your butterflies are ready!

Try experimenting with different details, colors, and compositions!

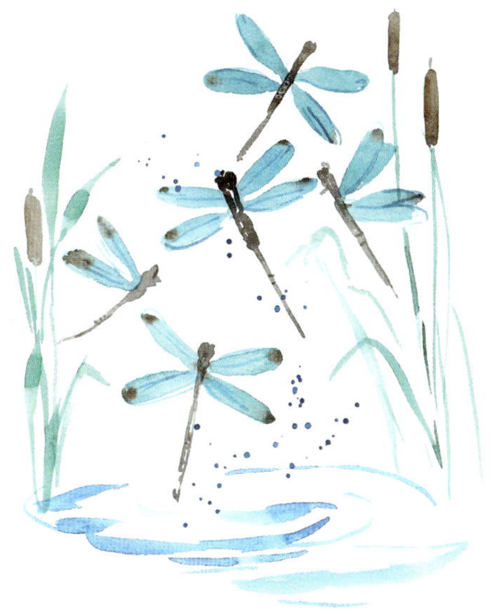

Dragonflies on the Lake

Welcome to this beautiful, easy, and fun project: a scene featuring dragonflies on a lake. I've limited the color palette to focus on the shapes and the process, and to demonstrate how watercolors work together to create this stunning painting. This project is straightforward, yet you'll learn so much about shapes, blending colors, and composition.

SUPPLIES

- Watercolor paper
- Pencil and eraser (optional)
- Masking tape (optional)
- Round brushes: small (sizes 1–4), medium (sizes 6–8), and large (optional, size 8)
- Toilet paper roll

PROJECT COLORS

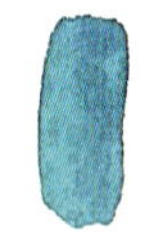 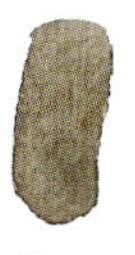 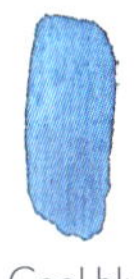 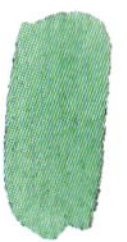

Blue green tint   Burnt Umber   Cool blue (see note)   Green tint

COLOR MIXING

- Blue green tint: Mix Prussian Blue with Viridian.
- Green tint: Add a little bit of Burnt Umber to the Viridian.

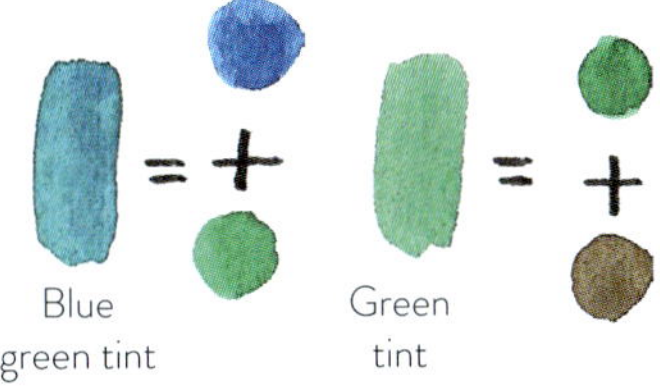

Blue green tint   Green tint

NOTE: You can pick a cool blue such as Prussian Blue, Cerulean Blue, or Indigo.

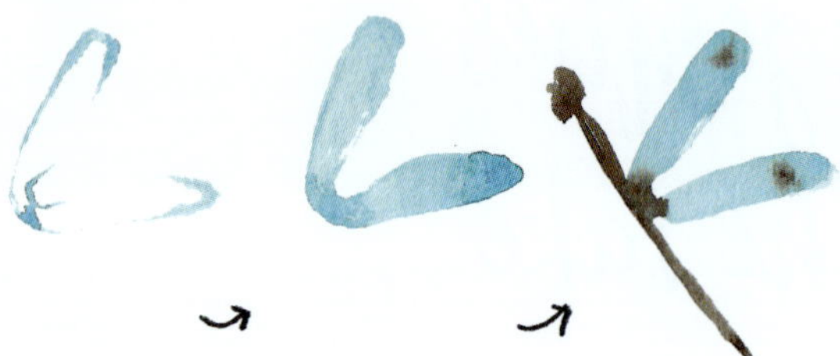

Figure 1

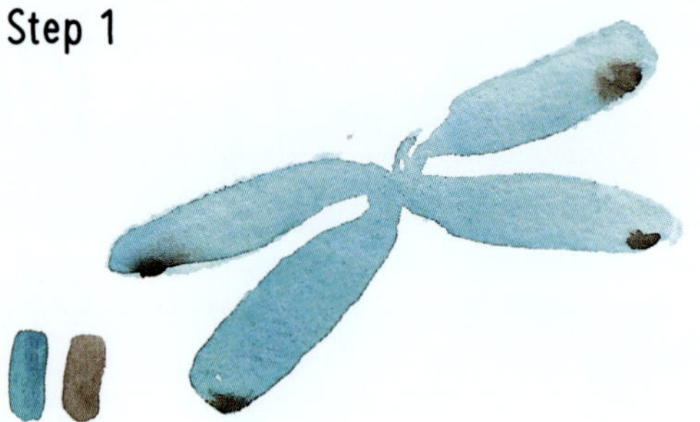

Step 1

PREPARATION WORK

Let's start our work with some preparations. The first thing we need to understand is the composition of our project. You can follow my composition or take a pencil and mark where you're going to place your dragonflies. Just lightly add some marks where they will be placed. However, I advise you to let go and embrace some creative flow in this project and skip any preliminary sketches.

Next, using washi tape is optional but highly recommended. It helps secure your paper to the table, prevents the paper from wrinkling, and creates a border, enhancing the overall look of your final project.

Once you've set up your paper and decided on your composition, you'll need to do a magic trick with a toilet paper roll. Shape it into a heart with long wings. We'll use this shape to create the wings of our dragonfly. If you look at Figure 1, you'll see how we will create a dragonfly using a technique called stamping. It's very easy to do.

I advise you to try this technique on a piece of paper first before starting our project together. First, load the shaped paper roll with watery consistency paint in any color. Press the paper roll onto the paper to get the outline of the dragonfly's wing. Then, fill the inside of the shape with the same color as the contour. Next, you can add extra color using wet-on-wet technique and add details to complete the shape of the dragonfly.

STEP 1

We'll start by painting the wings of one dragonfly.

We'll use the same method as described in the preparation section. First, prepare two colors: a watery blue green and medium consistency Burnt Umber. Also, have your medium round brush ready. And, of course, you'll need our secret tool—the shaped paper roll.

The first thing you need to do is understand where you're going to place the dragonfly wings. Take your paper roll and load it with blue green tint, ensuring that all edges of the paper roll are covered with paint. Then, press the paper roll onto the paper to create the wings of the dragonfly. Once you've made the stamp, lift it up, and you'll have the wings. Now you can fill in the wings with the same blue green tint.

Next, reload the paper roll with the blue green tint. Press it symmetrically to the wings you've already painted, then lift it up to create another set of wings. Again, use the brush to fill the shapes inside with the same color. While it's still wet, you can add another color. It can be any color, but I'd like to introduce some contrast, so we'll use Burnt Umber. With the tip of the brush, gently touch the wings to use the wet-on-wet technique to blend the colors and create a beautiful spread on the watercolor paper.

STEP 2

Create more dragonfly wings in different poses using the same technique as in Step 1. You can follow my composition and how I place the wings using the stamping technique or you can create your own composition. Please note that I have two types of dragonfly poses: one with open wings and one with slightly folded wings (Figure 2). If you choose to create your own composition, ensure that you make the wings in realistic shapes.

Once you have completed all of the dragonfly wings, allow them to dry completely before proceeding to step 3.

STEP 3

Let's refine our shapes to resemble dragonflies. For this, prepare a Burnt Umber of medium consistency and take your small brush; I suggest using a size 4 brush. With this brush, start painting the thorax along with all the body details of the dragonflies, as shown in the example. Ensure that you make them stunning and not too thick. You can always adjust their width or thickness, but it's difficult to make them thinner once applied. Once you're done with all the centers of the dragonflies, allow them to dry completely before adding further details.

For the details, we will use two colors in thick consistency: blue green tint and Burnt Umber. For the wings, I advise adding details with a small round brush using blue green tint, and for the bodies of the dragonflies, use Burnt Umber. Make sure to add these details imperfectly. While it makes sense to create symmetrical details for the wings, the body details should not be repeated for each dragonfly in the same way. Instead, create these details in random ways, with some small brushstrokes, to give a feeling of looseness.

Once completed, allow it to dry before proceeding to the final step.

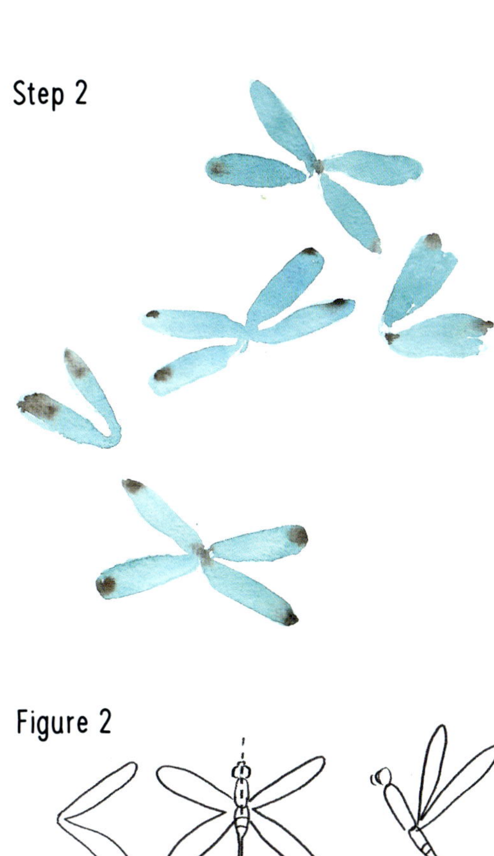

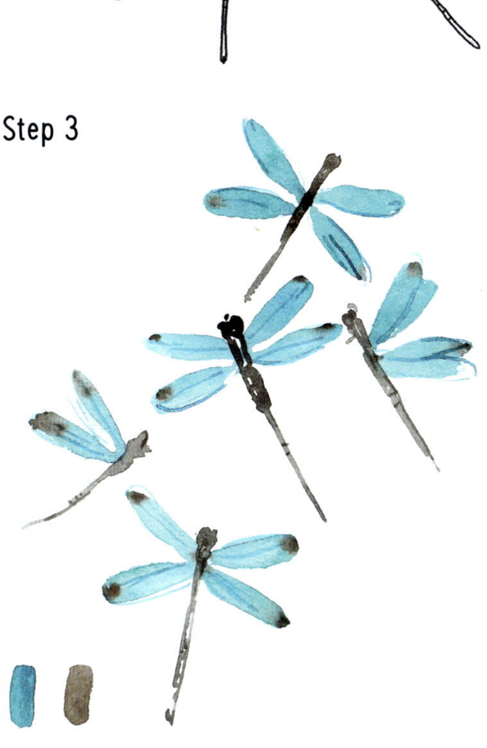

Step 4

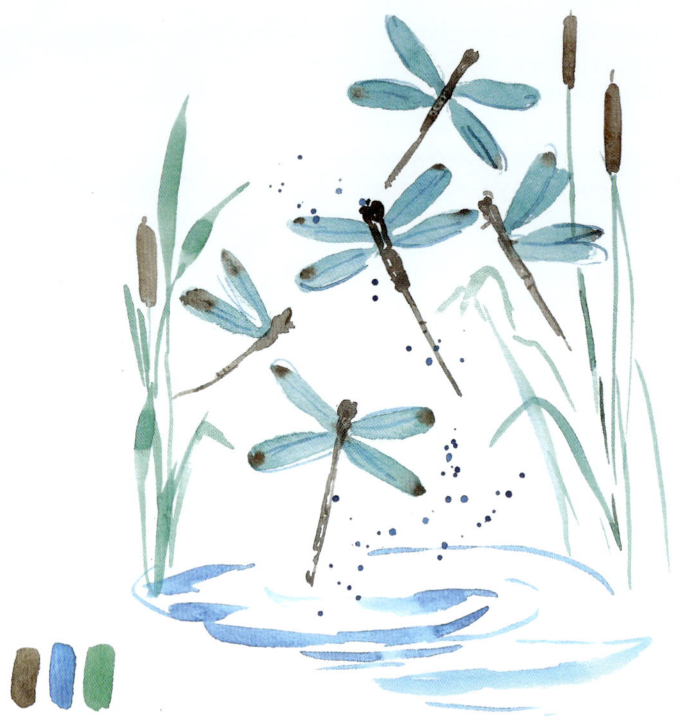

STEP 4

Let's add details to create the scenery. Prepare the following colors in medium consistency: Burnt Umber, cool blue, and green tint.

First, take a big brush and load it with some blue color. Try to create, as shown in the example, an imitation of lake water with these brushstrokes. You don't need to cover everything with blue; just create the illusion of lake water.

Once that's done, you can add some plants. We'll paint reeds with green tint and cattail-like spikes at the ends of the reeds with Burnt Umber.

You can follow my composition again, or you can let your creativity guide you.

TIP: In this step, you can use a big round brush do everything. For the thin lines, you can use the tip of the round brush, and for the leaves and other details, you can use a wide brushstroke. It's a great opportunity to practice.

Once you're done with all these details, I advise you to pick up some blue and just splatter it on the top of the painting. One or two splatters will be enough.

Try experimenting with different details, colors, and compositions!

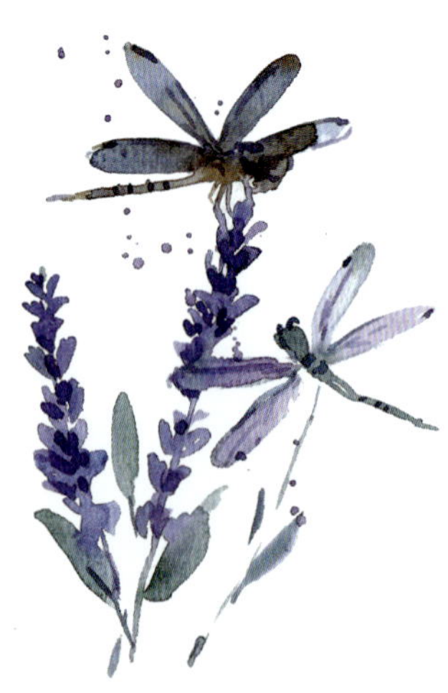

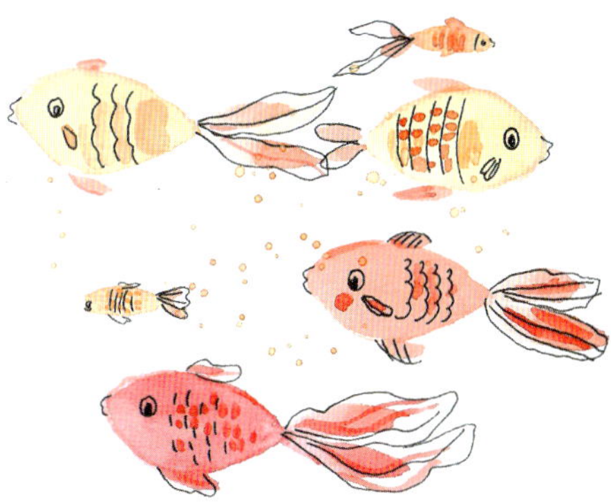

Colorful Happy Fishes

This lesson is dedicated to painting colorful watercolor fish. It's a cute project that won't take much of your time but will provide a lot of inspiration and joy. It's also great practice for applying both creative and traditional watercolor techniques without pressure—just enjoyment of the process. It includes a bit of brush-stroke practice, but the focus will be on the stamping technique. Be sure to share it with creative friends and kids—they're sure to love it.

SUPPLIES

- Watercolor paper

- Washi tape or masking tape (optional)

- Toilet paper roll

- Round brushes: small (sizes 1–4) and medium (sizes 6–8)

- Black pointed ink pen, waterproof (size 0.5 mm)

NOTE: For this project, it is especially important to use a waterproof ink pen, because we will be adding watercolor on top of the black lines for extra details. If you don't use a waterproof liner or pen, I recommend skipping step 4.

TIP: For this project, you can experiment with colors. However, I advise you to select two or three colors that are adjacent on the color wheel if you want to create your own palette. For example, if you use orange, you might also choose yellow, orange-yellow, or red tints. If you use blue, you might also choose blue tints, green-blue, or purple-blue tints. Three tints will be enough.

PROJECT COLORS

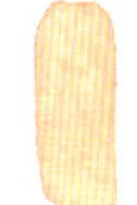 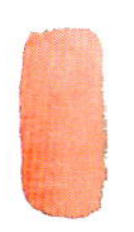 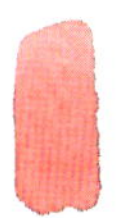

Orange   Cadmium Red   Deep red tint

COLOR MIXING

- Orange: Add just a little bit of Permanent Red or Cadmium Red to Cadmium Yellow.

- Deep red tint: Mix Alizarin Crimson with a little Permanent Red.

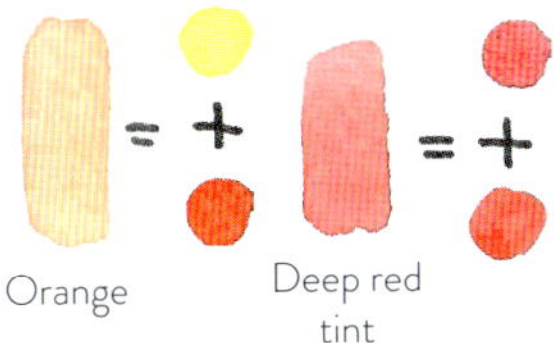

Orange   Deep red tint

PREPARATION WORK

Secure your paper if you prefer. You can tape it to the table using washi tape to prevent any wrinkling. We won't do a preliminary sketch, as this project is very creative, and we'll be using the stamping technique, letting the process flow naturally. Refer to the project images or create your own.

Prepare a stamp using a paper roll. Slightly squeeze one end to create the fish's body, leaving the other end slightly oval. The oval end will represent the head, while the squeezed end will form the tail, creating a drop-like shape.

(Continued)

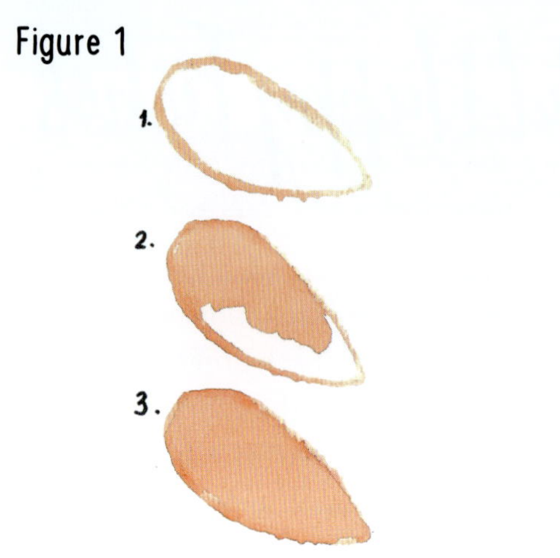

Step 1

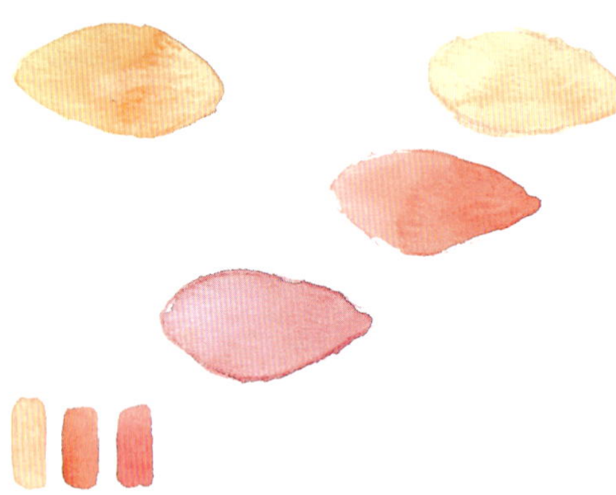

Step 2

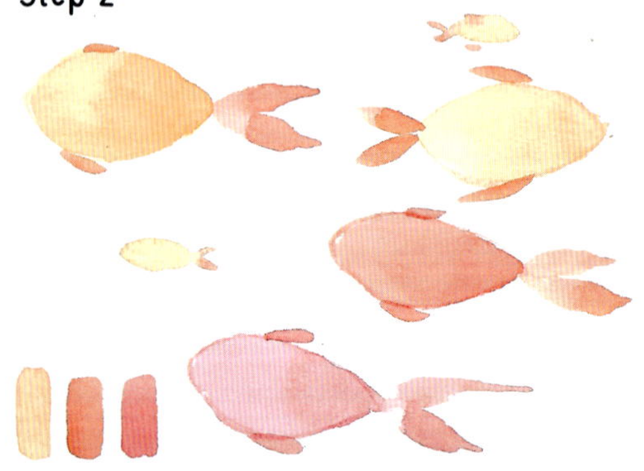

Once your stamp is ready, prepare your watercolor in a watery to medium consistency. Test the stamp by dipping it into the watercolor and pressing it onto the paper. When you lift it, the shape will resemble a fish's body. Don't worry if it's not perfect—the natural, irregular lines are part of the beauty of this project. Feel free to make a few attempts until you're satisfied with the shape.

Finally, I recommend preparing all three colors (orange, Cadmium Red, and deep red tint) ahead of time, in a watery to medium consistency, with a generous amount of each color.

STEP 1

In this step, we will create the fish bodies using the stamping technique. You should have all three project colors prepared in watery to medium consistency. Have a medium-soft brush ready as well.

Take the stamp shape you prepared earlier and start by dipping it into the orange color. Press it onto the paper and lift it to create one, two, or three fish.

Once you've stamped the outline of the fish, fill in the shape with the same color using the brush (see Figure 1).

After finishing with orange, make a few fish in Cadmium Red and a few in a deep red tint.

TIP: For different colors, you can use the opposite side of the paper roll, or you can cut off the colored end of the paper roll to apply another color.

Once you have created all the fish bodies in three colors, let everything dry before moving on to the next step.

STEP 2

Now let's add fins and tails to our fish.

Use a medium round brush and a small round brush. We will use orange, Cadmium Red, and deep red tint, and I recommend preparing them in a medium consistency.

I suggest practicing some brushstrokes first. Paint the details with just one brushstroke—press your brush down and, depending on the shape you want, move it in the desired direction. If you'd like to create a small tail or fin, simply press the brush and lift it up. In Figure 2, you'll find examples. You can follow my example or experiment; just make sure your details are unique and done in a loose style.

You can paint the fins and tails in the corresponding colors—for example, for an orange fish, you can use orange—or you can experiment by using Permanent Red.

Once you're satisfied with the results, allow all the details to dry completely before proceeding to the next step.

STEP 3

In this step, we will add the final details using a waterproof ink pen. If you look at the example image, you'll see various ink details on the fish. Now, take your pen and start adding details such as patterns on the body, eyes, lips, outlines on the fins and tails, and any extra details you'd like. You can either follow my example or be creative.

Keep in mind the importance of balance—avoid adding too many details. The goal is to make the watercolor illustration interesting and fun, while ensuring each fish is unique. It's better to vary the fish, but they should still be recognizable.

STEP 4

Now, pick your small round brush and prepare orange, Cadmium Red, and deep red tint in a medium or even thick consistency. Use each color to start adding extra details to the fish using the layering technique. Add these details randomly—extra brushstrokes, lines, dots, or spots— anything you feel will make the illustration more interesting. Remember, less is more, so stop when you feel it's enough.

Once you're satisfied, flick orange paint (or any other color of your choice) once or twice onto your work to add a beautiful final touch using the splattering technique.

That's it! Our happy, colorful fish painting is complete.

Try experimenting with different details, colors, and compositions!

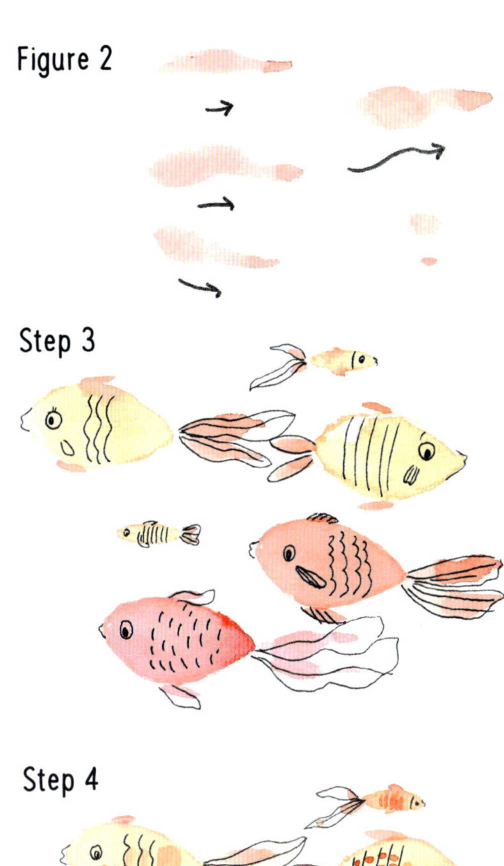

Figure 2

Step 3

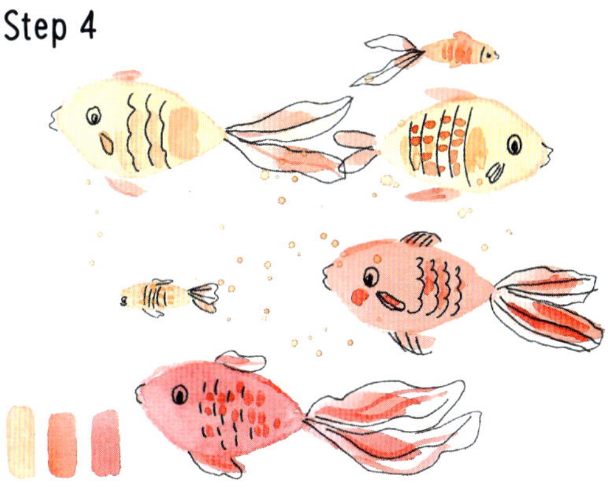

Step 4

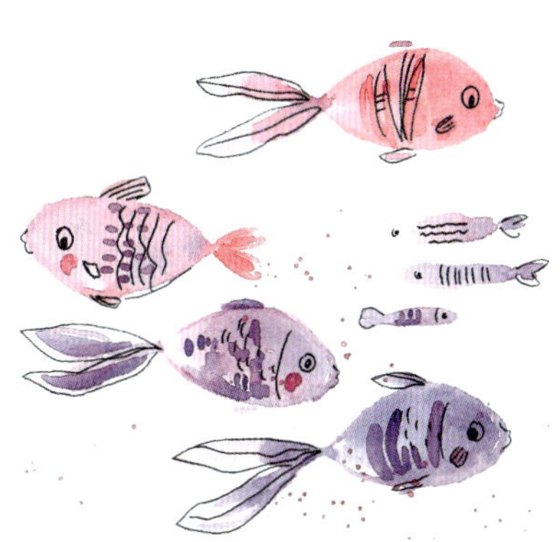

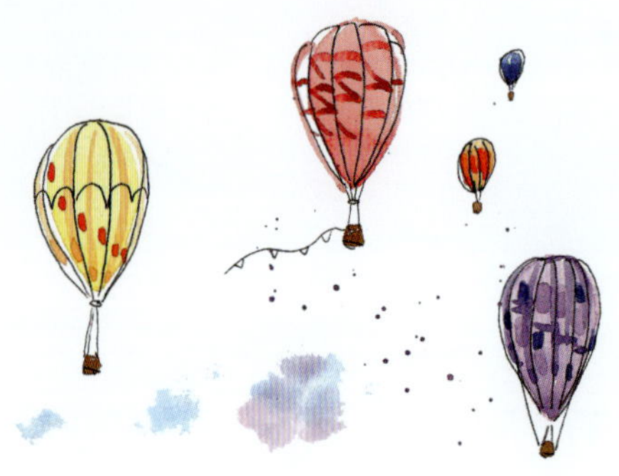

SUPPLIES

- Watercolor paper
- Washi tape or masking tape
- Pencil and eraser (optional)
- Toilet paper roll
- Round brushes: small (sizes 1–4) and medium (sizes 6–8)
- Black pointed ink pen, waterproof (size 0.5 or 0.8 mm)

NOTE: For this project, it is especially important to use a waterproof ink pen, because we will be adding watercolor on top of the black lines for extra details. If you don't use a waterproof liner or pen, I recommend skipping Step 4.

Dreamy Air Balloons

If you're looking for a quick, fun, and colorful project, this one is perfect for you. It features a variety of creative techniques. We will create a dreamy scene with hot air balloons. The happy colors always bring a smile, while the transparency of watercolor adds an airy feeling of joy and delight!

PROJECT COLORS

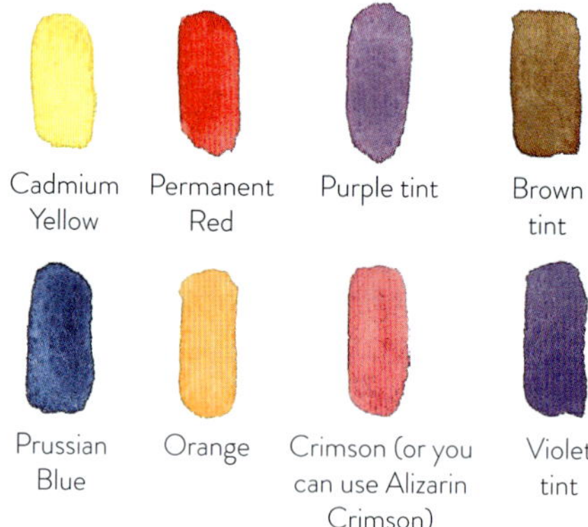

Cadmium Yellow	Permanent Red	Purple tint	Brown tint
Prussian Blue	Orange	Crimson (or you can use Alizarin Crimson)	Violet tint

COLOR MIXING

- Purple tint: Mix Opera with a little Ultramarine.
- Brown tint: Add a little Burnt Umber to Burnt Sienna.
- Orange: Add a little red to Cadmium Yellow.
- Violet tint: Mix Ultramarine with some Opera.

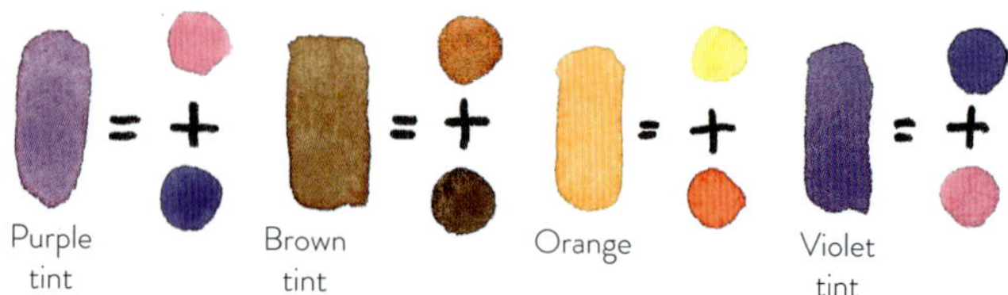

PREPARATION WORK

Prepare your piece of watercolor paper by securing it with washi tape. We won't be doing any preliminary sketches, but if you'd like, you can mark the places where you'll add the hot air balloons with the stamping technique; for example, mark where the base of the balloon will be. Once that's done, prepare a generous amount of Cadmium Yellow, Permanent Red, and purple tint in watery to medium consistency.

TIP: Before starting this method, I advise you to try the stamping technique on a separate piece of scrap paper.

STEP 1

Form a toilet paper roll into a drop shape—squeeze one side and round out the other. To create a balloon shape, load the stamp with Cadmium Yellow, ensuring it fully covers the edges of the paper roll, then press it onto the watercolor paper where you are going to create the air balloon. Using the same color, fill in the shape of the air balloon. See the stages in Figure 1.

Repeat this method for making air balloons in Permanent Red and purple tint. Once it's done, proceed to the next step.

NOTE: For different colors of air balloons, use different rolls. Or, you can cut off the used edge of the roll and then apply another color.

STEP 2

Pick up a small round brush and paint small air balloons in medium to watery consistency blue and orange. You can create your own composition and add even more balloons or follow mine.

Then switch to brown tint and add a basket to each balloon. Don't aim for a perfect basket; try to paint them differently for each balloon.

Finally, let's add the clouds using the wet-on-wet technique. For this, carefully wet the paper around the balloons with a medium round brush, and on the wet layer, add touches of purple tint and blue. Let everything dry completely.

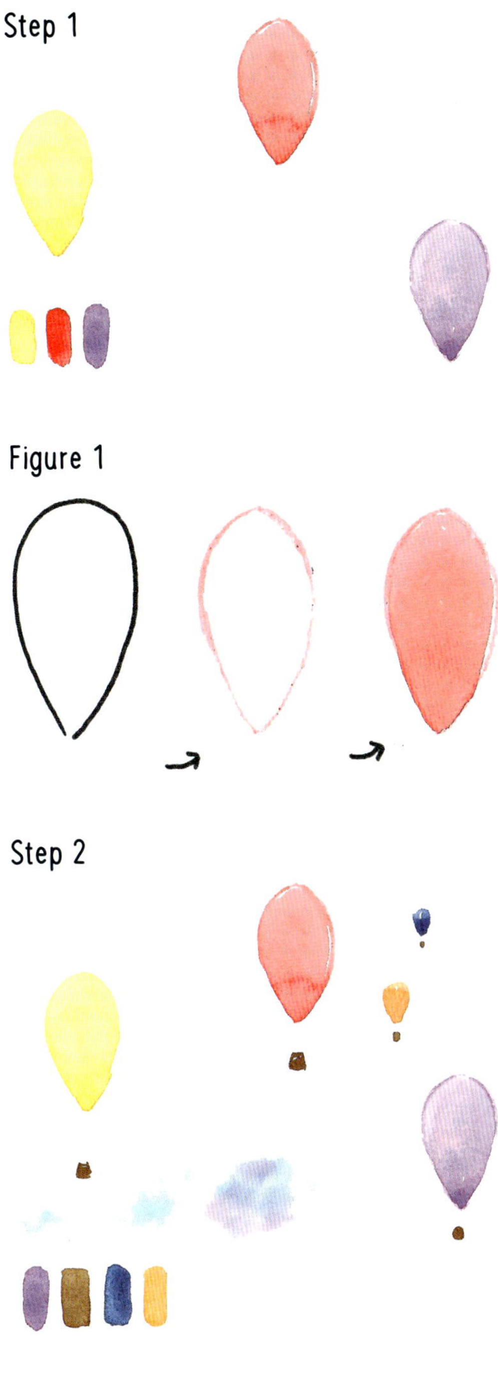

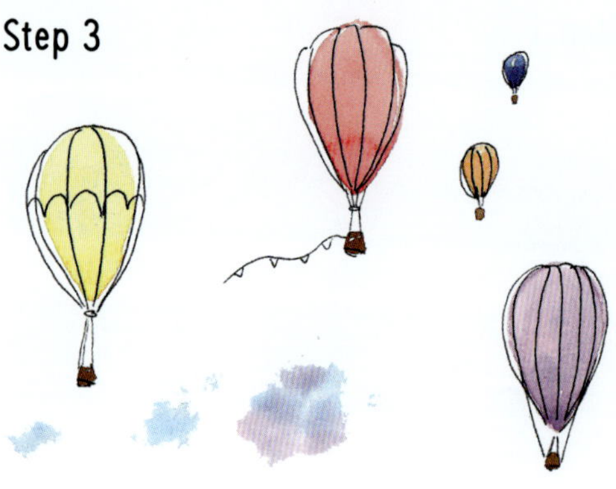

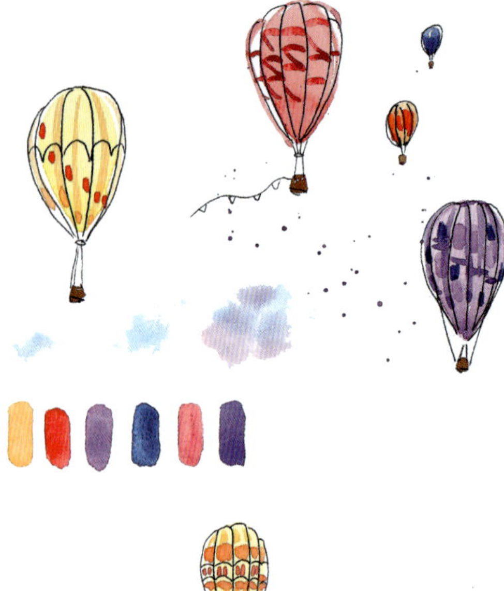

STEP 3

Now, draw details with a black ink pen. Outline each of the balloons, and then define all the parts of each balloon. I suggest adding extra details such as a cord with flags and extra ropes.

For inspiration, you can look at photos of real balloons and notice the shapes of the top parts, baskets, and all the other details.

If you prefer, you can follow my design or play with your own. Once all the details are added, let the ink pen dry for a minute and then proceed to the next step.

NOTE: Don't add details to the smallest air balloons. You can emphasize them somewhat, but the smaller the object, the less detailed it should be.

STEP 4

Our painting looks pretty and colorful, but the final touches will give it a more complete look. Take your small round brush and prepare the following colors in medium to thick consistency: orange, Permanent Red, Crimson, purple tint, violet tint, and blue.

In real life, hot air balloons have patterned designs. Let's add these pattern details to each of the balloons using the layering technique. You can follow my design or create your own if you prefer, based on inspiration from photos of real balloons. But remember to add colors that will look harmonious with the base color. For example, for a yellow balloon, add orange and red details. Also, limit colors to two or three.

It doesn't have to be perfect, but remember that the design on air balloons is usually a repeated pattern.

You can also correct the inner shape of the balloon and add brushstrokes on the sides. Play with these details, but at the same time remember that less is more.

Finally, add splattering on top using purple or any other project color.

Try experimenting with different details, colors, and compositions!

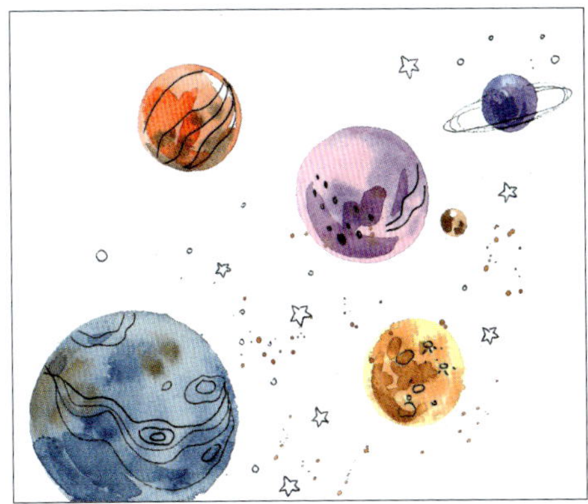

The Magic of Planets

In this project, I'll share an easy method for painting cute, colorful planets. You'll learn how to paint with joy, blend colors beautifully on paper, add doodles for contrast, and play with composition to create a delightful final watercolor illustration. I'll share all my tips, allowing you to recreate these charming planets with your own personal touch!

SUPPLIES

- Watercolor paper
- Washi tape or masking tape (optional)
- Lids, cups, or jars of various diameters
- Round brushes: small (sizes 1–4) and medium (sizes 6–8)
- Black pointed ink pen, waterproof (size 0.5 or 0.8 mm)

NOTE: The sizes of the lids, cups, and jars should range from the size of a very small pen lid to the size of a larger lid from a jar.

NOTE: For this project, it is especially important to use a waterproof ink pen, because we will be adding watercolor on top of the black lines for extra details. If you don't use a waterproof liner or pen, I recommend skipping Step 4.

PROJECT COLORS

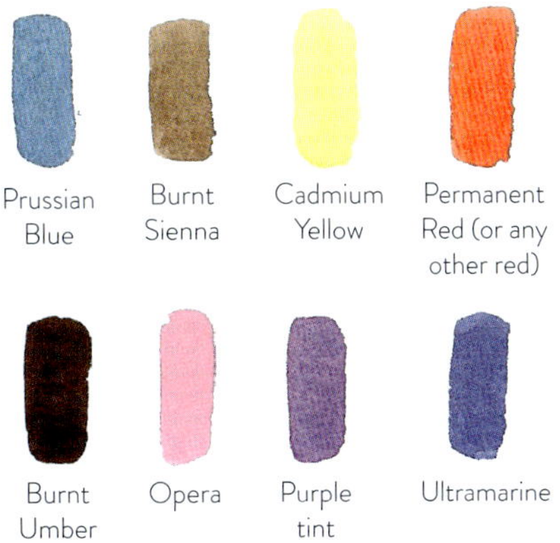

Prussian Blue	Burnt Sienna	Cadmium Yellow	Permanent Red (or any other red)
Burnt Umber	Opera	Purple tint	Ultramarine

COLOR MIXING

- Purple tint: Mix Opera (or any pink or rose you have) with a bit of Ultramarine.

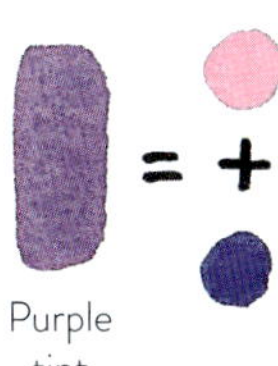

Purple tint

NOTE: For this project, you can use the colors I've chosen or explore your own palette and play with different colors.

PREPARATION WORK

First, if you like, you can secure your paper with washi tape.

You can find all the steps for creating a planet with the stamping technique in Figure 1. We'll use this method to create all the planets, so it's best to prepare at least three lids in different sizes, along with all the project colors (blue, Burnt Sienna, Cadmium Yellow, Permanent Red, Burnt Umber, Opera, purple tint, and Ultramarine) in a medium consistency.

Practice creating a circle. Take a lid, cup, or jar and load the edges with paint. Press the object onto scrap paper in your desired spot to create a circle. Fill in the circle with the same color, either covering it evenly or leaving some unpainted areas. While the layer is still wet, you can add one or two extra colors.

STEP 1

Let's begin by painting the largest planet. First, decide where you want to place it. In my case, I positioned it at the bottom of the painting.

Using the stamping technique with a lid, cup, or jar, create a blue outline. Then, fill in the inside with the same color using a medium or large round brush. While the circle is still wet, add a few extra touches of blue and a bit of Burnt Sienna. Allow it to dry completely.

STEP 2

Create the remaining planets.

You should have prepared Burnt Sienna, Cadmium Yellow, Permanent Red, Burnt Umber, Opera, purple tint, and Ultramarine in a medium consistency. Gather your round brushes—medium or small, depending on the circle size. Also, prepare all your lids and cups in various sizes, including a pen lid for the smallest planet.

Start by adding the largest planets. For the first planet, use Opera and add touches of purple tint while the layer is still wet. Then, move on to smaller planets: For the red planet, use Permanent Red and add Burnt Sienna; for the yellow planet, use Cadmium Yellow and add Burnt Sienna. Paint a smaller circle with Ultramarine, adding some purple tint. For the smallest planet, use the pen lid—use Burnt Sienna and add a few touches of Burnt Umber.

Once finished, let everything dry completely.

NOTE: When adding details to the planets while they're still wet, avoid using too much of the second color, as it can create a mess.

STEP 3

Once the planets are completely dry, pick up a waterproof ink pen and start adding details to the planets.

I suggest adding different doodles to each planet, such as curved lines, dots, spots, rings like Saturn's, and various patterns. You can refer to real planets for inspiration on what to add. I also recommend adding some extra doodles around the planets on the white paper, like circles and stars. This will help enhance the composition and give your artwork a more complete look. Be careful not to add too many details around the planets; aim to find a balanced composition. Once you're satisfied with the result, let the ink dry for about a minute, then move on to the final step.

STEP 4

We've already created cute, colorful planets. Now, if you used a waterproof ink pen, you can still add a second layer on top.

To add a second layer, simply apply another coat in each planet's base color. Prepare the following colors in a medium consistency: blue, Permanent Red, Cadmium Yellow, Burnt Sienna, purple tint, and Ultramarine. Have your round brushes (medium and small) ready.

Add details to each planet: Use blue for shadows on the blue planet, Permanent Red for the red planet, purple tint for shadows and details on the purple-pink planet, and Burnt Sienna for the yellow planet. For the blue-purple planet, add details with Ultramarine.

Feel free to add your own details to the planets or follow my design. As a final touch, I suggest adding some splattering. Pick up Burnt Sienna (or any other project color) with a small round brush and make one or two flicks on top. This will be a great finishing touch to complete your composition.

Try experimenting with different details, colors, and compositions!

Step 3

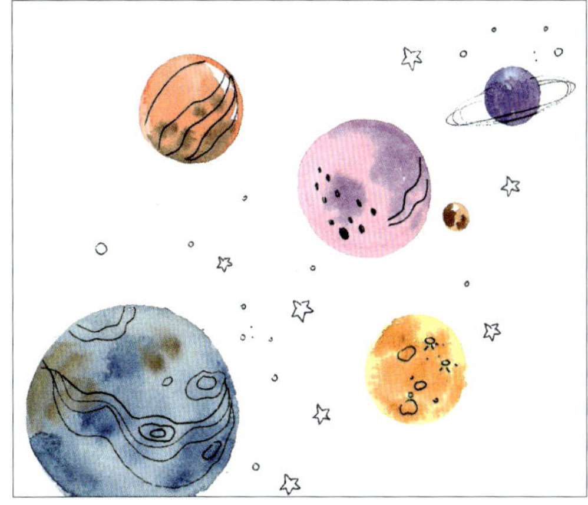

Step 4

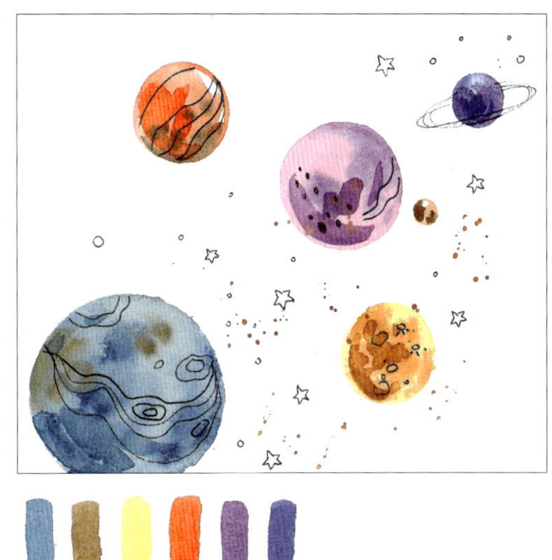

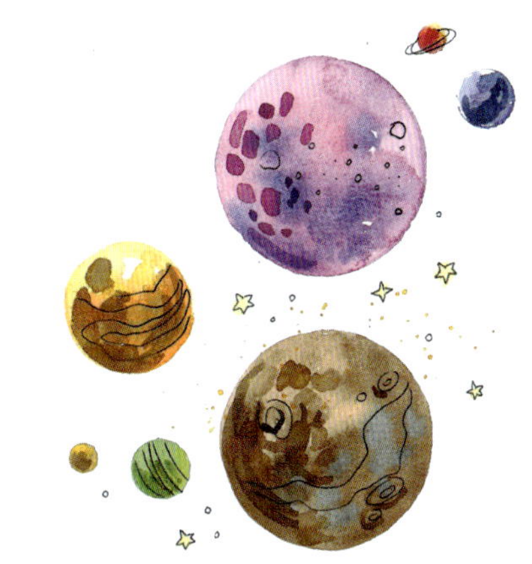

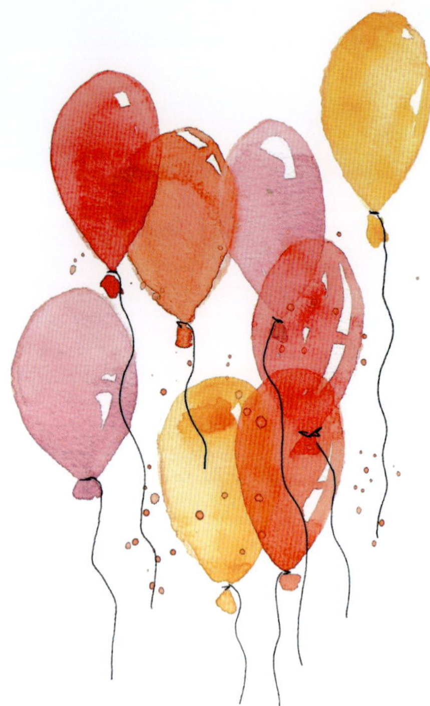

Happy Balloons

Let's paint some vibrant, translucent balloons together using the stamping technique. This project isn't about creating something epic or impressive, but about having fun and relaxing. It's excellent for experimenting with color combinations and also for practicing your paint consistency skills. So, let's do this!

PROJECT COLORS

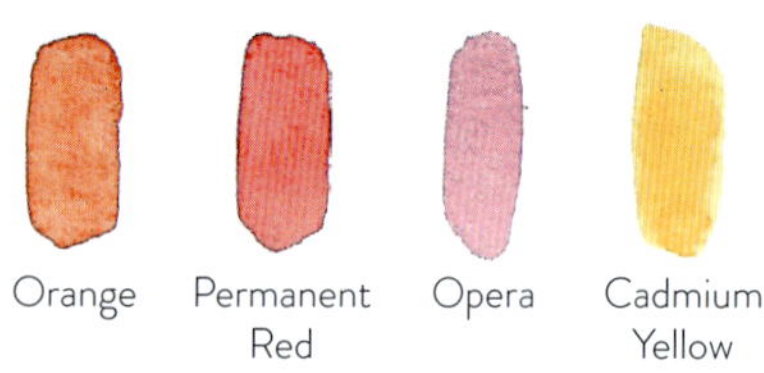

Orange   Permanent Red   Opera   Cadmium Yellow

COLOR MIXING

- Orange: Add just a little bit of red to Cadmium Yellow. It can be Permanent Red or Cadmium Red.

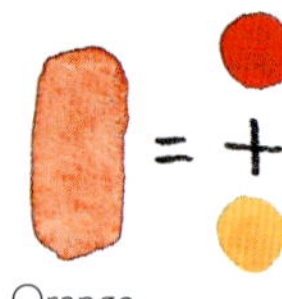

Orange

NOTE: It's possible to do this project using only one brush. It can be a medium-sized brush, such as a size 8, but make sure that your brush has a thin tip so you can add details with it. For this project, I prefer a very soft brush like one that imitates natural hair.

NOTE: For this project, it is especially important to use a waterproof ink pen, because we will be adding watercolor on top of the black lines for extra details. If you don't use a waterproof liner or pen, I recommend skipping the final splattering technique.

SUPPLIES

- Watercolor paper
- Washi tape or masking tape (optional)
- Round brushes: small (sizes 1–4) and medium (sizes 6–8)
- Toilet paper roll
- Black pointed ink pen, waterproof (size 0.5 or 0.8 mm)

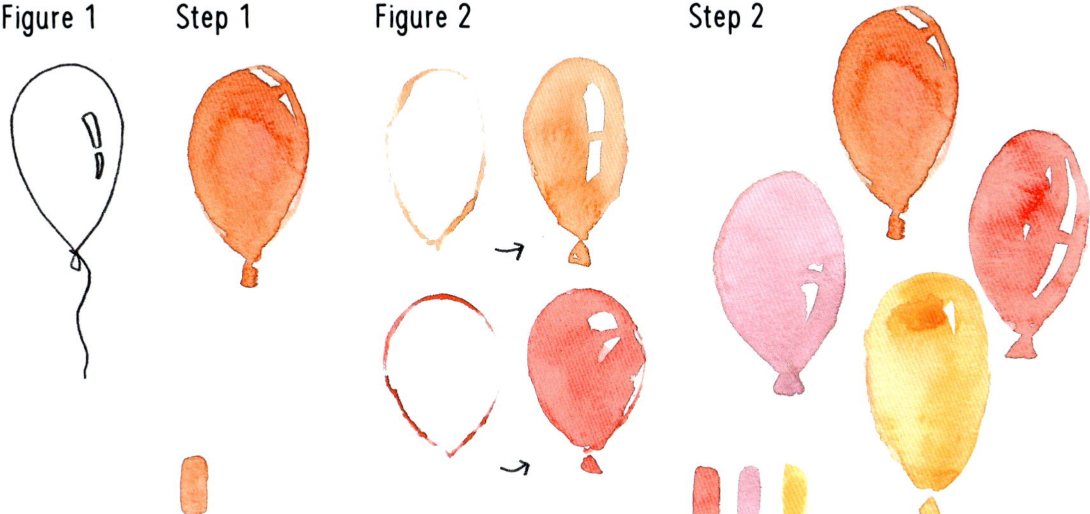

PREPARATION WORK

If you'd like, you can secure your paper with washi tape. Using washi tape also helps create borders, which can be useful for framing your painting. This project does not require a preliminary sketch; the goal is to create fun and quick balloon shapes using the stamping technique with a paper roll.

Next, prepare a toilet paper roll. Try to shape the roll into a balloon-like form. It can be more oval with a thinner end, or you can keep it simply oval. Feel free to experiment. In Figure 1, you can see the shape of the paper roll that I use in the project.

STEP 1

Take a look at Figure 2, where you can see the outline that transforms into the balloon shape. We begin by using the stamping technique to create the outline of the balloon and then fill it with watercolor. Then, we'll add a bit of the same color at the ends of the balloons.

Let's implement this approach. Prepare orange in a fairly watery consistency. Load your shaped roll with the orange color and press it onto the watercolor paper. Then, using a large or medium round brush, pick up some extra orange paint and fill in the shape, leaving

some areas unpainted to create a glossy effect on the balloon. Finally, with the tip of the brush, add a bit of orange to the end of the balloon.

STEP 2

Continue creating balloons using the same method, but in different colors. Prepare the next set of colors in a transparent consistency: Permanent Red, Opera, and Cadmium Yellow. Using the method described in Step 1, paint three balloons, one in each color. You can either copy my composition or play with it and create your own. At this step, don't add too many balloons.

The balloons shouldn't be perfect; the most important aspect here is to create a sense of transparency and airiness, and to make them look fun. Once all three balloons are added, let everything dry completely.

NOTE: If you use multiple colors for the stamping technique in this project, you can use different toilet paper rolls for each color. Alternatively, you can cut them into pieces. This way, you have several paper rolls in different colors. When using a paper roll, if you dip it into paint with a watery consistency, the paper may soften. In this case, you can cut it and then dip it again.

Step 3

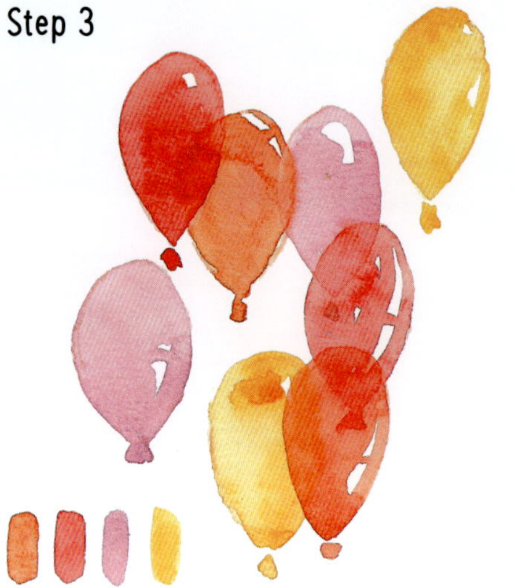

STEP 3

Let's add more balloons, layering them on top of the ones we've already painted. We will use both the layering and stamping techniques in this step.

Prepare the following colors in medium consistency: orange, Permanent Red, Opera, and Cadmium Yellow. Begin adding balloons using the method described in Step 1: First, load the paper roll with paint, then press it onto the paper, lift it up, and fill in the shape with the same color. Again, you can either copy my composition or create your own and have fun experimenting with it. Once everything is done, allow the painting to dry completely.

STEP 4

And finally, let's add the strings. For this, use a waterproof pointed pen. I prefer using size 0.8 or 0.5 mm, but you can use any ink pen you have. Then start to add strings, which extend downward from the balloons.

You can make them straight or in wavy lines. The most important thing here is to make them imperfect and not too thick. Don't cover everything with these lines; they should complement your painting and merely complete your work.

Once that's done, take a brush, pick up some paint, and using the splattering technique, flick the paint over the top for the perfect final touch. I used orange for splattering, but you can use any color from the project.

And that's it. Our painting is complete. It's colorful, lovely, and cheerful!

NOTE: If you would like to add splattering technique as the final touch, make sure that your ink pen is waterproof to avoid making a mess at the end of this project.

Try experimenting with different details, colors, and compositions!

Step 4

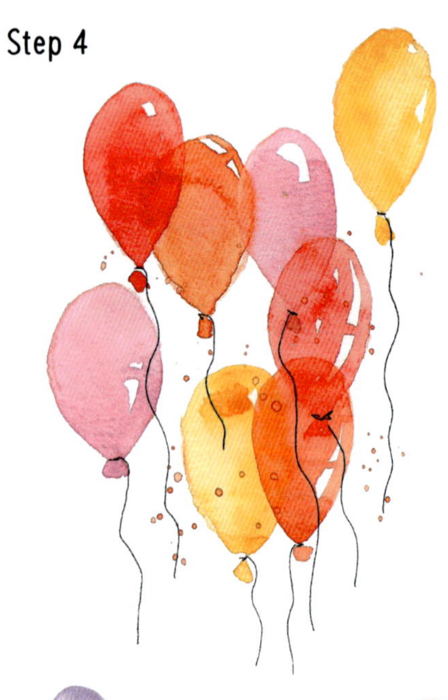

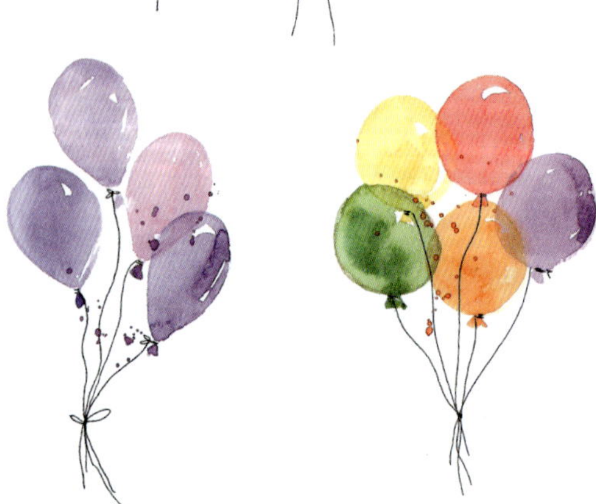

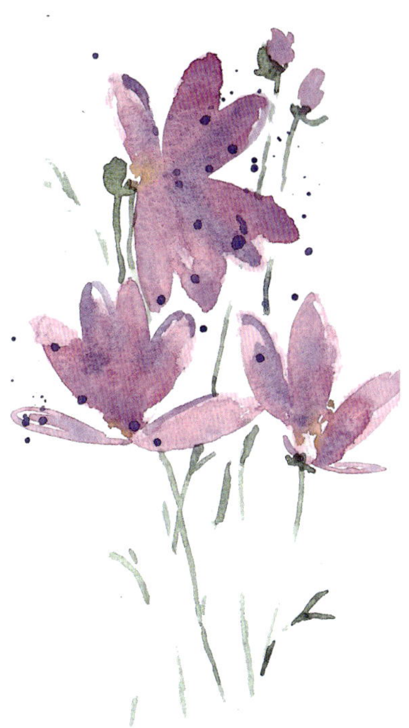

Abstract Floral Creations

Let's paint a beautiful abstract project with the stamping technique. I will show you how to use a paper roll to form the shapes of flower petals.

This project is not only joyful and relaxing but also a great way to explore how to blend colors, build compositions, and create loose watercolor flowers.

This abstract style of painting can be used to decorate your home, make greeting cards, or design other creative watercolor flower projects. If you're looking for a quick project or a warm-up exercise, this is exactly what you need!

SUPPLIES

- Watercolor paper
- Washi tape or masking tape
- Pencil and eraser (optional)
- Toilet paper roll
- Round brushes: small (sizes 1–4) and medium (sizes 6–8)

NOTE: Instead of moss green, you can use any green tint. However, if you want to emphasize the flowers and keep the stems and green details more muted, I recommend using a less vibrant green. For this purpose, I mixed moss green, but you can use any green tint and make it less vibrant by mixing Cadmium Yellow with some Prussian Blue.

PROJECT COLORS

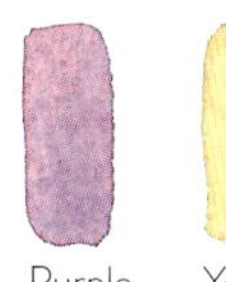
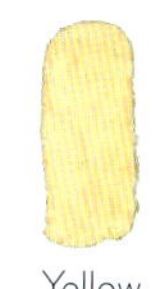
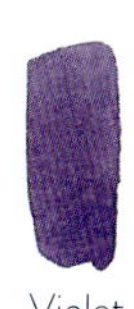
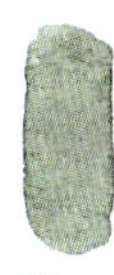

| Purple tint | Yellow Ochre | Violet tint | Moss green |

COLOR MIXING

- Purple tint: Add a little Ultramarine to Opera (or any other pink or rose you have).
- Violet tint: Mix Ultramarine with some Opera.
- Moss green: Mix a little Indigo with Yellow Ochre.

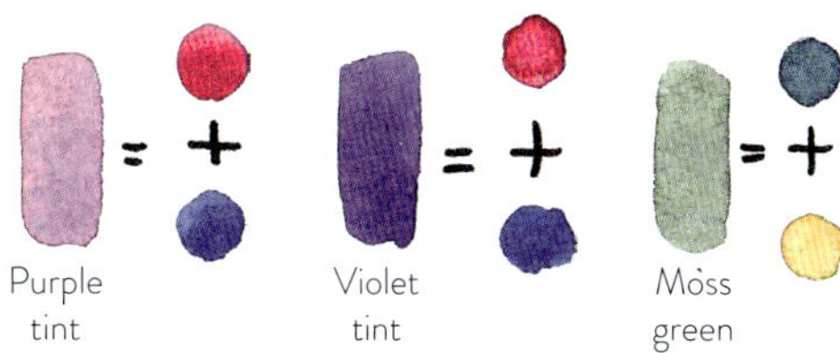

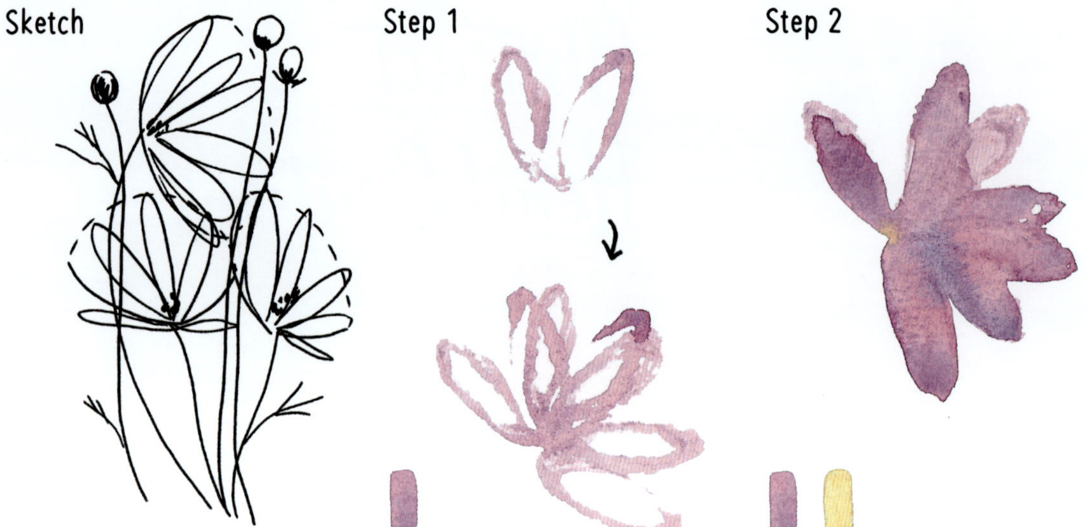

PREPARATION WORK

First, secure the watercolor paper with washi tape to prevent it from wrinkling.

We don't need to make a preliminary sketch, as this is a very loose and abstract project. However, if you look at Sketch, you'll see a draft for how I'm going to place the flowers. You can use this as a guide for where to place your flowers, or you can make a rough sketch on another piece of paper to plan the composition you'd like.

Next, prepare your colors in advance. Mix a large amount of purple tint in a watery to medium consistency. Also, prepare the rest of the colors in medium consistency: Yellow Ochre, violet tint, and moss green. You don't need as much of these, but it's good to have them ready in advance.

Once you're ready, grab a paper roll and move on to the first step.

STEP 1

Let's start by creating one flower for our composition using the stamping technique.

First, use your paper roll to form a heart shape, then extend both sides of the heart to make them longer. This will create a shape resembling two petals. You can play around with this shape, but the most important thing is that the petals look somewhat similar.

Next, load the paper roll well with purple tint. I recommend testing the shape by pressing the paper roll with the color onto scrap paper to see what kind of shape and outline you create. You can experiment by combining a few shapes to form a flower.

Once you're happy with the result, try it on your watercolor paper in the spot where you want to place the first flower. After creating the petals by pressing the paper roll onto the paper, lift it up and then add another pair of petals in the same way. This process will allow you to form the edges of the petals for your first flower.

STEP 2

Now, pick your medium round brush and, using the same color (purple tint), fill in the petals of your first flower.

While the layer is still wet, you can use the same brush to add a little Yellow Ochre to the center or base of the flower (if your flower is partially opened).

Additionally, I recommend adding a few brushstrokes with violet tint for a more interesting effect.

Let the layer dry, then move on to the next step.

Step 3   Step 4

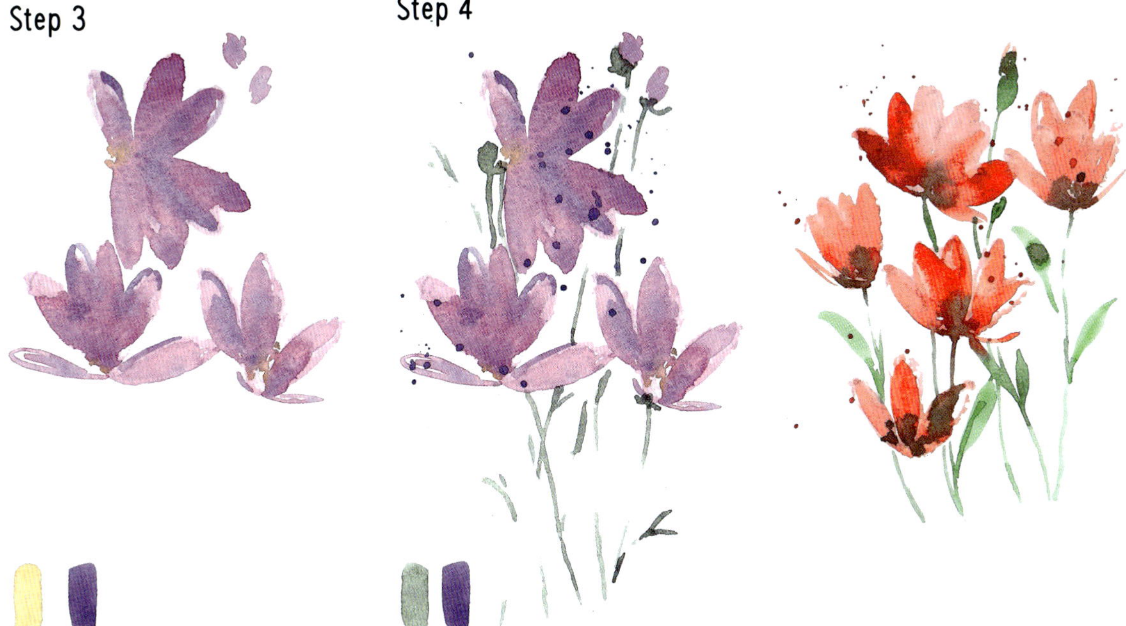

STEP 3

Let's add some more flowers using the stamping technique with purple tint. Then, add details while the paint is still wet using Yellow Ochre and violet tint.

You can follow the composition I created or design your own. Make sure your flowers have different shapes, as this will make your painting look more natural, even in a loose style. You can also add extra petals with a brush if needed. I recommend adding a few buds with purple tint. Play around until you're happy with the result.

For your first attempt, I suggest not adding too many flowers. Once you're satisfied, let everything dry completely before moving on to the final step.

STEP 4

Now, let's add the green parts to our flowers. Take a small round brush and, using moss green, start adding details such as the stems of the flowers, small leaves, and the tiny parts of the buds. You can even add some extra buds in green.

Make sure your stems are as thin as possible, as this always adds elegance to your loose flowers. Also, ensure that your flowers are logically built. Each stem should have a clear beginning and end. You can play around with the composition, but I advise you not to add too many green details.

Once you're happy with the result, I recommend adding some splattering on top. In this abstract painting style, splattering is more than welcome. I did mine in violet to add intensity to the composition.

Try experimenting with different details, colors, and compositions!

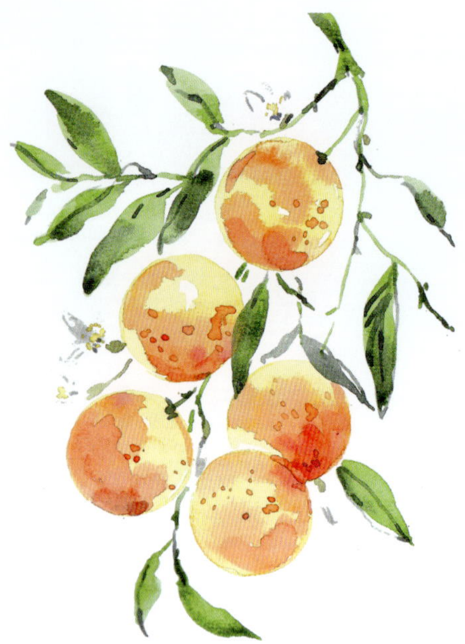

Sunny Oranges

Let's create a sunny and beautiful painting of oranges. Just like the other projects in this section, we'll use the amazing stamping technique.

Remember, it doesn't need to be perfect. Just focus on the process. This project is perfect for practicing your color mixing skills and developing a sense of composition. You'll create oranges, leaves, branches, and flowers. Enjoy!

SUPPLIES

- Watercolor paper
- Masking tape (optional)
- Pencil and eraser (optional)
- A glass or cup with a small diameter
- Round brushes: small (sizes 1–4) and medium (sizes 6–8)
- Quill brushes (sizes 1–4, optional)

PROJECT COLORS

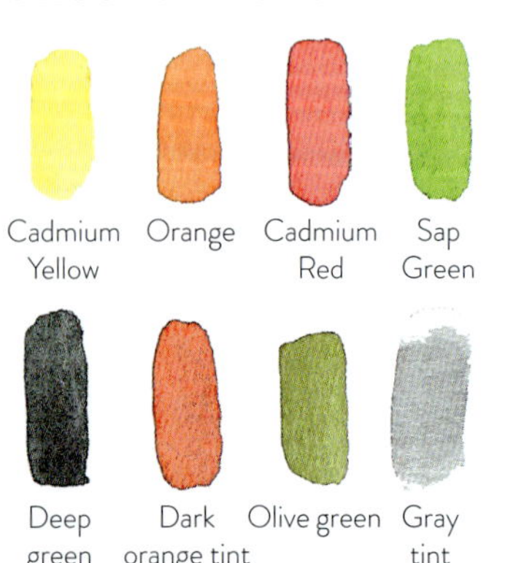

Cadmium Yellow   Orange   Cadmium Red   Sap Green

Deep green   Dark orange tint   Olive green   Gray tint

COLOR MIXING

- Orange: Mix Cadmium Yellow with a little bit of Cadmium Red.
- Deep green: Mix Sap Green with any blue. I use Indigo.
- Gray tint: Mix Ultramarine with Burnt Umber.
- Dark orange tint: Mix Crimson with a little bit of Cadmium Yellow and just a bit of Ultramarine.
- Olive green: Add a little Burnt Umber to Sap Green.

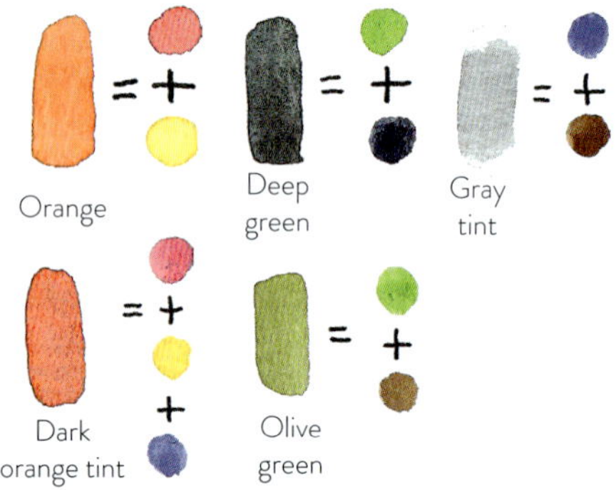

Orange   Deep green   Gray tint

Dark orange tint   Olive green

PREPARATION WORK

If you prefer, you can use washi tape to secure the paper to the table or a board.

Next, we need to create a basic outline of the composition. If you're following my composition, you don't need to do any preliminary sketching. However, if you're creating your own composition, you'll need a pencil to lightly sketch the general layout: Mark where you want to place your oranges and possibly add a few lines for where you plan to add branches.

STEP 1

Now, let's start by using the stamping technique to create oranges and establish the base of our composition.

Prepare three colors in medium consistency: Cadmium Yellow, orange, and Cadmium Red. Dip the rim of a glass or cup into a generous amount of Cadmium Yellow, ensuring the edges are evenly coated. Press the cup onto the paper to create a circle, then use a clean, damp medium round brush to blend the yellow inside. Add more yellow if needed to intensify the color.

While the yellow is still wet, use the wet-on-wet technique to add touches of orange and a bit of Cadmium Red inside the circle. That's it! Refer to Figure 1 for all the stages of painting an orange.

Repeat this process for the remaining oranges as shown in the example, or create your own composition. Once finished, let the painting dry completely.

TIP: For better control, instead of dipping the cup directly into the paint, use a large round brush to apply the paint to the edge of the cup. This way, you can ensure even coverage and consistent results.

STEP 2

Let's add branches and leaves. For this step, prepare a small round brush with a thin tip and a quill brush. If you don't have a quill brush, a soft large round brush will work for painting leaves. Also, prepare medium consistency Sap Green and deep green.

Start by adding the branches in Sap Green, as shown in my example. If you're using your own composition, I recommend using a reference photo to guide you in creating and adding the branches. Once the branches are done, switch to a large round brush or quill brush and start painting the leaves with Sap Green. Add the leaves in varying sizes and arrangements to make the composition look realistic.

After the leaves are in place, use deep green to add touches to the leaves and branches while the Sap Green layer is still wet. This will allow the colors to blend directly on the paper. Once you've completed this step, let everything dry completely before moving on.

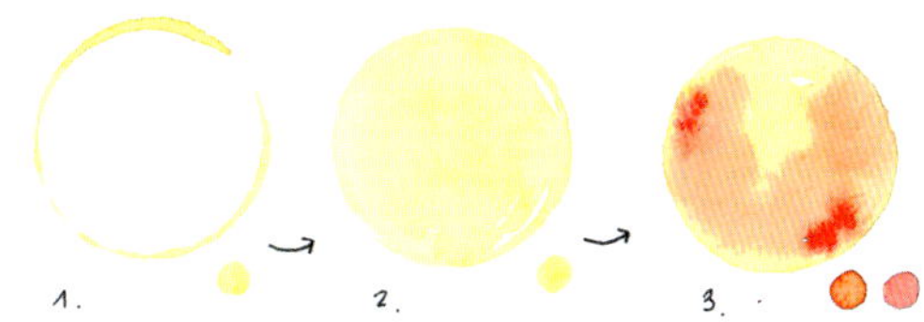

Figure 1

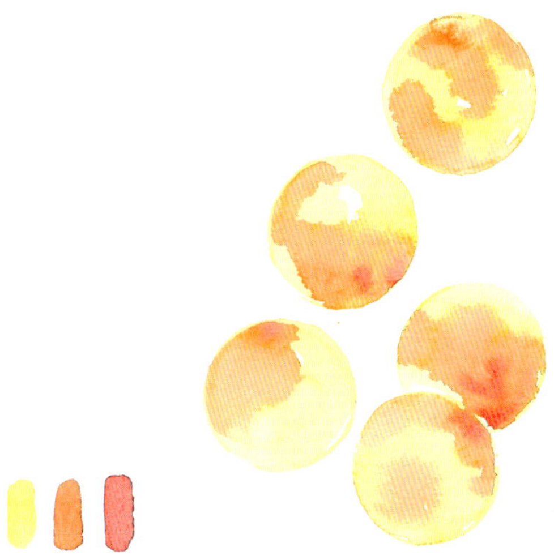

Step 1

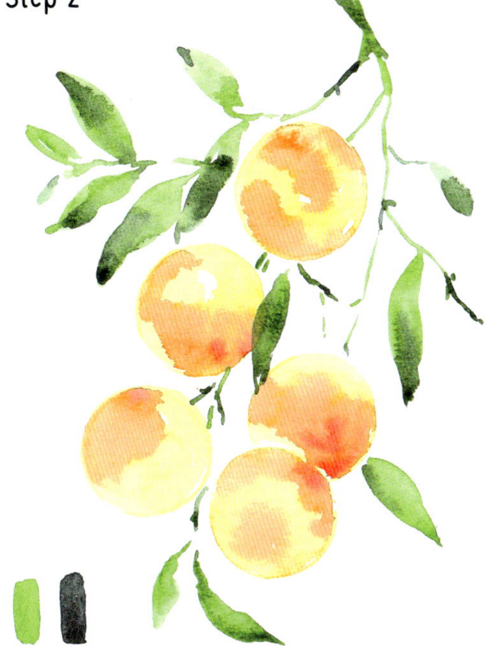

Step 2

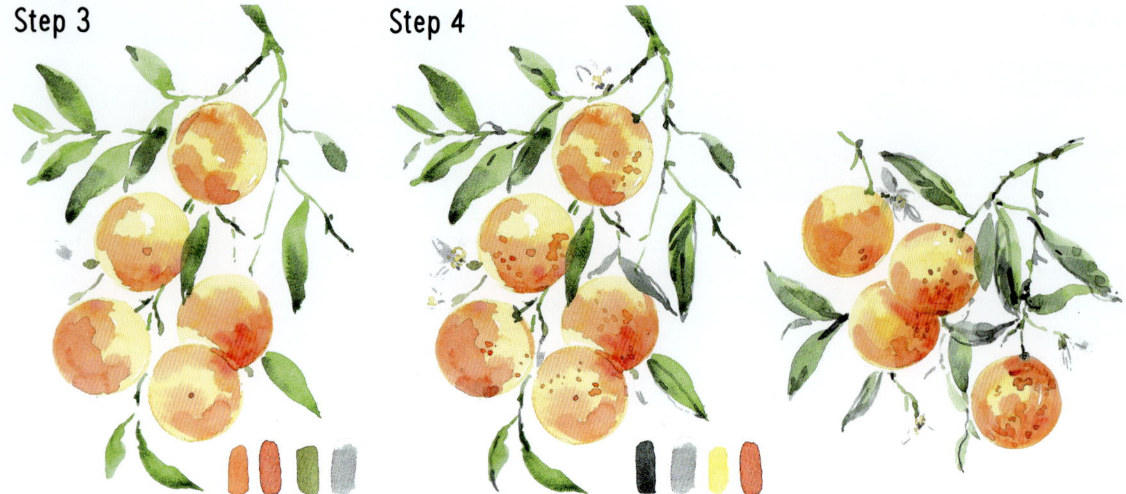

STEP 3

Let's add depth to our painting by adding more layers. First, prepare medium consistency dark orange, orange, and olive green. Also, prepare a gray tint in a watery consistency. I recommend using a medium round brush for this step.

Start by adding a second layer to the oranges using the dark orange and orange colors. I suggest applying these details in random spots, dots, and washes on one side of each orange. If light is hitting the oranges, some areas will have shadows, so we need to emphasize these shadows with dark orange. Additionally, you can add a few touches of orange to give each fruit more dimension and a more natural look.

Once you're satisfied with the oranges and they resemble the example image, you can move on to the flowers. I recommend starting with the buds and some branches, which connect the buds to the rest of the composition, using olive green. Then, use a very watery gray tint to add some flowers and buds.

Once everything is done, allow the painting to dry completely before moving on to the next step.

STEP 4

Our project is almost finished, and we just need to add the final details to make it look stunning. For this, prepare the following colors in medium consistency: Cadmium Yellow, deep green, gray tint, and dark orange. You can also use any other project colors if you'd like to add your own touch and vision to the piece.

For this step, I suggest using a small round brush.

Let's start by adding details to the oranges. Use dark orange to add extra spots and dots, emphasizing the texture of the oranges. With the same color, you can also enhance the shadow details to make them more visible. Once that's done, use deep green to add the final details to the green parts of our composition, such as veins and accents on the leaves, as well as small details on the branches.

Next, switch to Cadmium Yellow to add details to the centers of the flowers. Let it dry slightly, and then use the gray tint to add details to the flower petals, emphasizing both the petals and the centers.

You can add some extra branches to complete the composition or play with additional details. However, remember that sometimes less is more!

Try experimenting with different details, colors, and compositions!

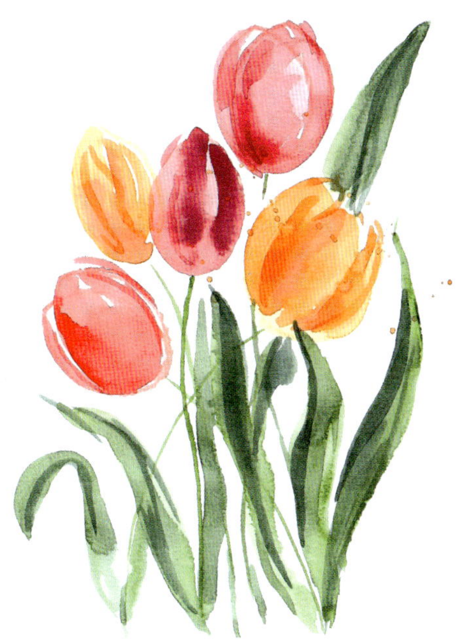

Tulips Bloom

In this project, we will create beautiful blooming tulips using watercolors and a very creative stamping technique. This project showcases the beauty of watercolors, highlighting their airiness and transparency as well as their bright, vivid colors. I believe this project can be recreated in variations many times. Feel free to invite your friends or children to join in! I am sure they will enjoy this lesson.

SUPPLIES

- Watercolor paper
- Washi tape or masking tape (optional)
- Pencil and eraser (optional)
- Round brushes: small (sizes 1–4) and medium (sizes 6–8)
- Quill brush (sizes 1–4, optional but highly recommended), mop brush (size 4), or large round brush
- Toilet paper roll

PROJECT COLORS

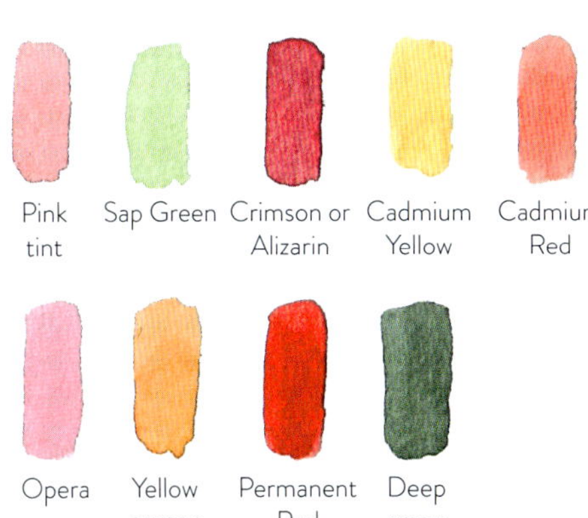

Pink tint   Sap Green   Crimson or Alizarin   Cadmium Yellow   Cadmium Red

Opera   Yellow orange   Permanent Red   Deep green

COLOR MIXING

- Pink tint: Add a little bit of Crimson to Opera.
- Yellow orange: Mix Cadmium Yellow with a pinch of Cadmium Red.
- Deep green: Mix Sap Green with any blue. I use Indigo.

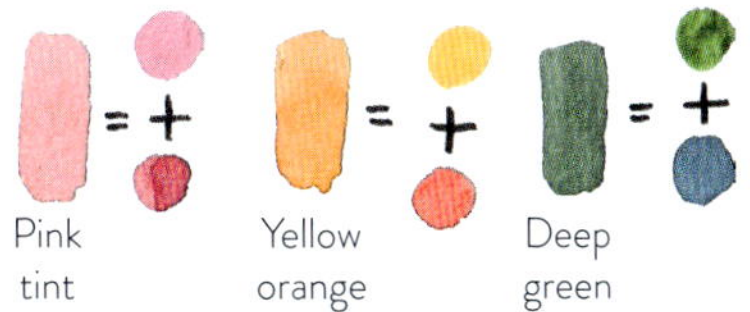

Pink tint   Yellow orange   Deep green

PREPARATION WORK

I recommend securing the watercolor paper with washi tape to prevent wrinkling and keep the paper from moving while you work.

For this project, we will paint in a loose style, which means we won't do any preliminary sketching. However, if it helps, you can make very light pencil lines to indicate, for example, the stems of the tulips. This may help you with the composition and keep you oriented during the painting process.

Please refer to Figure 1, where you can find the three types of tulips we will create using the stamping technique: a tulip bud, a slightly open tulip, and a more open tulip. If you look at Figure 2, you'll see how to create a slightly open tulip using the stamping technique. First, create an outline with watercolor using the stamping technique. Then fill it with the same color used for the outline. While it's still wet, add some extra colors and brushstrokes to complete the tulip.

(Continued)

Figure 1

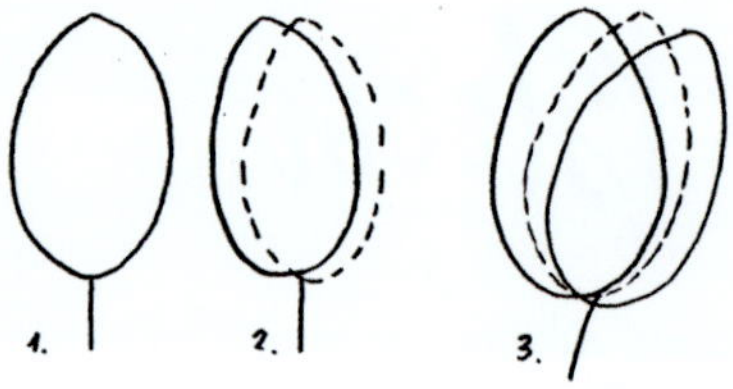

Figure 2

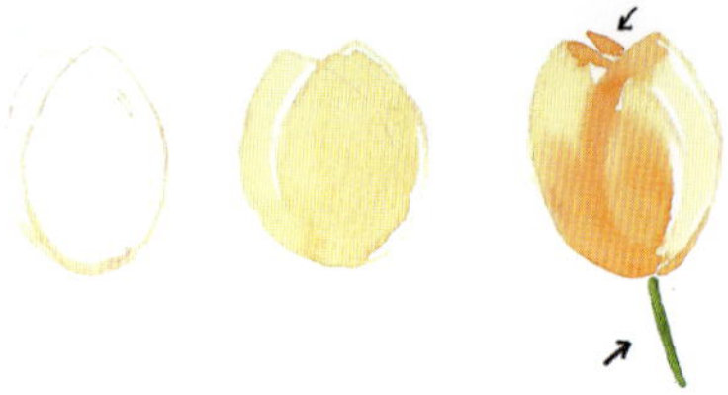

Step 1

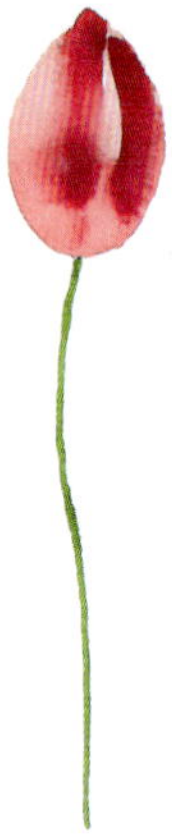

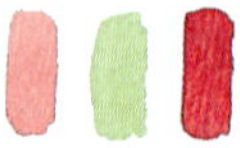

Step 2

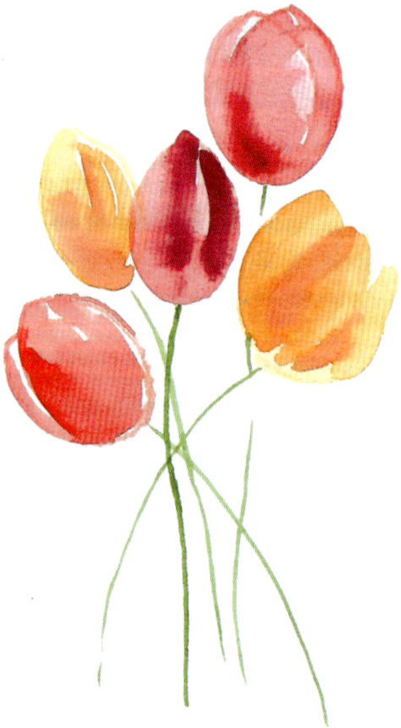

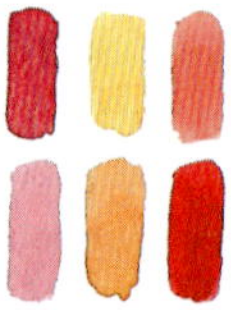

This is the primary method that will be used in this lesson to create a tulip. Don't worry, I will guide you step by step through the process.

STEP 1

Let's start painting our first tulip, beginning with a bud. For this shape, you'll need just one stamp. Prepare three colors: a large amount of pink tint in watery consistency, and Sap Green and Crimson in medium consistency. Also, prepare two brushes—a small round brush and a medium round brush—and a toilet paper roll. Shape the roll into an oval, sharpening one end to resemble the top of a tulip.

TIP: Before starting to paint on your main area, use a piece of test watercolor paper to practice this first step.

Load the shaped paper roll with pink tint, and then make a stamp by pressing the paper roll onto the watercolor paper. Lift it up to reveal the outline. Then, using your medium round brush and the same pink tint, fill the shape. Leaving a few small areas free from paint is okay; it adds contrast and more volume to your base layer.

Once this is done, switch to Crimson, using the same brush, and add one or two brushstrokes to create shadows on your tulip using the wet-on-wet technique. Finally, take your small round brush, pick up Sap Green, and paint the stem of the tulip. Aim for a thin stem, not too thick. Allow everything to dry completely before moving on.

STEP 2

Let's add more tulips to our composition. Prepare the following colors in watery consistency: Cadmium Yellow, Cadmium Red, and Opera. Prepare the following colors in medium consistency: yellow orange, Permanent Red, and Crimson. In this step, we'll add four extra tulips, each with a different shape. Arm yourself with a medium round brush and an already shaped paper roll.

First, let's paint two yellow tulips. Using Cadmium Yellow, create a bud shape with the stamping technique. Then add some details with yellow orange on the still-wet layer. Repeat the process for another yellow tulip, but this time use three stamps close to each other to form a more open tulip.

Next, paint a red tulip. Create the shape of a slightly opened tulip with Cadmium Red, stamping twice. Fill in the shape with the same color and add one or two brushstrokes of Permanent Red on the still-wet layer.

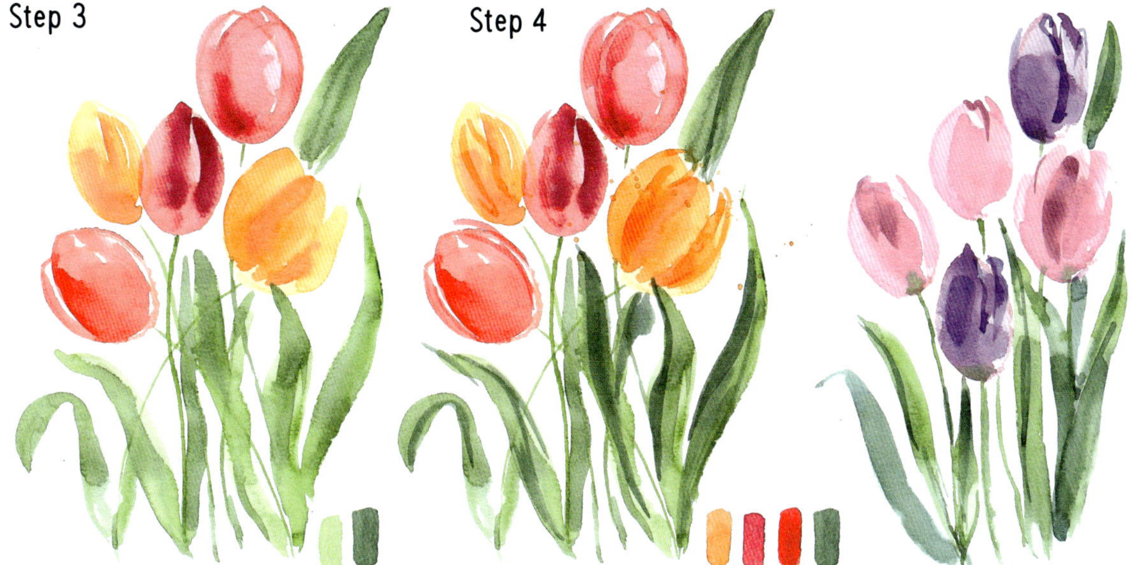

Finally, paint a pink tulip. Stamp three times with Opera for a more open tulip shape, fill in the shape with the same color, and add one or two brushstrokes of Crimson on the wet layer.

Switch to the small round brush and pick up Sap Green. Paint the stems of the tulips as shown in my example, or as you prefer.

Allow everything to dry completely before moving to the next step.

TIP: If you're using the stamping technique with different colors, it's better to use different paper rolls. Alternatively, you can use one roll but cut it into a few pieces. For example, if you use two rolls, you can cut each in half and use them from both sides. In this case, you will have four stamps.

STEP 3

In this step, we will add some leaves to our tulips to complete the composition. Prepare your quill brush. Also, prepare Sap Green in a watery consistency and deep green in medium consistency. Once you are ready, begin by applying Sap Green to your brush and start painting the leaves as shown in the example, or create your own composition. On the still-wet layer, add some accents with deep green. Once you have painted all the leaves, allow everything to dry completely before moving to the next step.

STEP 4

We have already created an elegant and bright composition. Now, let's add some accents to complete our painting. For this, take a small or large round brush and prepare yellow orange, Crimson, Permanent Red, and deep green in medium consistency. Add extra brushstrokes: On the pink tulips, add accents with Crimson; on the red tulips, add details with Permanent Red; and on the yellow tulips, paint details in yellow orange. Make these details very loose and asymmetrical. Emphasize certain areas, create accents or shadows, or even add some extra petals at the top or in the top corner.

Finally, add some extra details with deep green on the leaves. Once you're happy with your composition and its final look, you can leave it as it is, or add splattering with any of the tulip colors. I used yellow orange and made a few flicks with a large round brush to add some extra accents to my painting.

Try experimenting with different details, colors, and compositions!

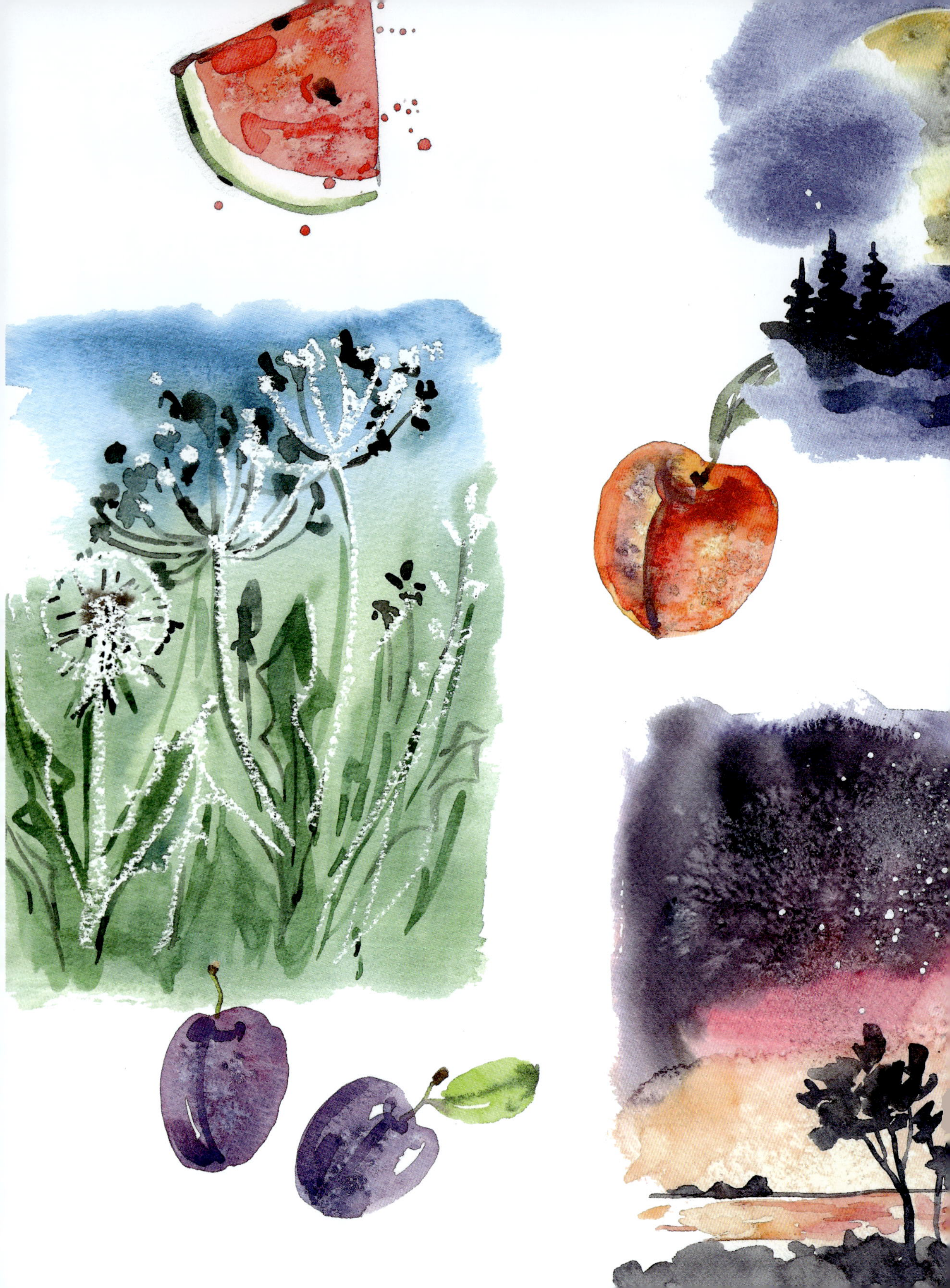

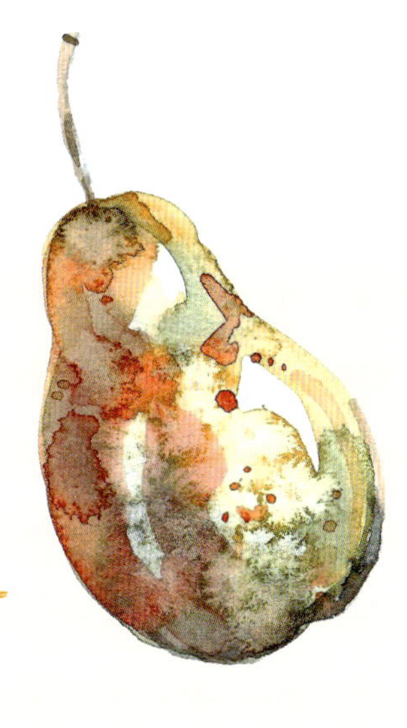

Salt TECHNIQUE

TECHNIQUES USED IN THIS CHAPTER

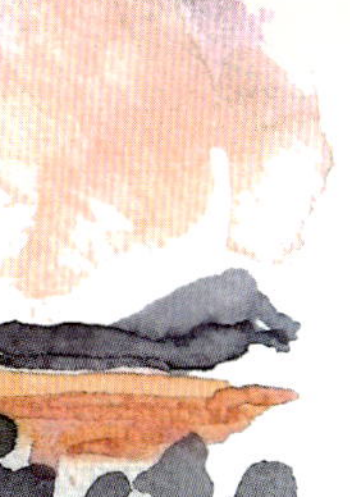

Mystery Night Sky

In this project, I will show you how to create a beautiful starry night landscape using the lovely salt technique. This project is very relaxing and yields an impressive result that anyone can achieve. With the salt technique, you can execute many diverse projects. So grab your brushes, clear your mind, and enjoy the process because it's worth it.

PROJECT COLORS

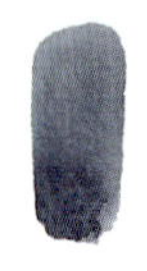 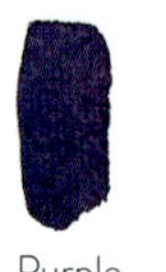 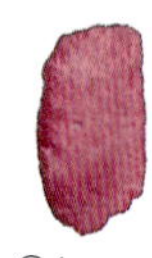 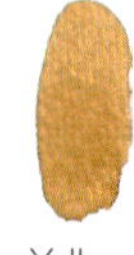 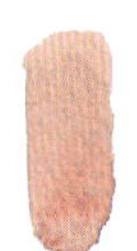

Deep purple blue   Purple   Crimson   Yellow Ochre   Warm rose tint

SUPPLIES

- Watercolor paper
- Washi tape or masking tape
- Pencil and eraser (optional)
- Quill brushes (sizes 4–6) or a round brush
- Kitchen salt
- Round brushes: small (sizes 1–4) and medium (sizes 6–8)
- White gouache
- Toothbrush (optional)

NOTE: Please note that if you don't have a quill brush, you can use any round watercolor brush you have. However, the best option for this project is to use a quill brush, as it can hold a large amount of water and distribute it effectively.

COLOR MIXING

- Deep purple blue: Mix purple with a little Indigo. If you don't have Indigo, use any blue with a little Burnt Umber.
- Purple: if you don't have purple, mix Prussian Blue with Crimson.
- Warm Rose tint: Mix Yellow Ochre with Crimson.

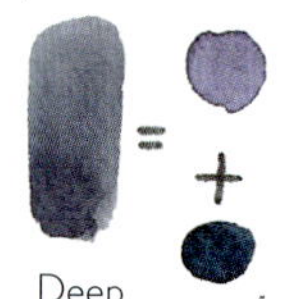  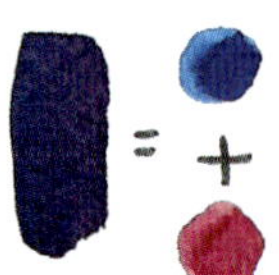 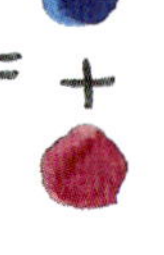 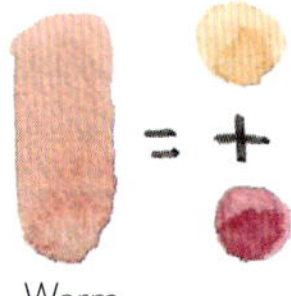

Deep purple blue   Purple   Warm rose tint

PREPARATION WORK

I recommend securing your paper with washi tape to a table or a board. This prevents any wrinkling or damage to your paper, since we'll use a wet-on-wet technique. This project doesn't have a sketching stage, since we are creating a very abstract and loose watercolor landscape. However, if you feel more comfortable, you can do a basic sketch just to feel confident.

Step 1

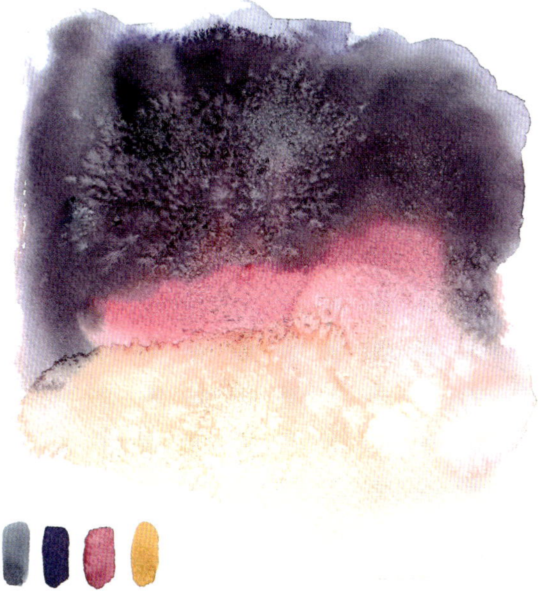

Step 2

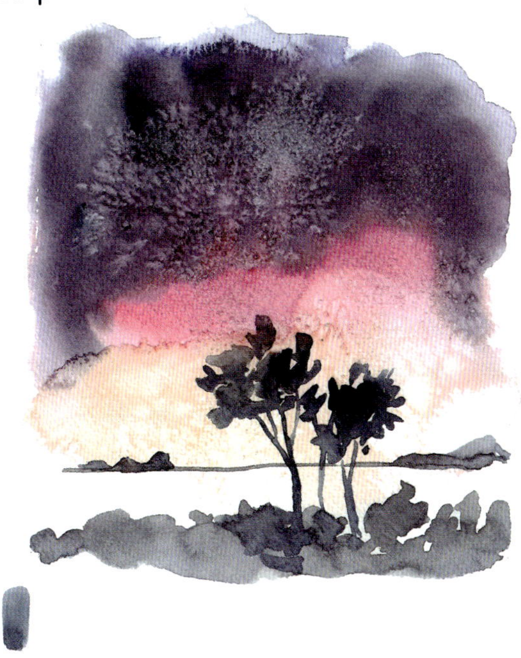

STEP 1

NOTE: Please note that you can paint across the entire page you've already outlined with washi tape, or create loose, abstract borders like I have.

TIP: During this step, work quickly because wet paper dries quickly, and colors applied to wet surfaces can also dry rapidly. Keep this in mind for successful execution of the project.

Begin by preparing the following colors: medium consistency deep blue purple and purple, along with watery consistency Crimson and Yellow Ochre. Make sure you have enough paint on your mixing palette. Take your quill brush or a big round brush and moisten the area of the painting. Don't make it too wet or too dry. Then, start adding colors to the still-wet layer. Begin at the bottom with Yellow Ochre, making horizontal brushstrokes. Then apply Crimson towards the top of our scenery. Working from the top, add purple and finally some touches of deep blue purple. You should get a kind of imperfect gradient with rich colors at the top and transparent brightness at the bottom.

Then, on the still wet layer, add salt; a few pinches will be enough. Make sure you spread the salt evenly, not just in one area. Allow the layer to dry completely.

Since we are using the salt technique, it may take some time. Once the salt and watercolor layer are dry, carefully remove the salt. You will have a lovely texture on your watercolor base layer.

STEP 2

In this step, we will add another layer to our landscape. We'll use just one color, so prepare a medium consistency of deep blue purple, and take your medium round brush. You may also need a small round brush for adding extra details. In this project, we'll add silhouettes of trees, a horizontal line, and other elements that bring contrast and make the painting less abstract.

Begin with your bigger brush to add foreground shapes like bushes, and then the crowns of the trees, as shown in the example. Using the same color and consistency, switch to the smaller round brush to paint the horizontal line, the trunks of the trees, and some silhouettes of the hills in the background. You can follow my composition, or feel free to create your own, whether it's very abstract or more defined with silhouettes like mountains, trees, and various types of bushes. Allow everything to dry before moving to the next step.

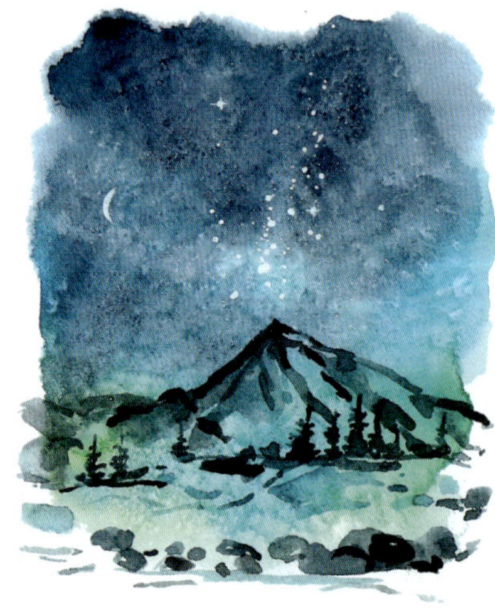

STEP 3

Let's continue using the layering technique to add more depth to our painting and bring some color to the lower part of our landscape. We'll use two colors in medium consistency: Crimson and warm rose tint. You can opt for a very watery consistency if you prefer a more tender result.

Take your medium round brush. We are painting a reflection of the sky on the water, so carefully begin by adding some loose Crimson brushstrokes to the water. Then, add a few brushstrokes from the sides with warm rose tint. That's it! You can also add some extra brushstrokes to the sky if you'd like, but it makes sense to just bring in some color without making the landscape too abstract or covering the lovely texture effect we achieved with the salt technique. Let everything dry.

STEP 4

We just need to add some extra final details. For this project, you will need thick consistency warm rose tint and white gouache. First, with a small round brush, add some final details onto the water, such as horizontal brushstrokes that imitate the waves on calm water. Don't overdo these lines; just add a few to emphasize the water and its texture. Then let these details dry.

Add a little water to the white gouache to make a creamy consistency, and then protect the bottom part of the painting with some paper towels or anything that will shield the trees and horizontal line from the gouache splatters. Then, just do a splattering using a medium round brush or toothbrush. I advise you to limit the splattering to just a few flicks, mostly towards the center of your painting, angling to the top right corner. You can also take a small round brush and, with white gouache, add one or two tiny stars to bring some interesting details. These elements should catch the viewer's eye.

Try experimenting with different details, colors, and compositions!

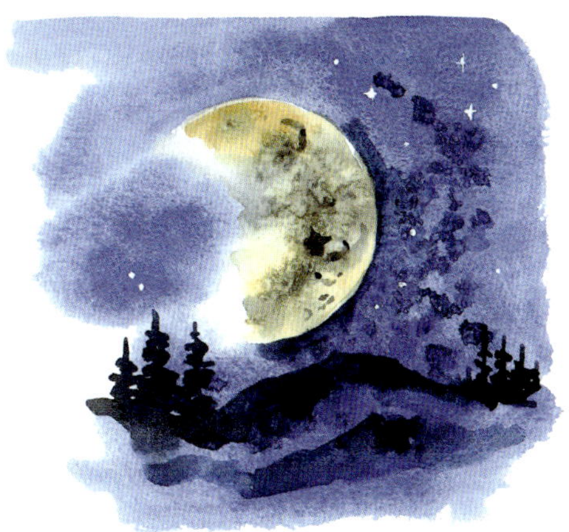

Moon in Beauty

Let's paint a beautiful moon. The salt technique creates a beautiful texture on both the moon and the night sky. I encourage you to try this method to create more paintings of the moon or planets. So, let's have fun and paint the Moon in Beauty!

SUPPLIES

- Watercolor paper
- Washi tape or masking tape
- Rounded object (cup, glass, or jar) the desired size of your moon
- Round brushes: small (sizes 1–4) and medium (sizes 6–8)
- Quill brush (size 4)
- Kitchen salt
- White gouache
- Liner brush (size 0 or 1)

PROJECT COLORS

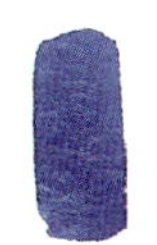 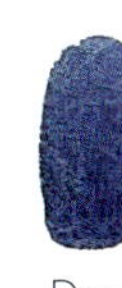 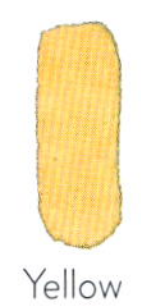 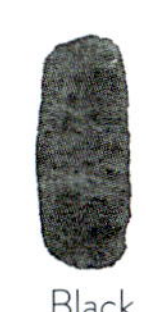 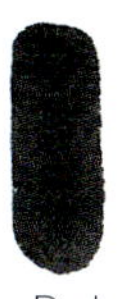

Ultramarine   Deep blue   Yellow Ochre   Black   Dark blue gray

COLOR MIXING

- Deep blue: Mix Ultramarine with a bit of Prussian Blue (or Indigo).
- Dark blue gray: Mix Burnt Umber with a bit of blue (I used Prussian Blue).

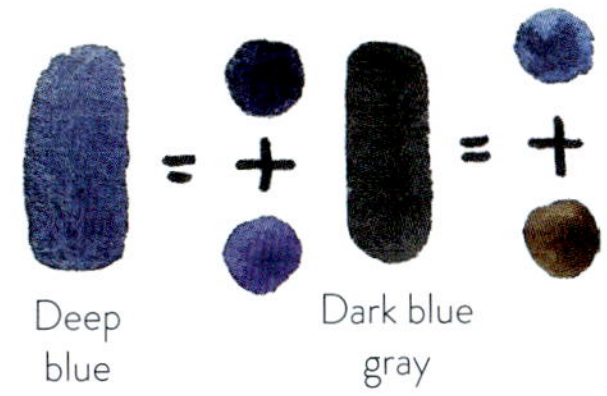

Deep blue   Dark blue gray

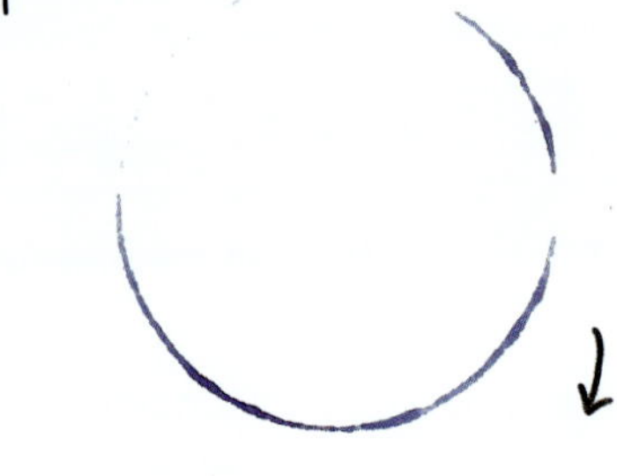

Step 1

Step 2

PREPARATION WORK

First, we need to secure our paper with washi tape. You can make strong, defined borders with the tape, or you can secure the paper but leave the borders loose to add charm to your work.

This project does not require any sketching. However, I suggest preparing all the colors in advance, especially a large amount of Ultramarine in a medium to thick consistency, and a large amount of deep blue in a medium consistency. Also prepare medium consistency Yellow Ochre and Black and thick consistency dark blue gray.

STEP 1

We'll create the moon outline using the stamping technique. Load your rounded object (I'm using a glass) with Ultramarine, then press the glass onto the paper where you want to place your moon. Lift the glass.

Now, using a medium round brush or a quill brush, start blending with a bit of water on the sky to the left of the moon. This will create a half-moon effect, as we blend only one side.

Next, begin adding Ultramarine to the outer area around the moon, filling the background consistently with a medium round brush or quill brush using the same color (Ultramarine and slightly diluted Ultramarine).

STEP 2

Work quickly during this step, as we'll be adding salt to a wet layer.

Continue adding Ultramarine around the moon with a medium round brush or quill brush until you have created a square or another shape to frame the scene. If you decide to create stronger borders, fill in the entire area around the moon.

While the paint is still wet, add a few touches of deep blue on the sky to the right of the moon. Then, on the still-wet layer, sprinkle a few pinches of salt over the sky area. Leave it to dry completely.

Step 3

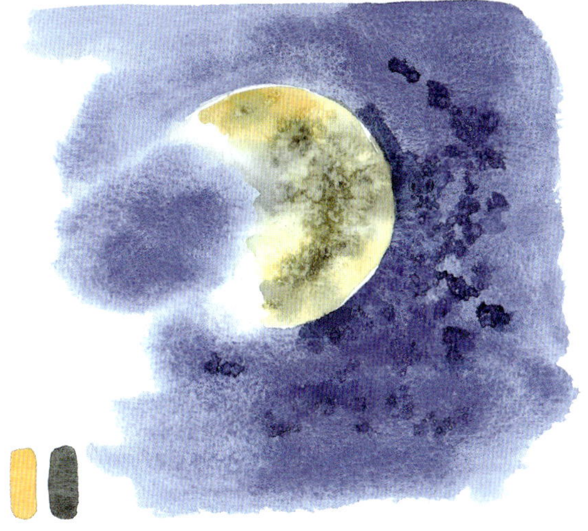

Step 4

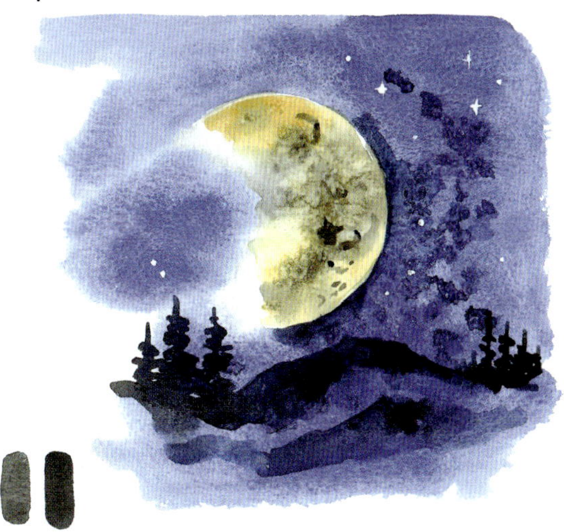

STEP 3

Once the salt is completely dry, you can remove it with your finger, but be careful not to smudge the rest of the painting. After removing all the salt, we can begin painting the moon.

Prepare Yellow Ochre and black in medium consistency. Then, using a medium round brush or quill brush, moisten the area of the moon with clean water, being careful not to disturb the already painted blue sky.

On the still-wet area of the moon, add Yellow Ochre. Then, add a few touches of black.

While the moon layer is still wet, sprinkle a few pinches of salt on the area. This effect is especially magical because we're using two colors.

Now, let everything dry completely.

STEP 4

Once you are sure the salt is dry, carefully remove it from the moon. Be careful here, as you could smudge or stain your painting with your fingers. After you've removed the salt, we can begin adding details.

To make the painting less abstract, I recommend painting silhouettes of mountains or trees. You could even add some clouds. Let your imagination flow. For my version, I added silhouettes of hills and pine trees. I used a small round brush and thick dark blue gray to paint these details.

Once you're happy with the result, add a few touches and details, like craters, to the moon with medium consistency black. Be careful not to overwhelm the texture created by the salt.

Finally, with white gouache and a liner brush, you can add a few stars in the sky area.

Avoid adding too many details.

Try experimenting with different details, colors, and compositions!

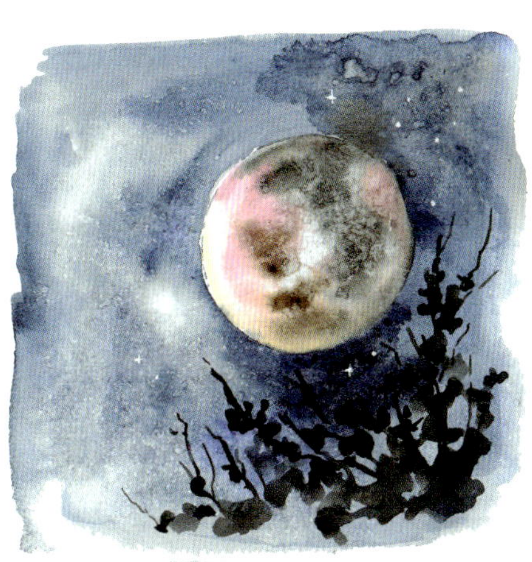

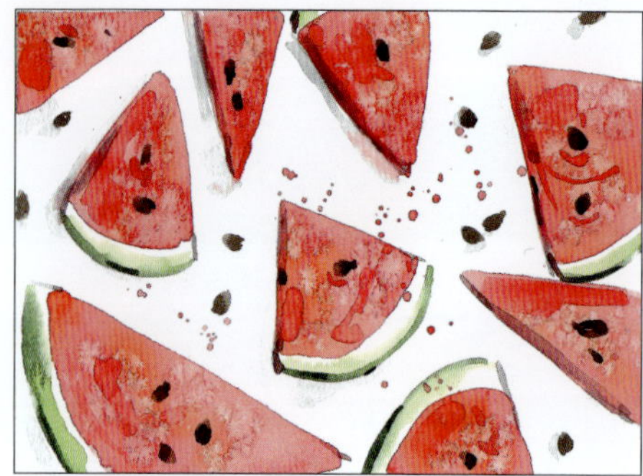

Sun-Kissed Watermelon Slices

Let's paint sun-kissed watermelon slices. It's a very fun project that's not only about using salt; it's also about playing, making and discovering shapes, and seeing how everything comes together to create a simple yet colorful pattern illustration. The principles of this project can be applied to other patterns or paintings that contain fruits, vegetables, or even other simple shape patterns. Even kids enjoy it!

SUPPLIES

- Watercolor paper
- Masking tape or Washi tape
- Pencil and eraser (optional)
- Round brushes: small (sizes 1–4) and medium (sizes 6–8)
- Quill brush (size 1)
- Kitchen salt

NOTE: If you don't have a quill brush, you can use a soft round brush, for example, size 8. Make sure it's pretty soft and can hold a significant amount of watercolor paint.

NOTE: To mix a beautiful gray tint, you need to mix green and red in equal proportions. If you change the proportions, you can still get a gray, but it will have more red or green.

COLOR MIXING

- Sap Green tint: Add a little Lemon Yellow to Sap Green.
- Deep green: Mix Sap Green with Prussian Blue.
- Brown tint: Add just a hint of Ultramarine to Burnt Umber.
- Gray tint: Mix Permanent Red with deep green, or you can mix any green color with red.
- Red brown tint: Add a little deep green to Permanent Red to make it more brownish.

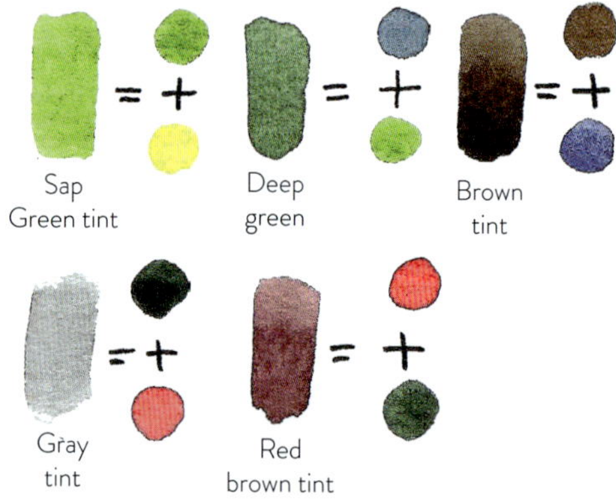

Sap Green tint

Deep green

Brown tint

Gray tint

Red brown tint

PROJECT COLORS

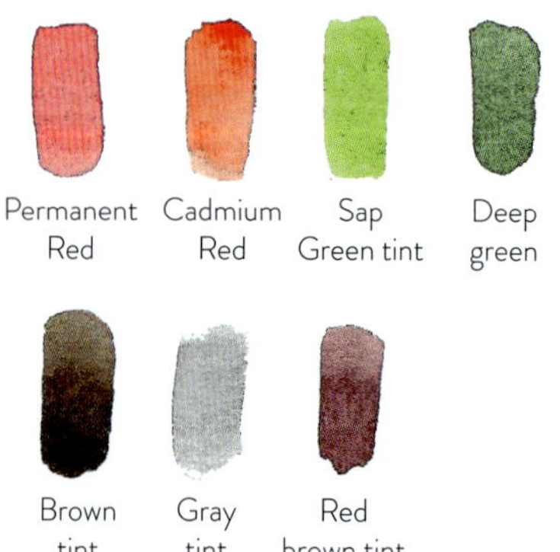

Permanent Red

Cadmium Red

Sap Green tint

Deep green

Brown tint

Gray tint

Red brown tint

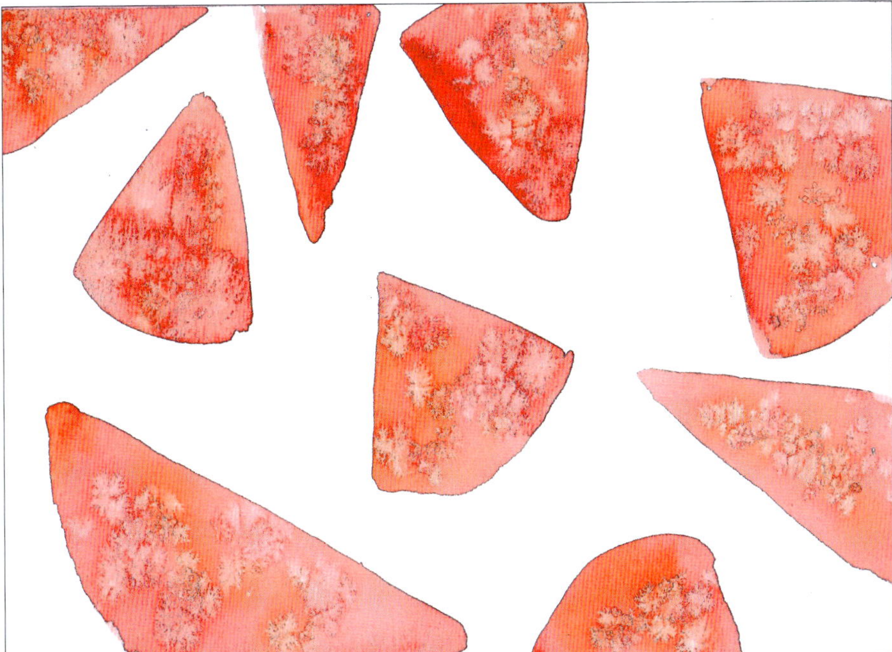

PREPARATION WORK

Let's start our project with some preparation. First, we need to secure the paper with washi tape. This tape will help us create a beautiful white border.

The beauty of this project lies in playing with shapes and embracing a loose style, so I don't recommend a sketch. However, you can do some preliminary sketching to mark the slices of watermelon if it makes you feel more comfortable. Refer to the final step to see the completed project and use it as a guide for your preliminary sketching.

STEP 1

Let's paint our sunny watermelon slices. For this step, you will need medium consistency Cadmium Red and watery consistency Permanent Red. I also recommend using a quill brush and a medium round brush (I use a soft round brush in size 8).

With the quill brush, use Permanent Red paint to paint a watermelon slice. While the slice is still wet, add a few touches of Cadmium Red using the round brush, then sprinkle a little bit of salt on the wet layer. Try to spread the salt evenly over the slice rather than concentrating it in one area. Repeat this process for painting the rest of the slices.

You can follow my composition or create your own. Just make sure to fill the painting area evenly while also playing with the sizes and orientations of the watermelon slices. The composition should not be symmetrical but rather have a natural, chaotic order.

Now, let everything dry. For the best results with salt, allow the paint to dry naturally for at least 5 minutes or more. This will give you a beautiful texture. Once everything is completely dry, carefully remove the salt. I prefer to do this with a paper towel, but make sure not to touch or stain the clean paper areas with watercolor.

Step 2

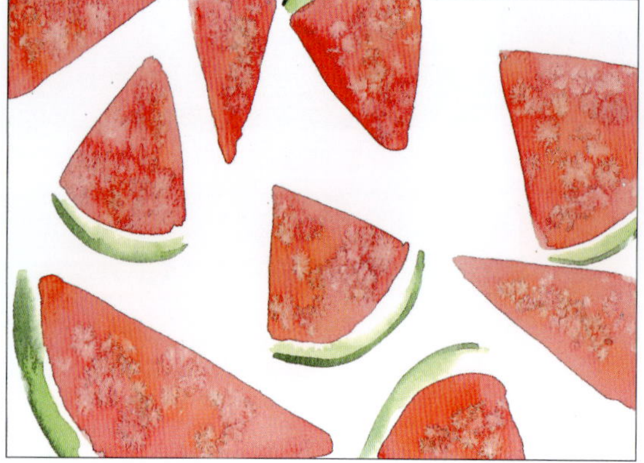

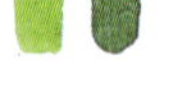

Step 3

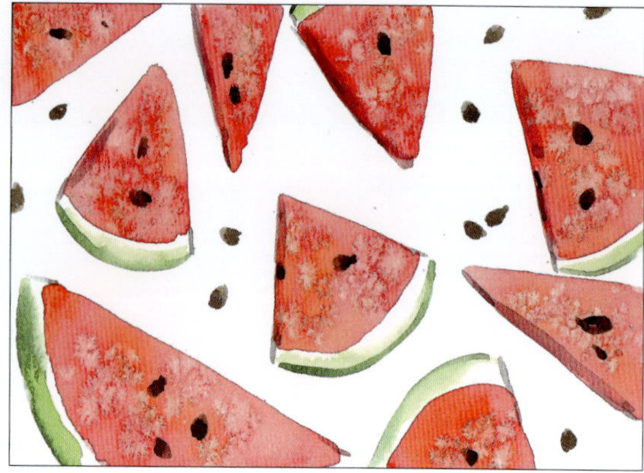

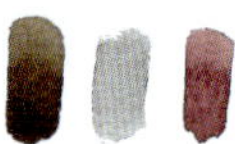

STEP 2

Now, to turn our red shapes into watermelon slices, we need to add green skin to each one. Prepare watery consistency Sap Green tint and medium consistency deep green, and use a small round brush and a soft medium round brush.

First use the small round brush to paint the edge of the green part of a watermelon with Sap Green tint. Then, using a wet medium round brush, blur the edge into the slice to create a soft transition effect. Add deep green to the Sap Green tint on the paper. You don't need to wait until the Sap Green tint dries; these two greens together will achieve a beautiful blending effect.

Repeat these actions for each slice of watermelon. Allow everything to dry completely before proceeding to the next step.

STEP 3

Let's now make our watermelon slices more defined. For this, prepare medium consistency brown tint, gray tint, and red brown tint. I recommend using a small round brush, or if you can handle it, a big round brush.

Start by adding seeds to your slices. As with any composition, you don't need to make it symmetrical or perfect. Add the seeds in a chaotic order, and you can even place some seeds in the white spaces between the slices to balance the composition. Once that's done, take the gray tint and use it to paint the details that connect the red part of the watermelon to the green part.

Next, pick the red brown color and thicken one side of some slices. I added the paint to the left sides of each slice. This will add volume to your watermelon slices and make the white parts stand out.

Once everything is done, you can let it dry naturally or speed up the drying process with a hairdryer.

Step 2

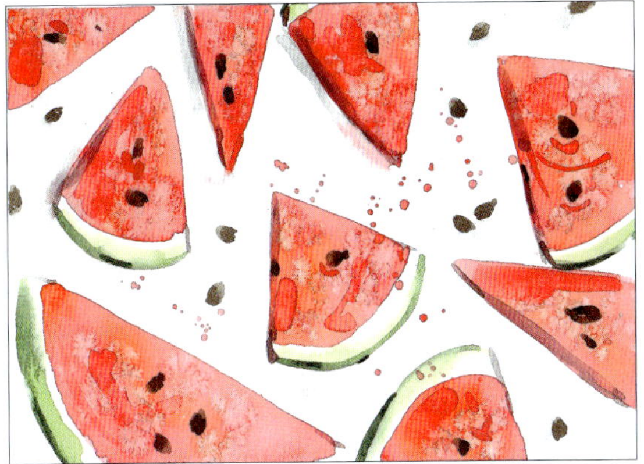

STEP 4

We just need to add some final details to balance our composition.

First, using a very watery consistency gray tint, add shadows with a medium round brush for each slice and seed. The shadows should be placed consistently for all objects in the composition. If the light comes from the top right corner, add the shadow to the left side and bottom.

Next, we need to add more details, but not too many, so as not to cover the beautiful texture created by the salt. You can switch to the small round brush or keep working with the medium round brush. Emphasize the green skin with deep green using some very loose touches to the edges of the slices to create contrast.

Then, pick a medium round brush, and with medium to thick consistency Permanent Red, randomly add some details to the red, juicy parts of the watermelons: texture details, shadows from the seeds, and some other brushstrokes.

I recommend adding splatters of Permanent Red. One or two flicks on the paper will make a big difference and bring freshness and airiness to the painting.

NOTE: You can experiment with splattering more colors, but remember, less is more.

Once everything is done, remove the washi tape, and voilà, your sunny, juicy watermelon slices full of summer vibes are complete. If you enjoyed this project, the process, and the final effect the salt brings to the layout, you may enjoy recreating it with different fruits. You can experiment with adding salt when painting the first layer for plums, peaches, apricots, apples, and pears (see below). Don't be afraid to experiment and be creative. Remember to maintain some consistency, as we have in this project, and consider other techniques we have used, as well as important points like composition and contrast.

Try experimenting with different details, colors, and compositions!

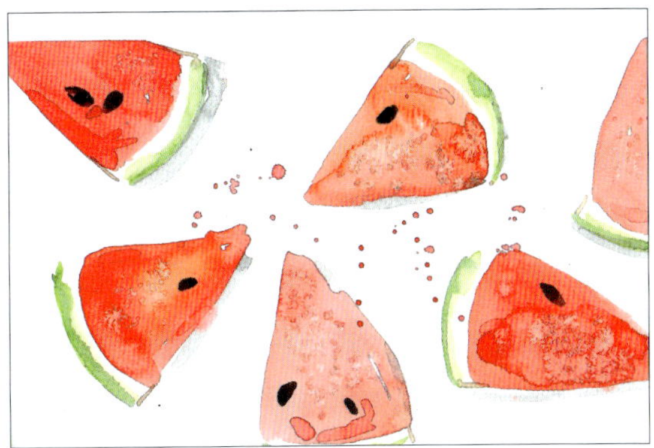

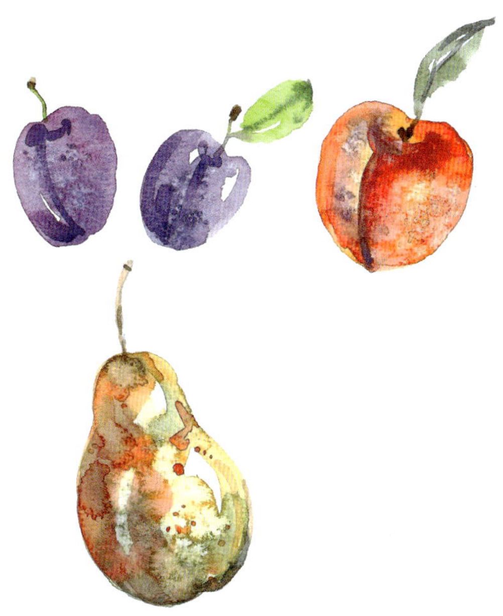

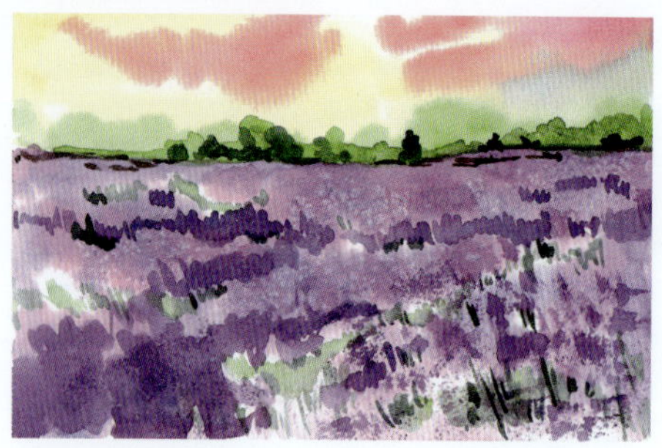

Dreamy Meadow

This project is truly magical. You'll create beautiful textures, emphasize details, and add contrast to your composition. You'll see how easily we can create a bright, transparent landscape with texture and details. I encourage you to enjoy the process. Let's paint a dreamy meadow together!

SUPPLIES

- Watercolor paper
- Washi tape or masking tape
- Pencil and eraser (optional)
- Quill brushes (sizes 4–6)
- Round brushes: small (sizes 1–4) and medium (sizes 6–8)
- Kitchen salt
- Kitchen sponge

NOTE: If you don't have Opera, you can use Alizarin, Rose, Madder Rose, or any other pink or rose tint of watercolor to mix purple and violet tints.

PROJECT COLORS

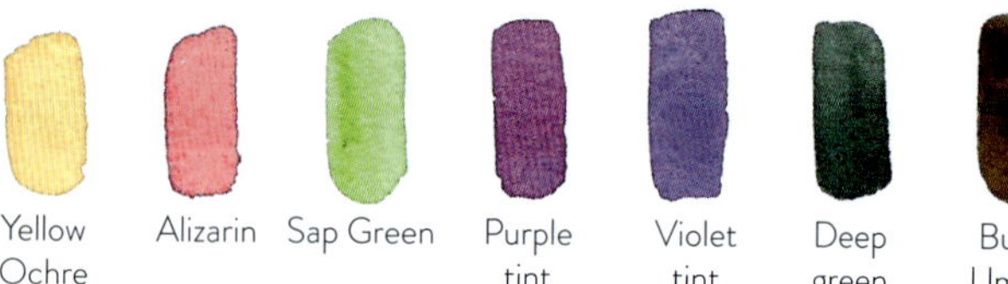

Yellow Ochre · Alizarin · Sap Green · Purple tint · Violet tint · Deep green · Burnt Umber

COLOR MIXING

- Purple tint: Mix Opera with some Ultramarine.
- Violet tint: Add a little Opera to Ultramarine.
- Deep green: Add a hint of Sap Green to blue (I use Indigo).

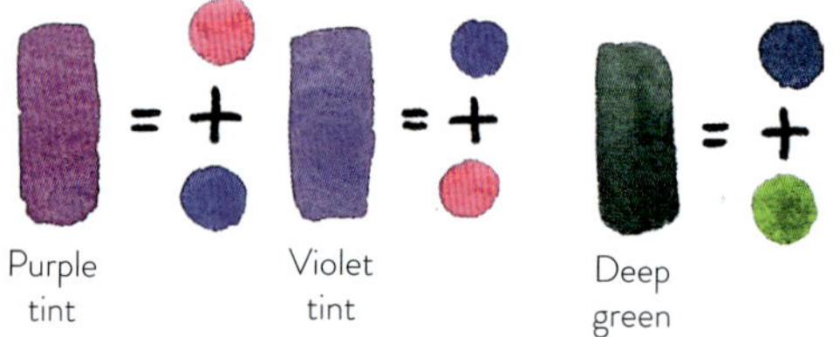

Purple tint · Violet tint · Deep green

Sketch

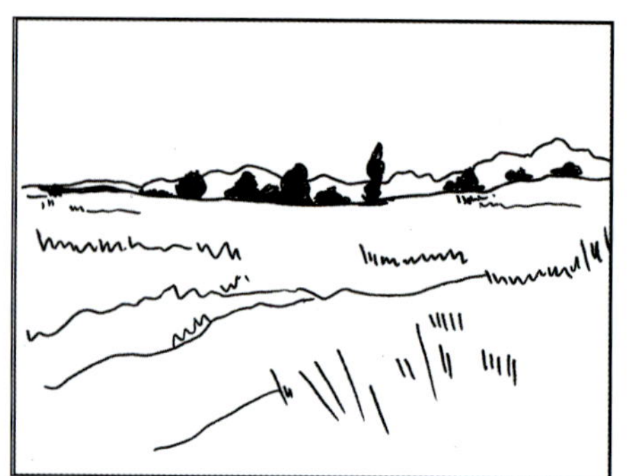

PREPARATION WORK

We need to secure our paper with washi tape to prevent any wrinkling because we will use the wet-on-wet technique, and the paper may curve.

You don't need to do a preliminary sketch, but for this project, I recommend at least marking the horizontal line with a pencil, along with some basic landscape lines to help you feel more confident. You can refer to the very simple sketch in Sketch.

Step 1

Step 2

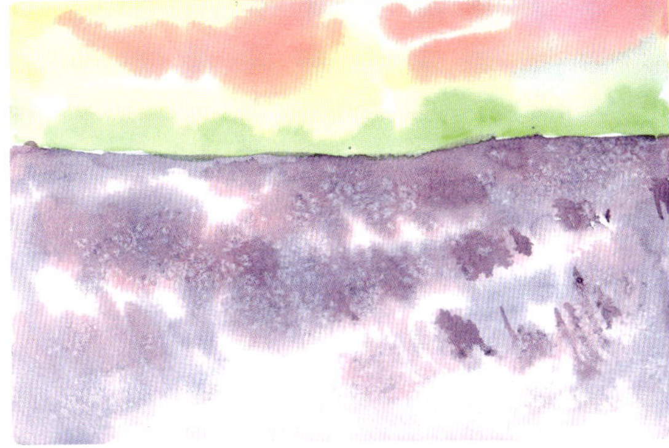

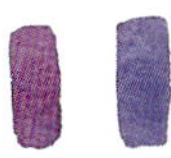

Step 3

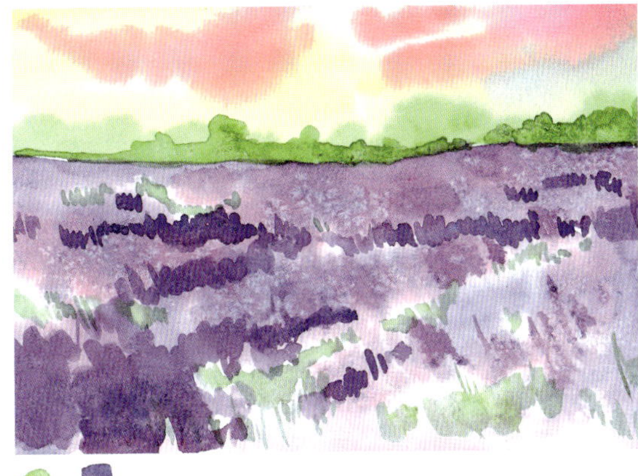

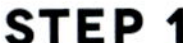

STEP 1

Prepare Yellow Ochre in a watery consistency, and Alizarin and Sap Green in a watery to medium consistency. Start by wetting the sky area with clean water using a quill brush or a soft medium round brush. Once that's done, begin adding Yellow Ochre on the wet paper with the same brush. You don't need to spread the color evenly; instead, make some brushstrokes, especially to the borders of your painting. While the layer is still wet, add some brushstrokes of Alizarin, mostly at the top of the painting and in the middle part of the sky. Then, add a line with Sap Green near the horizon by spreading the paint naturally on the wet layer to create soft bushes using the wet-on-wet technique.

Allow the painted layer to dry completely before moving on to the next step.

STEP 2

It's time to paint the meadow itself. We will use the wet-on-wet technique as well as the salt technique.

Prepare purple and violet tints in medium consistency. First, using the same medium round brush or quill brush as in Step 1, start wetting the meadow area, which is the bottom part of our landscape. Then, on the wet layer, begin adding lines and random brushstrokes with the purple and violet tints. Let the colors bleed on the paper to create beautiful blends. You don't need to create an even layer—leave some gaps and areas free from paint, as we will add green there later.

While the layer is still wet, sprinkle just a little salt over it. Make sure it's spread evenly over the meadow area. Then, allow everything to dry completely so the salt can work. Once it's fully dried, gently remove the salt with your finger or a paper towel, being careful not to smudge the paint.

STEP 3

In this step, you can use a medium round brush and a small round brush rather than a quill brush if it's easier for you. Prepare violet tint in a thick consistency and Sap Green in a medium consistency.

First, using Sap Green, paint another layer of bushes closer to the viewer. These will appear more saturated and less blurred than the background. You can paint similar shapes to mine or create your own above the horizon line. Once that's done, use a small round brush to add grass strokes in the gaps we created in the meadow. Make sure the strokes closer to the viewer are larger, while those farther away are smaller for a realistic look.

Next, use violet tint to add random brushstrokes to the middle ground of the meadow, focusing more on one side of the landscape for emphasis.

Once finished, sprinkle a bit of salt on the wet layer and let it dry. When dry, carefully remove the salt to reveal the texture, then move on to the final stage.

STEP 4

It's time to add the final details and bring contrast to our painting. For this, prepare deep green and Burnt Umber in a medium consistency, as well as purple tint in a medium to thick consistency. Take your small round brush, or if it's easier, a medium round brush, and start adding more bushes and tree silhouettes above the horizon line with deep green. Using Burnt Umber, add some brushstrokes and dashes near the horizon in the middle area. Then, with deep green, emphasize details in the grass, varying the shapes and sizes. Don't add too much detail with the green—just a little. Remember to vary the size of the details based on distance: The farther away they are, the smaller they are, and the closer to the foreground they are, the larger they are. Let this layer dry a bit.

For the final stage, I suggest using the sponge technique. Dip a dry sponge in purple tint and lightly add some touches to the foreground of the middle area. Be careful not to overdo it, as too much could cover the beautiful effect we created with the salt.

Remove the washi tape, and voilà—your dreamy landscape is complete!

Try experimenting with different details, colors, and compositions!

Step 4

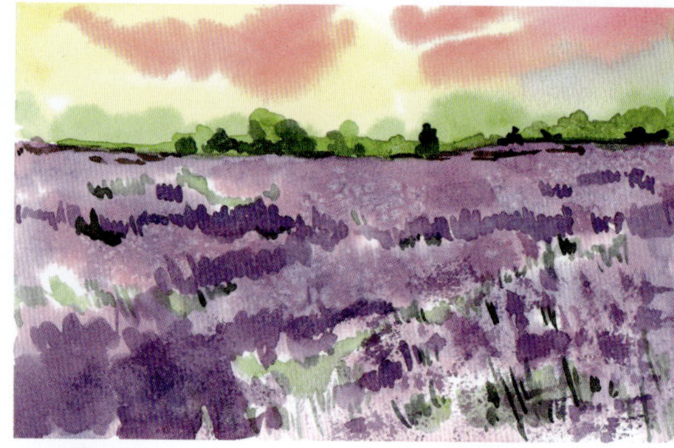

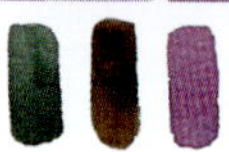

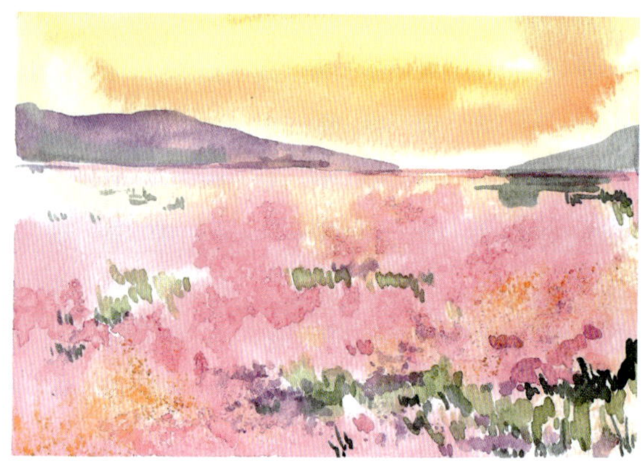

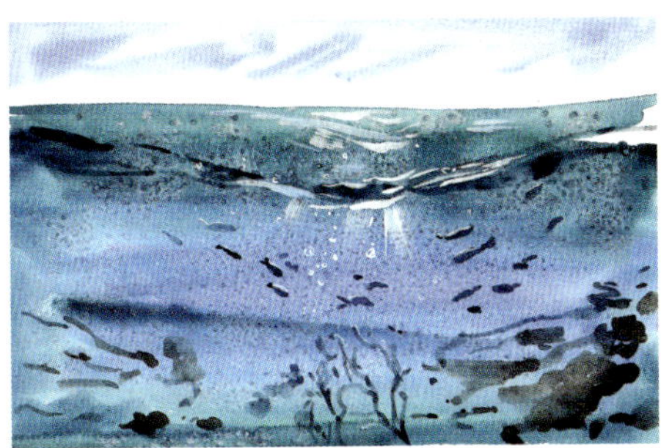

Deep Underwater Mystery

This project is amazing because you'll see how easily you can create beautiful, deep colors in an underwater scene. By adding texture with salt, we create a lovely effect that imitates bubbles in water. The salt texture combined with layered details adds depth and makes the scene more dynamic.

This project is ideal if you like precision, as it requires patience. Let's create a mysterious underwater scene together!

SUPPLIES

- Watercolor paper
- Washi tape or masking tape
- Pencil and eraser (optional)
- Quill brushes (sizes 4–6)
- Round brushes: small (sizes 1–4) and medium (sizes 6–8)
- Flat brush
- Kitchen salt
- White gouache

NOTE: You can experiment with colors in this project, especially with the tints created by mixing blue with Viridian. You can blend these two colors in different proportions to create a variety of mixtures that can be used for the base layer. Additionally, instead of Prussian Blue, you can try other blue shades.

PROJECT COLORS

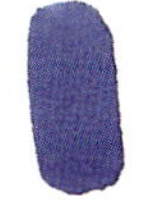
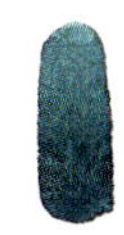
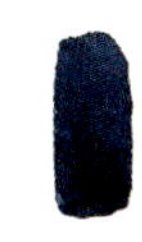

Ultramarine | Green blue tint | Blue green tint | Blue gray tint

COLOR MIXING

- Green blue tint: Mix Viridian with a bit of blue (I use Prussian Blue).
- Blue green tint: Add a little Viridian to Prussian Blue.
- Blue gray tint: Mix blue (I use Indigo) with Burnt Umber.

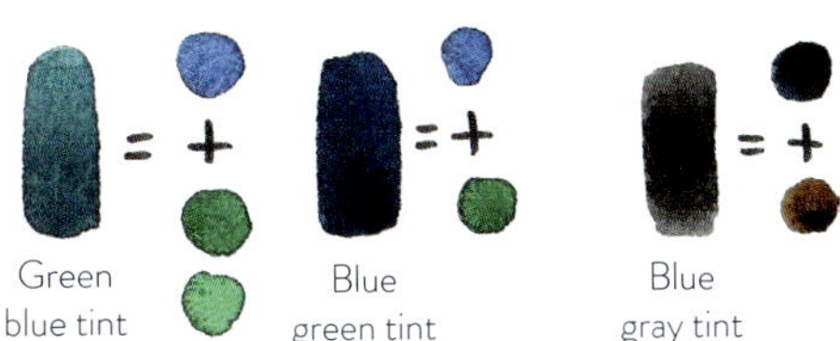

Step 1

Step 2

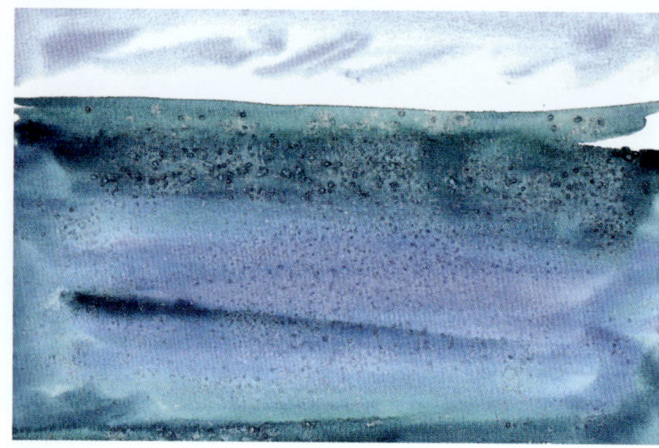

PREPARATION WORK

Secure your watercolor paper to a table using washi tape to prevent it from warping.

A detailed sketch is not required for this project. However, if you prefer, you can use a pencil to lightly mark the waterline that divides the sky and the underwater scene. It doesn't need to be a perfectly straight line; it's better if it's slightly curved.

STEP 1

Let's start painting our underwater scene. First, use a quill brush to lightly wet the underwater area with water. Then, while the layer is still wet, start adding colors with the same brush. You can use Ultramarine, green blue tint, or blue green tint in a medium consistency, applying them to different parts of the wet underwater area.

In my example, I add a few brushstrokes of Ultramarine in the center, followed by some brushstrokes of blue green and green blue tints at the top and bottom of the water area.

While the layer is still wet, generously sprinkle salt, but be sure to spread it evenly and avoid adding too much salt in any one area.

Let everything dry completely before moving on to the next step.

STEP 2

First, once the salt is completely dry, carefully remove it from the paper. Be cautious, as you can smudge the painted layer with your fingers, and take care not to move any salt particles into the white area of the sky. Once you've removed the salt, you'll have a beautifully textured base.

Now, let's move to the sky. Lightly moisten the sky area with a medium-sized round brush, or you can continue using the same quill brush from the underwater area. Then, using Ultramarine in a watery consistency, begin adding blue to the sky from the top, gradually fading it as you approach the waterline. This creates a transition from transparent Ultramarine to white. You can also add a few extra brushstrokes to mimic sky textures.

Once everything is ready, allow it to dry completely before moving on to the next step.

Step 3

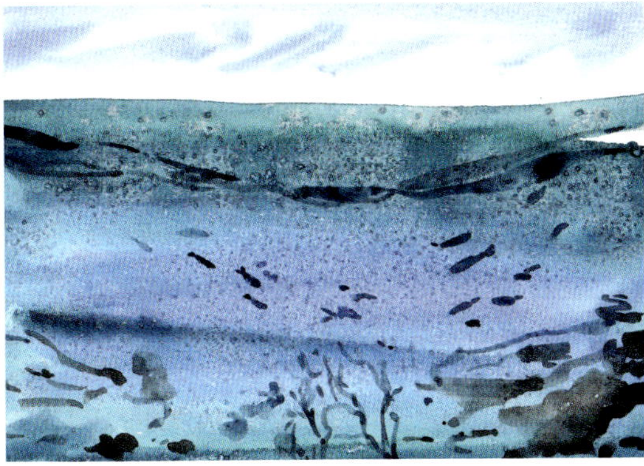

Step 4

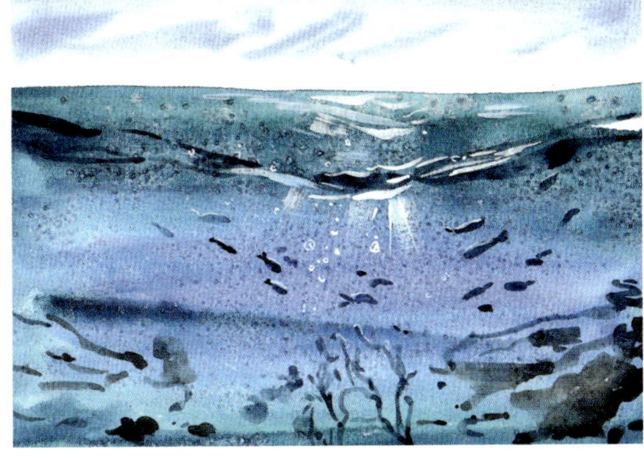

STEP 3

We've already created texture and deep colors. Now let's turn this painting into a true underwater scene. For this, we'll use the layering technique. Take a small round brush; you can also use a medium round brush for larger details. Then, prepare a thick consistency of blue gray and blue green tints.

Now, start adding details. You can add stones, seaweed, and fish silhouettes, and emphasize the wave that flows through the underwater scene. The most important thing when adding details is to keep them imperfect. Once you're happy with the result, let everything dry completely before moving on to the final step.

STEP 4

Now, let's turn this painting into a true masterpiece. For this step, you can add extra details using the project colors, but it's optional, and I don't recommend overloading the painting. Instead, I suggest using a small round brush with a fine tip and white gouache paint to add highlights and lighting effects to the scene.

Add a bit of water to the white gouache, but keep the paint fairly thick. Begin adding highlights and light details to the underwater area: some bubbles, light reflections on the water, and a light effect in the large wave. Also add light along the contours of silhouettes, such as fish and seaweed. Feel free to experiment, but be careful not to overdo it.

Next, take a flat brush (or, if you don't have one, a round brush will work). Moisten it lightly, then dry it with a paper towel so it's almost dry. Use this brush with white gouache to add light brushstrokes that imitate sunlight streaming through the water. These details make your painting look more interesting and complete, as if real light is filtering through the water.

When adding the white highlights, ensure they come from the same side as your light source, so the lighting feels logical. Once you're satisfied with the results, your painting is finished!

Try experimenting with different details, colors, and compositions!

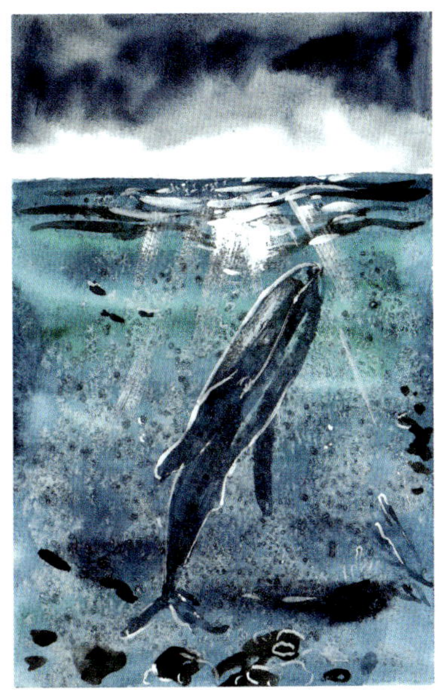

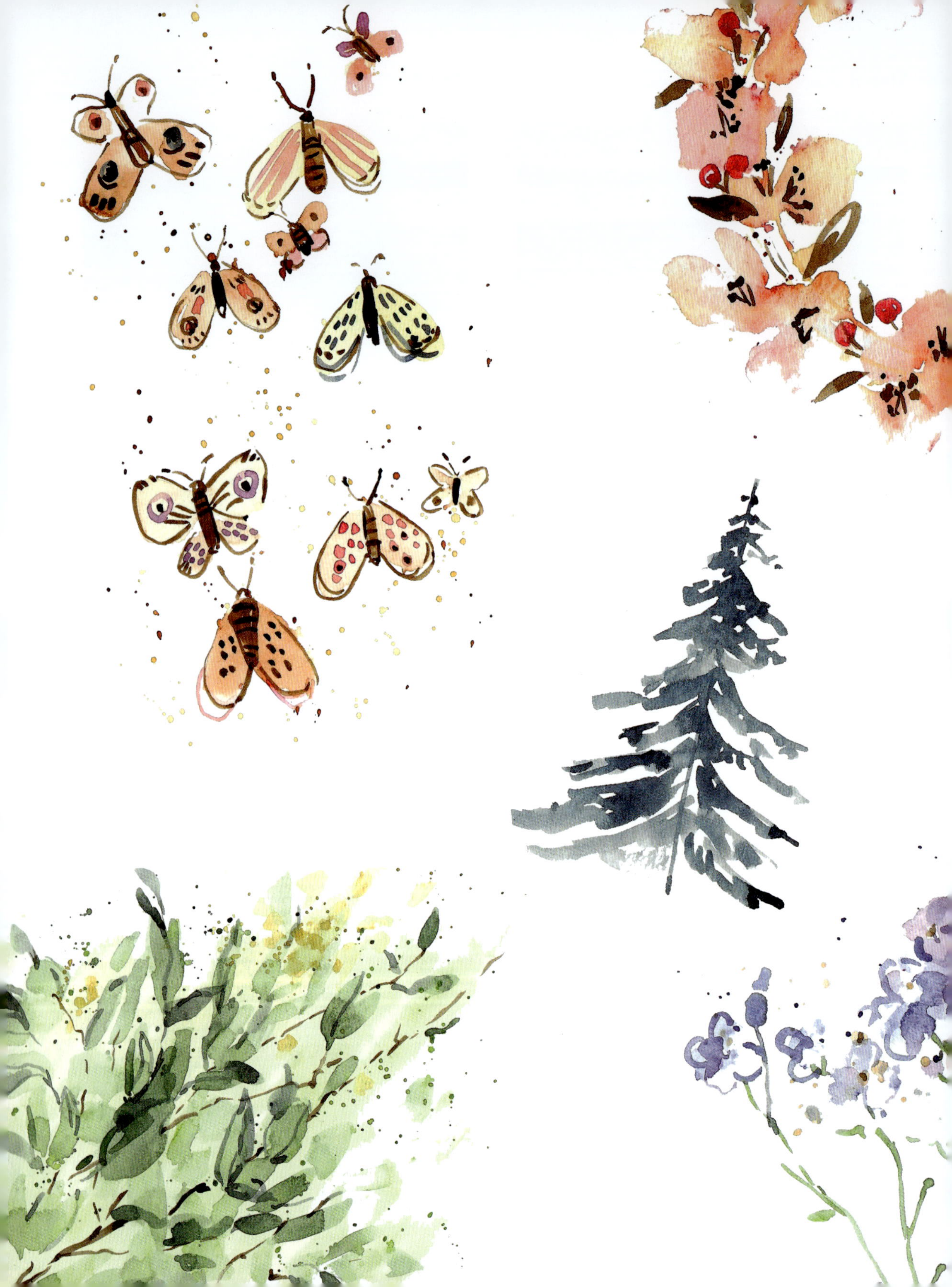

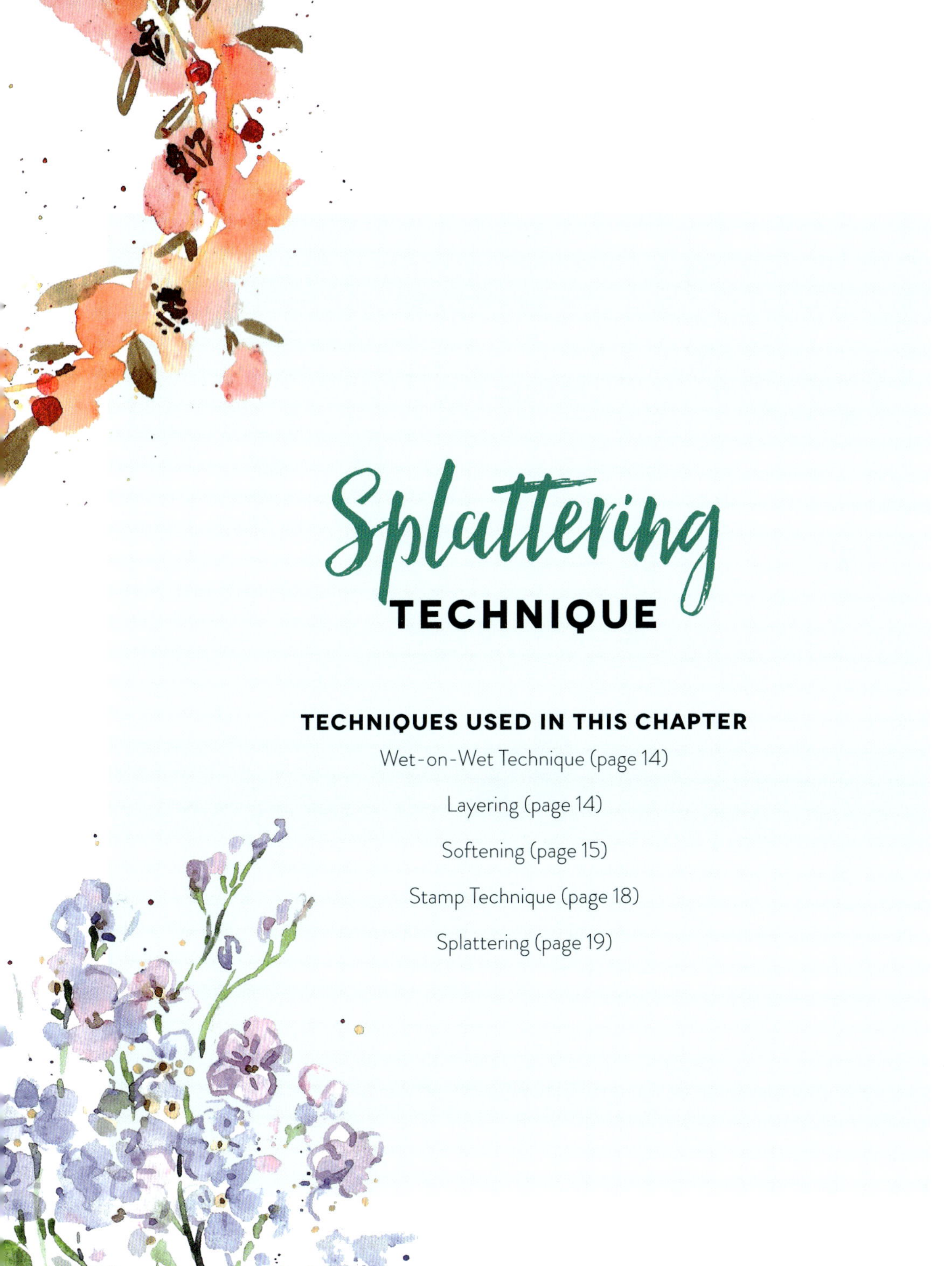

Splattering
TECHNIQUE

TECHNIQUES USED IN THIS CHAPTER

Wet-on-Wet Technique (page 14)

Layering (page 14)

Softening (page 15)

Stamp Technique (page 18)

Splattering (page 19)

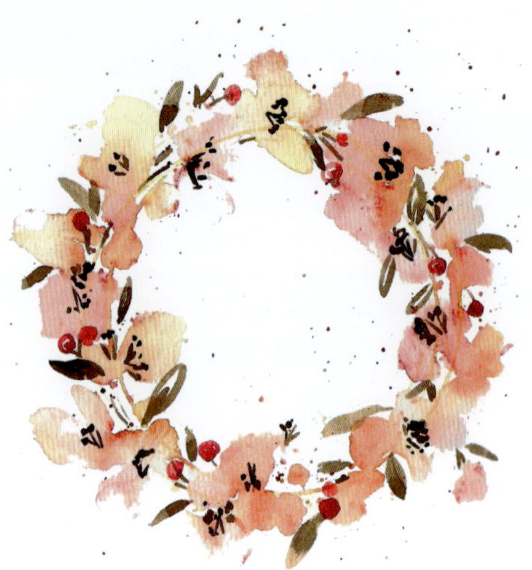

Delicate Wreath

This project is a wonderful way to create quick and impressive watercolor floral wreaths by using the splattering technique. It's absolutely fun, and you'll see that watercolor can truly give you a sense of freedom. Let's paint a delicate and tender wreath.

PROJECT COLORS

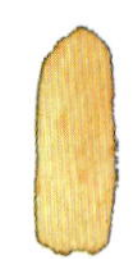 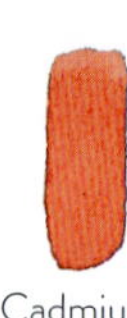 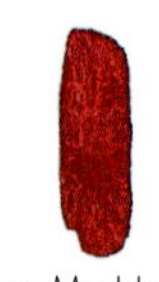 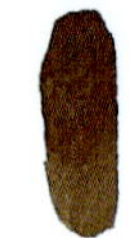

Yellow Ochre   Cadmium Red   Rose Madder or Alizarin Crimson   Brown tint

COLOR MIXING

- Brown tint: Add a little Yellow Ochre to Burnt Umber.

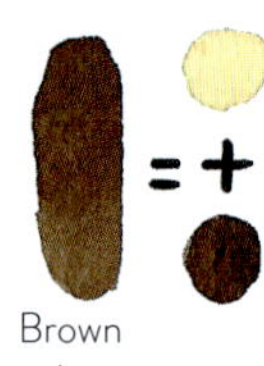

Brown tint

TIP: When painting a wreath, I don't recommend choosing too many colors. It's best to plan your project colors in advance and keep your palette limited. For example, you can select a few colors and mix them together to create new shades. This approach will help you achieve a more harmonious and natural-looking result. Additionally, I encourage you to experiment with colors. Instead of traditional green for leaves, try using unconventional shades like brown or blue green, which can often look stunning.

SUPPLIES

- Watercolor paper
- Washi tape or masking tape (optional)
- Pencil and eraser (optional)
- Rounded object (cup, glass, or jar) the desired size of your wreath
- Round brushes: small (sizes 1–4) and medium (sizes 6–8)

NOTE: This project can get quite messy, so make sure you have an apron and cover your table to keep it clean, as we'll be using the splattering technique a lot.

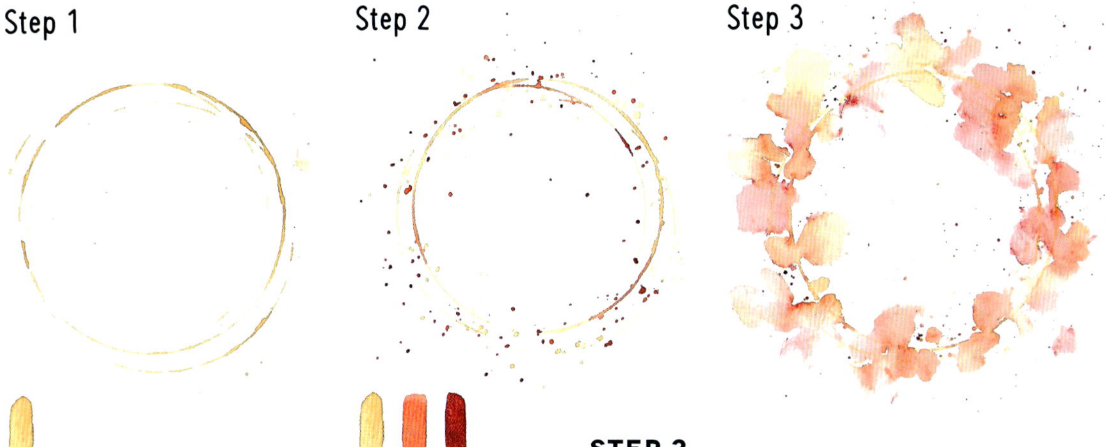

PREPARATION WORK

If you'd like, you can secure your paper to the table or a board using washi tape. We won't be making any preliminary sketches, but make sure you have a clear idea of where you want to place your wreath—for example, at the center of the paper. You can even use a pencil to lightly mark the center of your wreath.

STEP 1

Prepare a medium consistency Yellow Ochre. Then, take your medium round brush, pick your round object, and start applying the paint to the edges of the object. Make sure all the edges are evenly covered with paint. Next, turn the cup upside down and press it onto the paper where you want to add your wreath.

Repeat this process a few times—at least two or three, or even four if you prefer. Three is usually ideal, but make sure you slightly change the position of the cup each time you press. In the end, you should have a few thin, imperfect circles in Yellow Ochre. These form the base for the wreath and add a playful, natural look.

Now you can move on to the next step, or, if you'd like, let everything dry first and then continue. Either way will work.

STEP 2

Prepare the following colors in a medium consistency: Yellow Ochre, Cadmium Red, and Rose Madder. Then, using the medium round brush, start adding splatters around the entire diameter of your wreath with each color.

If you feel nervous about splattering, you can practice on a separate piece of paper first. However, I assure you that we'll blur the splatters in the next step to make them look like flowers, so it's okay if some splatters aren't perfect.

Work quickly! Start by splattering Yellow Ochre, then move on to Cadmium Red, and finally add a few splatters of Rose Madder. Add the splatters randomly along the circles. Make sure to work quickly, as you'll move on to the next step as soon as you finish splattering.

STEP 3

Now, take your medium round brush, clean it, wet it, wipe off the excess water, and start blurring the splatters you've created with the brush. Using just water, you can create shapes, petals, or flowers of various sizes.

I recommend cleaning your brush from time to time and wiping off the excess water so it's damp but not too wet. Just enjoy the process and ensure the entire wreath is filled with blossoms.

Once you're happy with the result, let everything dry completely and move on to the final step.

Step 4

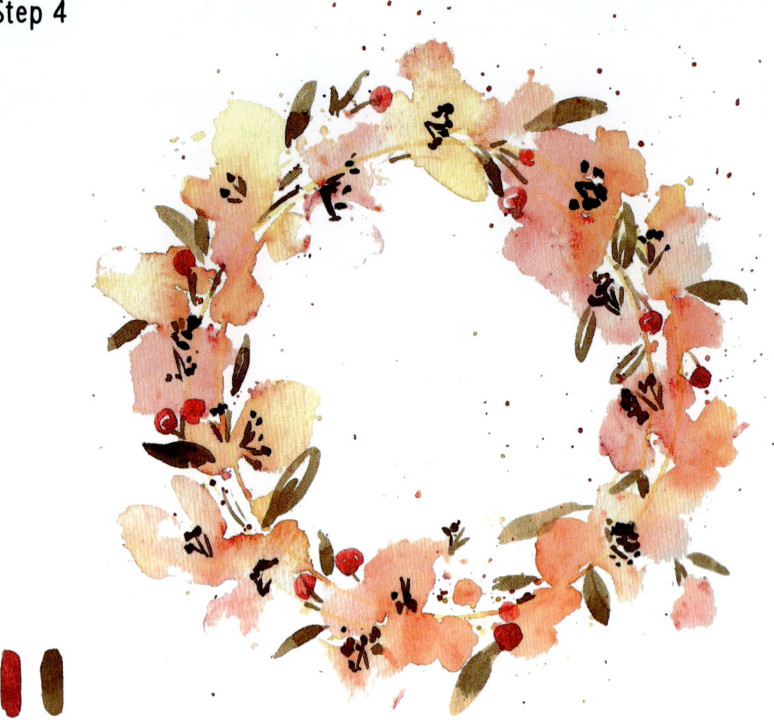

STEP 4

Now it's time to add the final details and bring some contrast and a finished look to your wreath. Prepare medium consistency brown tint and Rose Madder.

Start by picking your medium round brush and adding leaves along the wreath. Ensure the leaves follow a logical direction around the wreath, and vary their shapes and sizes for a more natural look. Then, switch to a small round brush and use it to add small details to the flowers, such as their centers, as well as some small branches and other fine details.

Don't worry about making them perfect or identical—variation always adds charm. Just make sure everything aligns with the overall direction and flow of the wreath.

Finally, using the small round brush and Rose Madder, add a few berries to the wreath. Vary their sizes and placement to make the composition more interesting. Avoid placing berries too evenly or symmetrically. Play with these details to enhance the visual appeal of your wreath.

And that's it! Your wreath is complete. Remember, don't add too many details—simplicity is key.

Try experimenting with different details, colors, and compositions!

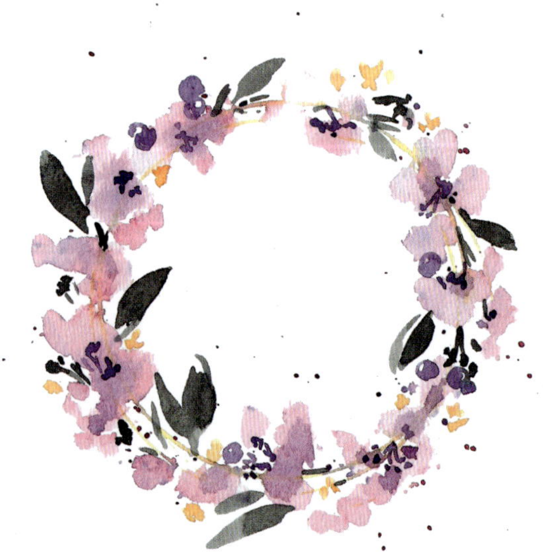

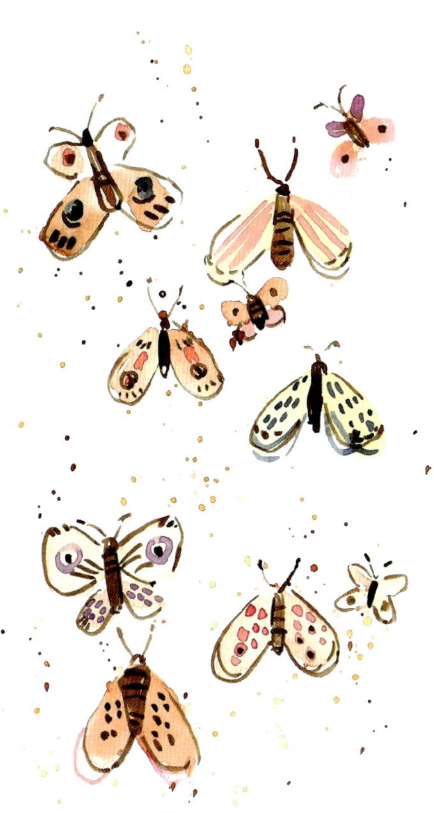

Flowing Moths

Let's paint beautiful and elegant Flowing Moths. This project is so much fun to create and very quick, making it perfect for a warm-up, a way to ease back into watercolor painting, doodling, or kicking an art block!

PROJECT COLORS

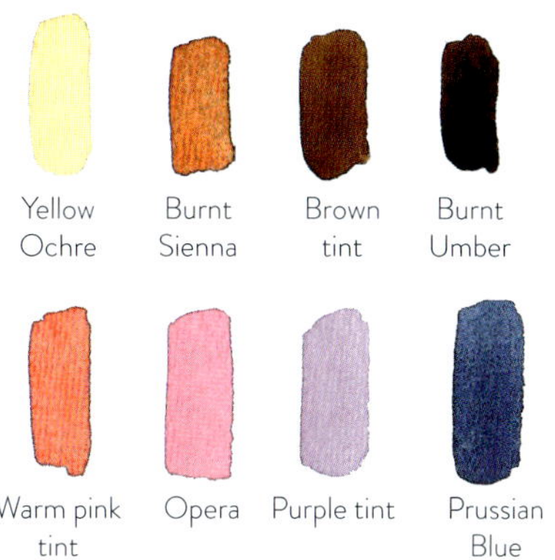

Yellow Ochre

Burnt Sienna

Brown tint

Burnt Umber

Warm pink tint

Opera

Purple tint

Prussian Blue

SUPPLIES

- Watercolor paper
- Washi tape or masking tape (optional)
- Pencil and eraser (optional)
- Round brushes: small (sizes 1–4) and medium (sizes 6–8)

COLOR MIXING

- Brown tint: Add a little Burnt Umber to Burnt Sienna.
- Warm pink tint: Mix Opera with a bit of Yellow Ochre.
- Purple tint: Add a little Ultramarine to Opera.

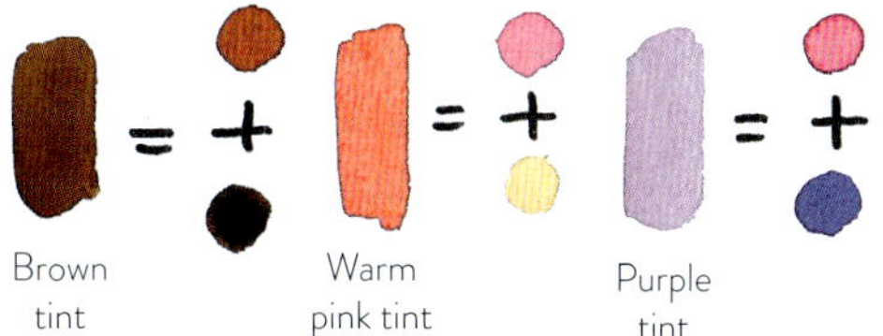

Brown tint

Warm pink tint

Purple tint

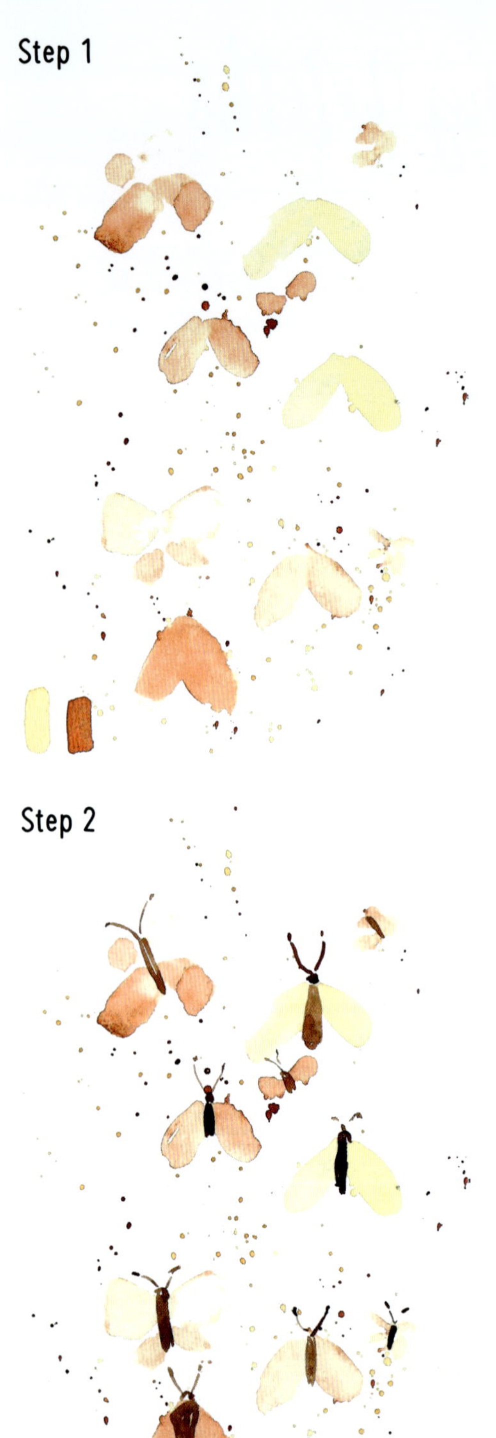

PREPARATION WORK

For this project, it is not mandatory to secure the watercolor paper to the table with washi tape, but if you prefer, you can do so. Also, there is no need for preliminary sketching—just let the splattering technique do all the work for you.

However, if you feel more confident with some guidance, you can lightly mark the centers of your moths with a pencil to plan the flow and composition of your project. Make sure the marks are barely visible.

STEP 1

Prepare Yellow Ochre and Burnt Sienna in medium consistency. Using a medium round brush, and working quickly, start adding generous splatters with both colors.

You can create a flow with the splatters or add them in any way you like. However, the splatters should mainly be chaotic and freestyle. Again, work quickly, because once the paint starts to dry, you won't be able to blur it with water.

Clean the same medium round brush and use it wet to blur some of the splatters to form wings.

These can look like fully open wings or partially closed ones. You can follow my composition as closely as possible or create your own, depending on your splatter patterns.

NOTE: Be sure to clean your brush frequently to avoid transferring pigment from one area to another. You don't need to blur all the splatters. Just make sure you have enough shapes to represent the wings of your moths.

Once you are happy with the result, let it dry completely before moving on to the next step.

STEP 2

Now, prepare medium consistency brown tint and Burnt Umber, and switch to a small round brush. Start adding details to the center of your moths' bodies as well as the antennae of your moths.

You can follow my design or create your own. Just make sure they are not all the same—experiment with different types of details.

Let everything dry completely before moving on to the next step.

Step 3

Step 4

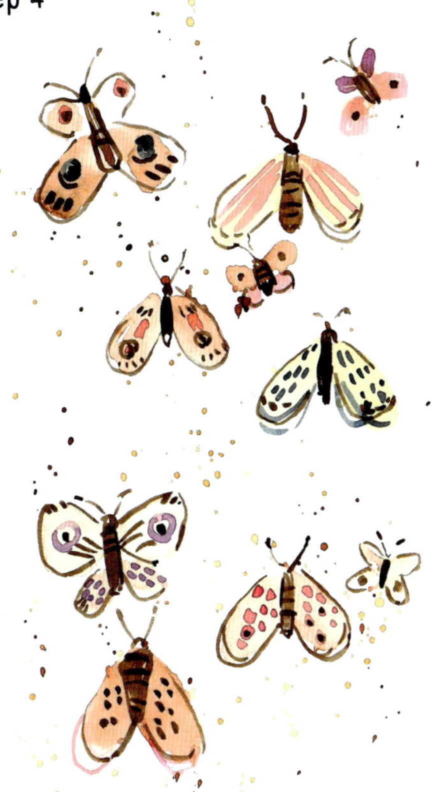

STEP 3

Prepare warm pink tint, Opera, purple tint, and blue in medium consistency. Using a small round brush, start adding details to the wings or the body, such as spots, dashes, circles, stripes, and lines.

Feel free to experiment and play with the details, or you can follow my design. Make sure the details are loose with some imperfections.

Let everything dry completely before moving on to the final step.

STEP 4

Prepare Burnt Umber in medium consistency and start adding the final details to your moths. Focus on the bodies and antennae, and especially on defining and detailing the wings. Know when to stop.

Try experimenting with different details, colors, and compositions!

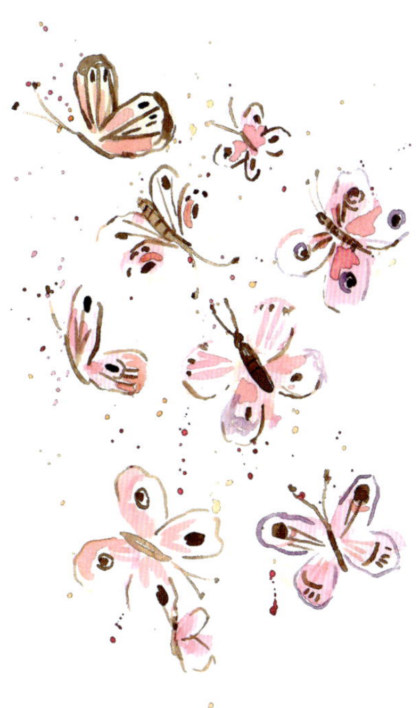

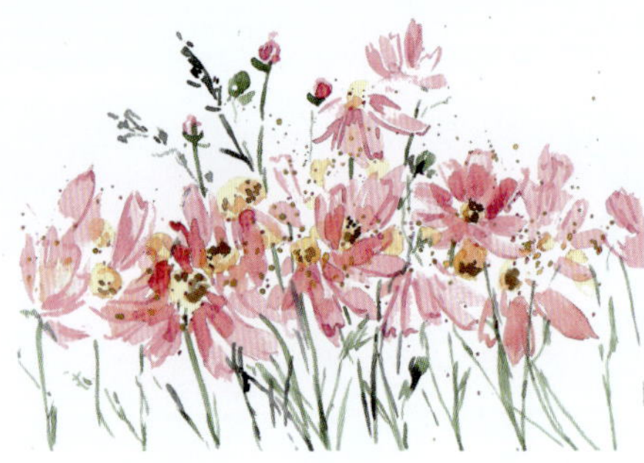

Splatter of Wildflowers

Let's explore the splattering technique to create tender, delicate wildflowers. You'll be amazed at how quickly you can paint these! The splattering does most of the work for you. All you need to do is follow the flow and enjoy the process. Let's get started!

SUPPLIES

- Watercolor paper
- Washi tape or masking tape (optional)
- Pencil and eraser (optional)
- Round brushes: small (sizes 1–4) medium (sizes 6–8)

PROJECT COLORS

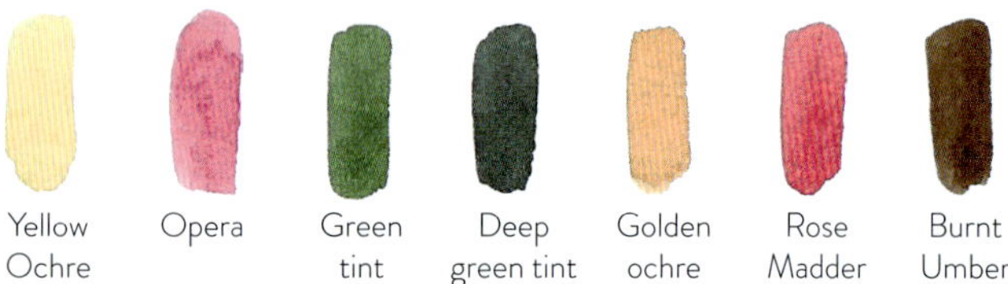

COLOR MIXING

- Green tint: Add a little Indigo (or any other blue) to Sap Green.

- Deep green tint: Mix Sap Green with blue (Indigo or Prussian Blue) to achieve a rich and deep green tint.

- Golden ochre: Add a little Burnt Sienna to Yellow Ochre.

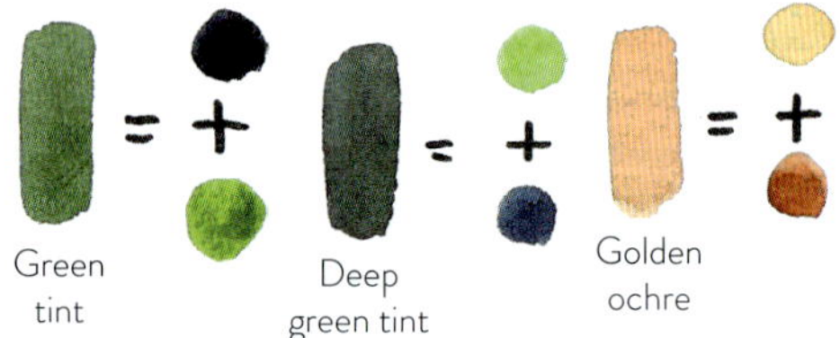

NOTE: For this project, you can experiment with colors, but I advise you to limit them. For example, use three to a maximum of four colors for the flowers. If you use more, it might make the painting look muddy instead of delicate. I love starting this project with Yellow Ochre to create the centers of the flowers.

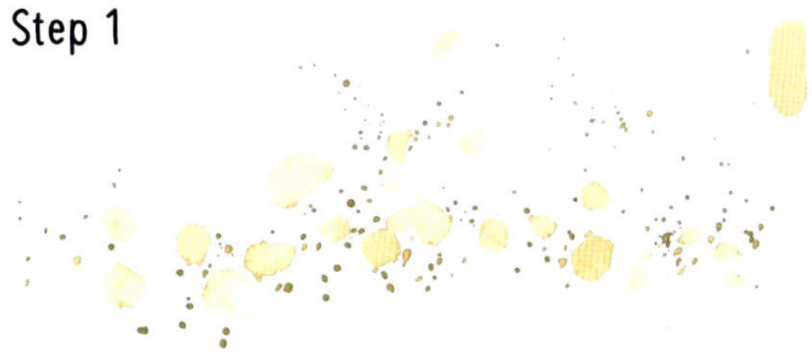

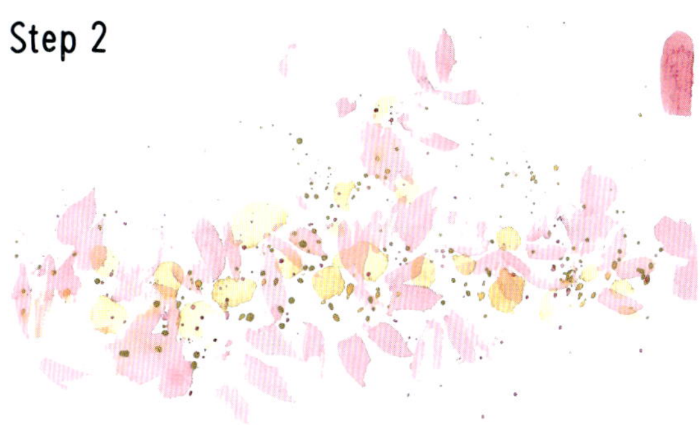

PREPARATION WORK

If you'd like, you can secure your paper to the table with washi tape to prevent wrinkling or movement while working.

This project doesn't require any preliminary sketching, and we will paint it in a very free and loose style. However, if you find it helpful, I suggest lightly sketching some stems of the flowers.

STEP 1

Let's start by adding the centers of our flowers. For this, prepare medium consistency Yellow Ochre. Use a medium round brush and begin adding splatters to the central part of your painting, focusing on a horizontal line in the middle. You can add a few extra splatters above this line to create a composition base.

Next, clean the same brush, wet it, and remove the excess water. Use it to blend some of the splatters to form the centers of the flowers. You don't need to blur all the splatters—just some of them. Make sure they vary in shape, size, and direction to create visual interest and balance.

Once you're done, let it dry completely before moving on to the next step.

STEP 2

Now, we will use the same method to add petals to our flowers. Prepare Opera in medium consistency and use the same medium round brush. Generously load your brush with Opera and start adding splatters on top of the flower centers you've already painted. Focus on the middle of the paper and the areas where you placed the centers.

Once you're happy with the result, take a clean, wet medium brush and start blurring the splatters to form the petals. Make sure the petals have a defined shape. Work quickly because the splatters will dry, and you won't be able to shape them afterward. The petals should vary in size, shape, and direction to make the composition more dynamic.

If you need to add more petals, you can carefully do so while the layer is still wet. However, avoid adding splatters on already painted areas, as it might make the painting less delicate. Instead, it's better to add more splatters first and then blur them.

Finally, let everything dry completely before moving to the next step.

STEP 3

Now it's time to add the green parts of our flowers. For this, prepare medium consistency green tint and deep green tint. For this step, you can use both brushes: a small round brush for the stems and small details, and a medium round brush for the leaves.

Start by adding the green parts using both colors. I recommend beginning with the stems of the flowers. Then, add some buds, small leaves, and other details. If you'd like, refer to a photo of real flowers to observe how their leaves, stems, and other parts look and grow. This can help you replicate their natural appearance.

For this project, I am aiming to create cosmos flowers, so I try to include their recognizable details.

Once you're happy with the result, let everything dry completely before moving on to the next step.

Step 3

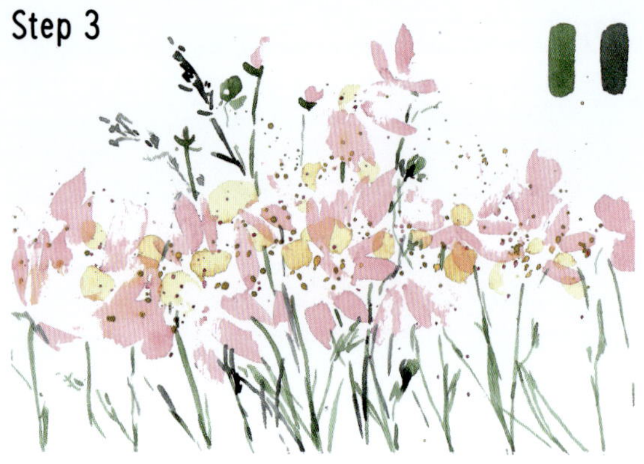

Step 4

STEP 4

Now let's add a second layer to our flowers using the layering technique.

Prepare golden ochre and Opera in medium consistency and pick up your small round brush.

Using Opera, I suggest defining the petals further. Refine their shapes if you'd like and add extra brushstrokes inside some petals. You can also add details to the buds. However, try to keep these details freestyle; avoid making them too perfect or symmetrical.

Next, use golden ochre to add details to the centers of the flowers with small touches, spots, and dashes. You can also emphasize the bottom parts of the centers, but again, keep them varied and avoid making all the centers look the same.

Allow everything to dry completely, and then move on to the final step.

STEP 5

You can skip this step, but I believe it makes this piece complete! Prepare Rose Madder and Burnt Umber in medium consistency, and pick up your medium round brush. If you prefer, you can continue working with a small round brush.

I suggest choosing a few flowers to act as the foreground, closer to the viewer, and making them more saturated by adding extra brushstrokes to the petals using Rose Madder. Additionally, you can enhance their centers with Burnt Umber.

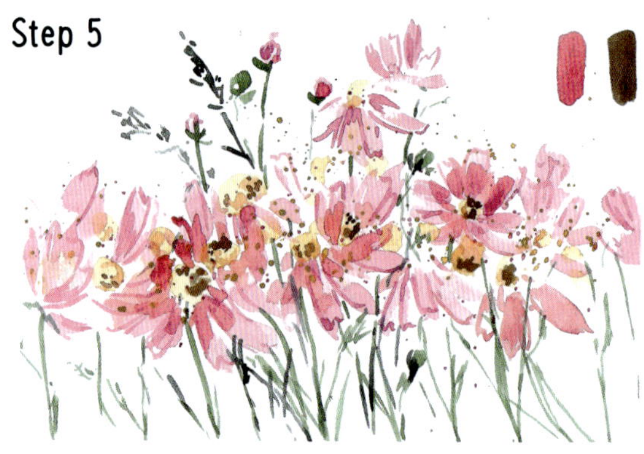

Step 5

And that's it! Leave the painting as it is, because your delicate wildflowers are complete.

Try experimenting with different details, colors, and compositions!

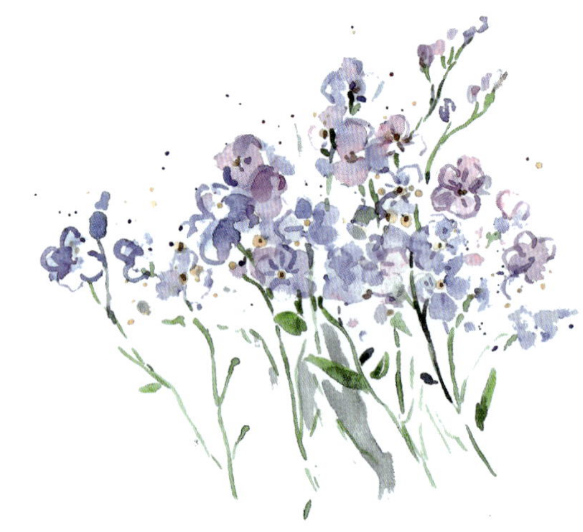

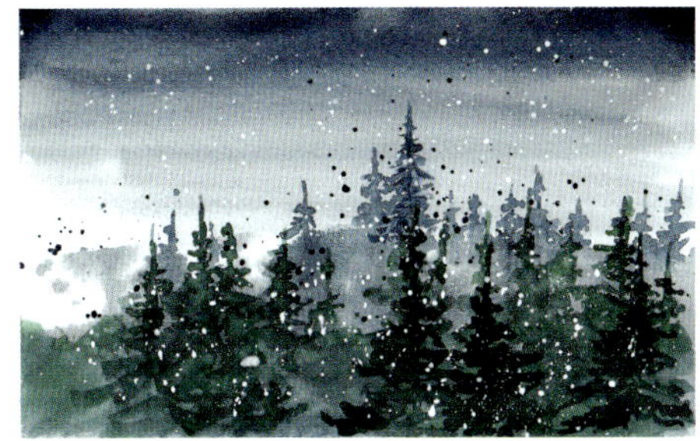

Fir Trees in Snow

Dive into this impressive and quick project. Step by step, you'll enjoy creating a beautiful, wintry landscape. You'll learn how to use splattering to create an expressive, transparent watercolor background, how to add layers one by one, and finally, how to add a contrasting final touch using splattering and white gouache. This project doesn't require much time but always turns out beautifully. Let's let the flow inspire us!

SUPPLIES

- Watercolor paper
- Washi tape or masking tape
- Pencil and eraser (optional)
- Quill brushes (sizes 1–4) or soft large round brush (sizes 9–12)
- Round brushes: small (sizes 1–4) and medium (sizes 6–8)
- White gouache
- Toothbrush (optional)

NOTE: For this project, it is especially important to use thick watercolor paper, as we will be using a lot of water.

PROJECT COLORS

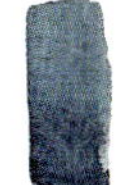 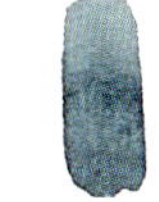 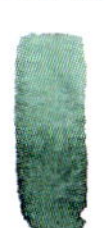

Indigo   Blue green tint   Green tint

NOTE: If you don't have Indigo, you can use Prussian Blue or any other cool blue tone you have. Add a little Burnt Umber to mute it slightly.

COLOR MIXING

- Blue green tint: Add a little Viridian to Indigo.
- Green tint: Add a touch of Indigo to Viridian.

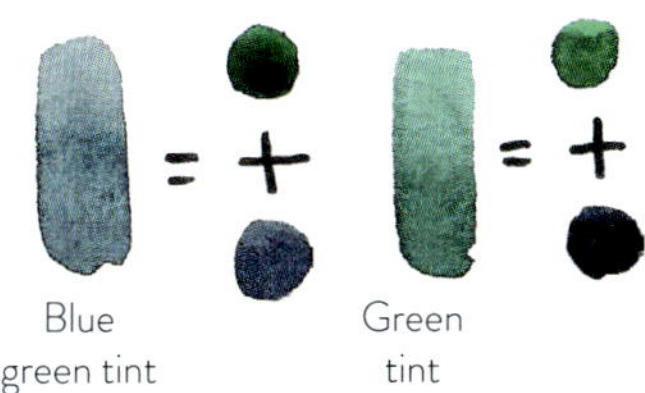

TIP: You can experiment with these colors and try mixing more shades, such as green and blue green tints. Add a little Sap Green or Burnt Umber to create natural colors, which you can also use for the project.

PREPARATION WORK

Secure your watercolor paper to your table or board with washi tape.

You will not need to do any preliminary sketching, but if it makes you feel more confident, you can lightly mark a few trees in the foreground with a pencil.

Step 1

STEP 1

First, pick your quill brush and begin wetting the top part of your paper, moving down to the middle section. While the paper is still wet, use the same brush to add horizontal brushstrokes of Indigo in medium consistency.

(Continued)

As you move toward the middle section, gradually reduce the intensity of the Indigo by blending it with water until it becomes fully transparent.

Let everything dry completely before moving on to the next step.

STEP 2

Now, prepare a blue green tint in medium consistency. This time, use a quill brush to wet the bottom part of the paper up to the middle with clean water. While the layer is still wet, use a medium round brush to add some splatters of blue green tint.

NOTE: Some splatters might end up in the sky, and that's perfectly fine. It will add extra charm to your work.

The paint will spread on the wet layer, creating the illusion of blurred trees in the background. You can add more splatters if you feel the layer should be more intense.

Then, using the same medium round brush and the same blue green tint, start forming the tops of some fir trees. This helps create more defined background shapes in our landscape.

Once everything is done, let the painting dry completely before moving on to the next step.

STEP 3

Now let's add middle-ground fir trees. For this, prepare a green tint in medium consistency and thick consistency. We will use the layering technique to build the layout of these trees in two stages.

Use a medium round brush along with a small round brush for finer details.

First, start by painting the bottom area using a medium round brush and green tint in medium consistency. Form the shape of the middle-ground trees by creating the base shape, then add the tops of a few trees using the same brush and color (see Figure 1). Let everything dry completely.

Once it's fully dried, use the thick consistency green tint to add a few trees in the foreground. Start by painting the trunks, then add the branches, and finally fill them in with some loose brushstrokes. The brushstrokes should be loose and natural (see the stages of painting a fir tree in Figure 2).

Let everything dry completely before moving on to the final step.

Step 2

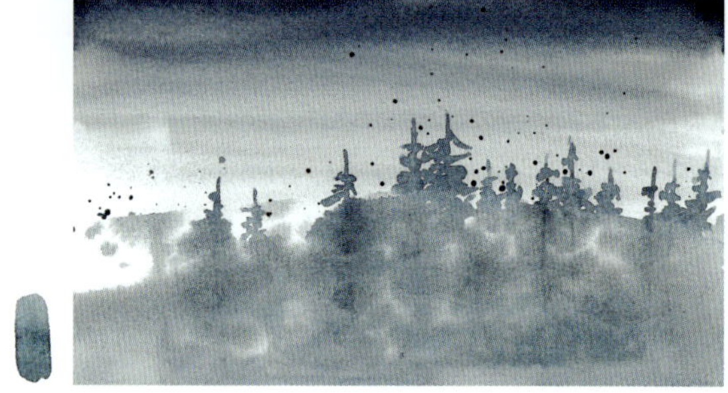

Step 3

Figure 1

Figure 2

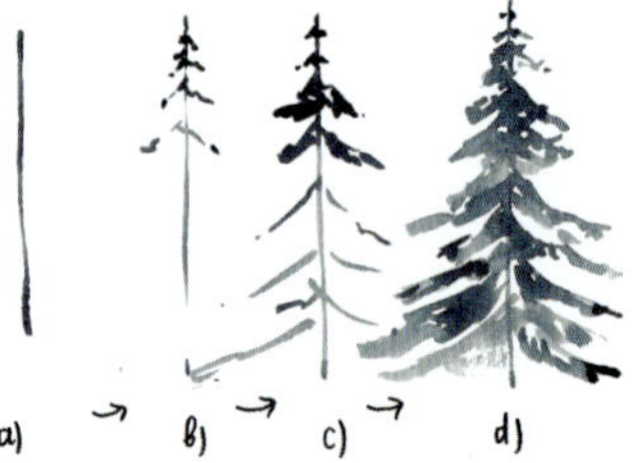

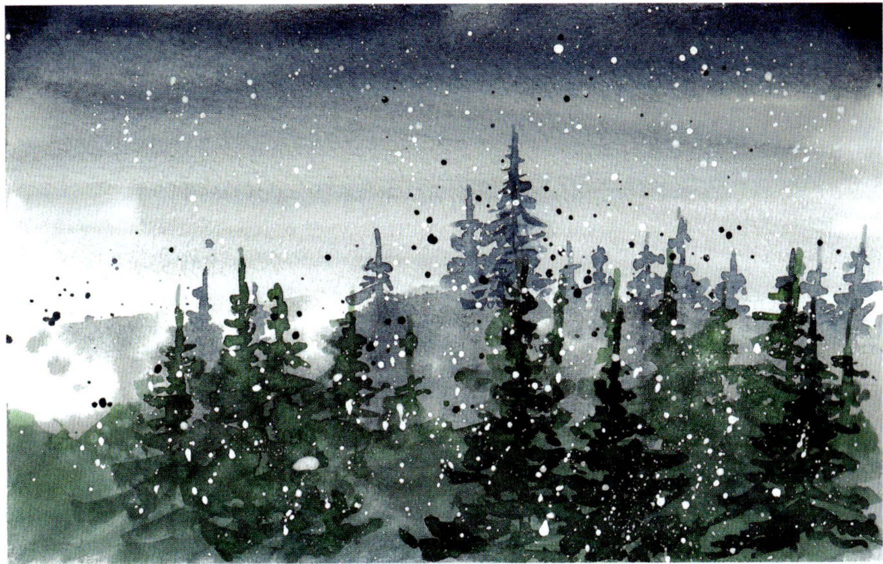

STEP 4

It's time to add the final touch to our painting. We will use white gouache to create the effect of snow using the splattering technique.

First, squeeze some white gouache onto your palette and gradually add water, little by little, until you reach a creamy consistency.

Next, prepare a medium round brush and your toothbrush, if using; if you don't have a toothbrush, use a small round brush.

Start by loading your medium round brush with white gouache and adding two or three splatters at the top of your painting. Let it dry slightly. This will create the effect of snow in the foreground.

Then, use your toothbrush to generously add splatters all around your piece. Once you're happy with the effect of snow on your scenery, your painting is complete.

TIP: If you're not confident about using white gouache for splattering, you can practice first. Take a piece of paper, paint a deep layer of any color (such as Indigo or another dark shade), and practice splattering with white gouache on it. Once you're comfortable with the technique, move on to your main piece.

Try experimenting with different details, colors, and compositions!

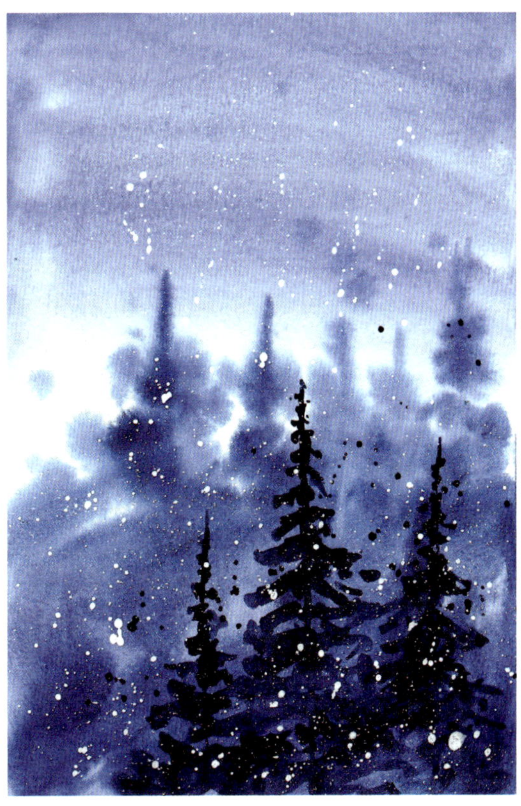

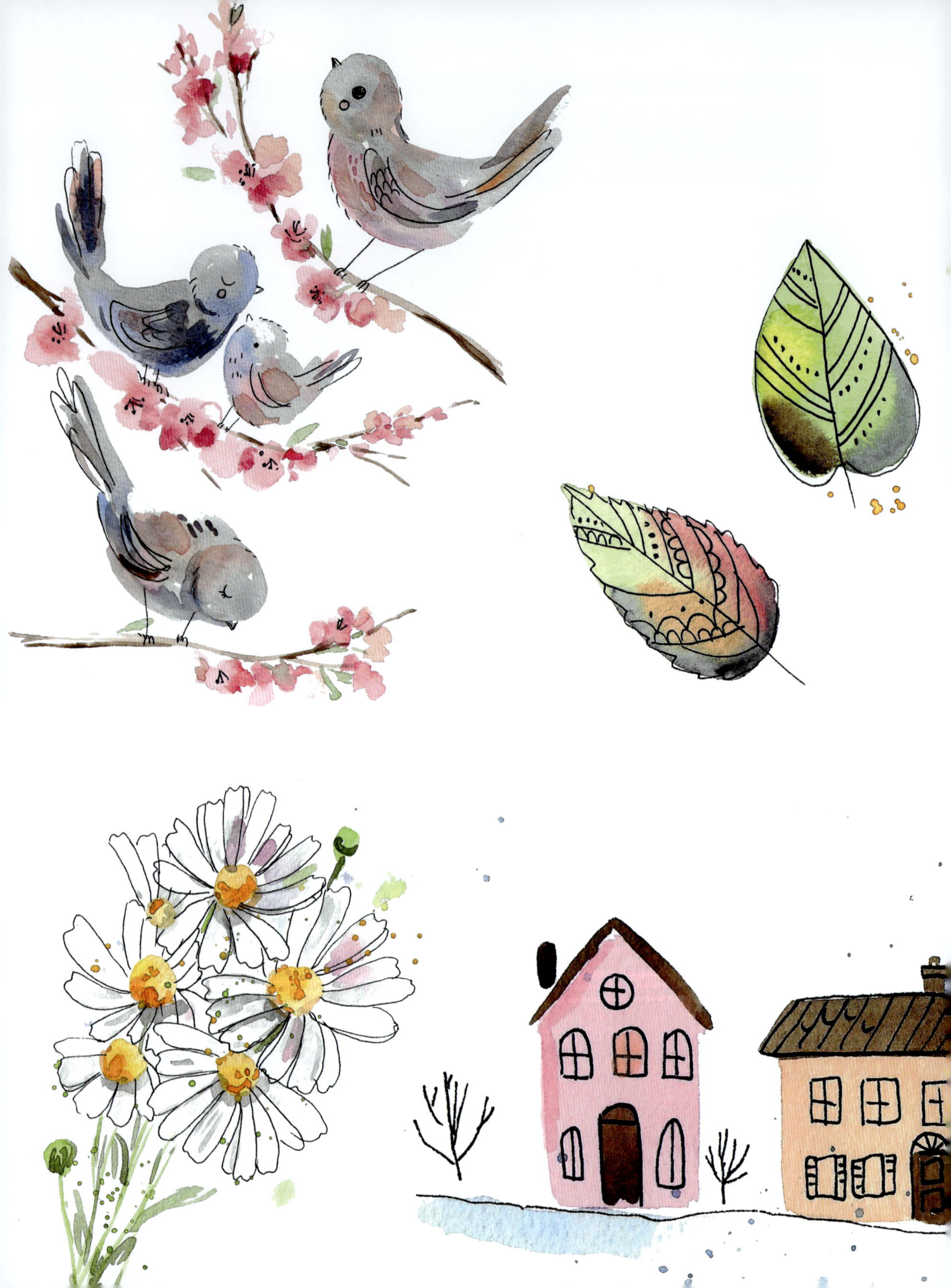

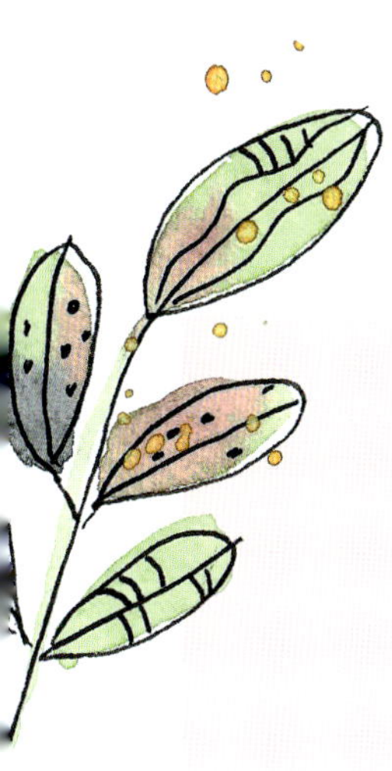

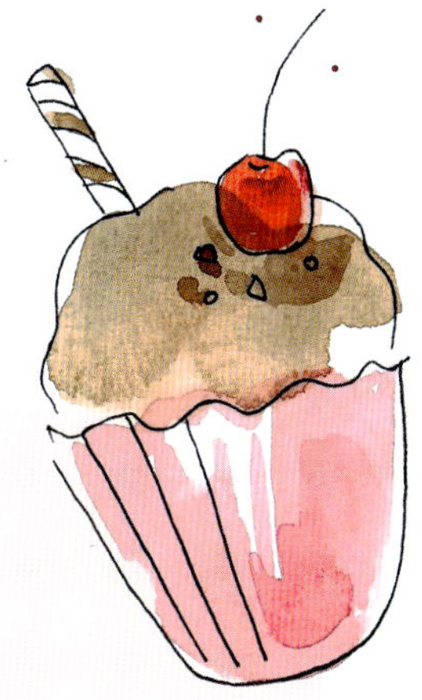

Black Ink Outlining
TECHNIQUE

TECHNIQUES USED IN THIS CHAPTER

Wet-on-Wet Technique (page 14)

Layering (page 14)

Splattering (page 19)

Outlining (page 20)

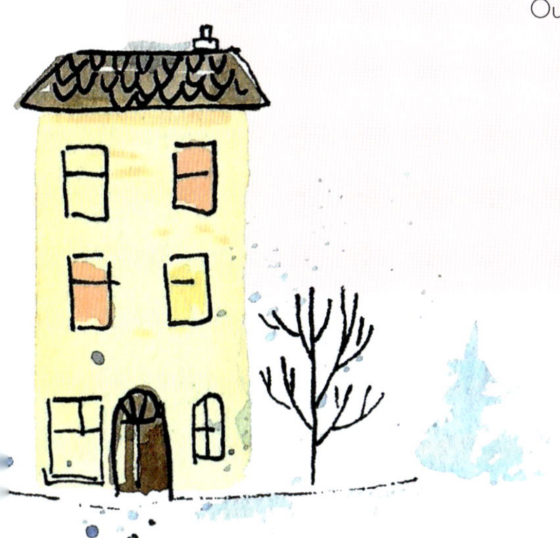

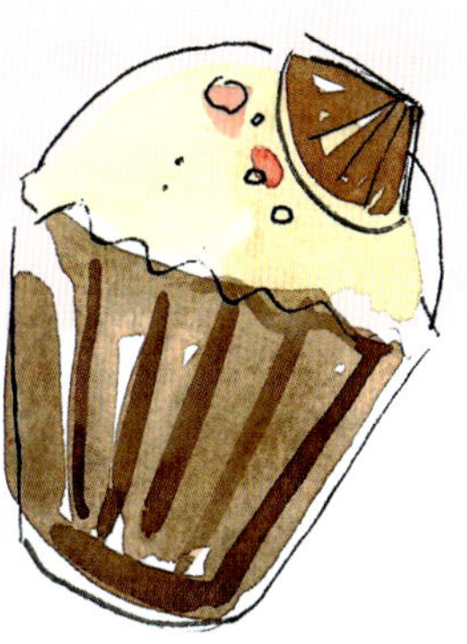

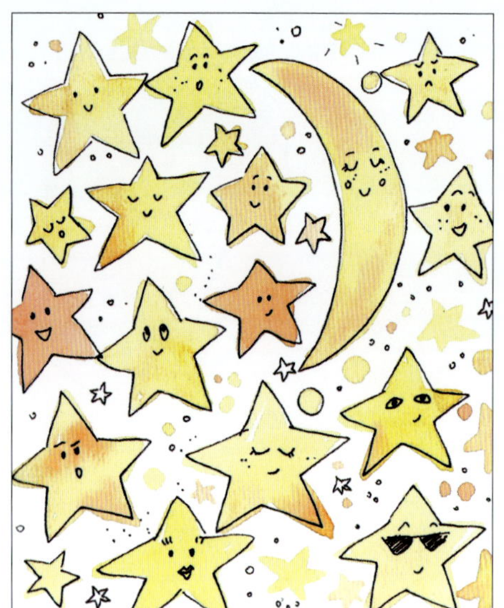

Cute Stars

With watercolor, you can create so much more than landscapes, fruits, or portraits. And it's easier than you think, especially if you use watercolor along with an ink pen for outlining and adding details.

In this project, I will show you how to paint whimsical watercolor stars. This project is simple, and its lessons can be applied to creating other cute illustrations too!

PROJECT COLORS

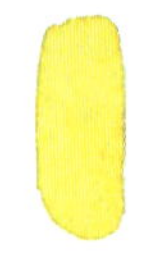 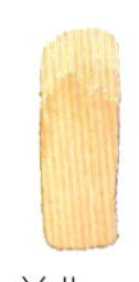 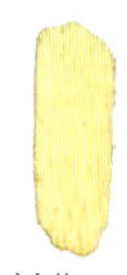

Cadmium Yellow   Yellow orange tint   Yellow Ochre

COLOR MIXING

- Yellow orange tint: Add a little Cadmium Red to Cadmium Yellow.

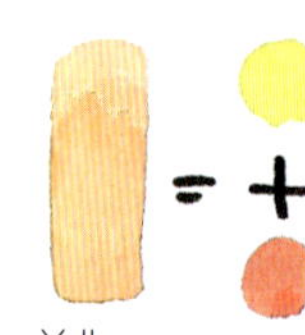

Yellow orange tint

NOTE: You can add more shades of yellow and yellow orange to this project if you'd like, but I believe simplicity always looks best. That is why I recommend keeping your colors limited and using just three or four colors for this project to achieve a clean and balanced look.

SUPPLIES

- Watercolor paper
- Washi tape or masking tape
- Pencil and eraser (optional)
- Round brushes: small (sizes 1–4) and medium (sizes 6–8)
- Black ink pen (size 0.5 or 0.8 mm)

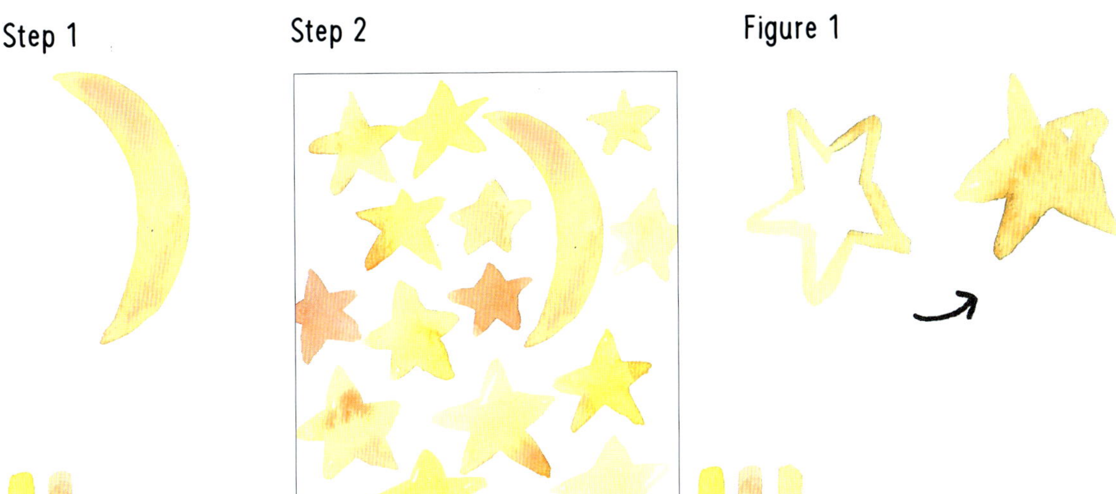

PREPARATION WORK

Let's begin by defining the area where we will paint our watercolor illustration. I recommend using a piece of watercolor paper and securing it with washi tape. This helps define the area where we will add our stars. The tape also prevents the paper from wrinkling while using watercolor.

We will not do any preliminary sketching, and I do not recommend it because it is better to paint directly on the paper with watercolor. This is great practice for loose painting and improving control over your brushstrokes.

STEP 1

First, we will paint the largest object in our illustration. Start by preparing Cadmium Yellow in a watery consistency and a yellow orange tint in a medium consistency. Then, take your medium round brush and use it to paint the shape of the moon with Cadmium Yellow. While the layer is still wet, add a few touches of the yellow orange tint.

You can place the moon, or a big star if you prefer, anywhere you like in your composition. Once the main object is painted, we will add more elements around it. For now, let it dry completely before moving on to the next step.

STEP 2

Now let's add more stars around the new moon shape we have created. Prepare all three project colors in both watery and medium consistencies: Cadmium Yellow, yellow orange tint, and Yellow Ochre. Keep working with the medium round brush and start adding the stars.

I recommend starting by painting the outline of the star shapes and then filling them with color (see Figure 1). You can choose any color, but I suggest using a watery consistency for the base color and adding some brush touches on the wet layer with a different color in a medium consistency.

As you add stars, you can also paint some closer to the border. Even if they are not fully visible, that's okay because we are creating an illustrative style. Make sure your stars are not perfect or symmetrical, as this adds interest to the composition. You can also leave some white space inside the star shapes to create a shining effect.

Once the bigger stars are painted, let everything dry completely.

Step 3

Step 4

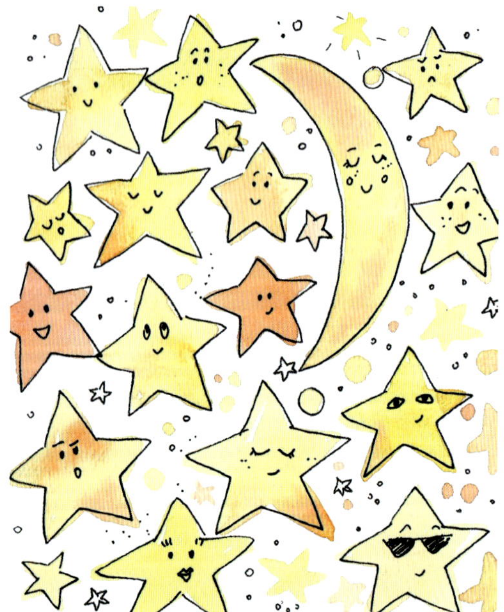

STEP 3

You can skip this step, but I think it's a great idea to add some extra details like spots, dots, and tiny stars around the composition. So, if you'd like, pick a small round brush and use watery or medium consistency project colors to add small details around the painted objects.

Focus on filling the empty areas to make your composition look balanced and complete.

Once you are happy with the result, let everything dry completely before moving on to the final step.

STEP 4

Transform your painting into a cute and whimsical illustration. Take your black ink pen and start by outlining the moon and stars. Don't worry about making the star outlines perfect. You can go slightly outside the watercolor shapes and play with the lines. Make sure the outlines are loose and continuous, without interruptions, as this adds to the charm of the illustration.

Let the ink dry for a moment to avoid smudging, and then begin adding cute details, such as facial features like eyes, cheeks, and mouths.

Have fun and experiment with different emotions on your stars. This is a great exercise if you want to create more children's book–style illustrations with watercolor.

Using the same pen, add small details like dots, tiny circles, or extra stars around the composition.

Try experimenting with different details, colors, and compositions!

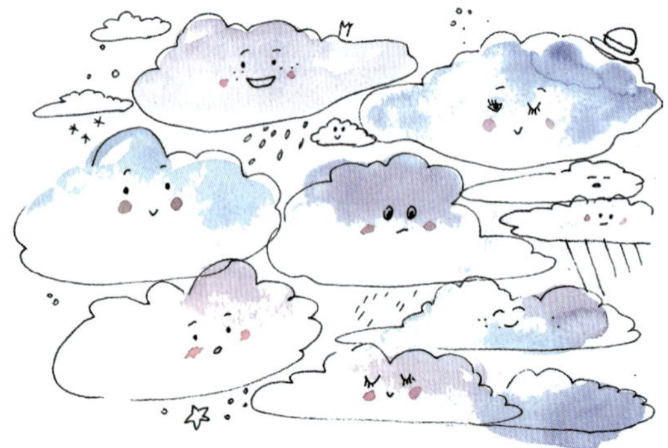

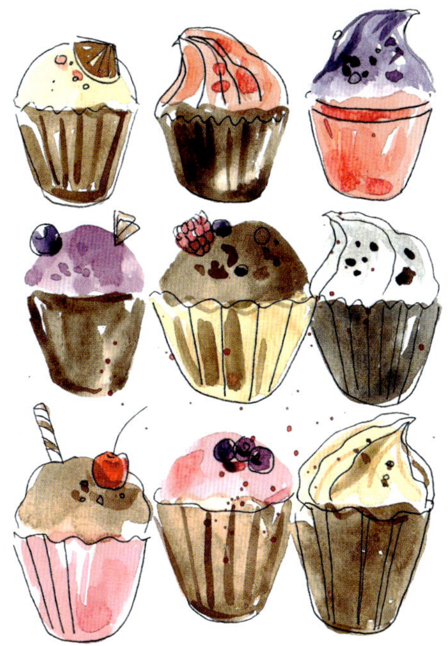

Yummy Colorful Cupcakes

In this project, I will show you how to paint cupcakes and other desserts using outlines and watercolor. As someone who loves painting food, I can promise you'll enjoy using black outlines to add details in your paintings. This project has an illustrative style, but you can make it as realistic or playful as you like—it's all up to you. Let's paint some yummy desserts!

COLOR MIXING

- Warm brown tint: Add a little Burnt Umber to Burnt Sienna.
- Warm pink tint: Mix Opera with a bit of Yellow Ochre.
- Deep brown: Add a little Ultramarine to the Burnt Umber.
- Cool pink tint: Add just a hint of Yellow Ochre to Opera.
- Purple tint: Add some Ultramarine to Opera.
- Violet tint: Mix Ultramarine with a bit of Opera.
- Deep blue purple: Add a little Madder Rose to Ultramarine.

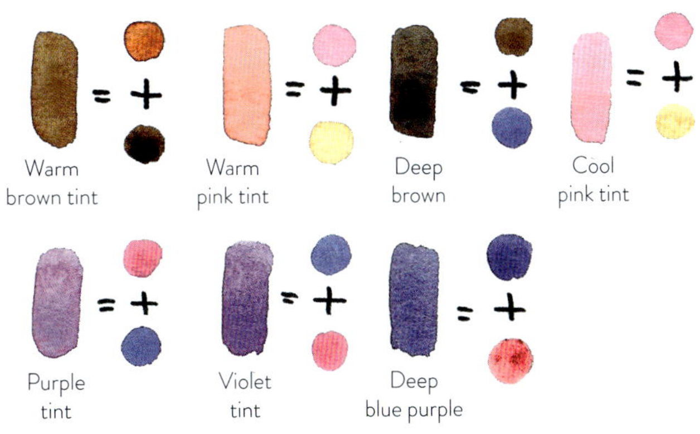

SUPPLIES

- Watercolor paper
- Washi tape or masking tape
- Pencil and eraser
- Round brushes: small (sizes 1–4) and medium (sizes 6–8)
- Waterproof black ink pen (size 0.5 or 0.8 mm)

PROJECT COLORS

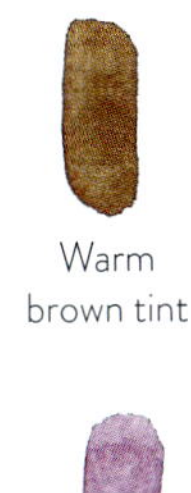
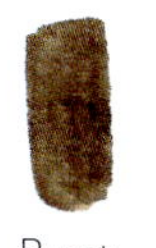
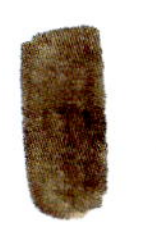
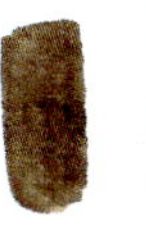
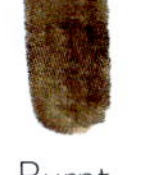
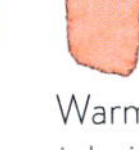
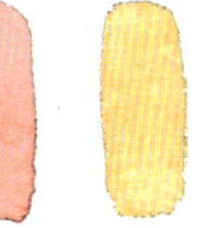
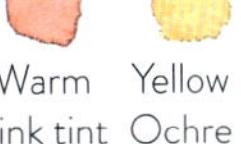
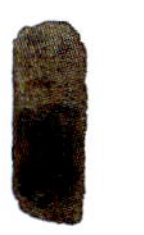
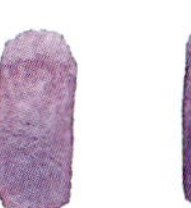

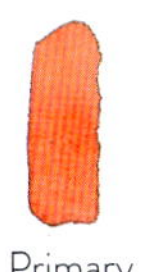
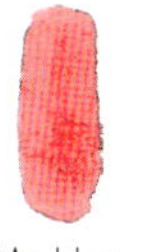
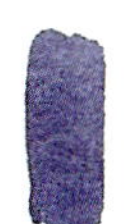

Warm brown tint · Burnt Umber · Warm pink tint · Yellow Ochre · Deep brown · Cool pink tint

Purple tint · Violet tint · Primary Red · Madder Rose (or Alizarin or Crimson) · Deep blue purple

Step 1

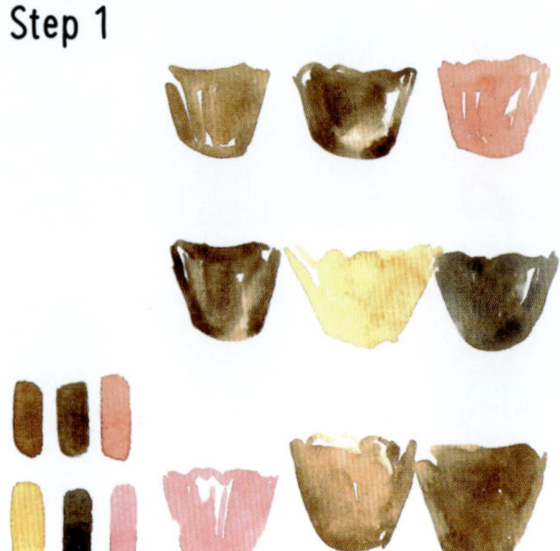

Step 2

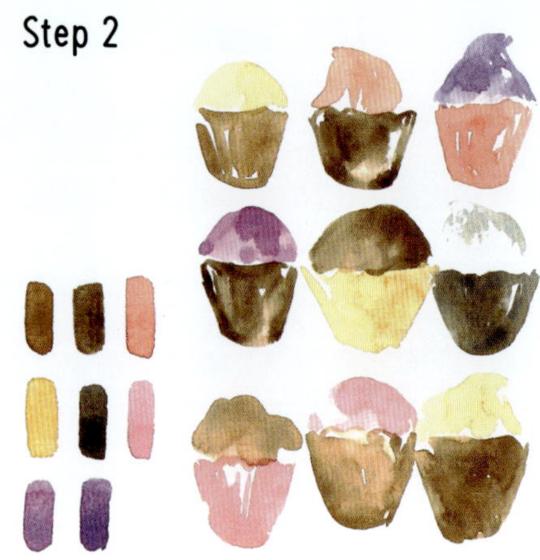

NOTE: For this project, it is especially important to use a waterproof ink pen, because we will be adding watercolor on top of the black lines for extra details. If you don't use a waterproof liner or pen, I recommend skipping step 5.

NOTE: Project colors for this project don't need to be exact. You can experiment with them; for example, instead of purple and pink tints, you can try other options. The most important thing is to have one or two base colors that can unite the project, such as Burnt Umber, Burnt Sienna, or Yellow Ochre.

PREPARATION WORK

Let's begin with some preparations. First, secure your paper with washi tape. The washi tape will also work as a border for our painting. This project is done in a loose, illustrative style, so we won't be doing any preliminary sketching. However, I suggest you lightly draw a grid with a pencil to divide your paper into nine cells: three rows and three columns. The grid doesn't need to be perfect; it's just a guide to help you start painting directly on the paper without sketching.

STEP 1

Let's start by painting the bottom part of our cupcakes. Prepare the following colors in watery to medium consistency: warm brown tint, Burnt Umber, warm pink tint, Yellow Ochre, deep brown, and cool pink tint. Then, take a medium-sized brush and begin painting the cups of the cupcakes. You can follow the colors and shapes in my example, or you can create your own.

The most important thing to remember is that the cups don't need to be perfect. Leave some areas unpainted inside the cups to create an airy effect and highlights. Avoid making them overly symmetrical; experiment with their positioning. Some cups can even touch each other, and you can allow the colors to blend naturally. Lastly, vary the shapes of the cups to add charm and character to your painting.

Once you're happy with how the cups look, let them dry completely before moving on to the next step.

STEP 2

Now, let's add the top parts of our cupcakes. Prepare the following colors in watery to medium consistency: warm brown tint, Burnt Umber, warm pink tint, Yellow Ochre, deep brown, cool pink tint, purple tint, and violet tint. Using the same medium round brush, start adding the top part to each cupcake.

Just like with the cups, make sure the tops are not perfect. Vary their shapes, and try to avoid using the same color for the cup and the top part. For example, if the bottom of a cupcake is brown, you can make the top part yellow, purple, or pink to keep it colorful and diverse.

Don't worry about imperfections. We'll correct everything later with a black ink pen. You can follow the shapes I created, or you can create your own.

Let everything dry completely before moving on to step 3.

TIP: Please note that for the white whipped cream swirls, I used deep brown in a watery consistency. With just a few brushstrokes, the deep brown creates the appearance of shadows. This is a great approach you can use for any watercolor dessert illustrations.

STEP 3

Now, let's bring our cupcakes to life by adding details to the dry layer. Prepare the following colors in a medium consistency: warm brown tint, Burnt Umber, Yellow Ochre, deep brown, purple tint, violet tint, Primary Red, Madder Rose, and deep blue purple.

You can continue using the same brush or switch to a small round brush to start adding the details. You can follow my example, but the beauty of this step lies in the freedom to explore. Add your own unique touches, like fruit pieces, berries, or decorative elements on top of the cupcakes. You can also enhance the cups by emphasizing shadows and textures.

Avoid overloading with too many details. The key here is variety: Create an interesting mix of colors and textures that draw the viewer's eye.

Let everything dry completely before moving on to the next step.

STEP 4

Now it's time to bring everything together. Arm yourself with your pen and get ready to add the finishing touches.

Start outlining the details. Focus on the swirls of the cream, the tops of the cupcakes, and the cups. Add small accents, outline the decorations, and highlight additional elements like berries, fruits, or pieces of chocolate. You can even add outlines to areas you didn't paint with watercolor if you feel it enhances the composition.

You can follow my design, but feel free to create your own unique style. Remember, outlining serves as a way to refine shapes, fix imperfections, and bring symmetry where needed, but without aiming for perfection. Let the black outline highlight what you want to showcase.

Once you're satisfied with the result, give the ink a minute to set, and then move on to the final step.

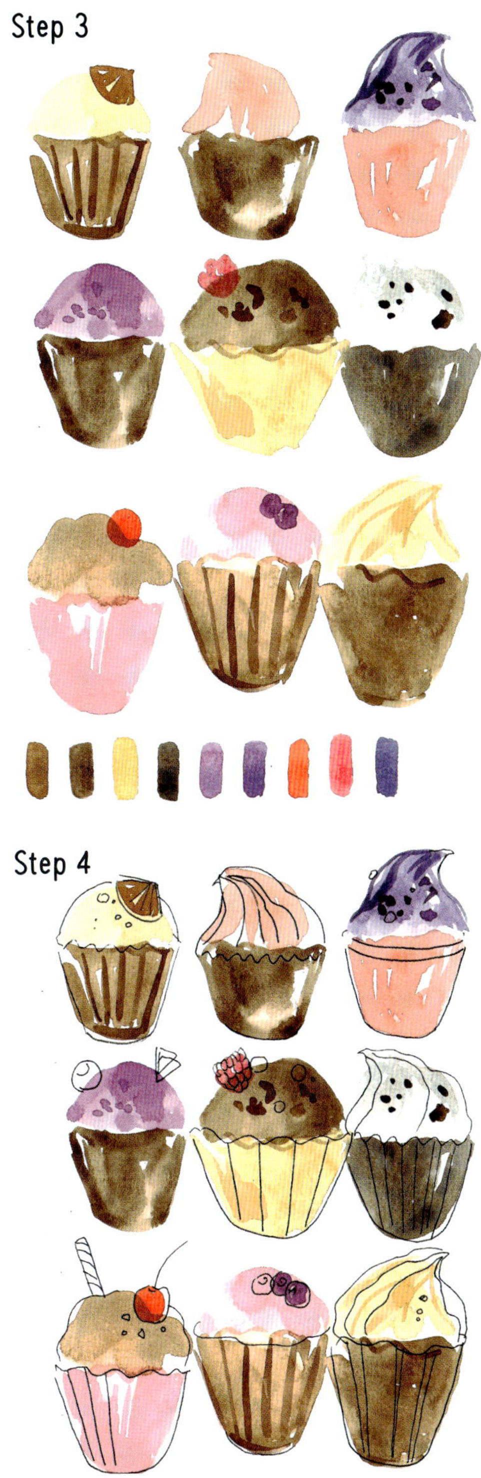

Step 5

STEP 5

We already have the base layer painted and the details outlined with ink, but now we need to add more depth and make our cupcakes look complete.

For this step, prepare any colors from the project in a medium to thick consistency. Additionally, prepare medium to thick consistency deep blue purple for some extra details. Take a medium or small round brush and begin adding finishing touches to the cupcakes. This could include brushstrokes on the cups to emphasize the folds of the paper, shadows, details on the berries, or refining the outlines you created earlier.

I used deep blue purple to add highlights on the purple cream and blueberries. Feel free to experiment and create as many details as you like. However, remember to stop when you feel it's enough.

For the final touch, I recommend using a medium round brush to add one or two flicks of splatter to the painting. I used the Madder Rose, but you can choose any color from the project.

Try experimenting with different details, colors, and compositions!

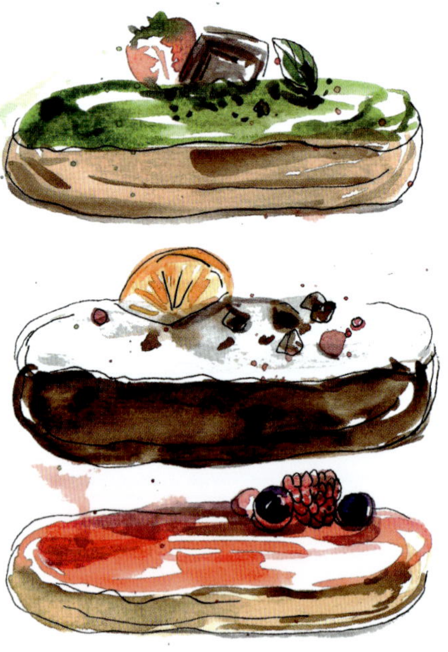

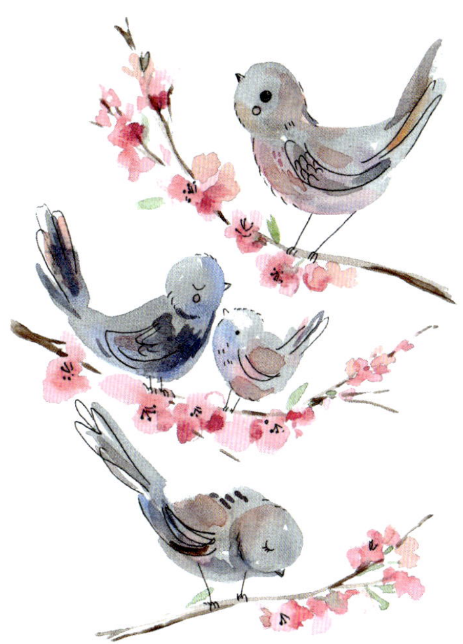

Garden Birds Harmony

In this project, I will share with you a delightful method for painting various garden birds in any color variation using watercolor and an ink pen. You can paint any real garden bird or use your imagination and create a stunning project in just a few easy steps!

SUPPLIES

- Watercolor paper
- Masking tape
- Pencil and eraser (optional)
- Quill brush (size 2 or larger) or soft-bristled medium round brush
- Round brushes: small (sizes 1–4) and medium (sizes 6–8)
- Waterproof black ink pen (size 0.5 or 0.8 mm)

NOTE: For this project, it is especially important to use a waterproof ink pen, because we will be adding watercolor on top of the black lines for extra details. If you don't use a waterproof liner or pen, I recommend skipping step 4.

PROJECT COLORS

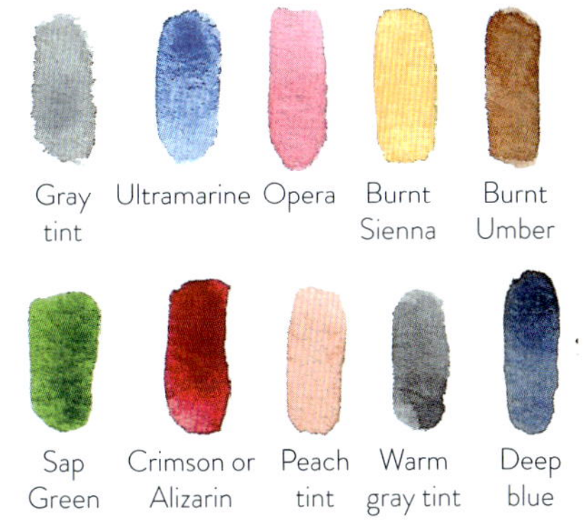

| Gray tint | Ultramarine | Opera | Burnt Sienna | Burnt Umber |

| Sap Green | Crimson or Alizarin | Peach tint | Warm gray tint | Deep blue |

COLOR MIXING

- Gray tint: Mix Ultramarine with Burnt Umber.
- Peach tint: Mix Opera with Yellow Ochre.
- Warm gray tint: Mix Ultramarine with Burnt Umber and a little bit of Crimson.
- Deep blue: Mix Ultramarine with just a little bit of Burnt Umber.

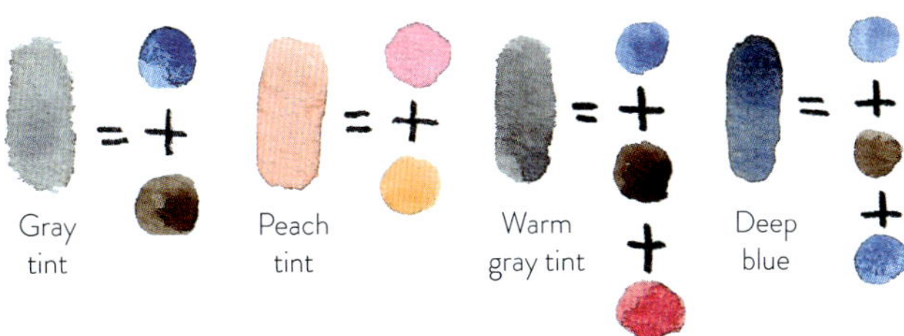

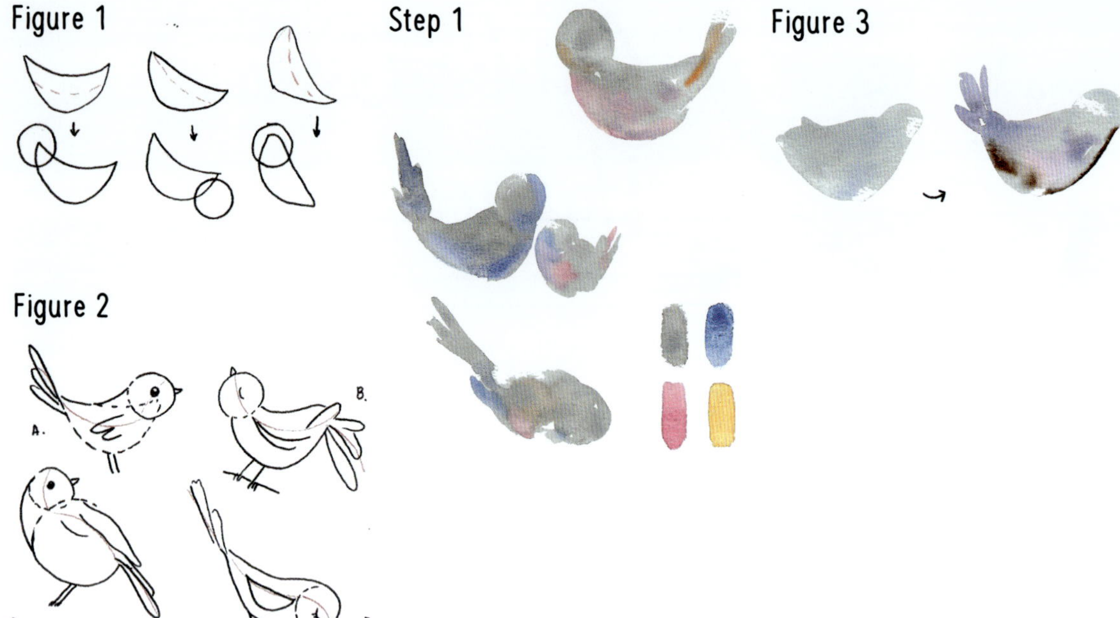

PREPARATION WORK

I recommend securing your watercolor paper with washi tape.

This project does not require preliminary sketching because we work in a loose, freestyle manner, and you can correct and complete the shapes of the birds using a black ink pen. However, if you feel more comfortable, you can use a pencil to make some very light, thin lines. Mark the axes of each bird or outline the bodies.

Next, I would like to emphasize the importance of understanding how to paint the birds in this project. Basically, any bird you paint will have a head, body, tail, feet, and wings. To make the shapes look different, you just need to change the pose. The most important thing is to understand the orientation of the body, and from this, you can build and add the other parts of the bird. In Figure 1, you can find a few examples of how you can start with different bird body poses and then add the head.

In Figure 2, you can find four examples of different birds, but each of these birds is built using the same principle: First, draw the body, then add the head, tail, and other parts, and finally, add the details.

From these images, you can see that the most important thing is to understand how to build the bird's shape before painting. Once you figure this out, you can paint or draw any bird you like. These shapes are simplified, which is acceptable for our illustrative and loose style. However, if you would like to paint something in more detail and a realistic style, it's better to have some references.

STEP 1

Prepare your quill brush. Then prepare watery consistency gray tint and medium consistency Ultramarine, Opera, and Burnt Sienna.

Using my example as a reference, start painting the shapes of the birds in gray tint. Don't aim for perfect shapes; try to create them using loose brushstrokes. While the first layer of the birds is still wet, add some details using Ultramarine, Opera, and Burnt Sienna.

You can follow my bird shapes and composition or create your own based on the principles I described earlier. Once the first layer is done and you are happy with it, allow everything to dry before moving to step 2.

TIP: To paint the first layer of the bird, start with the body and head, then add the tail and details while the paint is still wet. Repeat this for each bird (see the example in Figure 3).

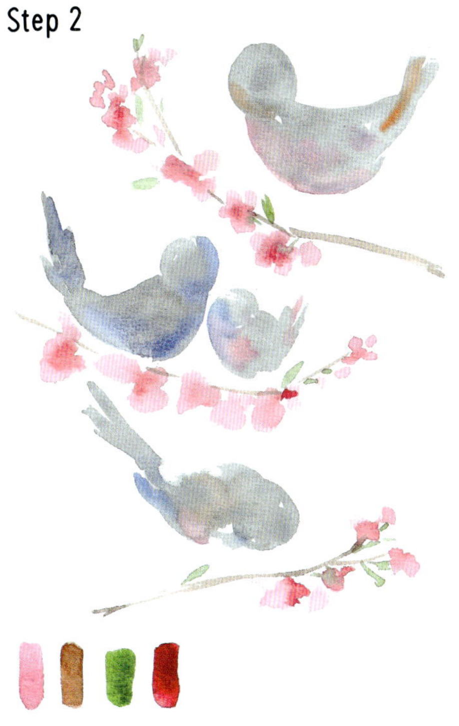

Step 2

STEP 2

Prepare watery consistency Burnt Umber, Opera, and Sap Green, and medium consistency Crimson. Continue working with the same brush.

First, start painting the branches where the birds are perched. Make thin lines, leaving some gaps for adding blooms later. You can follow my example for painting branches or create your own. Once the branches are done, wait until these details are completely dry.

Using the same brush, start forming blossoms with Opera. Use loose brushstrokes and add some blossom buds at the ends of the branches. While the blossom layer is still wet, add Crimson to the center of each blossom flower. It creates a beautiful blend and brings some contrast to the blossoms.

Add some leaves to the branches using Sap Green.

Once all the details are painted, allow everything to dry completely.

STEP 3

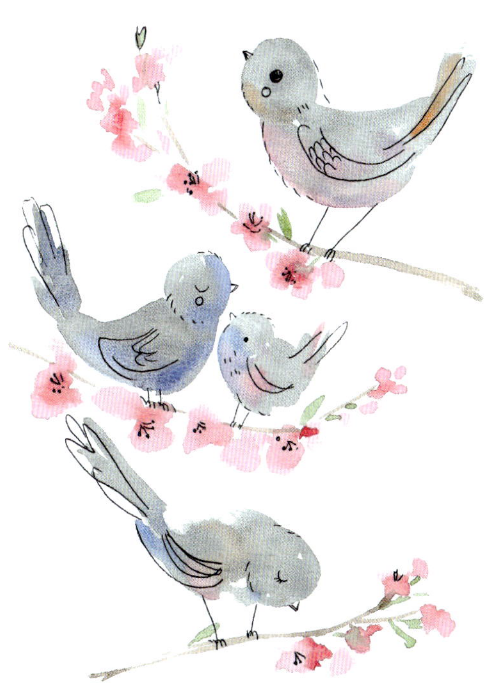

Step 3

We have already created a beautiful, transparent watercolor base for our project. Arm yourself with a pen and start drawing the details. I recommend beginning with the birds' details, such as eyes, beaks, and feet. Draw or emphasize the birds' tails. Also, add extra details like wings, feather imitations, and some extra texture. Here you can use your imagination and add different details and accents—but don't overdo it.

The birds should not lose their individuality. Draw their details differently; for example, create different eyes or wings.

Lastly, add black line details to the blossoms' flowers, especially to the centers, to bring some contrast there. If you are happy with all the black details, let the ink dry for about a minute, then move on to the final step.

STEP 4

This step only makes sense if you used a waterproof ink pen. Otherwise, you will smear your black ink lines. You can use a small round brush or a medium one with a thin tip. Prepare the following colors in medium consistency: Burnt Umber, peach tint, warm gray tint, Crimson, and deep blue.

We will add brushstrokes to emphasize and add details, making our birds look less flat. It's always better to have two or three layers in watercolor instead of just one base layer.

Start by adding brushstrokes to the birds using deep blue, warm gray tint, and peach tint. Add some details randomly to your birds. You can absolutely follow my example, but the main purpose is to add contrast and emphasize different parts of the birds' bodies. For example, it's great to add shadows under the head, shadows on the wings, and extra feathers to the tail.

After you finish the birds, use Burnt Umber to add the final details to the branches. You can make some parts thicker or add extra branches, especially thinner ones at the branch tips.

Finally, take Crimson and add extra accents to the blossoms. You can emphasize the petals and shadows. However, it's very important not to overdo it and to maintain a balance between composition, contrast, and added details.

This work is quite detailed and has many accents, so splattering is not necessary, but you can express your creativity and personality here and add some if you would like.

Try experimenting with different details, colors, and compositions!

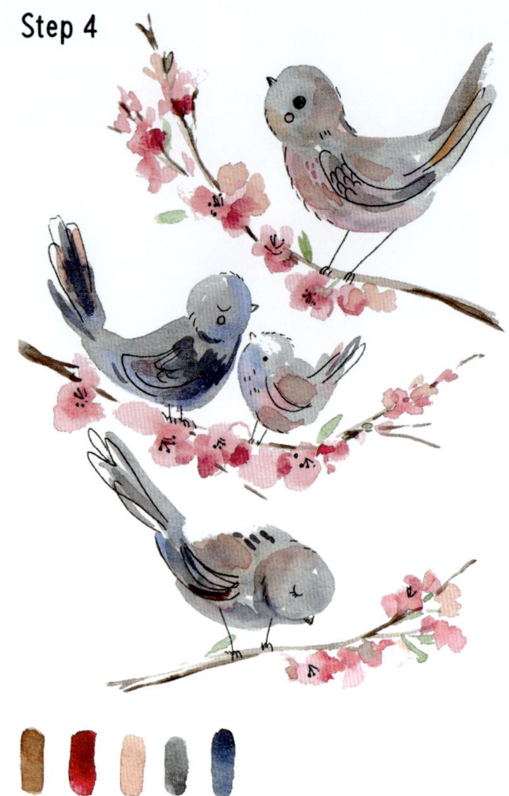

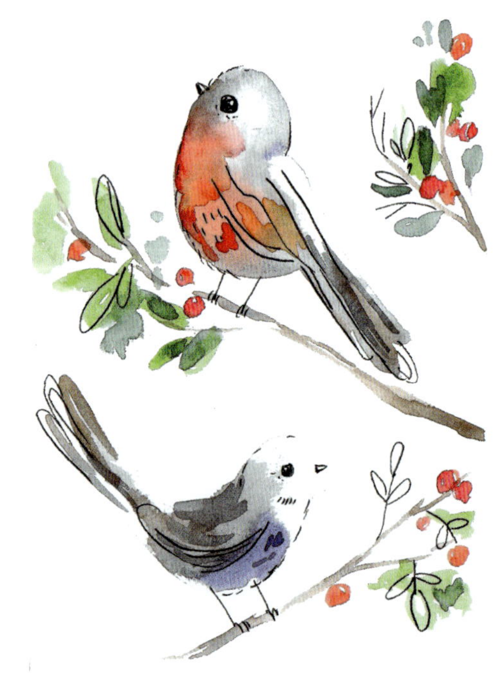

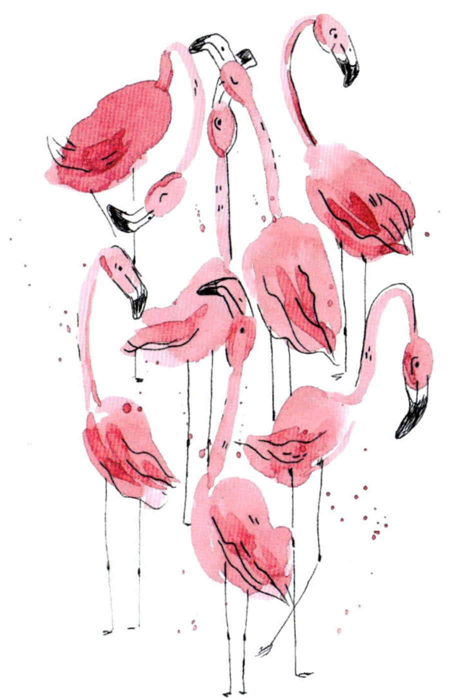

Graceful Flamingos

This amazing project is simple in one sense because you'll use only one color and outlines, yet you'll create a beautiful and impressive illustration. It will help you focus on creating shapes, the overall look of the composition, and adding details to enhance depth. Sometimes, with just one or two layers and a few added details, you can achieve the desired result!

PROJECT COLORS

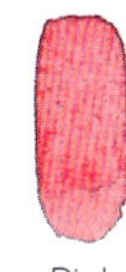

Pink
tint

SUPPLIES

- Watercolor paper
- Washi tape or masking tape (optional)
- Pencil and eraser (optional)
- Round brushes: small (sizes 1–4) and medium (sizes 6–8)
- Waterproof black ink pen (size 0.5 or 0.8 mm)

NOTE: For this project, it is especially important to use a waterproof ink pen, because we will be adding watercolor on top of the black lines for extra details. If you don't use a waterproof liner or pen, I recommend skipping the final splattering step.

COLOR MIXING

- Pink tint: Add a little Yellow Ochre to Opera.

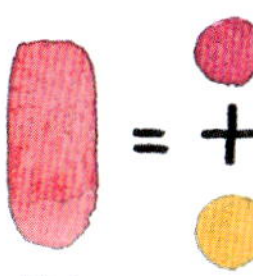

Pink
tint

PREPARATION WORK

Using washi tape to secure the watercolor paper is optional—you can do it if you'd like, but it's not mandatory.

It's not necessary to do any preliminary sketching. However, if it makes you more comfortable, you can very lightly create a basic sketch. In this case, I recommend only a light outline of the bodies, and maybe the heads and necks, of the flamingos.

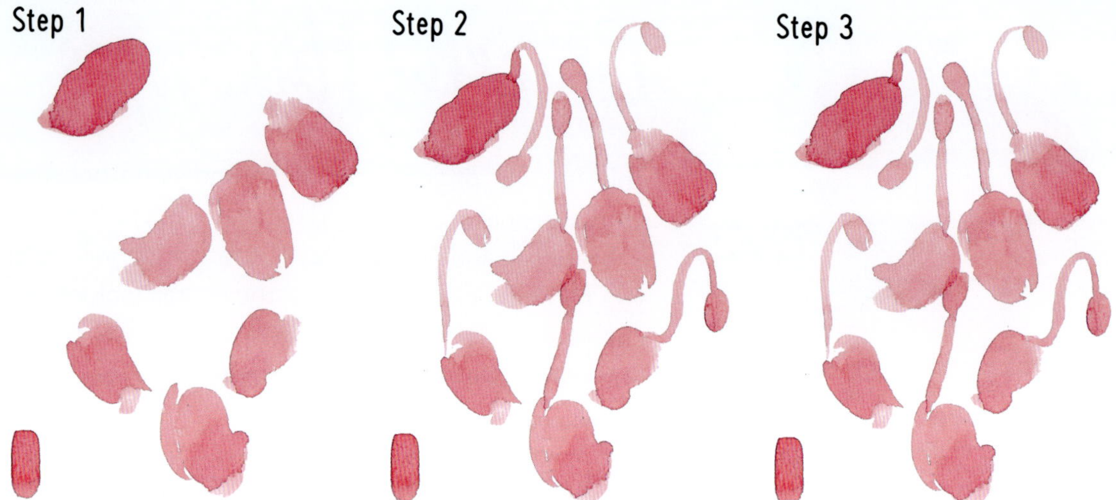

STEP 1

Let's begin our project. First, using a watery to medium consistency pink tint and a medium round brush, paint the shapes of the flamingos' bodies. You can copy the placement of the bodies in the example or create your own arrangement. Don't worry about making these shapes perfect. We'll add more defined lines with a pen later. Keep the project loose and expressive and let your creativity flow.

Once you're done, you can either let the paint dry completely before moving to the next step, or, if you work carefully, you can continue adding the details described in step 2 without waiting for it to dry.

STEP 2

Let's add the heads and necks of the flamingos to the already painted bodies. Using the same pink tint in a watery to medium consistency, start adding these details. You can switch to a small round brush if it feels more convenient.

Place the heads and necks in your own way or follow my example. Just remember to keep a logical flow so that the body parts look connected. If you look at real flamingos, you'll notice they can turn their heads or lower them in different ways. You can refer to these natural positions to add character.

Allow it to dry completely before moving on to the next step.

STEP 3

Now, let's add the second layer to our flamingos. Prepare the pink tint paint again, this time in a slightly thicker, medium consistency. Continue working with a small round brush or use a medium round brush for bolder brushstrokes.

Begin adding strokes to emphasize the feathers, heads, and necks of the flamingos. Each bird can have its own look—make some more detailed, others less so.

Be careful not to overdo it with these second-layer details, as we'll be adding more with a black ink pen later. Once you're finished, let everything dry completely before moving to the next step.

Step 4

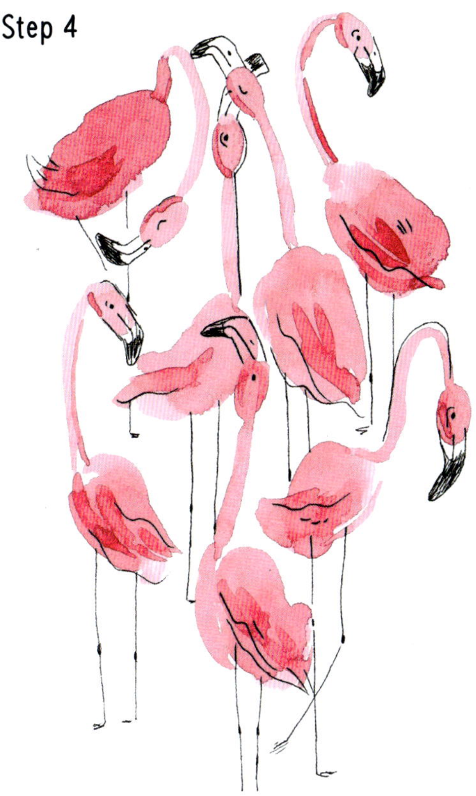

STEP 4

Now it's time to take your waterproof ink pen and draw the eyes, beak, and feet of the birds. You can also add small details to emphasize the necks and tail feathers.

Follow the design shown in my example or create your own.

Let the pen lines dry for a minute or two, then move on to the final step.

STEP 5

Our illustration already looks lovely, but these last details will allow us to play with the composition a bit more.

First, use your ink pen again to add even more detail to the flamingos. Perhaps add some feather texture or emphasis on certain parts of their bodies, like the heads, necks, or tails. Feel free to experiment with different types of lines and strokes to add variety and character.

For the final touch, consider adding some splattering. This step is optional, but it can help fill any empty spaces in your illustration. Using a medium consistency pink tint and a medium round brush, add some flicks of color to areas that feel a bit empty.

Once you're satisfied with the result, let it dry completely. And there you have them—your happy flamingos!

Try experimenting with different details, colors, and compositions!

Step 5

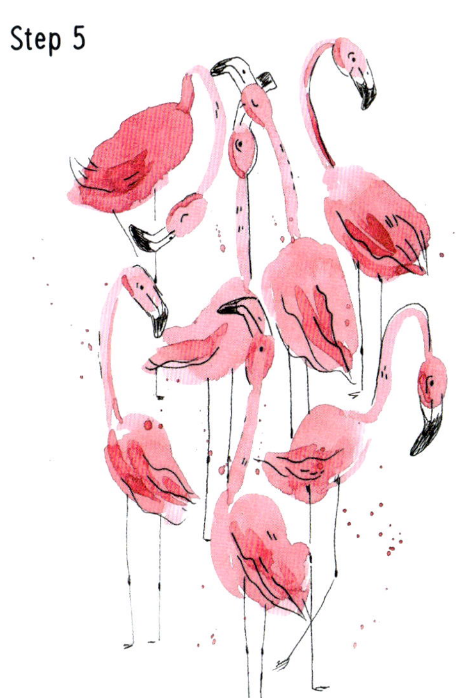

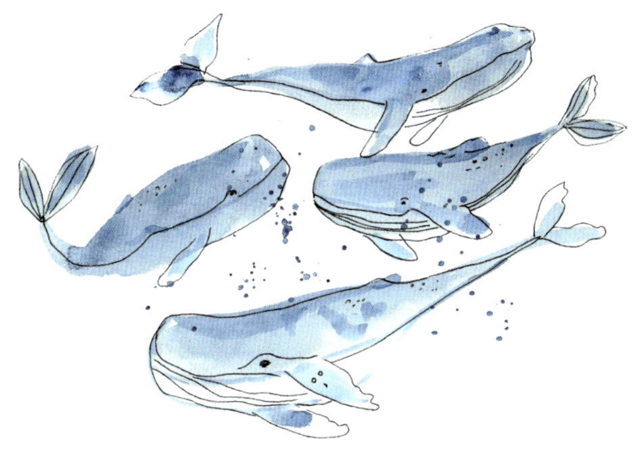

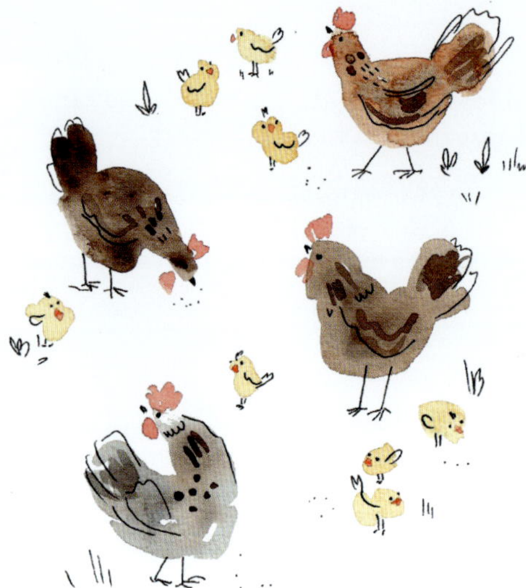

Chicks and Hens

In this project, I will show you how to paint a lovely scene of chicks and hens with watercolor and a black ink pen. I love this project because of its simplicity, the cute and impressive results, and its many possible variations. So let's do this together in just four easy steps!

PROJECT COLORS

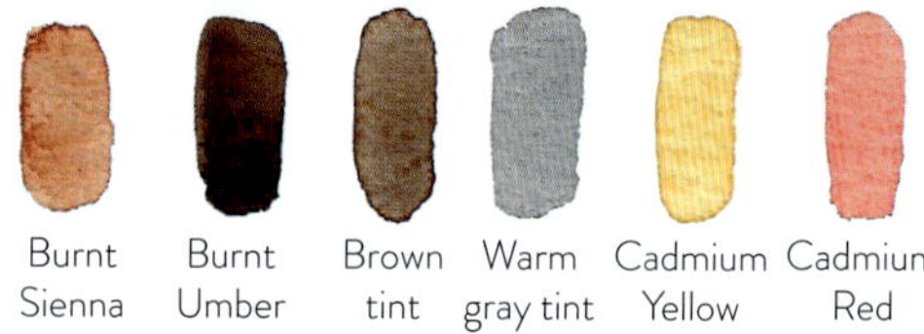

Burnt Sienna	Burnt Umber	Brown tint	Warm gray tint	Cadmium Yellow	Cadmium Red

COLOR MIXING

- Brown tint: Add a little Burnt Umber to Burnt Sienna.

- Warm gray tint: Mix Ultramarine with Burnt Umber and a little Burnt Sienna.

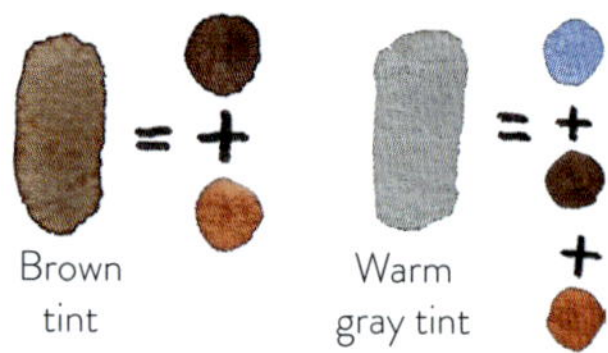

Brown tint

Warm gray tint

SUPPLIES

- Watercolor paper

- Round brushes: small (sizes 1–4) and medium (sizes 6–8)

- Waterproof black ink pen (size 0.5 or 0.8 mm)

NOTE: If you don't have a waterproof black ink pen, you can use any black ink pen or regular black pen. If you don't use a water-proof liner or pen, don't paint over it with watercolor.

Sketch

PREPARATION WORK

For this project, we will work in a loose, illustrative, and very simple style, so we won't do any preliminary sketching. Watercolor serves as the base, and then we will use a black ink pen to shape the forms of our chicks and hens.

Decide on the poses of your chicks and hens. A hen generally has a body, tail, neck, and head. Depending on the pose, you will need to create different shapes, but they don't need to be perfect. You can then refine the shapes with lines and pen details. The same goes for the chicks. You just need to paint a very simple body and spots—either one or two—and later we'll add the beaks and some small details to make it clear that they are chicks.

Step 1

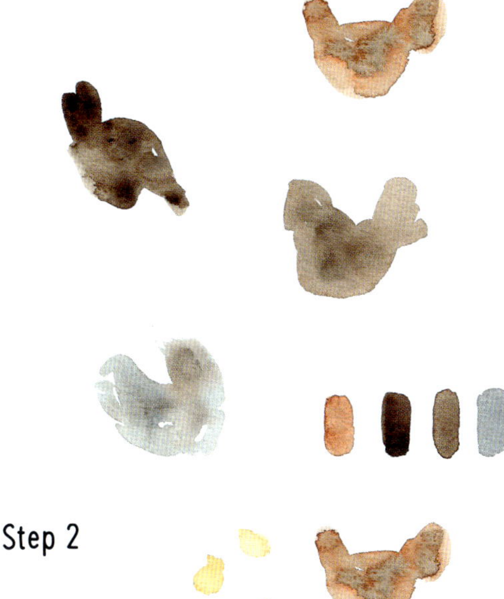

If you look at the sketch on the previous page, you'll see two hens and some chicks in a very basic sketch, just to give you an idea of the shapes we are aiming to create. However, I advise you to look at some reference photos to understand the basic shapes of hens and chicks in real life.

STEP 1

We will begin by painting the shapes of our hens. For this step, I recommend using watery consistency Burnt Sienna, Burnt Umber, brown tint, and warm gray tint. Use a soft round brush, size 8.

For the first attempt, paint no more than four or five hens. You can paint their poses as you like, or you can follow the poses and shapes I have created.

Paint the body shapes of our hens, combining the colors you've prepared. For example, for a base feather color of Burnt Sienna, you can use the wet-on-wet technique to blend in Burnt Umber. For warm gray tinted feathers, you can add brown tint. Play around to create a beautiful blending effect.

Don't aim to make the hens' bodies perfect; just ensure each has a head, neck, body, and tail.

Allow everything to dry before moving on to the next step.

Step 2

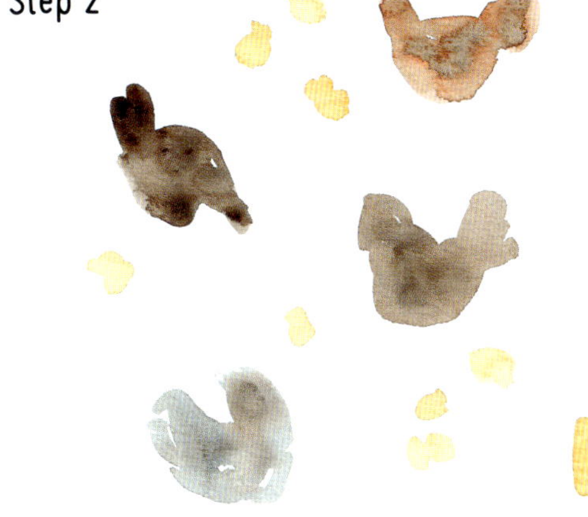

STEP 2

Continue working with the same brush. Prepare watery consistency Cadmium Yellow and start painting the first layer of our chicks. The chicks should be very loose and abstract; they can be recognizable as chicks, but they don't need to be perfect. We can always correct the shape with black lines later. You can follow my composition and add the chicks where I did, or you can play around. Once you are happy with the result, let everything dry, and move on to the next step.

Step 3

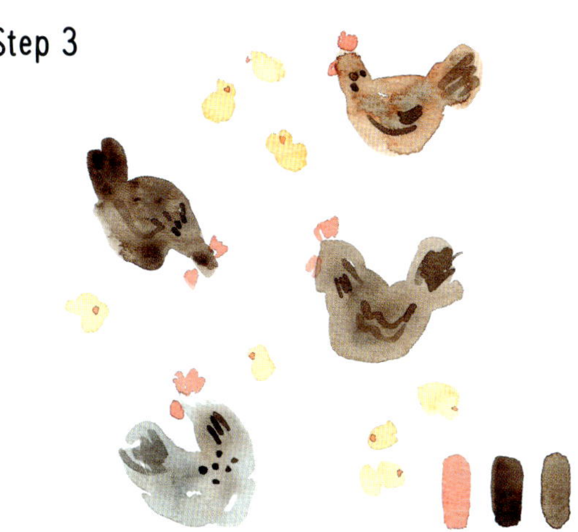

STEP 3

To make these shapes look more recognizable, let's add some details. Prepare the following colors in a medium consistency: Cadmium Red, Burnt Umber, and brown tint. You can keep using a big round brush and work with its tip, or you can use a smaller round brush, for example, size four. It depends on the format of the paper you use and what is easier for you to work with.

(Continued)

Start adding the red details to the hens: the combs (top parts of the beaks) and the wattles (bottom parts of the beaks). Also, use the same Cadmium Red to add beaks to the chicks.

Use Burnt Umber and a tint of brown to add some details to their bodies, like dashes, spots, and feather lines on their wings and tails.

Once you're happy with the result, allow everything to dry before moving on to the final step.

STEP 4

In this step, we won't use watercolor; we'll just use a black pen. It's best to use an ink pen as the lines are smoother. You can experiment with the thickness of the lines, though I prefer a thicker line, like 0.8 mm.

In this step, we'll make our cute hens and chicks look more like an illustration by adding their final details. First, for the hens, you need to add beaks, eyes, legs, and feet. These are necessary elements. I also recommend adding wings and extra lines to emphasize them. The same goes for the tails—adding extra feathers would be great.

Next, move to the chicks and add their wings, legs, feet, tails, and eyes. Play around and use your imagination to add some extra details. Once you are happy with the hens and chicks, you can add some details to the white, empty background. Consider line doodles like grass, small leaves, bushes, flowers—whatever you like. Just make sure you don't overdo it and that the composition looks balanced.

Once you feel happy with the result, your painting is done. You can add some extra watercolor details on top, but make sure that your black ink pen is waterproof.

Try experimenting with different details, colors, and compositions!

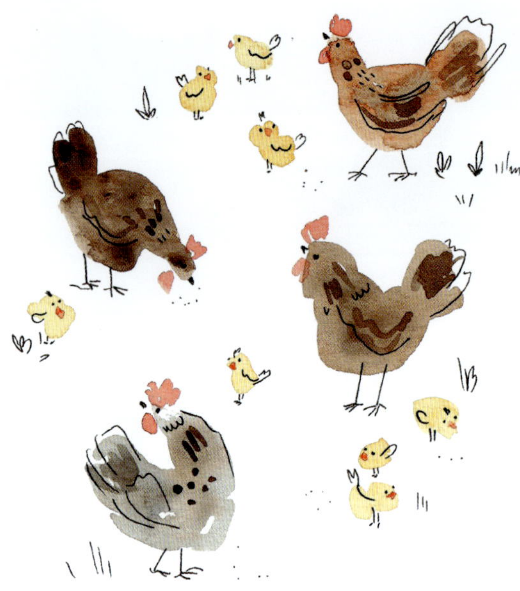

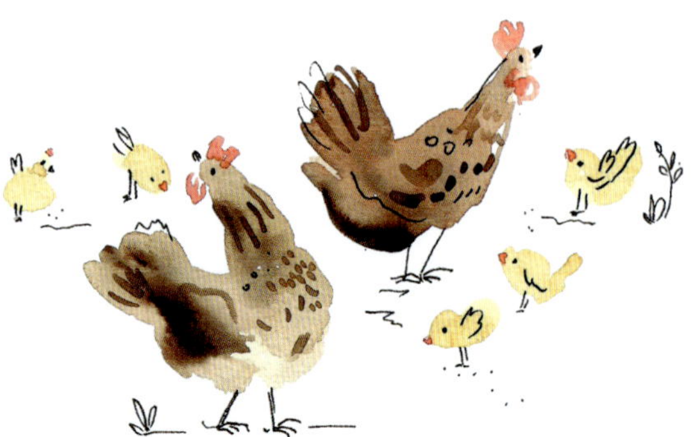

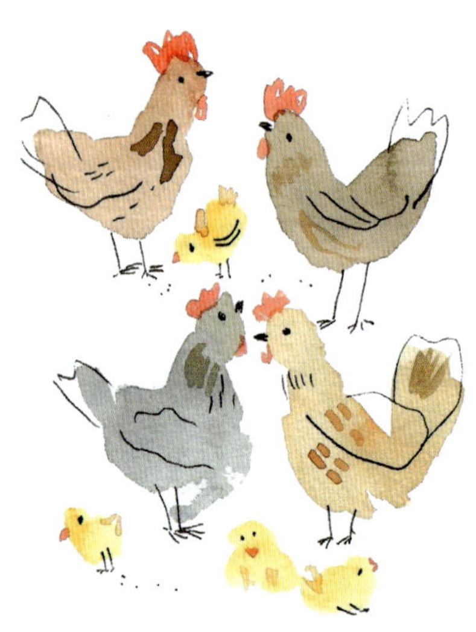

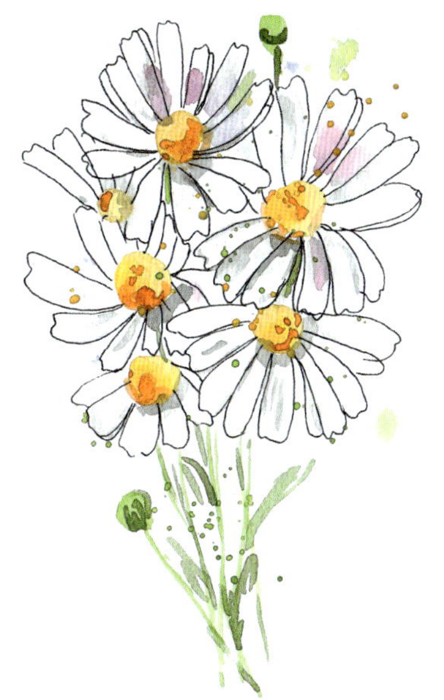

Delicate Daisy Bouquet

In this project, I will show you how to paint a daisy bouquet with watercolor and a black ink pen. It's easy with an impressive result, and you'll explore how contrast works and how white paper helps you to paint and intentionally create white areas.

SUPPLIES

- Watercolor paper
- Washi tape or masking tape
- Pencil and eraser (optional)
- Round brushes: small (sizes 1–4) and medium (sizes 6 and 8)
- Waterproof black ink pen (size 0.5 or 0.8 mm)

PROJECT COLORS

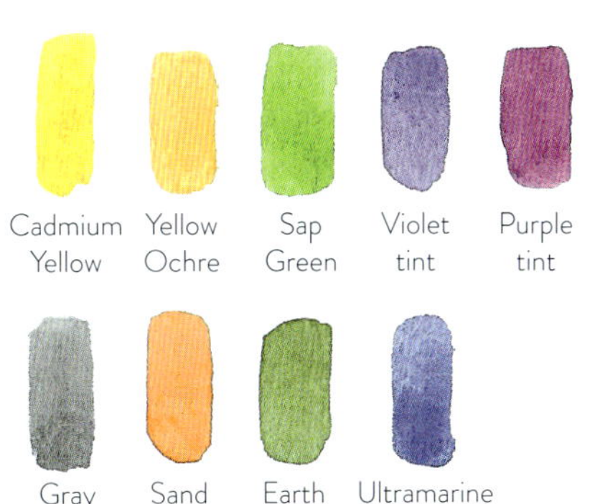

Cadmium Yellow Yellow Ochre Sap Green Violet tint Purple tint

Gray tint Sand tint Earth green Ultramarine

COLOR MIXING

- Gray tint: Mix Ultramarine with a little Burnt Umber.
- Violet tint: Add a little Opera to Ultramarine.
- Purple tint: Mix Opera with a little Ultramarine to get a bright, warm purple.
- Sand tint: Add a little Burnt Sienna to Yellow Ochre.
- Earth green: Mix Sap Green with a little blue (I use Indigo) and just a bit of Burnt Sienna.

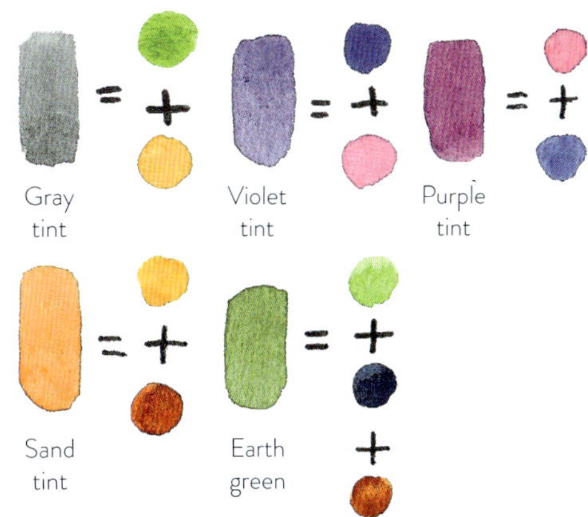

Gray tint Violet tint Purple tint

Sand tint Earth green

NOTE: It is important to use a waterproof black ink pen if you want to complete the entire project and all the steps, especially the background.

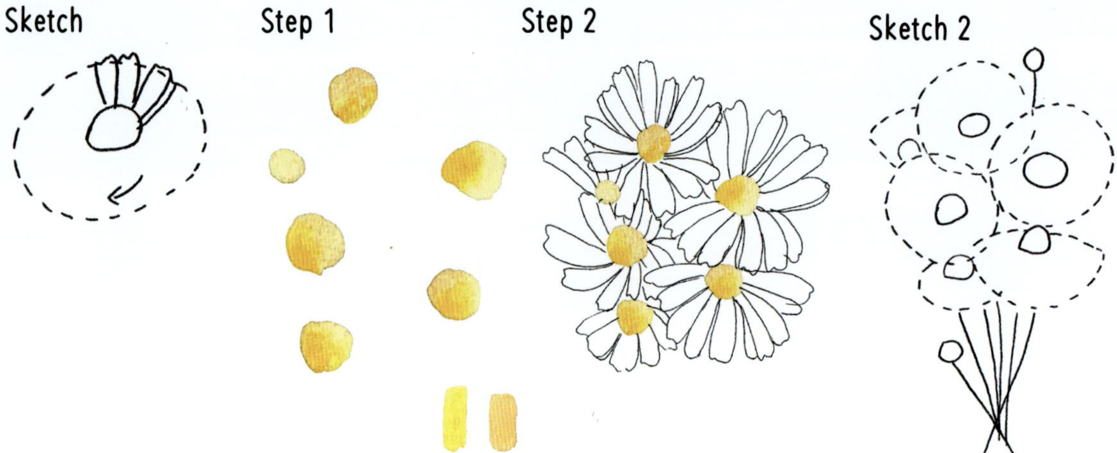

PREPARATION WORK

Secure the watercolor paper to the table with washi tape. It's mandatory for this project because we'll be using the wet-on-wet technique, and we'll paint a beautiful, transparent, and bright watercolor background.

If you'd like to make a sketch, you can refer to Sketch, where you'll find a very basic sketch of the flowers. However, it's not detailed; in this case, it's more about composition—where the flowers are located. I do not advise you to add petals with a pencil; just mark the overall shape and orientation of each flower. You can also add very light lines for the stems, and that's it. It will be enough. Make sure your lines are very, very thin and barely visible.

If you'd like to approach this project in your own way or with a loose style, you can skip the sketching and simply mark the centers of the daisies. Or, you can opt not to create a sketch.

STEP 1

We start the project by coloring the centers of our daisies. If you've made a sketch, you can follow it and fill in the centers as planned. If you haven't, simply take your brush and start adding the spots. They don't have to be perfect. Prepare Cadmium Yellow and Yellow Ochre in a watery to medium consistency.

Use a medium round brush, such as a size 6, to create round spots with Yellow Ochre. Then, while the layer is still wet, randomly add a few touches of Cadmium Yellow to each spot. Once you're done, allow everything to dry completely before moving to the next step.

STEP 2

Let's add petals. In the image for Step 2, I suggest choosing one flower and adding the petals one by one using the waterproof ink pen until the flower shape is filled. Petals can be round, oval, or arched, depending on the daisy's orientation in the composition.

Keep the ink lines consistent and avoid interruptions. If a line gets distorted, stop and restart, but it's better to continue the line to the center. Petals don't need to be perfect—slightly different sizes work as long as they fit the flower's shape.

Remember, petals on lower flowers may be hidden, so you don't need to draw them. You can follow my example or create your own; just ensure the petals look natural. Once you've drawn all the petals, let the ink dry for a minute or two.

STEP 3

We can already see our daisies, but we're adding more colors to complete the painting in just a few extra stages. Prepare medium consistency Sap Green, violet tint, and purple tint. Prepare watery consistency gray tint. Finally, prepare two medium brushes—size 8 and size 6—and a small brush for adding stems.

With a soft medium brush, randomly add some brushstrokes with gray tint, especially at the bases of the daisy centers. You can also add a few touches of purple and violet tints, even if they blend with the gray tint—this is fine, as the wet-on-wet technique will begin to take effect.

Once you've added these color touches with purple and gray tints, switch to a small round brush and paint the stems and buds, as shown in the example, or feel free to go your own way. Once you're done, let everything dry before proceeding to the next step.

STEP 4

Let's make our painting look deeper and more colorful. Prepare medium consistency sand tint, earth green, and gray tint. Use a medium brush—I suggest size 6.

First, add details to the centers of the daisies. These can be random spots, and you should also emphasize the bottom of each center. Keep the details random—they don't need to be perfect or the same. Once you're done with this, I suggest using gray tint to add more details to the petals. This time, try to emphasize the shadows that each petal casts on the others, as shown in my example.

Lastly, use earth green to add some extra details to the stems and buds, and some leaves. A few brushstrokes and accents will be enough. Let everything dry completely before moving to the final step.

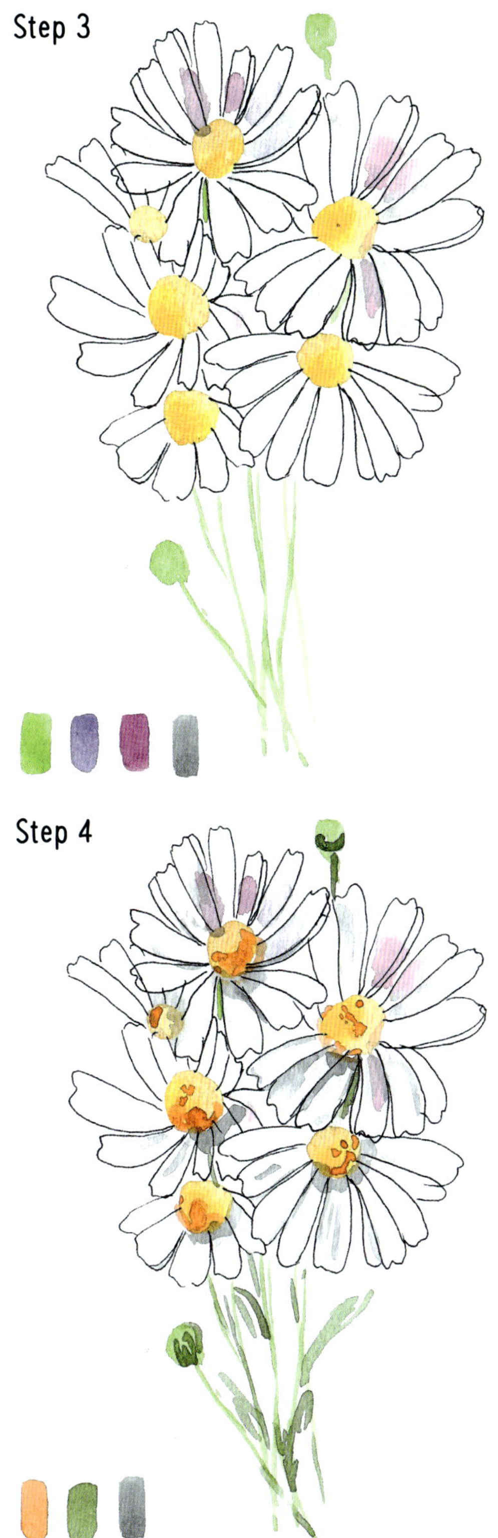

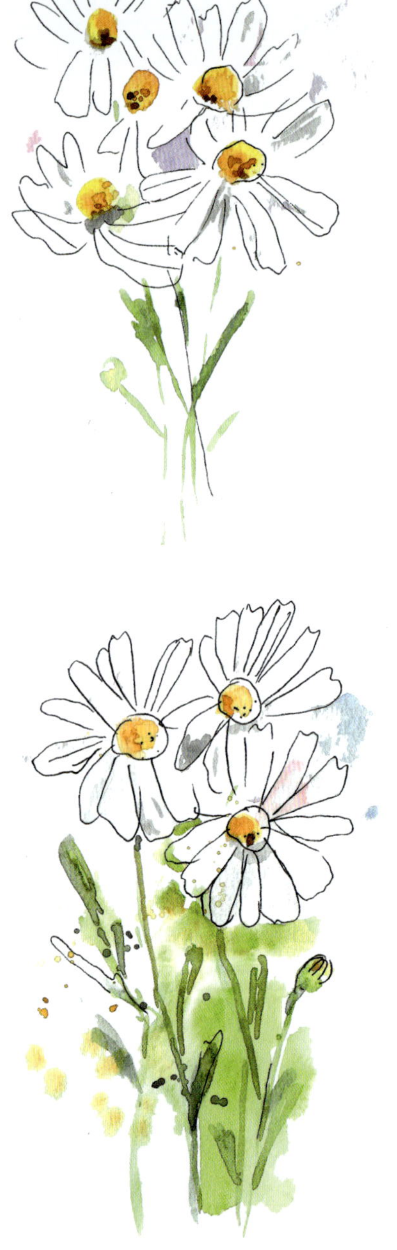

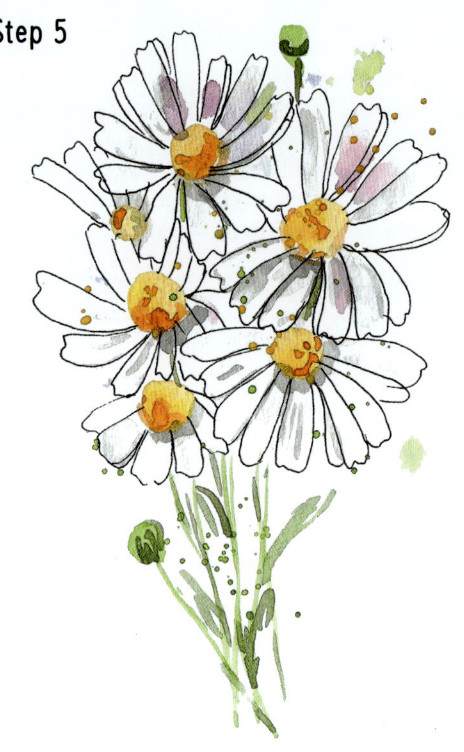

Step 5

STEP 5

Let's move on to the final step. You could leave the project as is, but I suggest adding a background and some splatters. For this step, prepare Ultramarine in watery consistency, and Cadmium Yellow and Sap Green in medium consistency. Use soft medium brushes in sizes 6 and 8.

Using your size 8 brush, start by adding the background with watery Ultramarine. Begin in the top left corner, leaving gaps for the flowers, and move down towards the bottom right corner. The goal is to fill the background with soft brushstrokes, just enough to make the white petals stand out. The contrast will help the daisies pop as the focal point.

For the bottom, add a few random brushstrokes with Ultramarine. Then, using your size 6 brush, flick Cadmium Yellow onto the paper for splatters. Repeat with Sap Green.

That's it. You can add more details if needed, but remember—less is more. Let everything dry completely.

Try experimenting with different details, colors, and compositions!

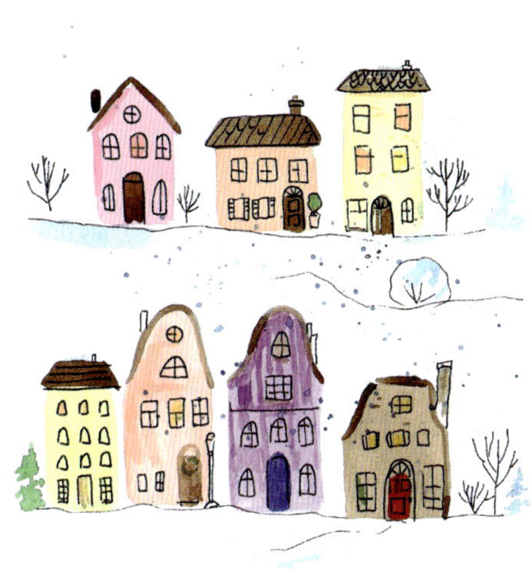

Adorable Houses

Let's paint some colorful houses using watercolor and the black ink outlining technique. This project is quick and doesn't require much concentration. It's super fun to follow step by step—you can relax, doodle, and enjoy how the watercolor blends to bring your cute little houses to life. I think this project is also perfect for painting with kids. You can use this method to paint urban-style illustrations or travel illustrations that include houses and streets. Let's have fun!

SUPPLIES

- Watercolor paper
- Washi tape or masking tape
- Pencil and eraser (optional)
- Round brushes: small (sizes 1–4) and medium (sizes 6 and 8)
- Waterproof black ink pen (size 0.5 or 0.8 mm)

NOTE: For this project, it is especially important to use a waterproof ink pen, because we will be adding watercolor on top of the black lines for extra details. If your ink pen is not waterproof, you won't be able to add details or complete step 4.

PROJECT COLORS

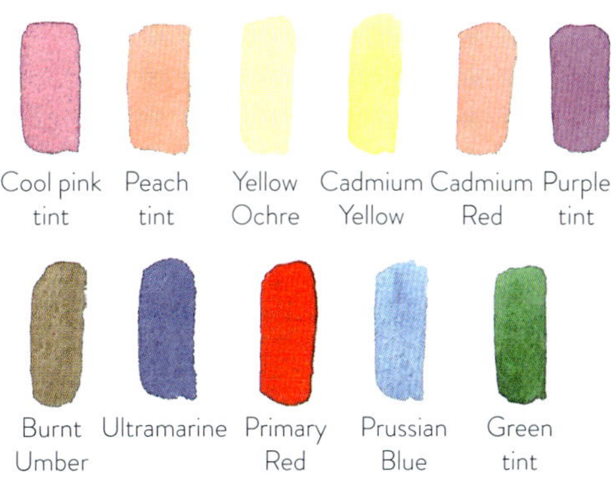

| Cool pink tint | Peach tint | Yellow Ochre | Cadmium Yellow | Cadmium Red | Purple tint |

| Burnt Umber | Ultramarine | Primary Red | Prussian Blue | Green tint |

COLOR MIXING

- Cool pink tint: Add just a hint of Ultramarine to pink (I used Opera).
- Peach tint: Mix Opera with some Yellow Ochre.
- Purple tint: Mix Opera with a little Ultramarine to create a bright, warm purple.
- Green tint: Mix Sap Green with some Viridian.

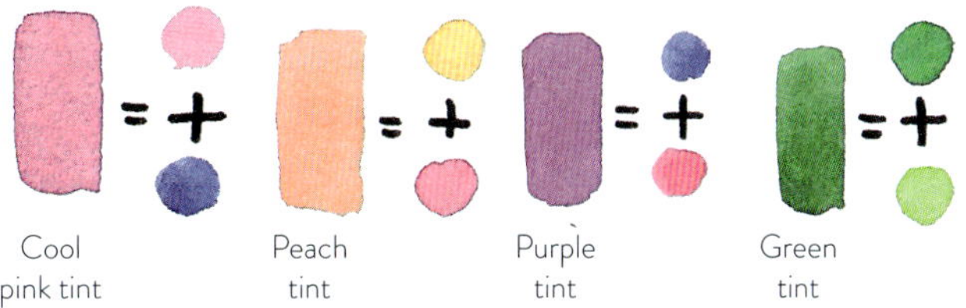

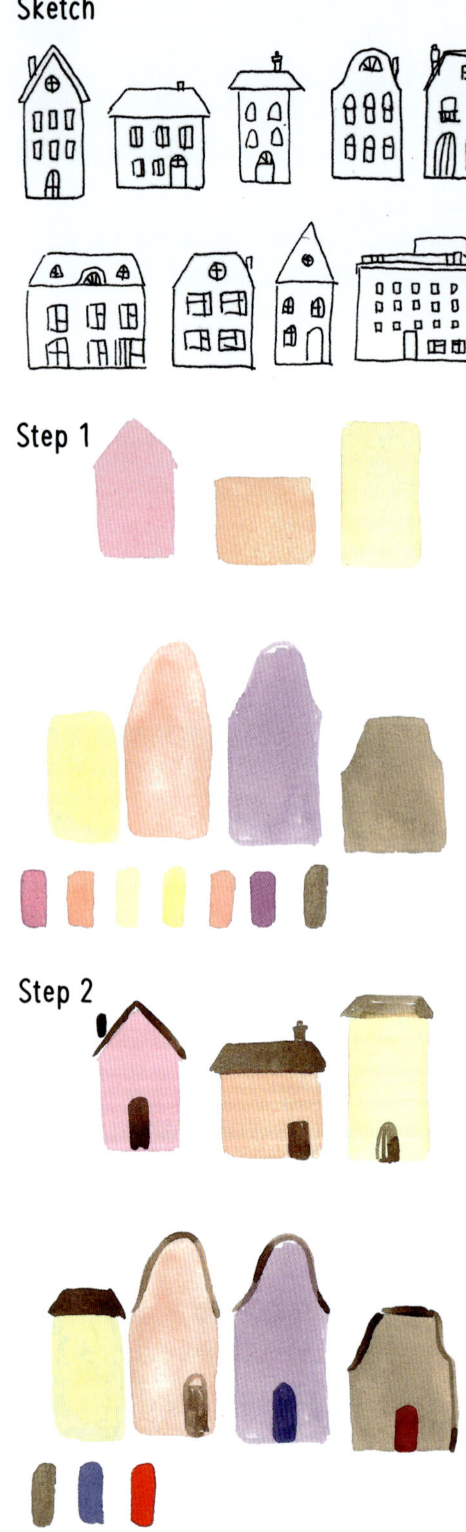

PREPARATION WORK

Secure your paper with washi tape to protect it from wrinkling while we apply watercolor and from moving while we create doodles.

For this project, I don't recommend making a sketch because it's fun to try painting the shapes of the houses freehand without any preliminary drawing. However, if you feel more comfortable sketching, you can either design your own composition or follow my composition in Sketch. You'll find sketches of different house types, but they're not strict and you can modify them and play with the details.

If you decide to make a sketch, avoid adding details like windows and doors with a pencil. Add those details later with a black ink pen. For now, just use a pencil to outline the basic composition and shapes of the houses.

STEP 1

Let's start by coloring the bases for our houses. If you have done the sketch, you just need to trace the houses. If you don't have a sketch prepared, you can paint them directly onto the paper. Make sure you've decided where you want to place your houses and what colors to use.

In my composition, I have seven houses, but you can change this and play with the arrangement. Prepare watery to medium consistency cool pink tint, peach tint, Yellow Ochre, Cadmium Yellow, Cadmium Red, purple tint, and Burnt Umber.

Once your colors are ready, arm yourself with a medium round brush and start painting the houses.

Let everything dry completely before moving on to the next step.

STEP 2

Let's make our house shapes look more like houses. For this step, prepare medium consistency Burnt Umber, Ultramarine, and Primary Red. Using a small round brush, paint the roofs, chimneys, doors, and other details. These don't need to be perfect, just neat enough to bring some contrast to your illustration and make the houses more recognizable. You can create your own designs here or follow mine.

Let everything dry completely before moving on to the next step.

STEP 3

Now we can enjoy adding details with a black ink pen.

First, decide on the scene you want to create based on the houses. For example, you might start by defining the ground where the houses are standing. Then, add tree trunks and other elements. Finally, add details to the houses, such as windows, door details, roofs, chimneys, and anything else you'd like—streetlights, small decorative touches, or other creative ideas. Adding these details will transform your work into a true watercolor illustration, full of interesting elements for viewers to discover.

Let your illustration dry completely before moving on to the final step.

STEP 4

Let's add some final details. You can use either small or medium round brushes, depending on what feels easier for you.

If you are following my example, we're illustrating houses on a winter day, so prepare Prussian Blue in a watery consistency and green tint in medium consistency. Also, prepare medium consistency cool pink tint, peach tint, Cadmium Yellow, and any other colors you might want for extra details.

I use Prussian Blue to add snow on the ground, snowy hills, tree crowns (on trunks drawn earlier with black ink), and roofs. Use the same color to add splatters that imitate falling snow. You can also add fir trees with this color.

Once that's done, let it dry a little before adding more details. With green tint, paint potted plants outside a house, a wreath on one of the doors, or a hidden tree visible in a window.

Use Cadmium Yellow and peach tint to color a few windows.

Finally, add some details to each house. For example, I emphasized the pink house with a cool pink tint, and on the purple house, I added vertical brushstrokes with the same purple to create texture.

Keep adding details until you're happy with the result.

Try experimenting with different details, colors, and compositions!

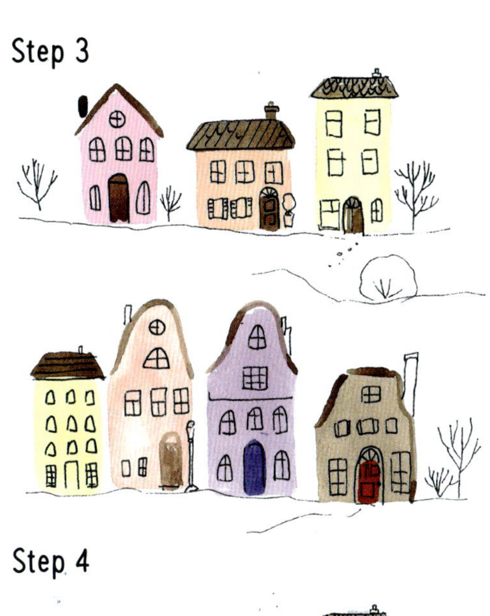

Step 3

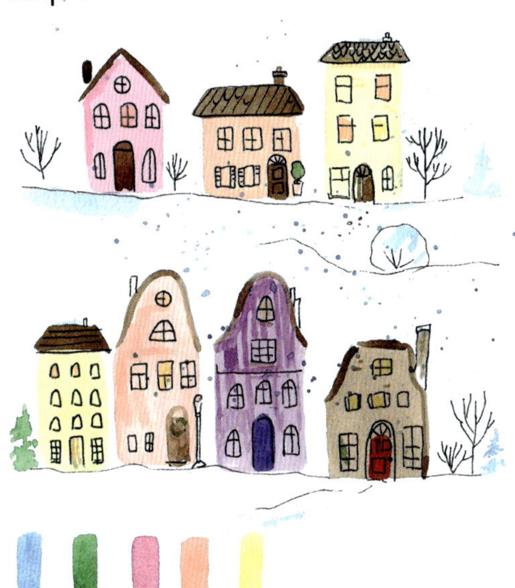

Step 4

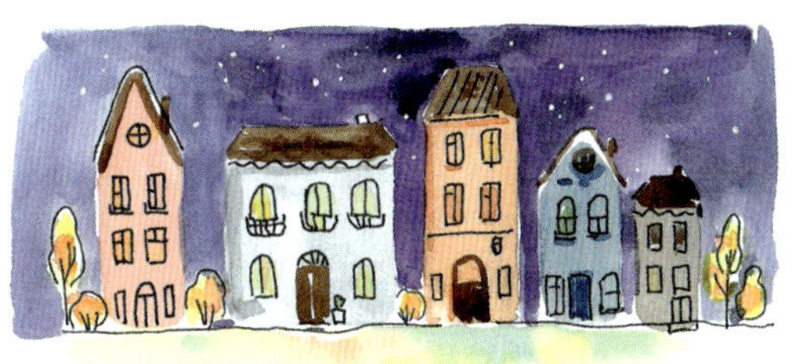

SUPPLIES

Although we use a fun and easy approach in this book, it's still important to use good-quality watercolor supplies. The right materials will make a big difference in your results. In this section, I will share what you need to know when choosing watercolor supplies for this book.

WATERCOLOR PAPER

In my opinion, watercolor paper is a game-changer. Using drawing paper or other unsuitable paper will never give you the desired result. That's why the first and most important thing is to always use watercolor paper.

There are three types of watercolor paper: cold-pressed, hot-pressed, and rough. Cold-pressed paper is the most common and popular type. It has a slight texture and works well for most watercolor techniques and styles. Hot-pressed paper is smooth and ideal for detailed work, such as illustrations or botanical paintings. Rough paper has a strong texture and is great for creating bold effects, especially in landscapes.

You can use any type depending on your goals, but for beginners and most projects in this book, cold-pressed watercolor paper is the best option.

The next thing to consider is the weight of the paper. The thicker the paper, the better it will handle water without warping or wrinkling. The most common and recommended weight is 300 gsm.

Watercolor paper comes in various formats. Pads or albums are perfect for larger projects, such as landscapes, while smaller sizes, like postcards, are great for practicing small projects. You can also cut sheets into pieces for practice or specific projects. For this book, I suggest using pads or albums for bigger projects and postcard-sized paper for smaller practice pieces.

The brand is up to you. Choose one that fits your budget and personal preferences. You don't need the most expensive option—just make sure it's good quality.

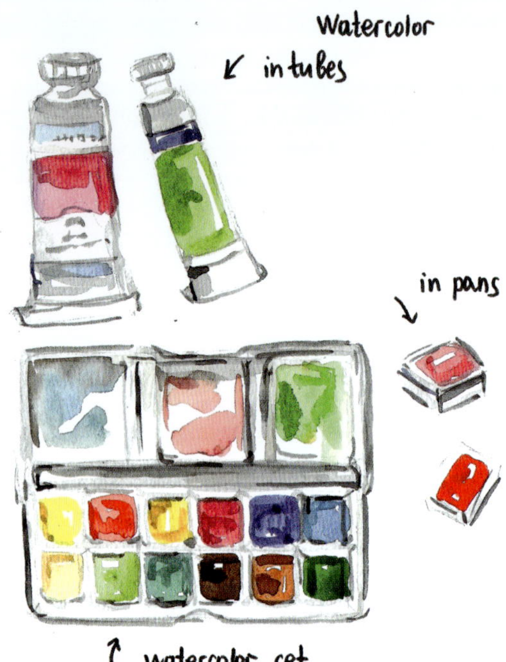

WATERCOLOR PAINTS

The next essential supply is watercolor paint. There is a huge range of watercolors available, but the most important thing is to choose student-grade or professional-grade watercolors. Never use children's watercolor sets, as they are not suitable for practice and will limit your progress.

Watercolor paint comes in two main forms: pans and tubes. Pans are solid blocks of paint that activate with water. They are portable and easy to use. Tubes contain creamy paint that's more concentrated, which allows you to control paint consistency better.

You can choose a set or buy individual pans or tubes depending on your preferences. For this book, I've included a section on the essential palette I used. You can find it on page 11.

You don't need a lot of colors. Most tints can be mixed using just a few basics. I recommend starting with primary colors like red, blue, and yellow, along with neutrals like Burnt Sienna and Burnt Umber. Ultramarine is another useful color to have. For more on color mixing, refer to page 12.

TIP: If you use watercolor in tubes, I recommend pairing it with a plastic palette with a lid. This kind of palette is reusable. Squeeze the paint from the tubes into the palette, and when a color runs out, you can just add more paint. This helps keep the paint from staying too wet or drying out completely.

WATERCOLOR BRUSHES

The next essential supply is watercolor brushes. There are many types and sizes available, but you don't need an extensive collection to get started.

For most of the projects in this book, you'll ideally have at least one small round brush (size 1 to 4) for adding fine details and at least one medium round brush (size 6 to 8). A large round brush (size 9 and up) is useful for washes and larger areas. You can also choose to use only one medium round brush, such as size 8, to complete most projects.

If you'd like to expand your collection, I also recommend a quill brush (size 1 to 4), which is great for creating soft washes. A flat brush is another must-have, in my opinion. It's perfect for smooth washes, creating gradients, and making straight edges.

In every project, I give specific recommendations for brushes in the supplies section. In the end, though, the choice of brushes depends on you and how you like to work, and is often intuitive.

The size of the best brush also depends on the size of the paper. For example, if the project suggests using a small brush for a certain step, but your paper is large, it doesn't make sense to use a small brush. Instead, you can use a medium round brush with a thin tip for the same step.

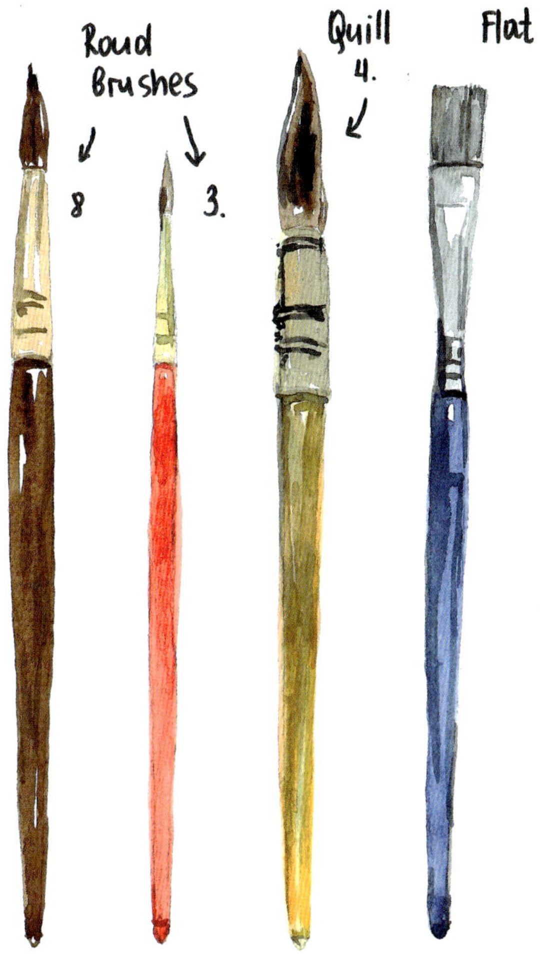

Brushes can be expensive, so focus on quality over quantity. For beginners, synthetic brushes are a great option. They are affordable, durable, and work well for most watercolor techniques. As you gain more experience, you can add natural hair or imitation brushes to your collection.

ADDITIONAL ESSENTIALS

Watercolor painting is not just about having watercolor paper, paints, and brushes. There are also some additional materials you need to buy or find at home.

Water Containers

To dilute colors and clean your brushes, you'll need some water containers. These can be jars, glasses, or cups. I recommend having three large containers. Glasses are the best because you can always see how dirty your water is and change it when needed.

I use the first jar or glass for warm colors like yellow, red, and orange. For cool tones like green and blue, I use a second one. The third container is for cleaning brushes or when I need clean water. Make sure to change the water whenever it gets dirty.

Spray Bottle

A spray bottle with clean water is, in my opinion, a must-have for painting with watercolor. I use this bottle to activate watercolor paints if they are in pans, and when I squeeze tube paint onto the palette, I spray water on top before I start painting. When I stop to clean the palette, I also spray some water on the watercolor to keep the paint fresh and prevent it from drying out completely.

Towel

You'll need a towel for cleaning your brushes or removing excess water. You can use a paper towel, but a fabric towel is an eco-friendlier option. I now use only a fabric towel and recommend you do the same.

Pencil

Most of the projects in this book don't require detailed sketches, but having a pencil is still helpful for quick sketches or rough marks. I use a number 2 pencil and prefer a mechanical pencil, but you can use any pencil you like.

Eraser

I recommend a kneadable eraser because it's clean and doesn't leave a mess on your table.

Washi Tape or Masking Tape

Masking tape is used to secure your paper to a surface like a table or board. It removes easily and won't damage your paper. However, sometimes masking tape can tear your watercolor work, which is very frustrating. Recently, I've started using washi tape instead. It works the same way but is smaller and often comes in sets.

Palette

You'll need a palette for mixing colors. It can be porcelain, plastic, or even a white plate from your kitchen. If you use watercolor in tubes, it's helpful to have a palette with a lid to keep your paints from drying out. The lid of the palette usually has a surface inside for mixing colors.

Scrap Paper

Have some extra paper for testing colors, practicing techniques, or experimenting with mixes.

Hairdryer

A hairdryer can help speed up your painting process. Be careful when using it on a high setting, as it might blow the paint around and damage your work. It can also interfere with certain techniques, like the salt technique, if you don't allow enough time for the salt to interact with the paint.

White Gouache

For some techniques, you'll need white gouache. It usually comes in a tube and can be expensive, so you only need a small amount.

MATERIALS FOR CREATIVE TECHNIQUES

This book focuses on creative techniques. Here are all the materials you'll need to practice them. Remember, you can explore these materials on your own—I am giving my recommendations based on my experience, but you can always try different things. Have fun!

Wax Crayons

Wax resists watercolor when you paint over it. That's why this technique works. You can use any wax crayons you can find. I usually use wax crayons from kids' sets. You can buy them in art or stationery shops, and even in kids' stores. Always check if the set includes a white crayon, as it is used most often in the projects from this book. Try to find thin, pencil-style crayons, as they are easier to use for adding small details.

TIP: Make sure your crayons are sharp enough to draw small details. If not, you can use a knife or office knife to sharpen the crayons.

Instead of wax crayons, you can also use candles. I recommend thin candles, such as birthday candles.

I don't recommend spending a lot of money on crayons or candles—just make sure they work with watercolor.

Sponge

You can use simple, cheap sponges. I usually buy them in dollar stores and then cut them to use for the sponge technique. Sometimes, I find very soft and interesting sponges in craft stores. These are often used for working with clay or pottery, and they are suitable but more expensive. I have also found very soft sponges in the baby product sections of stores. Again, there is no need to spend a lot of money. Use the cheapest sponges you can find; you can reuse them by washing and drying them after use.

Household Items for Stamping

For stamping, you can use anything you find at home. The easiest materials to keep are paper rolls from toilet paper or paper towels. You can also use cookie cutters, glasses, cups, lids, or any other objects with interesting shapes. Focus on objects with defined edges for the best stamping results.

Cotton Swabs

For the Q-tip technique, you will need cotton swabs. These are usually sold in stores. I recommend reusing them by washing and drying them to avoid waste. Try not to use too many at once.

Toothbrush

For the splattering technique, I sometimes recommend using a toothbrush. You can use an old toothbrush or buy the cheapest one available.

Waterproof Ink Pen

Ink pens are great for outlining. To complete all the projects in this book, make sure your pen is waterproof. I recommend purchasing sizes 0.5 and 0.8 mm. Sets can often be more cost effective.

Salt

You can use regular kitchen salt, but I also recommend experimenting with different types and sizes of salt, as they have different results.

ABOUT THE AUTHOR

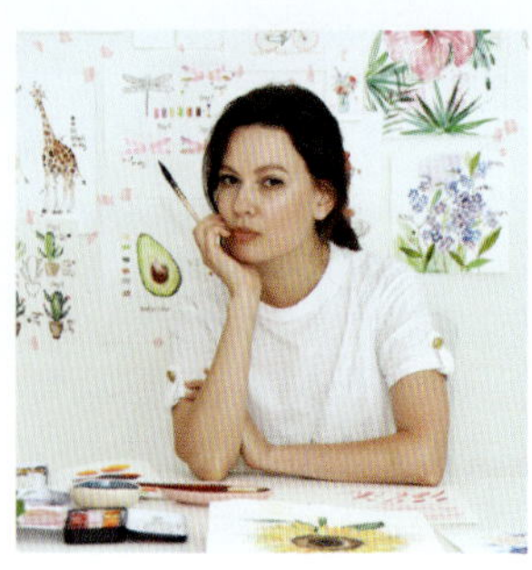

Anna Koliadych is a passionate watercolor, gouache, and oil pastel artist, illustrator, and teacher. She loves inspiring others to unlock their creative potential and enjoy the process of making art. As the founder of DearAnnArt, Anna not only shares her own artistic journey but also helps her students explore different techniques and ideas to discover their own unique style.

Anna was born in Ukraine and has lived in Malta, the UK, and Estonia. Recently, Anna and her family moved to sunny Spain, where they now reside. Before turning her art hobby into a career, Anna earned a master's degree in automation and engineering in Ukraine and worked as a graphic designer for international companies in Malta and Ukraine for five years.

Since childhood, Anna has loved creating art as a way to express herself. In the summer of 2014, Anna received her first watercolor set. After painting her first two illustrations, she fell in love with watercolor and started learning on her own. In 2015, she studied at a private art school in Kyiv, Ukraine. Later, she improved her skills in food, children's books, fashion, and street illustrations by attending an art school in St. Petersburg, Russia. By 2016, Anna had begun working as a freelance watercolor illustrator.

Since then, Anna has held over 20 watercolor workshops in London. She has also written three books: *15-Minute Watercolor Masterpieces* (2019), *Gouache in 4 Easy Steps* (2021), and *Oil Pastel Masterpieces in Four Easy Steps* (2022).

Anna is happiest when she's teaching and inspiring others to achieve their creative goals. She loves simplifying complex ideas to help her students succeed. Her authenticity and passion for art have made her a well-known watercolor, gouache, and oil pastel artist and teacher.

When Anna isn't teaching or working on her own art, she enjoys baking, experimenting with makeup, spending time in nature, practicing yoga, and, most of all, spending quality time with her husband and little boy.

ACKNOWLEDGMENTS

From the bottom of my heart, thank you to my followers and all my students for trusting me, for your kind words and your messages, and for staying with me for so many years. Your support means the world to me.

Thank you to my family and friends who have supported and encouraged me throughout this journey.

A special thank you to my little boy, Leo, who always paints alongside me and reminds me that art is all about creation. He shows me that we don't need to be afraid—we just need to move forward. There are no rules in art, only fun.

Thank you to Page Street Publishing, and especially Lauren, for believing in me and for doing incredible work behind the scenes.

And finally, the biggest thank you to my husband, my soulmate, Ignat, who has always supported me, even when I didn't believe in myself.

INDEX